Alternative Exchanges

International Studies in Social History
General Editor: Marcel van der Linden,
International Institute of Social History, Amsterdam

ALTERNATIVE EXCHANGES

Second-hand Circulations from the
Sixteenth Century to the Present

Edited by
Laurence Fontaine

Berghahn Books
NEW YORK • OXFORD

First published in 2008 by

Berghahn Books
www.berghahnbooks.com

© 2008 Laurence Fontaine

Library of Congress Cataloging-in-Publication Data
A C.I.P. catalog record for this book is available from
the Library of Congress

British Library Cataloguing in Publication Data
A catalogue record for this book is available from the British Library

ISBN 978-1-84545-245-2 (hardback)

CONTENTS

LIST OF FIGURES AND TABLES

List of Figures

List of Tables

ACKNOWLEDGEMENTS

This book is the result of a project that started in the Department of History and Civilization of the European University Institute (Florence) in the years 2000–3 and has now been completed at the Centre de Recherches Historiques at the Ecole des Hautes Etudes en Sciences Sociales. I want to express my thanks to both institutions, and in particular to the EUI for financing the project and a substantial part of the translations.

The chapters have three distinct origins: some derive from presentations in my seminars during the years 2000/3, others began as papers to the conference I organized at the EUI on the circulation of second-hand goods in October 2002, and some have been expressly written for this book. I would like to thank all the colleagues and research students who have improved the project through their invaluable comments and, in particular, the Eric Cochrane Foundation at the University of Chicago where I presented this research.

Susan Porter Benson's contribution to this book was her last written work before her final illness. We all remember her illuminating intelligence and the generosity of her comments. This book is our way to honour her.

INTRODUCTION

Laurence Fontaine

The circulation of used or second-hand objects has attracted little attention from the scientific community,[1] even though it was and still is central to a number of important economic activities, and lies at the heart of symbolic interests, revealing struggles and identity issues within different societies. In Europe second-hand circuits dominated the garment and furnishings markets until the nineteenth century. They were also important for the art, clothing, paper, construction and financial markets. While their economic importance has dwindled in developed countries today, it is still by no means negligible in many non-European countries; and such items remain excellent indicators of self-presentations worldwide.

This lack of interest on the part of the scientific community results from two forms of concealment. Firstly, the establishment, in the eighteenth century, of economics as an autonomous category relegated all kinds of monetary circulation not strictly based on currencies to the realm of the archaic, and therefore consigned to oblivion. When the notion of economics was created by the Enlightenment *Philosophes*, it was as much an ideological and performative category as it was descriptive, and in their grand project for severing economics from politics and making it a separate category, they placed paper money at the center of their construction. But currency was far from being the only kind of monetary circulation. In fact, as a way of compensating for a lack of regular income and cash, as well as to get through those times when bad money drove out good, alternative currencies have always existed alongside the official coin.[2]

This blind spot arising from the political will of the Enlightenment fathers to found a new society, based no longer on personal ties but on the will of the majority, was combined with the phenomenon of a material occultation due to the fact that everyday clothing had disappeared, having been worn out, restyled and ultimately recycled for industrial use. And the clothing museums, which had to make do with Sunday dress, almost forgot to mention the existence of ordinary clothes ...

The present book therefore sets out to examine the role, significance and functioning of this market, and to unveil the forgotten circuits and uses of these castoff items over the long term. In relation to these issues, the book addresses two large sets of questions. The first relate to the organization and functioning of these markets in terms of their material significance, the social spaces that they occupied, and the social interests that they represented; they pose questions about the objects, the actors and the reasons. The second take into account the fact that these markets were complex markets since it was not just a matter of buying and selling items that had an easily identifiable value. Even taking the view that each transaction was also an exchange of values, the second-hand objects – and this applies even if these objects circulated as an alternative currency – carried with them the traces of their previous lives; they embodied beings and values. The second set of questions addressed by this book is concerned with bringing these latter aspects to light.

To this end, the book has invited dialogue between historians, anthropologists, sociologists and economists, and brought together the contemporary and pre-industrial worlds of Europe and other continents. The editor had no ambitions to draw up an inventory of all of the trade circulations of used objects the world over. She simply espoused Marc Bloch's remark that comparison is "the most effective of all dowsing rods."[3]

The collection of essays can thus be read in several ways. Firstly, each chapter presents a condition or an aspect of these markets. Then, certain themes are pursued from one chapter to another, and the differences in the lines of inquiry adopted make it possible to ascertain certain evolutions in the situation and role of second hand goods. Finally, the book as a whole highlights the major reconfigurations between the objects, the actors, the social spaces and the values that these changes brought about between the sixteenth century and today.

Logics and the Diversity of Markets

During the entire early modern period, second-hand markets were dominant because industry did not produce enough and, above all, because the values extolling the new and the need for replacement to keep pace with fashion were late to gain precedence over those of conservation and tradition. Every sector was characterized by these circulations, from construction to food, not to mention consumer products such as clothing, books,[4] jewelry and furniture. Reprocessing, re-use and repair were usual and natural activities for everyone. However, historians have shown little interest in this *ancien régime* economy, preferring the study of progress and the advent of capitalism.

Up until the twentieth century, textiles and clothing were at the heart of these trade circulations, and every chapter is concerned with clothing, except for the penultimate one which brings the automobile on to the scene, a bright new second-hand object in the contemporary world. The strong presence of clothing is principally due to three reasons. On the one hand, to dress – and therefore to possess a few pieces of clothing and linen – is a necessity for everyone; but as the conditions of the time made their conservation over an extended period very difficult, they were systematically put into recirculation after each death; they were either altered and given away, or they were sold. They were also sold to pay bankruptcy debts. Lastly, pawnshops regularly put on to the market pawned items that had not been retrieved. However, clothing and textiles were not the only items to enter these markets, and the first six chapters also refer to furniture, jewelry and weapons, without, nonetheless, exhausting the list of second-hand objects that were circulating and that would be worthy of study.

The organization of second-hand markets was very diverse. Chapters 1, 5, 7, 10 and 12 show the great variety of actors who shared these markets and the principal evolutions that they underwent between the sixteenth and the twentieth century. For the early modern age, the example of the Netherlands (chap. 1) enables us to consider the diversity of actors and to gain an impression of the volume of their activity. This chapter starts from the corporations and shows that they were not present everywhere or homogeneous, and that they always had to struggle to maintain their privileges and prerogatives.

Some, as in Antwerp, were rapidly obliged to restrict their sales to second-hand clothes and demanded the monopoly on auction sales in exchange; others, as in Ghent, were able to freely mix old and new, and tailors had free rein in both trades.[5] Whatever the arrangement, however, tailors and pawnbrokers vied with the corporations for markets, since the first controlled the re-use of old clothes, while the second were among their main purveyors.[6] However, depending upon the places and the importance of demand, the guilds more or less left the terrain open to women and migrant networks.

In spite of protective practices and restrictive legislation, the women strove everywhere to meet the daily needs of their families, even though incomes and work were irregular. Thus, social roles that made them into great clothing specialists in an economy that was still not completely monetary, and in a legal environment that marginalized them, explain why they became one of the major actors in the circulation of second-hand goods. They are present in almost every chapter. The first explores the institutional battles engaged in by the men to exclude women from the guilds into which they had previously gained entry. In fact, the regional variation of the Netherlands makes it a good observatory for these struggles, which occurred everywhere in Europe. At the higher echelons of the profession, women came out losing, lacking the capacity to adapt themselves to the evolutions of markets that always required more capital; being unable to change the scale of their business, they were undoubtedly marginalized at the end of the eighteenth century.[7] On the other hand, they continued to drive the informal sectors and certain weekly markets, as the studies of Paris during the eighteenth and nineteenth centuries attest (chaps 5 and 7). Their knowledge of the districts and local families made them into intermediaries and irreplaceable actors in this economy.

The courtesans played a particular role in these markets. Chapter 3 examines all of the second-hand traffic generated by and around them. As they were remunerated with gifts as well as money, these items were central to their economy. They were equally important to their savings strategies for dealing with difficult times, whilst simultaneously signaling their status and contributing to their charms. Certain courtesans could thus add to the sale of their body the roles of dealer and pawnbroker for other women or for other social milieus. These circulations reveal unexpected social mixings whereby shirts given in friendship between aristocrats ended up as gifts to pay for the services of a courtesan. The renewal of wardrobes was also an indication of the role as "fashion leaders" that the more successful among them played, equivalent to that of women from the aristocracy in Renaissance Rome.

Migrants were the other great actors in these markets, as chapters 1, 5 and 7 show. Owing to their organization through diasporas they could be active across several terrains and develop international commercial routes. Their networks enabled them to bridge the gap between the different spaces and clienteles. These groups also connected town and countryside through a job chain running from the richest merchants, who had shops in town, to the peddlers, who combed town and countryside, buying up old clothes and objects. The castoff goods were then sorted and dispatched to the different markets, some to specialized shops, and others to industries. Jewish immigrants were among the first to go into the second-hand trade. Jewish dealers can be found in many Italian towns from the fifteenth century, in Holland from the sixteenth, in England in the eighteenth, and they arrived in the United States in the nineteenth century. Around 1850, the Irish broke into the English market, and today West Indians are entering the trade in increasing numbers. Elsewhere in Europe, other local groups coming from Auvergne, Scotland or the Alps filled the niche.[8]

The great diversity of actors conveys the extent to which these markets were totally integrated into the economy of the time, and were also an essential element in the survival strategy of the poorest. Chapter 1 clearly shows the contrast, in the Netherlands during the early modern period, between the very wealthy houses and the poor vendors, men and especially women whom the municipality did not pursue because this small trade was their only resource against destitution. These contrasts are equally visible in the Paris of the eighteenth century (chap. 5). In that of the nineteenth century (chap. 7), one can trace the general marginalization of the trade in second-hand clothing, with, nevertheless, the maintenance of great houses turned towards export, and more and more specialized upon certain segments of the market. Their success should not, however, mask the archaic condition and impoverishment of the profession as a whole. In fact, the major reorganizations occurred in the second half of the nineteenth century. Up until the middle of the century, merchants were able to prosper and to provide a living for numerous employees, by specializing, by opening attractive shops, and by successfully displaying carefully chosen items of clothing. At this time, shops and markets still occupied a central place in towns, and all places, streets as well as inns, were favorable to peddling. But, rapidly, concerns with regard to the aesthetics of towns, and then questions about hygiene, became a constant source of criticism that led to second-hand commerce being chased out of the centers of towns.

Alongside the analysis of the different actors, these essays taken as a whole show a progression toward the globalization of markets and, in particular, those of fabrics and clothing. Between the first chapter, where the market is regional, even if one considers that it also has an extraregional dimension, and the last, which shows the total globalization of trading channels, the intermediate chapters, in particular chapter 7, examine the transformations in the scales of commerce. These transformations reverberate upon the multiple functions of second-hand trade circulations. They drive regional commerce whilst simultaneously being an alternative currency that attaches the peasants to the itinerant traders, and a whole structure of bartering is put in place between the peddler and his practices (chap. 1). At the international level, the diasporas benefited from their becoming settled in different locations and from their structure of hierarchical networks, enabling them to control the channels of large-scale commerce. Reprocessing has been the great motor for the internationalization of markets: it was as raw material for industry that, with paper pulp from the sixteenth century onwards, used clothing entered commercial channels that passed beyond regional boundaries.

An examination of the actors involved conveys the complexity of these trade circulations. Under the *ancien régime*, alongside the traditional role of merchants that consisted of buying, even hiring, clothing and furnishings, organizing auction sales – and the monopoly of these sales was one of the major strengths of the profession – these sales also served as an alternative currency and were just as essential to the systems of credit. All these occupations reveal so many segments of the market, as well as actors, and even political economies that could vary.

In fact, these objects that circulated and were exchanged in early modern Europe, as an alternative currency, reflect several types of phenomena. They indicate the existence of payments in kind as well as in cash, and the savings function devolved to objects, even the most symbolic such as personal jewelery or those received as a dowry. In Renaissance Rome (chap. 2), as in the Paris of the eighteenth century (chap. 5), personal items were bought, sold and pawned without distress when it was a matter of renewing one's wardrobe, keeping up with fashion, paying one's debts or dividing up one's estate more easily. The twentieth century has known similar practices when economic crises have taken hold, as can be seen in the practice of American workers between the two wars (chap. 8), or the economic changes in Argentina during the 1990s (chap. 11). The Argentine experience shows how, in a completely monetarized world, certain elites thought of reviving the system of bartering to take the country out of crisis and to come to the aid of the ever increasing numbers of destitute. Even if it was not just second-hand trading that featured in this attempt to reestablish the economy upon a system of generalized bartering, it is interesting to consider the role as alternative currency played by second-hand products, and particularly clothing, in early modern Europe, alongside other attempts made in the contemporary context, which activated other social groups, other structures and other political economies.

The attention given to the political and economic contexts has enabled an exploration of the interactions between conflicting economies that coexisted under the *ancien régime*, and which can be detected in certain other countries during the last century. It has also made it possible to consider the boundaries that defined the categories of "the gift," "charity," and "the market" during different periods and to see how much they were being modified and that they were often fragile. These questions open up another field of research still largely unexplored. In fact, the societies of early modern Europe were societies of order founded upon aristocratic political regimes and upon nobiliary values. For a long time, both endured in spite of the rise of the capitalist economy. These conflicting and dual economies impacted on the ways people viewed money: the aristocratic economy of the gift was still thriving among aristocrats and it also appeared at important moments in the lives of ordinary people. Chapter 2 shows how aristocratic and papal Rome was permeated by the economy of the gift. Chapters 5 and 6 address more precisely the way in which the aristocracy entered the second-hand market in the eighteenth century, when the culture of novelty and fashion added a new dimension to the relationship of men to objects, and demanded that they replace clothing and accessories ever more rapidly. In Paris, as in the provinces, the aristocracy was a supplier to the second-hand market: there they resold clothing and objects to offset the purchase price of the new items they coveted. In the provinces, re-use reigned supreme, and silverware was periodically resold or melted down, to be renewed and modernized, or to allow for other, more necessary purchases. In Paris more than elsewhere, fashion and the craze for collecting speeded up these rhythms, placing fashionable items back into the flow of second-hand traffic more rapidly.

In parallel, protected by his status as connoisseur, the aristocrat openly entered the market. However, collecting formed part of a whole body of aristocratic practices that have always favored the circulation of objects. These characteristics are more or less ingrained in all the social groups. In fact, aside from the lack of currency, a disdain for the circulation of money in cash between people who were socially or intimately related is apparent in all the transactions. Moreover, the gift as a portion of salary was standard practice between masters and servants and, in a more general way, between employers and their workers, since everyone supplemented or gave a portion of salary in kind. In the twentieth century, in spite of the manifest domination of capitalism in the United States, gifts always circulated in families between generations, and also found their way into the market, when the need arose (chap. 8). Finally, the contemporary second-hand clothing market clearly illustrates the porosity of boundaries between charity and market with, from the start, gifts of western charity and the cascade of markets that they generated up to their final destination (chap. 12).

Favored by the economy of the gift and the lack of banking institutions aimed at ordinary people, a financial economy developed in early modern Europe around second-hand goods and clothing. Lending against security was the chief source of credit for the poor since it was actually a sale in which the lender risked nothing. This method, which has to date been neglected by researchers because these transactions are rarely found in the archives, was part of the common culture and a normal practice. Everyone was involved in this economy, men and women, aristocrats as much as courtesans, directly or through intermediaries, as lender or as borrower; and the court files contain many examples of ordinary men and women who had agreed to lend or receive, pending payment, in exchange for an item of clothing or a small piece of jewelery as security (chap. 5). This financial economy also engendered its middlemen and specialized shops. A number of pawnshop records can still be found in England. All show the importance of lending on security in everyday life, and the role of neighborhood women, who served as go-betweens or guarantors in many arrangements.[9]

Not only was there a good deal of lending, but also renting was widespread among the poor. Pawning one's clothes in order to procure the tools or the materials needed for the day's work was commonplace, just as it was to rent out one's clothes when money was needed or even to make a profit when they had been a gift – a frequent practice among servants. This economy of renting, still visible in Paris in the eighteenth century (chap. 5), was very much in evidence in Venice at the time of the 1557 plague, for the authorities worried about contagion from these shirts, caps, hose, shoes, skirts, scarves, hoods, veils and aprons, as well as the jewelry, which were thus handed around.[10]

Thus second-hand markets have always been a precious resource for the less well-off. Moreover, the practices of the popular Parisian classes, who were accustomed to acquiring items to build up portable savings for times of need, were still a reality among working-class families in America in the first half of the twentieth century (chap. 8). In the eighteenth century, every material possession had a savings function, while, two centuries later, it is furniture that would be at the heart of this strategy. These items were bought in the second-hand market and resold to make ends meet during periods of economic difficulty, or even to risk the enterprise of a small business and thus bring in capital to get started. In sixteenth-century Rome as in the Paris of the eighteenth century, one can detect the strategies of workers who used the pawnshops to make a few sous from unused tools and raw materials. In America of the interwar period, male workers used second-hand tools, received as presents or bought, and the women did the same thing with sewing machines. These examples make it possible to gain an understanding of one of the survival strategies of the poorest in society.[11]

In addition, certain exceptional circumstances were propitious to the second-hand markets. Chapter 4 is concerned with rediscovering those that the wars in early modern Europe brought forth. They spread out around military bases and campaigns, with victories as well as with defeats. This chapter shows that each stage of the war engendered specific second-hand markets. They sprang up around the construction of military apparatus, weaponry and the equipping of soldiers. The fruits of pillage quickly joined the ordinary traffic of goods for resale. Since the armies of the period consisted of between ten and forty thousand soldiers, the entire military operation provided a huge market, not including the artisans, peddlers, valets, and refugees who followed the troops and made a living from war. The culture of nobility also created a taste for expensive weapons and for their multiple possession. Military clothing and arms also circulated far from the battlefields, when the belongings of deceased soldiers were returned to their family who, in spite of prohibitions, hastened to resell them (chaps. 6 and 7). In the nineteenth century, military clothing once more activated a prosperous commerce: some of it was re-cut and transformed for civil use, and some was dispatched outside Europe to clothe the armies of poorer countries (chap. 7).

A study of these markets also reveals the blurring of categories between the old and the new. This is apparent in early modern Europe as regards the guilds and the shops (chap. 1): certain guilds officially mixed second-hand dealers and tailors while others made a clear distinction between the two functions. The clothes shop usually sold both new and old.[12] For tailors, this practice often reflected payments made partly in cash, partly in clothes.[13] Many shops also sold on consignment on behalf of individuals or peddlers,[14] and in some cases the consignment agreement would also contain a clause stipulating the purchase of another article.[15] The same confusions can be found in Parisian shops in the nineteenth century (chap. 7). Nevertheless, the history of these markets is also that of the progressive separation of new and second-hand.

The spread of Enlightenment ideas, with their emphasis on trade, currency and progress, as well as the birth of fashion, with its constant demand for the new, not to mention the *Philosophes'* urging to rehabilitate luxury living as a driving force of exchange and provider of work, gradually raised the status of the new and valorized the replacement of objects and wardrobes, to the detriment of their conservation and re-use. Later, progress in the field of medicine brought a new awareness of the dangers presented by previously worn clothes, the difficulty of cleaning them, the massive diffusion of clothing-borne parasitic vermin, and thus threw suspicion on cast-off clothes and, in particular, items of unknown origin (chap. 7). Even today, for health reasons, Spain and its former colonies have slapped prohibitive restrictions on the import of second-hand clothes, though importers and exporters regularly circumvent them.[16] Lastly, the craze for new possessions was favored in the nineteenth century by the development of the textile industry and the boom in inexpensive imports. For the emerging masses of unmarried wage-earning women, it became a point of pride to buy new as a testimony to their freshly acquired economic capacities, and second-hand thus became synonymous with poverty, charity and dependence.[17]

The example of cars perfectly illustrates this progressive partitioning of categories as industrial production intensified. In fact, even though the vast majority of businesses conducted in the car industry concerned second-hand cars, manufacturers have had great difficulty in managing the business challenges posed by used cars. Chapter 10 shows that the US between 1910 and 1940, France between 1930 and 1960, and Europe more generally up until these last ten years were unable to integrate activities linked to second-hand cars. In this sense, the study of the circulation of second-hand cars in non-Western countries, where the ratio of new cars to used cars sold is 1 to 10, and even 1 to 20, makes possible an analysis of an informal economy that provides a livelihood for numerous middlemen engaged in dispatch, sale and repair, on the edges of the automobile industry. To compare this economy with that which developed around clothing in early modern Europe, or in the contemporary world, also sheds light upon the role of fashion cycles that made clothes and then cars flow from the centers toward the peripheries (chaps 1, 10 and 12).

In outlying geographical areas, migrants always played a major role in the routing of deliveries and in selling, leaving to the locals the occupations of repair and fulfilling the many services arising from the needs of these trade circulations. On the social peripheries, the behavior of consumers of second-hand products was also very different from that of those who bought new, whether it was clothing or vehicles. Finally, the category itself can be subverted, as the study of Zambia shows (chap. 12). In fact, in Africa, the merchants were very solicitous that bales of used clothing were opened in front of consumers, to be hung up "fresh" from the bale; clothes too well ironed could be considered "third-hand," in other words already worn by other Zambians. Travel and baling created new categories of new and used. These relationships were complicated further when migrants and local peddlers (often female) brought cases of clothing straight back from the United States, Asia, the Middle East or South Africa.

Reorganization of Values and Identities

Second-hand objects are a complex raw material. On the one hand, the objects and clothing are anonymous and, on the other, they carry the mark and memory of those who used or wore them, of the societies that created them, of the events they have witnessed. They thus lie somewhere between anonymity, souvenir and fetish. Every circuit in which they are involved bespeaks the value system of the societies in which they circulate and the evolution of these values. With the change in political contexts comes a change in the position of second-hand goods in the hierarchy of values, thus showing what, too, is at stake in the struggle for appropriation. The path followed by these objects in the various contexts is marked by different appropriations, and reveals various kinds of sharing, which always involves objects, power, money, ideas and people.

A reconstruction of the life span of these objects shows that they circulated in every form from commercial exchange to gift or charity and that at certain times they could be withdrawn from the circuits of exchange to enter those of collections, of art or of sacred objects (chap. 2, 3, 9). Moreover, collecting, which was popularized in the nineteenth century, gave rise to new places for strolling toward these flea markets that were established in the suburbs, and that became hunting grounds for the acquisitive bourgeoisie in quest of emotions and adventures, as the study of Paris in the nineteenth century attests (chap. 7).

The transfer of items from one category to another occurred in all social classes. Thus, the practice of withdrawing personal objects from the market to convert them into ornaments of worship or sacred objects, and to thus perpetuate one's presence beyond death, by offering them to the Church on condition that they be made into altar cloths, or be used to decorate a statue, was common under the *ancien régime*. It occurred among women in high society, such as Dorotea Antolini, rediscovered by Renata Ago, just as much as courtesans like Isabella Galeotti, brought to light by Tessa Storey (chaps 2 and 3). But this retrieval from the market does not mean that the journey of objects stopped there, as Jackie Goode's study of the dispersal of collections in twentieth-century England demonstrates (chap. 9).

By stigmatizing the poor, charity developed feelings of shame combined with gratitude among those who benefited from it and, conversely, a desire for power among those who offered it, expressed through this practice of stigmatization as the need for evidence of recognition. These ambiguities may be read in the gestures of giving as well as the ways of receiving: certain donors recorded their generosity on the bodies of the poor via the clothes that they offered, and fought to ensure that traces of their generosity were conserved. In response, some of the poor obliterated the stigmatization and erased the personalities of the donors by transforming these clothes from charitable offerings into raw material. Chapter 7 shows how Parisian students in the nineteenth century knew how to create their own look from the bourgeois cast offs on sale in the multiplicity of shops established around the University of Paris. The example of American working class-families in the USA during the inter war period (chap. 8) also provides an impression of the wide variation in attitudes and appropriations, the shame attached to clothes derived from charity, as well as the pride and the ability of numerous families to conceal their source by transforming them and adapting them to their needs and to fashion. Today, where certain non-European countries dress themselves almost entirely with clothes from Western charity, personalized appropriations are the rule and in African towns and cities, for instance, sellers and buyers cut down trousers into shorts, unravel sweaters, make colorful drapes into dresses, add pockets and buttons or layer various items of clothing to create an original style. In doing so, they transform charity clothes into raw material, and, with this transformation, the shame felt by the poor inhabitants of the Western world when forced to wear hand-me-downs becomes for the poor a thing of the past. These reinventions do not just take place via the expert hands of tailors, but occur at every stage in the circulation of these items of clothing, from selection to presentation (chap. 12).

This play upon identities reveals a domain still largely unknown and which should be investigated further: the changing roles of these second-hand objects in the psychic economy of families. Chapter 6 shows that the French aristocracy of the eighteenth century shrank from providing for themselves from second-hand markets for fear that the former owners of clothing would recognize them. Chapter 8, because it tries to follow all the currents of these second-hand circulations in lower-class American families, sheds light upon several features besides the interests arising from social domination through charity. Within families, they ignited conflicts between parents and children relating to the frustrations of the latter at not being able to acquire the social symbols of the peer groups with whom they associated or they adversely affected families that had to part with objects carrying a heavy recreational or symbolic significance, such as the piano. These frustrations also had their own histories that would be worth exploring and contextualizing. The Argentine experience also provides evidence that, alongside the lower classes, who were the first to be affected by a crisis and who made a success of this alternative currency, the middle classes, when they were obliged to enter into the system of barter, experienced this economy as a source of shame and of fear (chap. 11).

A study of the disposal of collections provides another means of investigating this "mental" economy of families and individuals. The obligation to break up a collection through lack of space, because the couple who built it up were separating, owing to financial need, or because the collector needed to prepare at a particular moment in his life for the day when he would no longer be there to take charge of it, entailed the making of choices by the collector and his relatives that were emotionally fraught (chap. 9). At these moments too all the ambiguity of the boundaries between the gift, the market, the destruction and the sanctification of objects may be grasped; these contingencies obliged individuals to uncover the hidden motivations of their passion for collecting: they showed that behind the presentations of self as men of aesthetic passions and erudition, speculators were concealed, as the commentators of the eighteenth century have already been pleased to underline in relation to aristocrats with a craze for "curios" (chap. 5).

This "psychological" economy compounds the difficulty of precisely defining the value of second-hand objects in circulation. In fact, they incorporate all sorts of value: a value linked to their utility, to their plus or minus degree of rarity, a value linked to the price of the raw materials of which they are composed or to the cost of the labour involved in their production, and a changing value linked to the age of the object in relation to the fashion cycle. When they cease to be in use and become collectable objects or pieces of art, their value increases in proportion. But a downward trajectory might be observed when their commonality takes them outside the realm of objects promoted by fashion. We see this clearly today with regard to cars (chap. 10). In certain social milieus, the car, having become too commonplace, had ceased to be an object of desire, to become a thing of disdain. With this change of value, the second-hand car has found new favor with these consumers.

These threads, drawn from the essays contained in the present volume, show how, because of its position at the intersection of a number of economic circuits and sites where values are exchanged, the second-hand market, long judged too negligible and marginal to be deserving of attention, turns out to be a signpost, pointing to concealed economic, political and cultural mechanisms.

Translated by Nora Scott and Sheila Oakley

Notes

1. Apart from the pioneering studies of Beverly Lemire and Patricia Allerston.
2. Peter Spufford, *Money and its Use in Medieval Europe* (Cambridge, 1988), pp. 329–38; Peter Mathias, *English Trade Tokens: The Industrial Revolution Illustrated* (London, 1962), p. 191; Margaret Hunt, "Women, Credit and the Seafaring Community in London 1700–1740," paper presented at Session C 59 of the 12th International Congress on Economic History, Seville, 1988, "Les Femmes et les Pratiques du Crédit (XVIIe–XIXe siècles)," coordinated by M. Berg, L. Fontaine and C. Muldrew, shows that notes guaranteed on sailors' future salaries circulated in the port of London and vicinity as real money.
3. Marc Bloch, "Pour une histoire comparée des sociétés européennes," *Revue de synthèse historique*, Dec. 1928; reprinted in *Mélanges historiques* (Paris, 1963), vol. 1, pp. 16–40.
4. Frederic Barbier, "Bouquinistes, Libraires Spécialisés," in: Roger Chartier and Henri-Jean Martin (eds.), *Histoire de l'édition française*, vol. 3, *Le Temps des éditeurs, du romantisme à la belle époque* (Paris, 1990).
5. Harald Deceulaer, "Urban Artisans and their Countryside Customers: Different Interactions between Town and Hinterland in Antwerp, Brussels and Ghent (18th century)," in Bruno Blondé, Michèle Galand and Eric Vanhaute (eds.), *Labour and Labour Markets between Town and Countryside (Middle-ages–Nineteenth century)* (Turnhout, 2001), pp. 224–5 and 227.
6. Madeleine Ginsburg, "Rags to Riches: the Second-hand Clothes Trade 1700–1978," *Costume*, 14 (1980), pp. 121–35 (121).
7. Bibi Sara Panhuysen, *Maatwerk. Kleermakers, naaisters, oudkleerkopers en de gilden (1500–1800)*, (Amsterdam, 2000), p. 240. I wish to thank Harald Deceulaer, who gave me access to this work.
8. Laurence Fontaine, *History of Pedlars in Europe* (Cambridge, 1996).
9. Such as those of John Pope, haberdasher in St. Georges, one of the poorest parishes of Southwark, London, whose records are specially complete for the year 1669: see Beverly Lemire, "Petty Pawns and Informal Lending: Gender, Households and Small-scale Credit in English Communities, circa 1600–1800," in Kristine Bruland and Patrick O'Brien (eds.), *From Family Firms to Corporate Capitalism: Essays in Business and Industrial History in Honour of Peter Mathias* (Oxford, 1998), pp. 112–38; those of Phillip Henslowe, a south London theatrical entrepreneur during fourteen months in 1594–5, see Jeremy Boulton, *Neighbourhood and Society: A London Suburb in the Seventeenth Century* (Cambridge, 1987), pp. 88–9; or those of George Fettes from York, in 1777–9, studied by Lemire, "Petty Pawns," pp. 131–2.
10. Patricia Allerston, "Clothing and Early Modern Venetian Society," *Continuity and Change* 15: 3 (2000), pp. 367–90 (377).
11. Laurence Fontaine and Jürgen Schlumbohm (eds.), *Household Strategies for Survival, 1600–2000: Fission, Faction and Cooperation* (Cambridge, 2000).
12. Deceulaer, "Urban Artisans," pp. 218–35. See also Natacha Coquery, "The Language of Success: Marketing and Distributing Semi-luxury Goods in Eighteenth-century Paris," *Journal of Design History*, 17:1 (2004), pp. 71–89, Special Issue: *Disseminating Design: The French Connection*.
13. Elizabeth Sanderson, "Nearly New: the Second-hand Clothing Trade in Eighteenth-century Edinburg," *Costume*, 31 (1997), pp. 38–48.
14. Laurence Fontaine, "Pierre Rullier colporteur horloger-bijoutier savoyard au XVIIIe siècle," in Martin Körner and François Walter (eds.), *Quand la montagne aussi a une histoire. Mélanges offerts à Jean-François Bergier* (Berne, 1996), pp. 167–75; Coquery, "The Language of Success."
15. For example the woman in Edinburgh, who gave her tailor three shirts to restyle and suggested he use two old ones she gave him at the same time, which were wrapped around a pair of shoes, adding that "the old shoes if sold would purchase thread," Sanderson, "Nearly New," p. 40.
16. Steven Haggblade, "The Flip Side of Fashion: Used Clothing Exports to the Third World," *Journal of Development Studies*, 26:3 (1990), pp. 505–21, appendix 6 on restrictions and taxes imposed on used-clothes imports according to countries, pp. A53–A59.
17. Ginsburg, "Rags to Riches," p. 128.

1

SECOND-HAND DEALERS IN THE EARLY MODERN LOW COUNTRIES

INSTITUTIONS, MARKETS AND PRACTICES

Harald Deceulaer

Saying that markets and consumption have received a lot of attention in the last two decades in history, economics and politics is not a very original statement. However, the functioning of a "market" is not a self-evident or unproblematic phenomenon, as the concrete acts of buying and selling necessarily involve processes of acquiring information, assessment of quality, contracting, trust, credit or deceit. If possible, this applies even more strongly for the second-hand market. As most new commodities were rather expensive, and as the majority of inhabitants of pre-modern Europe owned so little that their livelihood was highly insecure,[1] second-hand goods were probably of paramount importance. But the exact definition, price or quality of a second-hand commodity is far from evident, and remains open to discussion. Rules and institutions influence(d) commercial transactions in the retail trade of both old and new commodities, but we don't know a lot about the regulation of distribution for non foodstuffs in the early modern period.

The second-hand trade comprised a wide social range of men and women, from destitute ragmen through small shopkeepers to rich entrepreneurs. Their practices were remarkably versatile: they bought, sold and rented out both old and new goods, they held auctions, lent out money, acted as subcontractors in the clothing trades and were active players in regional markets. But not all second-hand dealers engaged in all these activities, and opportunities and constraints varied from one town to another.

This chapter will mainly deal with second-hand dealers and their guilds in the Low Countries in the early modern period, and will mainly be based on primary sources. I will not deal with the attitudes of consumers toward second-hand goods, but I will study the interaction between markets and institutions, focusing on practices, incomes and living standards of second-hand dealers in the Low Countries, and their variation in time and space. Which activities predominated where, and how did these evolve over time? What did it cost to become a guild member in different towns? What was the role of women? How did the second-hand trade evolve during the commercial expansion of the late seventeenth and eighteenth century, which some authors have described as the period of a "consumer revolution"?[2] In many towns, guilds of second-hand dealers could be found, but they did not exist everywhere, and the relative numbers of second-hand dealers varied dramatically between different towns. Can we discern regional patterns in this variation and if so, how can we explain them? The differences in guild regulation and in the number of actors on the market between towns, regions and the Northern and Southern Netherlands will partly be explained by the various ways in which rural markets interacted with urban trade in a regional context.[3]

The literature on guilds or on urban history does not pay a lot of attention to the countryside.[4] As towns generally controlled the jurisdiction over the guilds, the individual town is generally the taken-for-granted level of analysis. Differences in space and time have mostly remained unclear, due to the lack of systematic regional, national or international comparisons. Yet, concerning second-hand goods, most historians will agree that they were not just bought and sold in towns. Rural consumption plays a pivotal role in the literature on proto-industrialization and the "industrious revolution,"[5] but we don't know much about the size, composition, regulation or evolution of rural consumption markets and their relations to urban distribution networks. The responsiveness of rural society to the commercial opportunities afforded by towns loom large in much recent work on rural society, but the concrete intermediaries connecting town and country remain generally rather obscure.[6] In this chapter, it will be argued that urban second-hand dealers were one of these intermediaries in the early modern period, as they controlled some of the flows of goods into the countryside, at least in certain towns of the Low Countries. However, their activities can certainly not be reduced to this one activity.

For the Low Countries, several historiographic and political tendencies have complicated the writing of broader overviews. The early modern Low Countries were divided in three different political entities: the Southern Netherlands, the United Provinces and the principality of Liège, giving rise to separate historical traditions. In the Belgian historiography, older regional entities have even persisted, with medieval and early modern historians of the University of Ghent largely specializing in the history of the County of Flanders (the area west of the River Scheldt), while their colleagues of the Universities of Antwerp, Brussels and Leuven usually focus on the Duchy of Brabant.[7] More recently, the strengthening of the Flemish and Walloon regional governments and the politically stimulated construction of a regional "cultural identity," do not encourage Flemish or Walloon historians to transcend the linguistic borders in Belgium today. Interurban comparisons or broader perspectives have thus remained an exception[8] (often limited to the export trades in general and the textile sector in particular).[9]

In this context, giving an overview for the entire Low Countries of the second-hand market, an area with a dazzling regional, social and temporal variety, is not an easy job. This chapter will certainly reflect the shortcomings of the existing literature, and will not be able to present a balanced view of all regions in the Low Countries. It combines broad perspectives on the Southern Netherlands with some sparse material on the Northern Netherlands, and more focused approaches for Antwerp, Brussels and Ghent. In the first part, I study some general features about the guilds in the second-hand trade: their origins, the main rules, their insiders and outsiders, and the role of women. Second, I present the various ways second-hand dealers made a living in early modern towns in the Low Countries. Regional variation will be the theme of the third part, where quantitative data on the occurrence of guilds, their barriers of entry and the strong variation in the number of their members will be related to a hypothesis about town–countryside relations. This hypothesis will reemerge in the fourth part about the evolution of living standards in the second-hand trade, where other explanations will also be investigated.

Guilds and Institutions

Origins and Rules

It is generally impossible to detect the precise date of foundation of the second-hand dealers' guilds in the Low Countries, but their first traces date from the late Middle Ages. The oldest guild of second-hand dealers was probably founded in Bruges, where the first registration dates from 1297, closely followed by Ghent, in 1302.[10] In Utrecht, Leuven and Dordrecht, second-hand dealers' guilds were first mentioned in 1347, 1360 and 1367, and in Antwerp, the guild certainly already existed in 1399.[11]

The guilds provided an institutional framework for the second-hand market, and several similar rules were found in many towns of the Low Countries. Second-hand dealers had the right to have a shop, and could participate in the drawing lots in which the places in the weekly market were allocated. Generally, they were not allowed to own more than one shop or stall in the market. Usually, they were also active in the auctions or appraisals of household effects. A wealth of bylaws existed to prevent deceit in these sales: second-hand dealers who organized an auction were not allowed to buy anything for themselves, and "combinations" with colleagues or family members during the sales were forbidden. Furthermore, most towns had repeatedly proclaimed measures to prevent the trade in stolen goods, a prohibition on selling clothing coming from plague-ridden towns, and one on buying clothes from soldiers, in order to fight desertion.[12] Such rules often also existed in towns without second-hand dealers' guilds.

Even in towns with such guilds, there were always actors at the low end of the market who escaped their control. On free market days, everyone was customarily allowed to sell second-hand goods. Slop-dealers, ragmen and women were a permanent feature of urban society, and their relation with the official guild often proved to be difficult. In Antwerp, Brussels, Ghent and Mechelen, their sphere of action was limited to a few squares or streets. Yet they perpetually tried to enlarge this area, and the Antwerp second-hand dealers stated in 1749 that it was very difficult to fight these trespasses, because the cost of the seizure did not match the value of the seized goods, and the ragmen were "generally a kind of folk of which one cannot recover anything."[13] In Ghent in 1773, the second-hand dealers asked to appoint two or three city's soldiers to remove the countless ragmen who mingled with them on the Friday's market.[14] In Mechelen, six ragmen succeeded in eliminating these spatial limitations in 1760. When the second-hand dealers had their goods seized, they reacted by filing a petition to the town's government in which they requested an official permission. The magistrate stated that they wanted to give these poor people a way to make a living, and allowed them to sell second-hand goods that were not more expensive than 28 stuivers.[15]

Yet, despite these conflicts, there are also signs of collisions of ragmen and certain second-hand dealers. In the early sixteenth century, the Brussels and Ghent magistrates prohibited second-hand dealers from supplying ragmen with goods, a way to circumvent the rule of one shop per person.[16] In 1703, rich second-hand dealers allegedly paid small junk-dealers to keep an eye on opportunities to buy second-hand goods, and to purchase these wherever they could.[17] Unfortunately, sources are scarce about this group of people, who acted in the twilight zone of illegality. Some of these junk-dealers were women, but the role of women did not remain limited to the low end of the second-hand market.

Men and Women

Guilds are generally portrayed as exclusively male organizations, but the second-hand dealers form a clear exception to this. In sixteenth-century Ghent daughters, wives, widows and even independent women were registered buying and selling second-hand goods, taking workers in their service, making requests to the magistrate to provide them with official documents and swearing oaths.[18] There seems to be no reason to assume that the role of women in the guild of the second-hand dealers declined after the sixteenth century, when we look at the number of female members on the lists of the new members, which have been preserved for the guild of the second-hand dealers in Ghent, in the seventeenth and eighteenth centuries (see table 1.1). Official lists of the new guild-members are probably a rather poor source to assess the real economic role of women in a trade, as research for Brussels has shown that women could operate independently in guilds under the cover of male members, sons or husbands.[19] Nevertheless, the sources for Ghent suggest that female involvement increased in the second half of the eighteenth

Table 1.1. Number of women on the total number of new members in the guild of the second-hand dealers in Ghent, 1601–1794

Period	No. of women	Total new members	% women
1601–1650	28	396	7
1651–1700	53	757	7
1701–1750	59	929	6.3
1751–1794	72	598	12

century (at least, when the criteria for registration did not change). This source does not make a distinction between widows and independent women.

The participation of women in the guilds of the second-hand dealers did not remain limited to Ghent. The statutes of the second-hand dealers of Mons and Namur explicitly spoke about "tous ceux *ou tous celles*" (my italics) who wanted to become a member of the guild.[20] In Nivelles, widows and young girls were allowed to practice the trade if they paid the master fee (4 guilders) and an extra of 2 guilders.[21] In Den Bosch, 8 percent of the new members between 1750 and 1810 were women. An overview of all members in 1774 even counted 27 women on 114 members, but 16 of them were widows.[22] In Brussels, the registration of women in the official guild lists of members could only be measured for the years 1745–52: 9 percent of the registered members were women.[23] The highest participation of women in the Low Countries seems to have been registered in The Hague in the second half of the eighteenth century, where 19.9 percent of all new members were female.[24] In many other European towns, women played a role in the second-hand trade.[25] Still, female participation was not as high everywhere. On the lists of all members preserved for Leuven in 1597–8, seven women were registered on 30 members, but, on a similar list of 1794, not one woman was enrolled on 113 members.[26] I will investigate the reasons for this regional variation. First, I will take a closer look at how second-hand dealers made a living.

Market Practices: Trade Profits, Rents, Subcontracting and Renting Out

The income of second-hand dealers could be earned through a wide variety of activities, which varied through space, time and the individual involved. A distinction will be made in five activities: buying and selling goods in the local market, in regional markets, holding public sales, organizing production through subcontracting arrangements and renting out goods.

Buying and Selling in the Local Market

Second-hand dealers were of course best known for buying and selling second-hand goods. In Dutch they are called *oudekleerkopers*, old clothes buyers, and second-hand clothing was probably their main product. Their purchases could happen through personal contacts, as in 1754 in the inn "The

Apple" in Ghent, when the second-hand dealer Pieter de Cock said to the innkeeper Jacobus de Smedt: "Smet, you have a beautiful buffet over there." When de Smedt replied that he was sorry about his purchase, as the buffet did not fit in the room in the basement, de Cock offered to buy it for 14 ducats.[27]

More often, however, they bought and sold goods in public sales of the household effects of deceased or indebted people, or in the sales in the *Berg van Barmharigheid*, the public pawnshop where uncollected pawns were regularly sold. In the 1660s, it was said of the Ghent second-hand dealers that they always bought the larger part of the goods of these public sales.[28] This created possibilities for de facto monopolization of markets. In 1627, the town government of Ghent prohibited implicit or explicit deals among women who attended the public sales, and who divided the market among themselves, or pooled resources to make purchases together.[29]

Second-hand dealers often bought their goods in public sales on credit, generally for three months.[30] More than once, this became an issue of conflict. In 1628, the Antwerp second-hand dealers guild protested against the actions of one Jan Lindemans, who had lent a lot of money to many of their members, and who had assigned the official city's bellman to call out for a payment of these debts within eight days. This action "shamed and insulted them for the whole world."[31] The guild itself became split over an issue of credit in 1642, when an attempt was made to organize a public sale where only cash payments were accepted. This caused outrage among the less well-to-do members of the guild, and these decided to boycott it, insulting and threatening those who stayed. Ten years later, the deans of the guild stated that they were still being mobbed when they refused to give credit to a potential buyer.[32]

Second-hand dealers sold their goods in their shops, on the weekly market and during public sales. Sometimes, they apparently used quite aggressive sales methods. In 1622, the deans of the Antwerp second-hand dealers' guild asked that their members would be forbidden "to stop potential customers outside their houses, pull them inside and force them to buy in one way or another."[33] In 1753, seven second-hand dealers in Ghent accused some of their colleagues in their street "to allure the countrymen and other passing people to their houses, whether they intended to buy something or not, taking their clothes with such a violence, that these are torn from their bodies, and that people who wanted to buy something did not dare to enter their street."[34]

Buying and Selling in Regional Markets

The "countrymen" in the last citation are not coincidental. Many contemporaries signaled the role of the rural hinterland or even other towns as a market for the second-hand dealers. In 1725, the magistrate of Veurne spoke of second-hand dealers "who sell clothes and rags to the people of the countryside and the poor people."[35] The Antwerp second-hand dealers stated in 1599 that they regularly sold to 'common people and countryside dwellers', in 1608 they received permission to sell ready-made clothing "for the convenience of both the townsmen as for the countryside dwellers who visit the urban market" and in 1610 they were even accused of selling goods to their colleagues in Brussels and Mechelen.[36] In the sixteenth and seventeenth centuries, the Ghent second-hand dealers visited several fairs in other towns, certainly that of Bruges.[37] Several early eighteenth-century probate inventories of second-hand dealers register debts to inhabitants of nearby villages. In 1753 and 1788, the city government accused the second-hand dealers of running after the villagers when they entered the town. In 1760, the Ghent second-hand dealer Frederik Van de Vijvere borrowed a small wagon from his colleague Louys van Rechem to drive to Brussels. Normally, this would have remained unnoticed by historians, but Van de Vijvere apparently also drove to Mechelen, Antwerp, Waasmunster and Lokeren (making it a trip of roughly 150 to 160 kilometers), and damaged the wagon on his way, which led to a trial.[38]

Second-hand dealers did not simply sell goods in regional markets, they bought them there as well. In 1630, the Ghent second-hand dealer Jan van Plassche apparently sold "camisolles" (waistcoats) which he brought in from other regions.[39] They even imported old clothes from Holland and Zeeland, but this became illegal in the early eighteenth century.[40]

A Rent on Appraising and Holding Public Sales

Another important element in the incomes of some – though not all – second-hand dealers constituted a rent on the appraisal and public sale of household effects. In most towns, the second-hand dealers' guilds held a monopoly on these activities. The organizers of these public sales seem often only a part of the guild, and they were paid 1 to 5 percent of the value of the goods appraised or sold. Some sources suggest that they sometimes charged small extras on top of this regular payment.[41] In a few towns, the public sales were also taxed by the city government, and the second-hand dealers played a part in the collection of these taxes.[42] Sometimes, the guilds had been given this monopoly after the payment of a serious sum of money to the authorities. The second-hand dealers of Mechelen claimed in 1760 that their forefathers had paid the magistrate an unknown sum in 1459.[43] In 1627, the Antwerp second-hand dealers had paid no less than 50,000 guilders to the central authorities, for the perpetual privilege of appraising and organizing public sales. They even allegedly sent a delegation to Spain, where Philip IV confirmed this arrangement.[44] The mobilization of such important resources points to the profitability of this activity, and many attempts were made by brokers, notaries or other individuals to appropriate this right from the second-hand dealers' guilds. Such endeavors are registered for Mechelen in 1684, 1750, 1759, 1766, 1769 and 1771, for Ghent in 1721, for Antwerp in 1760 and for Leuven in 1744, 1745, 1757, 1760 and 1780, but they generally failed.[45]

There were important discussions about the nature of the goods involved, and various rules created different kind of sales in different towns. Some household effects were difficult to consider as "second-hand" (e.g., wood, living animals or agricultural products) and they were sometimes the object of long discussions of encroachers of the second-hand dealers' privileges. In 1766 and in 1771 in Mechelen, a group of notaries tried to appropriate the right to sell these goods.[46] A wide variety of new goods were sold during the public auctions at the Friday Market in Antwerp until 1682, when this became illegal. In Namur, new goods such as damask, satin, cottons, linen, silk stockings, tea, coffee and groceries were still sold during public auctions at low prices in 1759. According to contemporary observers, these came partly from smugglers and frauds, and partly from small regular shopkeepers who were in need of cash. The latter were accused of bringing part of their stock under the hammer, even at a loss, to be able to pay their debts. The public sales were also portrayed as occasions for debtors to escape their creditors, as they could dispose of their goods without being noticed. Similarly, traders who had to pay a bill of exchange sometimes trusted part of their goods to peddlers to get cash quickly.[47]

Old Goods, New Goods, and Subcontracting

Second-hand dealers obviously sold used goods, but the boundaries between second-hand and new goods were clearly blurred, and different interpretations of these borders created various opportunities for second-hand dealers through space and time. In 1652, the Ghent second-hand dealers lost the right to sell old books, "as these could spread heresy and confusion among the people," but in Leuven this was only forbidden in 1751.[48] In 1672 in Antwerp and in 1739 in Ghent, they lost the right to sell new fabric by the ell. In the sixteenth and seventeenth centuries, the makers of beds were incorporated in the second-hand dealers' guild, but, in 1676, they succeeded in breaking away from the guild in Ghent.[49]

The best-known bone of contention consisted of the sales of new clothing. In Antwerp, the second-hand dealers sold new, ready-made clothing illegally in the sixteenth century, and legally between 1608 and 1740, after which this became forbidden. In Ghent, Mons and Namur second-hand dealers continued to sell new clothing until the end of the *ancien régime*, but it remained illegal to their colleagues in Brussels and Bruges. The new clothing sold by the second-hand dealers was not made to measure, but was ready-made. Usually, they were made by poorer tailors or poorer colleagues in subcontracting arrangements.[50]

Some sources suggest that second-hand dealers were also indirectly involved in the production of other new goods, but the information on this topic is scarce. The second-hand dealers of Ghent sold new cupboards, beds and all kind of hats, kettles, locks and several items of copper or ironware, but these activities came increasingly under attack. From 1739 onwards, selling new furniture or ironware became forbidden to them.[51] Yet in 1756 it turned out that they circumvented these prohibitions. First, they allegedly had new furniture made by outworkers, or had it imported from other towns, which was subsequently moved to houses of their friends or acquaintances, after which they could sell them as "second-hand goods." The second-hand dealers acknowledged these practices, and the cabinetmakers therefore requested that the second-hand dealers would only be allowed to sell furniture that had lost all polish and appearance of novelty. The Privy Council declined the petition of the cabinetmakers.[52]

Renting Out

Renting out clothes was another way for second-hand dealers to make money. In 1569, Hans van Ceulen said that "frivolous women" daily hired beautiful clothes. In 1611, François Mans declared that "he hired out clothes on all Sundays, Holy Days and especially on kermis days, to be worn for a day or two, by people who could not afford to buy them or have them made." In the eighteenth century, the Brussels second-hand dealers still hired out clothes, to go to balls.[53] Furniture was also rented out sometimes, as is shown by the probate inventory of Joseph Dael, a rich second-hand dealer in Ghent in 1780.[54] This part of their trade is very hard to reconstruct, and its relative importance or evolution remains a mystery.

Obviously, not all second-hand dealers were involved in *all* these five activities. The combination of their practices and strategies could vary from one individual to another, and could change over time and space. The urban population could grow or decrease, the range of hinterlands could expand or contract, new goods replaced older ones... A decline of one part of their income may have been compensated by a rise in another. In 1716, a few years after the War of Spanish Succession and during the demographic and economic crisis of the city, the second-hand dealers in Ghent claimed that the lease of the tax of second-hand goods had declined four- to fivefold.[55] Yet the numbers of second-hand dealers reaches a zenith in these years, which must probably be related to the expansion of their regional outlets (see below).

Furthermore, these five activities probably do not exhaust the practices and strategies of early modern second-hand dealers. Circumstantial evidence points to the fact that some second-hand dealers were also active on the credit market, as lenders of money,[56] but the scale of these activities remains unclear so far. Neither is it clear whether second-hand dealers could also practice other trades or be a member of other guilds. Double membership with other guilds was forbidden in Antwerp,[57] and in Nivelles, a second-hand dealer was not allowed to be a tailor or a draper.[58] In Ghent, Maastricht, Den Bosch and Namur, on the other hand, many second-hand dealers were also a member of the tailors' or mercers' guild.[59]

In different towns, various market situations and institutional settings created different opportunities and constraints. All these elements make it clear that clear-cut generalizations about their incomes are difficult to make. In order to be more precise, we need to look in more detail at regional variation.

Regional Variation: Guild-structures, Barriers of Entry, and Numbers of Players in the Market

Guilds and Their Geography

Guilds of second-hand dealers did not exist everywhere, and it would clearly be wrong to assume that they covered the whole of the second-hand market in the Low Countries. In the countryside, they obviously did not exist. Public sales in the countryside were generally held by notaries. A simple town–

country dichotomy will not do, however, because second-hand dealers' guilds certainly did not exist in all towns of the Low Countries. The (incomplete) general 1784 inquiry about the guilds in the Southern Netherlands,[60] supplemented by other sources, informs us that autonomous guilds of second-hand dealers could only be found in the largest towns: Antwerp, Brussels, Bruges, Ghent, Liège, Lier, Leuven, Mechelen, Namur, Mons, Tournai and Ypres.[61] In most other towns with roughly 5,000 inhabitants around 1500, the second-hand dealers constituted a branch of the tailors' guild, as in Ath, Diest, Geraardsbergen, Huy, Kortrijk and Turnhout.[62] There are also examples where second-hand dealers were member of the mercers guild (e.g., in Oudenaarde and Maastricht). Of the 26 towns in the Low Countries with 5,000 inhabitants or more around 1500, 20 had some kind of a guild organization of second-hand dealers, with the exception of Aalst, Dendermonde, Enghien, Nieuwpoort, Tienen and Tongeren.[63] For most towns smaller than 5,000 inhabitants, no traces have so far been found of an organization of second-hand dealers,[64] although there were other guilds in quite a lot of these places, e.g. in Arlon, Beaumont, Diksmuide, Echternach, Halle, Herentals, Jodoigne, Ostend, Roermond, Ronse, Weert and St. Niklaas.[65] The small towns of Menen and Veurne (3358 and 2200 inhabitants respectively) form an exception, as they did have a mixed tailors-second-hand dealers' guild. This guild landscape was rather stable over time: when towns became larger than 5,000 inhabitants in the sixteenth, seventeenth or eighteenth centuries, this generally did not cause the creation of new second-hand dealers' guilds in the Southern Netherlands.

This pattern, which links demographic data to the existence of second-hand dealers' guilds, does not apply in the Northern Netherlands. Autonomous guilds of second-hand dealers only existed in Utrecht, Dordrecht, Middelburg, Bergen op Zoom, Den Haag and Den Bosch. In Amsterdam and Haarlem, second-hand dealers were part of the tailors' guilds, but elsewhere second-hand dealers were apparently not organized in a guild structure. An absence of a second-hand dealers' guild does not necessarily imply an absence of second-hand dealers: in Aalst for example, a census of 1796 registered thirteen second-hand dealers, although they seem not to have been organised in a guild structure. An absence of a guild likewise does not necessarily implies complete freedom on the second-hand markets: indeed, several similar rules about the second-hand market existed in most towns in the Northern Netherlands.[66]

This strongly uneven regional occurrence of guild organisations is a characteristic feature of the second-hand dealers. Groups such as the tailors, shoemakers or bakers were organized in guilds in almost all towns; this is illustrated by the fact that ninety-five tailors' guilds have been counted in the Northern Netherlands, compared to only six guilds of second-hand dealers.[67]

Barriers of Entry

A similar variation existed in the rules of entry. As for most commercial guilds, a formal apprenticeship was generally not needed to become a member of the second-hand dealers' guilds in the Low Countries,[68] with the exception of Mechelen (where the second-hand dealers guild prescribed an unusually long three-year apprenticeship) and Ath and Namur, where an apprenticeship of two years was needed. Likewise, passing a formal master test was only demanded in these three towns.[69] Yet traces of apprenticeships do exist in other towns as well. Older statutes prescribed an apprenticeship of two years in Bruges, but this seems to have disappeared in the late eighteenth century.[70] In Menen, the guild of the second-hand dealers was open to those who had fulfilled an apprenticeship and those who did not, but the latter paid a larger fee (see table 1.2). In Antwerp, an apprenticeship of two years was necessary to become a "crieur juré," an official organiser of public sales.[71]

In many German towns and the eastern part of the northern Low Countries, religious criteria existed to exclude potential guild-members or citizens, be they Jewish, Catholic, Lutheran or Mennonite.[72] They were introduced in the 1620s in the eastern towns of the northern Low Countries dominated by middle-class guildsmen, as Arnhem, Deventer, Nijmegen, Utrecht and Zwolle, but were relaxed in the eighteenth century.[73] In the western towns of the Northern Netherlands, anti-Catholic measures were never enacted. In the Southern Netherlands, the guild statutes of the second-hand dealers never explicitly required an allegiance to the Catholic Church, with the exception of Namur, where the statutes of 1717 prescribed that aspiring members should prove "qu'ils sont de bonne fame, faisant profession de la foi catholique, apostolique et romaine."[74] As Jews or Protestants were hardly found in the Southern Netherlands between 1600 and 1800, it was probably not necessary to insist on the necessity of being Catholic.

The most important precondition to become a member of a second-hand dealers' guild consisted everywhere in paying a fee to the guild. This sum varied according to the person and the specific town involved. Sons of members generally paid only half the fee, and in a few towns they paid even less.[75] In most small towns, official citizens clearly paid a smaller sum than "foreigners" (noncitizens). This last distinction seems not to have existed in the larger towns. In some cases, the second-hand dealers' guild comprised several subsections, which all had other tariffs of entry (as in Mons; see table 1.2). All these local particularistic customs complicate a global comparison for the Low Countries. Nevertheless, an attempt is made in the table below. In order to facilitate international comparisons, I added the number of days an unskilled laborer had to toil to acquire this sum. Daily wages of unskilled building-workers varied according to the trade, the town, the season or the life cycle of the worker. Therefore, I calculated two figures, based on a minimum of 8 stuivers and a maximum of 12 stuivers a day. In order to explore possible explanations for variation, I added the population figures of the towns involved, and the status of the guild organization: whether the second-hand dealers had an autonomous organisation (A) or were part of a mixed corporatist organization (M).

The variation in tariffs of entry is amazing. In Nivelles and Diest, the cheapest fees consisted only of some 6 to 10 day wages of an unskilled labourer, while in Mechelen and Leuven the trade was hardly accessible for

Table 1.2. Master fees in the guilds of the second-hand dealers (or mixed guilds with the tailors) in 1784

Table 1.2a. Town with no explicit distinction between citizens and non-citizens

			Fee to become a guild-member	
Town	Population[a]	A/M	Guilders	No. of day wages of an unskilled laborer
Nivelles	6,370	M	4–0	6.6–10
Diest	5,368	M	4–0	6.6–10
Geraardsbergen	6,050	M	6–0	10–15
Ghent	51,069	A	6–0[b]	10–15
Ath	8,000/6,185[c]	M	16–10	27.5–41.25
			10–10[d]	10.8–16.25
Bruges	30,846	A	30	50–75
Mons	21,000	A	60	100–150
			30	50–75
			6[e]	10–15
Mechelen	20,350	A	94	156.6–235
			394[f]	656.6–985
Antwerp	54,000	A	150	250–375
Brussels	75,000	A	150	250–375
Leuven	20,831	A	200[g]	333.3–500

Notes:
(a) Claude Bruneel, Luc Delporte, and Bernadette Petitjean (eds.), *Le Dénombrement général de la population des Pays-Bas Autrichiens en 1784* (Brussels, 1996), *passim*.
(b) In 1540, the tariffs of entry for almost all guilds in Ghent were levelled to 6 guilders by Charles V, in his Concessio Carolina, as part of a punishment to the rebellious city.
(c) Bruneel et al., *Le Dénombrement*, p. 145.
(d) Aspirant members had to pay 10 guilders and 10 stuivers for the chapel, and 6 guilders for the experts who controlled the master test. If the second-hand dealers were not obliged to take a master test, they thus only paid 10 guilders and 10 stuivers
(e) Full members paid 60 guilders. Those who only bought and sold goods, "sans pouvoir travailler ni mettre en oeuvre les marchandises," paid only 30 guilders. Those who only sold old linen paid 6 guilders.
(f) The fee for aspirants who were not a son of a member was 80 guilders. Furthermore, they had to pay 14 guilders for "une petite fête," and a security of 300 guilders.
(g) The fee to become a member of the guild was raised to 50 guilders in 1670, to 80 in 1680, 100 in 1690, 150 in 1735 and reached 200 guilders in 1750, Arthur Meulemans, "Leuvense ambachten. III. De Oudkleeerkopers," *Eigen Schoon en de Brabander*, 40 (1957) p. 370.

outsiders without any capital. Any comparison of fifteen towns is, of course, likely to find differences in tariffs, but the variation in the tariffs of entry of the second-hand dealers was again more important than in other trades, e.g. the tailors or the carpenters.[76]

How to explain this variation? We might assume that the fees of entry were roughly correlated to the possible size of the market. Indeed, fees of entry were generally higher in larger towns, but there are a few remarkable discrepancies, such as the high tariff for Mechelen and Leuven, and the low rates for Ghent and for Bruges. In Menen, the fee of entry was twice as high as in Kortrijk, where the population was five times larger.

Population figures clearly do not explain everything. The tariffs of entry were generally the result of negotiations between the guild and the town

Table 1.2b. Towns with a distinction between citizens and non-citizens

			Fee to become a member of the guild of the second-hand dealers					
			Citizen		Non citizen		Son of a master	
Town	Population	A/M	Guilders	Unskilled day wages	Guilders	Unskilled day wages	Guilders	Unskilled day wages
Kortrijk	15,072	M	12	10–15	24	20–30	6	10–15
Menen	3,000	M	24	20–30	48	80–120	6	10–15
			36[a]	60–90				
Turnhout	8,345	M	20	33.3–50	100	166.6–250	10	25
Namur	14,728	A	24	40–60	30	50–75	6	10–15
					48	80–120		
					72[b]	120–180		

Notes:
(a) Citizens who had fulfilled an apprenticeship paid 24 guilders, those who had not 36 guilders.
(b) For Namur, the tariffs of 1717 are cited, as they are missing for 1784. An inhabitant of the County of Namur paid 30 guilders, other subjects of the Austrian Royal House paid 48 guilders, and those from other countries 72 guilders, J.B. Goetstouwers, *Les métiers de Namur sous l'ancien régime. Contribution à l'histoire sociale* (Leuven, Paris 1908) p. 54, ROPBA, III (Brussels, 1873), p. 88.

magistrate.[77] Local political circumstances are therefore important variables. In this sense, it is interesting to note that in the four towns with the highest tariffs of entry, the second-hand dealers were closely involved in local politics. In Leuven, the second-hand dealers formed together with the tailors and the hosiers one of the ten "Naties," a part of the city government that played an important role in the election of the mayor. The Antwerp second-hand dealers had a regular representative in the "Brede Raad" (the large council), a representative institution that had to approve the collection of the taxes, or changes in the existing privileges. In Brussels, the second-hand dealers had a similar position, together with many other guilds.[78] In Mechelen, six guilds had representatives in the bench of aldermen, and appointed one of the two treasurers, and the bailiff (*rentmeester*), but the second-hand dealers were not part of this politically privileged group.[79]

Conversely, the exceptionally low barriers of entry in Ghent can be related to an atypically strong restructuring of local political institutions in 1540, when Charles V broke the power of the guilds after a spectacular insurrection against rising taxes and for the restoration of medieval privileges. All privileges were revoked, the guilds lost all influence in local or regional politics, and all guild fees (of entry) were levelled at the low sum of six guilders. Smaller rebellions in Oudenaarde, Kortrijk and Geraardsbergen were punished in a similar way, albeit less drastically.[80] The curtailment of the political muscle of the guilds in these towns may have slimmed the fees of entry in the long run too (see table 1.2). Similarly, the relatively low barriers of entry of the second-hand dealers guild in Bruges may have been influenced by the anti-corporatist policy of its magistrate in the second half of the eighteenth century.[81]

Political clout may thus explain the higher or lower tariffs for some towns, but it remains unclear why other guilds such as the tailors or the shoemakers were generally more expensive in towns with the same political structure, and why the variation in the tariffs of entry of the guilds of second-hand dealers in the towns of the Low Countries was that important. One element may have been the role of the guild organization itself, as the variation becomes less striking, when the autonomous guilds are isolated. The lowest fees are clearly demanded in a few small towns where the second-hand dealers were part of the tailors' guilds. One can imagine that the existence of an autonomous guild may have gone hand in hand with higher costs (litigation, guild house, feasts) for which a regular income in the form of higher tariffs of entry may have been important. Still, there must have been some relation between the sum one was willing to invest, or which a guild was able to extract, and the expected returns in the future. We might get an idea about the range of the different markets by looking at the numbers of second-hand dealers in the various towns of the Low Countries.

Geography by Numbers: External and/or Internal Explanations

In table 1.3 I have collected all the data I could find in guild sources and population censuses on the number of second-hand dealers in the towns of the Low Countries in the early modern period. Figures for different towns are not always easy to compare, as several sources often measure in different ways. Moreover, dealing in second-hand goods was often combined with other activities, and some actors on this market were certainly not registered. In order to compare the absolute figures, I related them to the population figures (/1,000 inhabitants). As this data is highly disparate, relating to different years, I have presented them in five periods of twenty years to improve the readability.

Despite the shortcomings of these sources, the variation in relative numbers of second-hand dealers through space and time is again remarkable. Compared to the concentration of tailors or bakers in different towns, this variation is much more important.[82] The high figures for certain towns can theoretically be explained by differences in access to the guilds, by the existence of some kind of an external market, or by a different internal composition of the trade in certain towns (if, for example, second-hand dealers controlled a larger part of the distributive trades). Institutional differences in barriers of entry can easily be discarded. At first sight, the high figures for Ghent could be explained by the low official sum of only six guilders aspirant members had to pay to become a member. Yet the relative number of tailors or bakers (who had to pay the same low sum) in Ghent was not higher than in other towns. Furthermore, the relative figures for Leuven were even higher in the late eighteenth century, when potential members had to pay 200 guilders, one of the highest barriers of entry in the Low Countries (see table 1.2).

Table 1.3. Number of second-hand dealers in various towns of the Low Countries, 1580–1799

Town	1580–99 /1,000	Abs.	1660–79 /1,000	Abs.	1730–49 /1,000	Abs.	1750–79 /1,000	Abs.	1780–99 /1,000	Abs.
Antwerp	4.9	245					0.9	42		
Brussels					3.0	214	2.8	168	2.8	211
Ghent			3.28	164	6.7	264	5.1	228		
Leuven	0.3	30			6.4	98	3.6	60	5.6	113
Bruges					0.2	8			0.8	27
Mechelen					2.0	40	1.4	30		
Liège			4.25	170						
Den Bosch							7.0	88	9.0	114
Namur					1.0	14				
Nivelles							0.1	1	1.4	9
Lier									0.7	7
Aalst									2.5	13
Tielt									0.7	7
Geraardsb.									0.9	6
Lokeren									0.5	4
Oudenaarde									0.8	3
Izegem									0.1	1

Sources: Rijksarchief Anderlecht, Ambachten van Brabant, 550–1; AGR, CP PA, 405A and B; SAG, Reeks 199, 16–21; Jan Van Roey, "De sociale structuren en de godsdienstige gezindheid van de Antwerpse bevolking op de vooravond van de reconciliatie met Farnese (17 augustus 1585)," unpublished PhD thesis, University of Ghent, 1963, p. 112; J. Verbeemen, "Antwerpen in 1755. Een demografische en sociaal-economische studie," *Bijdragen tot de Geschiedenis*, 40 (1957), p. 46; Arthur Meulemans, "Leuvense ambachten III. De Oudkleerkopers," *Eigen Schoon en de Brabander*, 40 (1957), pp. 68, 374; J. De Nolf, "Socio-professionele structuren binnen de Brugse samenleving rond het midden van de achttiende eeuw," in Jos de Belder, Walter Prevenier and Chris Vandenbroeke (eds.), *Sociale mobiliteit en sociale structuren in Vlaanderen en Brabant* (Ghent, 1983), p. 85; Edouard Poncelet, *Les bons métiers de la cite de Liège* (Liège, 1900); Bibi Panhuysen, *Maatwerk. Kleermakers, naaisters, oudkleerkopers en de gilden* (1500–1800) (Amsterdam, 2000); Peter Stabel, "De-urbanisation and Urban Decline in Flanders from 1500 to 1800: The Disintegration of an Urban System?," in D. McCabe (ed.), *Eurocit. European Urbanisation, Social Structure and Problems between the Eighteenth and Twentieth Century* (Leicester 1995), pp. 87–108. The figures for Lier and Nivelles were communicated by Bruno Blondé. Population figures from Denis Morsa, "L'urbanisation de la Belgique (1500–1800), taille, hiérarchie et dynamique des villes," *Revue du Nord*, LXXIX (1997), pp. 303–30 and Claude Bruneel, Luc Delporte and Bernadette Petitjean, *Le Dénombrement générale de la population des Pays-Bas Autrichiens en 1784. Edition critique* (Brussels, 1996).

The decline of the relative numbers of second-hand dealers in Antwerp can be related to a weakening of external markets and to a loss of certain parts of the distribution sector. During the sixteenth century, Antwerp was the economic capital of the Low Countries, and its clothing entrepreneurs had many contacts and outlets around the country.[83] But the new border with the Northern Netherlands cut off a part of the traditional Northern Brabantian agrarian hinterland of the town after 1585.[84] In 1586, one year after the surrender of the town to the Spanish troops of Farnese, the second-hand dealers were explicitly allowed to sell their goods in the countryside and in the Campine area, and in the other "places of obedience to his majesty," but not in the rebellious provinces.[85] The remaining hinterland of Antwerp, the

Campine, was a relatively thinly populated area of poor sandy soils with plenty of forests and moorland, where most peasants had no other choice but subsistence farming.[86] Rural demand was probably maintained in the relatively prosperous first two decades of the seventeenth century, but weakened thereafter. The border region was regularly hit by military operations and plunder before 1648, and during the Dutch War (1672–8) and the War of Spanish Succession. In the late seventeenth century an anonymous tract complained that parts of the Antwerp hinterland were supplied by the Dutch towns of Breda and Den Bosch.[87] Furthermore, the Antwerp second-hand dealers lost the right to sell new goods at the public auctions in 1682, which seriously affected the volume of their sales. The growth of a rural service sector further weakened what was left of the rural outlets of the second-hand dealers, which were reduced to a small number in eighteenth century Antwerp.

The high figures for Ghent can also be related to rural markets. In 1536, the second-hand dealers of the town already affirmed that they "especially sold to the people of the countryside." The area around Ghent was a fertile, densely populated and highly progressive rural area. The custom of the fallow disappeared in the eighteenth century, when the region registered the highest yields of the southern Low Countries.[88] Furthermore, this region was the main centre of a very important proto-industrial linen industry, which developed strongly in the seventeenth and eighteenth centuries.[89] Twenty to 30 percent; sometimes even 50 percent of the population of many nearby villages engaged in spinning or weaving, and the weavers were obliged to have their pieces measured, sealed and sold in the linen market of Ghent. There, second-hand dealers and other artisans sold a large range of new and second-hand goods. The accounts of a rich second-hand dealer in the second part of the seventeenth century show that a large majority of his (registered) customers lived in the countryside, and several early eighteenth-century probate inventories of second-hand dealers register debts by customers in surrounding villages.[90]

In Brussels, the relative number of second-hand dealers was lower than in Ghent, but still more than average. Its gently sloping hinterland was a fertile, market-oriented area of commercial agriculture, with hardly any rural industry. The town was an important regional service and fashion centre, and five new paved roads reinforced its ties with small towns and the countryside during the eighteenth century.[91] The second-hand dealers of the town were not allowed to sell any new clothing, but this apparently did not harm their numbers.

The relative number of second-hand dealers was negligible in Leuven in the late sixteenth century, but they peaked in the second half of the eighteenth century. This boom can probably be related to the agricultural growth in the Walloon Brabantine area, and to the central place of Leuven in the grain trade. The grain market of the town grew strongly after the construction of the brick road to Namur in the 1750s. Also, the second-hand dealers obtained official permission to sell new, ready-made garments in 1758, when rural demand started to soar. The multiplication of opportunities for the second-hand dealers of the town might shed some light on the exceptionally high barriers of entry that the guild was able to impose in the course of the eighteenth century (see table 1.2). The smaller role of women in the late eighteenth century compared to the late sixteenth century (see earlier) may be related to strategies of men to push them out of a trade that had probably become more profitable in this town.

The high relative figures of Liège in 1676 may also be explained by rural stimuli. From the early seventeenth century onwards, the town had become the center of an important puting-out trade in nails, which were made in the surrounding countryside by some 15,000 nail-makers. These often brought their products to the towns themselves, where merchants paid them.[92] Moreover, the grain market of the town was traditionally very important in the seventeenth and eighteenth century, and regional grain production expanded strongly in the 1660s and 1670s.[93] Just as in Leuven, second-hand dealers were allowed to sell new goods in Liège.[94]

The highest figure was registered for Den Bosch in the northern Netherlands, which must probably be related to the restructuring of the Dutch economy in the late seventeenth and eighteenth centuries. From the last quarter of the seventeenth century, the maritime provinces in the west of the Dutch Republic declined due to a restructuring of international trade, foreign competition for urban industries, high taxation and a drop in agricultural prices. Conversely, the inland eastern and southern provinces profited from a growth in rural industry, lower taxes and a diversification in agriculture. From the mid-eighteenth century, the countryside began to profit from the recovery in agricultural prices. Several artisans in larger towns reoriented their production to rural markets.[95] In this sense, the fact that a guild of second-hand dealers was founded in Den Bosch in 1750 fits very well. Moreover, contemporaries explicitly acknowledged the importance of the *Meierij*, the hinterland of the town, for the outlets of the local second-hand dealers.[96]

The insight that town–countryside relations were shaped differently between regions and over time may also help us to explain some of the peculiarities in the geographical distribution of guilds in the Low Countries. For the northern Netherlands, second-hand dealers' guilds only existed from the late Middle Ages to the late eighteenth century in Bergen op Zoom, Dordrecht, Middelburg and Utrecht. These four towns were longstanding centers of regional trade, and nodal points for town countryside contacts.[97] Dordrecht exerted institutionalized coercive power over its hinterland, with the farmers in southern Holland being forced to sell their crops in the town's market.[98] Similarly, it may not be a coincidence that in the Southern Netherlands, a guild organization of second-hand dealers existed in Ath, Geraardsbergen, Kortrijk and Oudenaarde, which were markets for rurally made linen or small tapestries,[99] and in Diest and Namur, which had reasonably important grain markets.[100] Aalst became an important secondary linen market in the late seventeenth and eighteenth century.[101] A guild of second-hand dealers was not created, but their numbers were relatively high all the same. Conversely, Roermond and Luxemburg had grain markets, but no trace of a second-hand dealers' guild. This is not that surprising, as the relation between these towns and their hinterlands was very weak indeed, due to geographical or political circumstances.[102] Other towns without second-hand dealers' guilds, or with relatively low numbers of their practitioners generally had weaker (or weakened) relations with their hinterlands, e.g., Bruges, Lier or Mechelen.

Balancing the "external" and the "internal" explanation of high relative figures of second-hand dealers (rural markets versus a larger share of the distributive trades) is in need of further detailed research. I have the impression that the permission or prohibition to sell new clothing or new goods was certainly an important element which influenced the opportunities, profits and living standards of second-hand dealers, but I doubt whether this was a decisive factor influencing their numbers. In Antwerp, second-hand dealers could sell new clothing till 1742, but their downfall seems to have set in much earlier. In Brussels, second-hand dealers were never allowed to sell new clothing, but their numbers were significantly higher than in Antwerp. Conversely, their colleagues of Namur were allowed to sell new goods, but their relative numbers were not that impressive. In Leuven, Meulemans counted 98 second-hand dealers in 1748, while they only received the permission to sell new clothing in 1758. Furthermore, practices cannot be read as a mere execution of rules, and we already saw that second-hand dealers often ignored many prohibitions concerning their trade. The political permission to sell new goods or new clothing seems not create a new market situation from scratch, but rather appears to confirm an existing situation, legitimizing and regulating a growing market. Conversely, prohibitions on selling new goods were generally made in harsh times, when external markets were already weakened.

There is another way to test the validity of the two explanations. If the large number of second-hand dealers in certain towns could be explained by the purchases of rural clients on the urban market, these would logically also have effects on other trades, which produced simple consumer goods such as shoes, hats etc. But, if the higher number of second-hand dealers were to be explained solely by a different institutional organization of the distributive trades, there is no reason to expect any deviation in numbers in these production trades. We do no have all the data for every town, but the number of shoemakers and hatters is clearly higher in Ghent and Brussels than in Antwerp.[103]

Living Standards

Rich and Poor

In Antwerp, in 1621 the second-hand dealer Guillaume Willems had a total value of his stocks amounting to 43,557 guilders. After a deduction of his debts, he still had a nice sum of 36,653 guilders, which made him one of the most affluent artisans of his time. Yet the second-hand trade was clearly characterized by a strong social differentiation, with rich and poor actors both inside and outside the second-hand dealers' guild. The Antwerp tax rolls of 1584 show that 51 percent of the second-hand dealers had to pay taxes, while the other half were considered too poor to pay anything. The actual sum paid also varied strongly.[104] In 1631, the Ghent second-hand dealers' guild requested that the prohibition on owning two stalls in the market should be reenacted, as one of their members had one stall run by his daughter, and another by his servant.[105] Social irritations in the marketplace reappeared a decade later, when a group of second-hand dealers who called themselves "the uncovered stalls" ("de ongedeckte craemen") complained that their small trestle tables were hardly noticed when their richer colleagues set up their larger stalls with awnings next to them. They therefore asked for a physical separation between these two groups in the marketplace.[106]

When we look at the stocks of these shops, it becomes clear that the second-hand dealers were far from a socially homogeneous group. In table 1.4, I present the number of pieces of clothing and their prices found in thirteen probate inventories from second-hand dealers in Ghent between 1720 and 1740.

Some second-hand dealers owned substantially more clothing than others. Pieter Moerman owned 694 pieces, a stock that was four to five times bigger than his other colleagues in the sample.[107] The value of the stock varied as well. The 125 pieces of clothing of Livinus Antonius Martens at first sight seem slightly more important than the 113 items of his colleague Pieter Galendeyn, but the value of the former's stock exceeded ten times that of the latter (83 and 1029 guilders respectively).[108] The second-hand market was clearly not uniform, but consisted of different marketsegments.

Historical Evolution of Living Standards

How did the living standards of second-hand dealers evolve between the sixteenth and the eighteenth century? Reliable sources about living standards

Table 1.4. Prices of 2,246 pieces of clothing in the stocks of thirteen second-hand dealers, 1720–40 (in guilders)[a]

Price	'22	'23	'24	'24	'27	'27	'28	'29	'35	'36	'36	'38	Total	%
<2	–	69	30	–	5	19	11	50	77	4	151	5	421	19
2–<4	–	118	47	91	44	62	35	122	–	6	82	17	624	28
4–<6	–	158	41	27	35	27	37	–	–	1	13	31	370	16
6–<8	39	119	38	–	21	36	31	–	–	–	9	–	293	13
8–<10	–	78	14	–	7	15	28	–	–	–	4	12	158	7
10–<15	–	111	17	–	13	18	16	–	–	–	–	2	177	8
15<20	28	25	36	–	7	2	3	–	–	–	–	46	147	6
+20	–	16	15	–	–	–	21	–	–	–	–	–	52	6
Total	67	694	238	118	132	179	182	172	77	11	259	113	2242	100

Note:
(a) SAG, Reeks 332, 468, 21, October 3, 1722; 486, 30, February 22, 1723; 499, 2, April 22, 1724; 496, 8, May 25, 1724; 519, 9, February 26, 1727; 517, 2, October, 26 1727; 523, 3, Augustus 27, 1728; 530, 12, March 20 1729; 565, 3, June 30,1735; 568, 2, 1736; 572, 17, October 26, 1736; 578, 12, March 19, 1738.

Table 1.5. Supported members and total number of second-hand dealers in Ghent, 1673/74, 1738 and 1773

Year	Supported	Total	%
1673/74	23	164	14.0
1738	49	264	18.5
1773	86	228	37.7

Source: SAG, Reeks 199, 16 and 17.

are scarce for the sixteenth and seventeenth centuries. For Ghent, several sources point to a decrease in living standards of some second-hand dealers in the eighteenth century. A comparison of the books of the guild's poor box with the accounts of the guild allows us to relate the supported members to the total number of second-hand dealers who were active at the time.

The same evolution is shown in more detail in the guild taxes. The guild tax was a yearly sum paid by the members of the second-hand dealers' guild to cover its debts. The contributors were taxed according to their capacity. A distinction was made in three categories, and sometimes a fourth group of poor members who were exempted. In table 1.6, I present eight samples from the eighteenth century.

If we assume that the criteria to allocate group members in the different categories did not change, it seems that the social status of the Ghent second-hand dealers altered dramatically. Between 1705 and 1736, the total number of second-hand dealers increased, their number of rich members tripled, and the share of the poorest decreased. But after the 1730s, we witness a deterioration in their social positions. While a bit more than half of the members were classified among the two poorest groups between 1705 and 1736, this rose to three-quarters or more from the 1750s onwards.

It is not clear whether this trend for Ghent can be generalized for other towns, as the data are scarce and difficult to compare. We know, for example, that in Brussels 19 percent of the second-hand dealers paid the forced loan of 1796, and that a bit more than a third of all the Antwerp second-hand dealers were considered to have small fortunes in the same year,[109] we know that Daniel Roche even considers the *fripiers* of Paris a wealthy group,[110] but whether or not this points to another evolution is difficult to asses. The

Table 1.6. Social categories in the guild taxes of the Ghent second-hand dealers

	1705		1717		1727		1736		1747		1756		1766		1773	
	No.	%	No.	%	No.	%	No.	%	No.	%	No.	%	No.	%	No.	%
1	16	7	61	20	52	18.0	53	18	16	7	11	4.5	20	5.8	30	13.2
2	48	21	42	14	80	27.8	58	20	48	21	49	20.0	35	10.0	27	11.9
3	152	67	192	65	148	51.0	153	53	152	67	184	75.1	177	54.1	152	67.2
4	10	4			7	2.0	23	8	10	4	1	0.4	95	29.0	17	7.5
Total	226	100	245	100	287	100	287	100	226	100	245	100	327	100	226	100

Source: SAG, Reeks 199, 16 and 17

question is important, though, because it has implications for the possible explanations of the decline in living standards.

Indeed, an "external" and an "internal" explanation is possible (and the two do not exclude each other). A first explanation for the decrease in living standards among the second-hand dealers of Ghent, could be found in the weakening of their regional markets. In the region around Ghent, living standards of proto-industrial weavers and small farmers seem to have declined in the second half of the eighteenth century, due to the strong rise in lease-holds, the decline of the linen price and the rise in prices of foodstuffs and wood.[111] Commercial reorganizations also affected the role of the Ghent linen market. In the course of the eighteenth century, middlemen increasingly bought the pieces of linen of proto-industrial weavers, and brought them to urban markets. Many producers also preferred to sell their fabric in smaller regional markets, where the rules about length and quality were less rigid, and where supply was less concentrated. The expansion in the road network simplified the decentralization of the linen trade. This evolution evidently harmed the crafts and retail trades of Ghent.[112]

Larger farmers in the region did profit from the rise in agricultural prices, but their basic needs were increasingly met by rural shops and artisans. In the village of Lede, for example, only one tailor had been active in the seventeenth century, but this number grew to eight in the course of the eighteenth century, and in 1796, already sixteen tailors were counted. The number of shoemakers rose with the same intensity, and the number of shopkeepers increased from fourteen to thirty-five.[113] The growth of a rural service sector, supported by a rise in home demand among middle-sized and large farmers obviously also occurred in other regions. Research on the occupational structures of twenty-seven villages between Antwerp and Brussels shows that the number of shop-keepers quadrupled between 1702 and 1796, and the number of countryside tailors increased eight times in the same period.[114]

Another recently formulated explanation for the decline of living standards among second-hand dealers centers on the changing nature of second-hand goods themselves. In a highly stimulating paper about the Antwerp retail market, Bruno Blondé, Hilde Greefs and Ilja Van Damme presented the interesting hypothesis that the relative share of the second-hand trade declined in the course of the eighteenth century, as consumers increasingly preferred new, fashionable goods, which became more available due to a decline in prices: "While the early seventeenth-century consumer pattern was largely made up of expensive, durable consumer goods, with a high secondary market value and well-suited for repair and resale, the eighteenth-century consumer increasingly preferred cheaper and more vulnerable commodities."[115] In the international literature on consumption, there is indeed a lot of evidence for an increasing taste for novelty, in a time of ever quickening fashion cycles. The history of textiles and clothing in the eighteenth century – an important item for second-hand dealers – also endorses this hypothesis, as cheaper, lighter and less durable fabrics were increasingly used (especially for women's clothing). Due to new production methods and the substitution of expensive by cheaper raw materials, a drop in prices of industrial commodities certainly occurred.[116]

Linked to a loss of the right to sell certain new goods, this may have eroded the living standards of those second-hand dealers whose income was mainly based on the rent of public sales (as their income was directly related to the value of the goods sold). For sixteenth- and seventeenth-century Antwerp, the large accumulation of wealth, the importance of the luxury trades and the soaring of the art market probably offered exceptional opportunities for secondary markets. We know that Antwerp second-hand dealers were involved in the sales of paintings in the sixteenth and seventeenth centuries; certain deans even acquired connoisseurial skills and owned paintings of important artists.[117] The collapse of the Antwerp art market in the late seventeenth and early eighteenth centuries must indeed have harmed the incomes of these specialized second-hand dealers.

Yet, so far, and as the aforementioned authors acknowledge, it is not clear whether and how broader trends in the eighteenth century consumer (r)evolution(s) affected the second-hand trade in general, and the living standards of second-hand dealers in particular. Can the Antwerp case be generalized? We clearly need to know more about retail prices, and prices of second-hand goods to evaluate the relations between new and secondary markets. Not everyone agrees that new eighteenth century commodities were that cheap or easily available, nor is it certain that second-hand goods were generally scorned. John Styles has argued that "mass production" of cheap goods is not an appropriate concept to describe eighteenth-century manufacturing, and Maxine Berg has repeatedly stressed the importance of luxury and semi-luxuries in eighteenth century consumption.[118] Daniel Roche has shown that certain second-hand goods of a high intrinsic quality were still more expensive than new articles in the eighteenth century, and that even nobles, clerics, *officiers* and the professions were clients of the Parisian *fripiers*.[119] Stana Nenadic did notice a decrease in the value of second-hand goods in Edinburgh and Glasgow after 1800, but stressed that most second-hand goods maintained their value in the eighteenth century.[120]

Moreover, we may wonder whether a quickening of fashion cycles may not have stimulated the second-hand trade, as goods had to be replaced more often. Eighteenth-century consumers were not monolithic, but consisted of many social groups, tastes and market-segments, so that goods that had become terribly out of fashion for some, may have been still attractive for other, less fashion-conscious or poorer consumers, e.g. in the provinces or in the countryside. This seems to be the case in Paris.[121] Rose Bertin, the famous French *marchande à la mode*, was notorious for palming off out-of-date fashions (in Parisian terms) on to provincial clients.[122] These kinds of activities were probably more important in larger fashion centers such as Paris or Brussels, influencing the second-hand dealers in different towns in highly different ways. The question can also be raised whether the well-documented overall increase in the number of commodities in Western European households may not have somewhat compensated the decline in prices of individual articles, even if a smaller part entered the second-hand trade (because glass, pewter or porcelain broke more easily than silver or tin).

Yet the hypothesis of Blondé, Greefs and Van Damme is interesting, and the decreased value of goods, the encroachments of competitors on the second-hand market and the loss of the privilege to sell certain goods in certain towns could very well have affected the status, image and living standards of second-hand dealers in the Low Countries, compared to the sixteenth or seventeenth century. If a decrease in living standards could be shown for a town that had already lost its regional markets (e.g., Antwerp in the second half of the eighteenth century), this hypothesis would certainly be strengthened.

Conclusion

In this overview, we saw how a group of highly diverse individuals made a living in the second-hand trade in several towns in the early modern Low Countries. Differences in regulation, changing town–countryside relations and changes in the nature of goods offered both opportunities and constraints, which varied over time and in space. This chapter has argued that one way to understand these differences is to cross the city walls. The dominant local, urban level of analysis often taken for granted in guild histories needs to be transcended into a more regional, comparative approach, in which different dynamics of hinterlands and town–countryside relations shaped different trajectories of urban markets and trades. A detailed interurban comparison shows that no other trade working for the local market revealed such spectacular variations in the occurrence of guilds, in the barriers of entry or in the numbers of their members. Similarly, no other trade seems to register such discrepancies in historical evolution, with second-hand dealers declining in one town, booming in another, and remaining in the status quo in a third. External markets now seem to offer the best explanation for the strong variation in numbers and institutional settings of the second-hand trade (although this does not exclude other factors). In the Low Countries, the high population densities of the countryside and the short distances to most cities enabled intense and close contacts between town and countryside. In the eighteenth century, the demographic growth in the countryside, and the growth of home demand due to agricultural expansion and proto-industrial development at first strengthened the ties between certain towns and their hinterland, but the development of a rural service sector subsequently harmed the urban markets of simple goods, e.g., the trade in (second-hand) clothing. The timing and intensity of this phenomenon varied from one town to another. Regarding living standards, the decrease in value of many goods and the permission or prohibition to sell certain products probably also play a role. More research is needed on fashion, the cultural meaning of objects and the attitudes of consumers to assess the role of the second-hand market in early modern consumption.

Indeed, many questions remain unsolved, and alternative explanations remain open. I certainly do not intend to raise the role of regional markets to the level of a "grand narrative" that has to explain everything. The second-hand trade was far too multiform to be reduced to mono-causal explanations. In this sense, accepting the complexity, plural identity and multidimensionality of the second-hand trade seems the ineluctable fate of its historians today.

Notes

I thank Bruno Blondé for the many stimulating discussions we had over the years about the topic of this chapter. Abbreviations used: AGR: Archives générales du Royaume (Brussels), CP: Conseil Privé, PA: Période Autrichienne, PK: Privilegekamer, ROPBA: Recueil des Ordonnances des Pays Bas Autrichiens, SAA: Stadsarchief Antwerpen (Municipal Archives Antwerp), SAG: Stadsarchief Gent (Municipal Archives Ghent).

1. Laurence Fontaine and Jürgen Schlumbohm, "Introduction," in Idem (eds.), *Household Strategies for Survival 1600–2000: Fission, Faction and Cooperation* (Amsterdam, 2000), p. 1 (*International Review of Social History*, Supplement 8).
2. The concept is reviewed by several contributors to John Brewer and Roy Porter, *Consumption and the World of Goods* (London, 1993), and by many others including Stana Nenadic, "Middle-rank Consumers and Domestic Culture in Edinburgh and Glasgow, 1720–1840," *Past and Present*, 145 (1994), pp. 122–56 and Anton Schuurman, "Aards Geluk. Consumptie en de moderne samenleving," in: Anton Schuurman, Jan de Vries and Ad Van der Woude (eds.), *Aards Geluk. De Nederlanders en hun spullen van 1500 tot 1850* (Amsterdam, 1997), pp. 15–24.
3. This chapter is inspired by the regional approach in the history of proto-industry and industry, see among others Pat Hudson, *The Industrial Revolution* (London, 1992), pp. 101–32; Dieter Ebeling and Wolfgang Mager (eds.), *Proto-Industrie in der Region. Europäische Gewerbelandschaften vom 16. bis zum 19. Jahrhundert* (Bielefeld, 1997), Stephen R. Epstein, 'Introduction', in Idem, *Town and Country in Europe, 1300–1800* (Cambridge, 2001), p. 7; Steven King and Geoffrey Timmins, *Making Sense of the Industrial Revolution. English Economy and Society 1700–1850* (Manchester, 2001), pp. 33–66.
4. The countryside is hardly mentioned in the (otherwise most useful) overview by James R. Farr, *Artisans in Europe, 1300–1914* (Cambridge, 2000).
5. Jan de Vries, "The Industrial Revolution and the Industrious Revolution," *Journal of Economic History*, 54 (1994), pp. 249–270 and by the same author "Great Expectations. Early Modern History and the Social Sciences," *Review*, 22 (1999), pp. 130–142.
6. As remarked by T. Brennan, "Town and Country in France, 1550–1750," in Epstein (ed.), *Town and Country in Europe*, pp. 258, 264.
7. Regarding guild history, an interesting overview has been published for Brabant by Marc Jacobs, "De ambachten in Brabant en Mechelen (12de eeuw–1795)" in *De gewestelijke en lokale overheidsinstellingen in Brabant en Mechelen tot 1795*, 2 (Brussel, 2000), pp. 558–624, but we lack similar publications for the other regions of the Low Countries.
8. See the critique by Sophie de Schaepdrijver, "Some Remarks on the Urban History in Belgium," *Journal of Urban History*, 23 (1997), pp. 647–57.
9. Future comparative research can draw on the useful bibliography on guild history by Marc Jacobs and Marianne Vanbellinghen, "Ambachten in de Zuidelijke Nederlanden (voor 1795). Een bijdrage tot de samenstelling van een bibliografische lijst van studies verschenen in de 19de en 20ste eeuw," extra edition of *Oost-Vlaamse Zanten*, LXXIV (1999), 187–320. However, the authors acknowledge that their bibliographic research was not conducted "with the same intensity to the south of the linguistic border" (the French-speaking region) (p. 190).

10. Albert Schouteet, "Het ambacht van de oudkleerkopers te Brugge," *Handelingen van het genootschap voor geschiedenis gesticht onder de benaming Société d'Emulation te Brugge*, CVII (1970), p. 46. Frans De Potter, *Gent van de oudsten tijden tot heden, geschiedkundige beschrijving der stad*, VI, (Roeselare, 1969) (Ghent, 1882), p. 112.

11. Bibi Panhuysen, *Maatwerk. Kleermakers, naaisters, oudkleerkopers en de gilden (1500–1800)* (Amsterdam, 2000), p. 255; A. Meulemans, "Leuvense ambachten. III. De Oudkleerkopers," *Eigen Schoon en de Brabander*, 40 (1957), p. 61; Floris Prims, *Geschiedenis van Antwerpen*, XI, 2 (Brussel, 1927), p. 18.

12. E.g., see SAG, Reeks 156 bis, 85, August 6, 1627. Prohibitions on buying clothing from soldiers can be found in Reeks 108 bis, 88, June 30, 1672, June 25, 1742, July, 30 1756, June, 20 1763, Reeks 110/5, July, 6 1771.

13. SAA, PK 840, December 18, 1749.

14. SAG, Reeks 156 bis, 85, November 24, 1773 and February 17, 1774.

15. AGR, CP PA, 419 A, 1760. This confined them to the very low end of the market, as the sum equalled 3 to 4 times the daily wages of an unskilled worker.

16. SAG, Reeks 93, BB, November 20, 1508, Rijksarchief Anderlecht, Ambachten van Brabant, 677 bis, August 13, 1530.

17. Rijksarchief Anderlecht, Ambachten van Brabant, 677 bis, May 15, 1703.

18. Marianne Danneel, "Handelaarsters in oude kleren in de 16de eeuw te Brugge," *Brugs Ommeland*, 25 (1985), pp. 205–209.

19. Siska Vastesaeger, "Vrouwen in ambachten in Brussel in de achttiende eeuw," unpublished thesis for the degree of "licentiaat," Vrije Universiteit Brussel, 1997–8, pp. 89–93.

20. ROPBA, III (Brussels, 1873), p. 88, AGR, CP PA, 405B, 1784.

21. AGR, CP PA, 405B, 1784

22. Panhuysen, *Maatwerk*, p. 263.

23. Vastesaeger, "Vrouwen in ambachten," pp. 54–6.

24. Forty-two women on 211 members between 1751 and 1794, Panhuysen, *Maatwerk*, p. 271.

25. In sixteenth century Nuremberg, the second-hand trade was completely controlled by women, see Mary Wiesner, "Paltry Peddlers or Essential Merchants? Women in the Distributive Trades in Early Modern Nuremberg," *The Sixteenth Century Journal*, XII (1981), pp. 8–9.

26. Meulemans, "Leuvense ambachten," pp. 373–375.

27. SAG, Reeks 199-14, 1755.

28. SAG, Reeks 199-13, 1667.

29. SAG, Reeks 156 bis, 85, August 6, 1627.

30. Meulemans, "Leuvense ambachten," p. 187.

31. SAA, PK 727, June 20, 1628.

32. SAA, PK 727, June 27, 1642, PK 751, September 16, 1652.

33. SAA, PK 717, f° 163–164, June 20, 1622.

34. SAG, Reeks 108 bis, 88, petition 1753.

35. AGR, Raad van State, 2020, June 15, 1725.

36. SAA, PK 681, 7 March 1599, GA 4003, November 24, 1608, Stadsbibliotheek Antwerpen 582577, undated petition, probably 1610.

37. SAG, 47 registers, MM, September 27, 1561. Their ordinance in SAG, Reeks 156 bis, August 6, 1627 mentions three fairs outside Ghent.

38. SAG, Reeks 199, 14, 1760–1.

39. SAG Reeks 199-13, March, 12 1630.

40. The second-hand dealers protested against this, SAG, Reeks 199-7, March 17, 1738, January 6, 1739.

41. In 1689, the second-hand dealers of Mechelen were forbidden to extract such extras, for which the ordinance described 13 different names: "qu'il ne leur a été permis de se faire payer ce qu'ils appellent conditiegeld, drinckgelt, malteytgelt, banqueroutgeldt, ganck en vacatien, verteir, gelagh, slot, afschrijf van pennen, taefel, beddecraem en bancken, teeckenen van bellen, voddelien en verhooghers, ou quelque autre profit, sous quel nom que ce puisse être," cited in a document by the Great Council of Mechelen, April 16, 1774 in AGR, Algemene Regeringsraad, 810.

42. Meulemans, "Leuvense ambachten," pp. 187–189, SAA, PK 843, f° 10v–11v, September 20, 1751
43. AGR, CP PA 419 A, 1760.
44. SAA, PK 725, June 25, 1627 and PK 821, March 3, 1732.
45. Meulemans, "Leuvense ambachten," pp. 191–194, AGR CP PA 419 A, 1771; CP PA 431A, 1784–1785; CP PA 1158B, September 23, 1768, August 10 and November 9, 1770.
46. AGR CP PA 419 A, 1771.
47. AGR, CP PA 425A, November 13, 1759. These sales of new goods were forbidden on December 13, 1759.
48. SAG, verdict of 1652 cited in SAG Reeks 199-13, April 13, 1709; Meulemans, "Leuvense ambachten," p. 139.
49. SAG, Reeks 199-2, f° 85v–86, March 14, 1676.
50. I have studied this in more detail in Harald Deceulaer, "Entrepreneurs in the Guilds: Ready-to-Wear Clothing and Subcontracting in late Sixteenth- and early Seventeenth-century Antwerp," *Textile History*, 31 (2000), pp. 133–49.
51. SAG, Reeks 191-4, May 8, 1724 and September 12, 1739.
52. SAG, Reeks 199-10, 1756.
53. Harald Deceulaer, *Pluriforme patronen en een verschillende snit. Sociaal-economische, institutionele en culturele transformaties in de kledingsector in Antwerpen, Brussel en Gent, ca 1585–ca 1800* (Amsterdam, 2001), p. 49.
54. Reeks 332, 783, 17, February 11, 1780.
55. SAG, Reeks 199/7 December 16, 1721.
56. The accounts of Abraham De Buck, a rich Ghent second-hand dealer show that he lent out money from time to time, SAG, Familiefonds handboeken, 433. After his death, his heirs pressed charges against one of his debtors, AGR, Grote Raad van Mechelen, processen in eerste aanleg, 2136 (after 1692).
57. AGR, CP PA 431 A, May 11, 1785 and the advice of the second-hand dealers' guild, which cited statutes from 1436 and several verdicts against tailors, diamond cutters, ..., who wanted to become a second-hand dealer and were forced to leave their other guild. Such a case can be found in SAA, PK 793, November 5 and 17, 1706.
58. AGR, CP PA 405B, November 26, 1784.
59. J.B. Goetstouwers, *Les métiers de Namur sous l'Ancien Régime. Contribution à l'histoire sociale* (Leuven-Paris, 1908), p. 65; Panhuysen, *Maatwerk*, p. 264.
60. The inquiry of 1784 can be found in AGR CP PA 405A, 405B, 406 and was of course only held in the Austrian Netherlands, not in the principality of Liège or in the Northern Netherlands. Not all towns with guilds were addressed by the central government (e.g. Beamont, Enghien, Fleurus, Halle, Ronse, Soignies, Vilvoorde), and the local magistrates of Aarschot, Antwerp, Brussels, Leuven, Lier, Tienen and Vilvoorde did not send in information. The data for Antwerp, Leuven and Lier can be found in their town archives, the data for other towns were not found. Furthermore, the data for Ypres, Tienen and Tournai have been lost over the years, see Hilda Coppejans-Desmedt, "De enquête van 1784 over het ambachtswezen in de Oostenrijkse Nederlanden. Bijdrage tot een kritisch onderzoek," *Archief en Bibliotheekwezen in België*, XLII (1971), pp. 34–47 and Jacobs, "De ambachten in Brabant en Mechelen," *passim*.
61. Goetstouwers, *Les métiers de Namur*, pp. 8, 15–16; Meulemans, "Leuvense ambachten"; Edouard Poncelet, *Les bons métiers de la cité de Liège* (Liège, 1900) pp. 146–147, 157–159; E. De Saegher, *Notice sur les archives communales d'Ypres et documents pour servir à l'histoire de Flandre du XIIIe au XVIe siècle* (Ypres: Callewaer-de Meulenaere, 1898), p. 344; Arthur Lens, *Inventaris van het oud archief van de stad Lier* (Brussels, 1973), p. 79.
62. Data from AGR CP PA 405A, 405B, 406, supplemented by Fernand Discry, *Notice historique et nouvel inventaire des archives de la ville de Huy* (Huy, s.d.), p. 53 e.v., René Dubois, *La ville de Huy au XVIIIe siècle* (Huy , 1895), p. 23.
63. See the overview of population figures in Denis Morsa, "L'urbanisation de la Belgique (1500–1800), Taille, hiérarchie et dynamique des villes," *Revue du Nord*, LXXIX (1997), p. 329.

64. Data from AGR CP PA 405A, 405B, 406, supplemented by Henry Baillien, *Inventaris van de Fondsen van de stad Tongeren, de ambachten en genootschappen en weldadige instellingen* (Brussels, 1964); Theodore Bernier, *Histoire de la ville de Beaumont* (Mons, 1880), pp. 135–141, Jacobs, "De ambachten in Brabant en Mechelen," pp. 563–4, 586 (Tienen and Jodoigne); Gaston Renson, "Sociaal-economisch leven te Halle in de 17de eeuw," *Eigen Schoon en de Brabander*, 66 (1983), pp. 345–60; Herman Van Isterdael, *Stad en baronnie Ronse (Ancien Régime)*, Rijksarchief Ronse, Inventarissen, 20 (Brussels, 1998), pp. 105–109; Laurent M. Van Werveke, *Stad Nieuwpoort. Inventaris van het archief van het Oud Régime* (Brussels, 1937).

65. The situation for Aarschot, Vilvoorde, Dinant and Sint-Truiden is not clear at the moment. In 1784 Aalst had 5070 inhabitants, Arlon 2133, Beaumont 1645, Diksmuide 2500, Echternach 2318, Halle 5302, Herentals 2513, Jodoigne 2253, Nieuwpoort 3039, Oostend 7075, Roermond 4330, Weert 5583, Claude Bruneel, Luc Delporte, Bernadette Petitjean (ed.), *Le dénombrement général de la population des Pays-Bas Autrichiens en 1784* (Brussels: Archives générales du Royaume, 1996), *passim*.

66. Panhuysen, *Maatwerk*, pp. 249–55.

67. Ibid., p. 255.

68. Harald Deceulaer and Marc Jacobs, "Qualities and Conventions. Guilds in Eighteenth-century Brabant and Flanders: an Extended Economic Perspective," in C.E. Nunez (ed.), *Guilds, Economy and Society* (Sevilla, 1998), pp. 91–107.

69. For Ath an apprenticeship and a master test were demanded to become a member of "La confrérie de St Maur," the guild of tailors and second-hand dealers, but it is not altogether clear whether these rules also applied to the second-hand dealers. AGR CP PA 405A, 1784. The rules for Namur were prescribed in their statutes of 1717, ROPBA, III (Brussels, 1873), p. 88.

70. Schouteet, "Het ambacht van de oudkleerkopers te Brugge," p. 49. A fifteenth-century apprenticeship contract of three years with a second-hand dealer is cited for Ghent by De Potter, *Gent*, p. 114, but there are no traces of an obligation in the statutes.

71. AGR, CP PA 431 May 1 and 11, 1785. See also AGR, Algemene Regeringsraad 810 April 17, 23 and 26, 1787.

72. Piet Lourens and Jan Lucassen, "'Zunftlandschaften' in den Niederlanden und im benachbarten Deutschland," in: Wilfried Reininghaus (ed.), *Zunftlandschaften in Deutschland und den Niederlanden im Vergleich* (Münster, 2000), pp. 25–33.

73. Maarten Prak, "The Politics of Intolerance: Citizenship and Religion in the Dutch Republic (seventeenth to eighteenth centuries)," in R. Po-Chia Hsia and H. van Nierop (eds.), *Calvinism and Religious Toleration in the Dutch Golden Age* (Cambridge, 2002), pp. 167–74.

74. ROPBA, III, p. 88.

75. As in Menen or Namur, where a son of a master paid four to twelve times less, or in Bruges, where sons of masters simply paid 1 guilder and 6 stuivers (a pittance compared to the 30 guilders for non family members).

76. A comparison of the barriers of entry for tailors in different towns of the Northern and Southern Netherlands is presented in Harald Deceulaer and Bibi Panhuysen, "Schneider oder Näherinnen? Ein geschlechtbezogener Vergleich der Bekleidungshandwerke in den Nördlichen und Südlichen Niederlanden während der Frühen Neuzeit," in: Reininghaus *Zunftlandschaften*, p. 90 and for the carpenters in the Northern Netherlands by Lourens and Lucassen, "Zunftlandschaften," p. 24.

77. Lourens and Lucassen, "Zunftlandschaften," p. 12.

78. Karin Van Honacker, *Lokaal verzet en oproer in de 17de en 18de eeuw. Collectieve acties tegen het centraal gezag in Brussel, Antwerpen en Leuven* (Kortrijk-Heule, 1994), pp. 93–95, 137–142, 161–164, 632, 634, 636–637.

79. Henri Installé, *Patriciërs en ambachtslui in het stadsbestuur te Mechelen onder Maria-Theresia. De sociale status van burgemeesters en schepenen (1740–1780)* (Mechelen, 1982), pp. 14–16.

80. A recent synthesis of this episode is given by Johan Dambruyne, "Stedelijke identiteit en politieke cultuur te Gent," in: Hugo Soly en Johan Van de Wiele (eds.), *Carolus. Keizer Karel V 1500–1558* (Ghent, 1999), pp. 116–120

81. Yvan Vandenberghe, *Jacobijnen en traditionalisten. De reacties van de Bruggelingen in de Revolutietijd* (Brussels, 1972), pp. 62–70.

82. For the tailors guild, concentration figures per 1000 inhabitants are compared for the Low Countries and a few European towns in Deceulaer and Panhuysen, "Schneider oder Näherinnen?," pp. 87–89.

83. See for more details H. Deceulaer, Entrepreneurs in the Guilds, *passim*.

84. Ilja Van Damme, "Het vertrek van Mercurius of de semi-periferisering van Antwerpen in de tweede helft van de zeventiende eeuw," unpublished thesis for the degree of licentiaat, Katholieke Universiteit Leuven, 2001, p. 42.

85. SAA, PK 666 f° 29, September 22, 1586.

86. See among others Michael Limberger, "Merchant Capitalism and the Countryside in the West of the Duchy of Brabant (Fifteenth-Sixteenth Centuries)," in Peter Hoppenbrouwers and Jan Luiten Van Zanden (eds.), *Peasants into Farmers? The Transformation of Rural Economy and Society in the Low Countries (Middle Ages–Nineteenth Century) in Light of the Brenner Debate* (Turnhout, 2001), p. 161.

87. Van Damme, "Het vertrek van Mercurius," p. 94.

88. Guy Dejongh and Erik Thoen, "Arable Productivity in Flanders and the Former Territory of Belgium in a Long-term Perspective (from the Middle Ages to the end of the Ancien Régime)," in: Bas van Bavel and Erik Thoen (eds.), *Land Productivity and Agro-systems, Middle Ages–20thCentury. Elements for Comparison* (Turnhout, 1999), pp. 51, 57.

89. Detailed figures in Johan Dambruyne, *Mensen en centen. Het 16de–eeuwse Gent in demografisch en economisch perspectief* (Ghent, 2001), p. 257.

90. See for more details Harald Deceulaer, "Consumptie en distributie van kleding tussen stad en platteland. Drie regionale patronen in de Zuidelijke Nederlanden (zestiende–achtiende eeuw)," *Tijdschrift voor Sociale Geschiedenis* 28 (2002), pp. 453–457 and by the same author "Urban Artisans and their Countryside Customers: different Interactions between Town and Hinterland in Antwerp, Brussels and Ghent (18th Century)," in Bruno Blondé, Eric Vanhaute and Michèle Galand (eds.), *Labour and Labour Markets between Town and Countryside (Middles Ages–19th Century)* (Turnhout, 2001), p. 224.

91. See Bruno Blondé, "Domestic Demand and Urbanisation in Brabant: Demographic and Functional Evidence for Small Towns of Brabant," in Peter Clark (ed.), *Small Towns in Early Modern Europe* (Cambridge, 1995), p. 237, and Roger De Peuter, *Brussel in de 18de eeuw. Sociaal-economische structuren en ontwikkelingen in een regionale hoofdstad* (Brussels, 1999).

92. G. Hansotte, *La clouterie liégoise et la question ouvrière au XVIIIe siècle* (Brussels, 1972), pp. 3, 9, 13, 16.

93. Joseph Ruwet, "Mesure de la production agricole sous l'Ancien Régime. Le blé en pays mosan," *Annales ESC*, 19 (1964), pp. 631–32, 641–42.

94. Poncelet, *Les bons métiers*, pp. 146–47.

95. Marjolein 't Hart, "Town and Country in the Dutch Republic, 1550–1800," in Epstein (ed.), *Town and Country in Europe*, pp. 99–103.

96. Panhuysen, *Maatwerk*, p. 256.

97. Jan de Vries and Ad Van der Woude, *Nederland, 1500–18.15. De eerste ronde van de moderne economische groei* (Amsterdam, 1995), pp. 215, 412, 473, 599–600.

98. Erik Palmen, "Dordt en zijn ommelanden," in: W. Frijhof, H. Nusteling and M. Spies (eds.), *Geschiedenis van Dordrecht van 1572 tot 1813* (Hilversum, 1998), p. 183.

99. See about Kortijk, Oudenaarde and Geraardsbergen Peter Stabel, "Urban Markets, Rural Industries and the Organisation of Labour in Late Medieval Flanders: the Constraints of Guild Regulations and the Requirements of Export Oriented Production," in Blondé, Galand and Vanhaute (eds.), *Labour and Labour Markets*, pp. 146–53.

100. Leo Van Buyten, "De Diesterse Mercuriaal, XVIIe–begin XIXe eeuw" in Joseph Ruwet, Françoise Ladrier, Etienne Hélin and Leo Van Buyten, *Marché des céréales à Ruremonde, Luxembourg, Namur et Diest au XVIIe et XVIIIe siècles* (Leuven, 1966), and in the same volume Françoise Ladrier, "Prix des céréales à Namur, XVIIe–XVIIIe siècles," p. 284.

101. Herman Van der Wee and Peter D'Haeseleer, "Ville et campagne dans l'industrie linière à Alost et ses environs (fin du moyen âge–temps modernes)," in Jean Marie Duvosquel and

Erik Thoen (eds.), *Peasants and Townsmen in Medieval Europe. Studia in honorem Adriaan Verhulst* (Ghent, 1995), p. 765.

102. Luxembourg was enclosed by a thinly populated region of mountains and forests, Roermond was an enclave close to the Northern Netherlands and German lands, see Etienne Hélin, "Prix des céréales à Luxembourg," in Ruwet, Ladrier, Hélin and Van Buyten, *Marché des céréales*, p. 187.

103. Deceulaer, "Urban artisans and their countryside customers," p. 222.

104. More details in Harald Deceulaer, "Guildsmen, Entrepreneurs and Market-segments. The Case of the Garment Trades in Antwerp and Ghent (sixteenth to eighteenth centuries)," *International Review of Social History*, 43 (1998), pp. 1–29.

105. SAG, Reeks 199-13, August 18, 1631, 199-12, no date.

106. SAG, Reeks 156 bis 85, June 15, 1641, Reeks 199-12, June 21, 1644.

107. SAG, Reeks 332, 486, 30, February 22, 1723.

108. SAG, Reeks 332, 580, 5, June 17, 1739; Reeks 332, 578, 12, May 19, 1738.

109. Deceulaer, *Pluriforme patronen*, p. 102.

110. Daniel Roche, *La culture des apparences. Une histoire du vêtement XVIIe–XVIIIe siècle* (Paris, 1989), pp. 335–6.

111. Chris Vandenbroeke, "Sociale en konjunkturele facetten van de linnennijverheid in Vlaanderen (late 14de–midden 19de eeuw)," in *Handelingen der maatschappij voor geschiedenis en oudheidkunde te Gent*, XXXIII (1979), p. 149; Luc de Kezel, "Grondbezit in Vlaanderen 1750–1850. Bijdrage tot de discussie over de sociaal-economische ontwikkeling op het Vlaamse platteland," in *Tijdschrift voor Sociale Geschiedenis*, 14 (1998), pp. 76, 80, 85.

112. Rijksarchief Kortrijk, Oud Stadsarchief Kortrijk, 3182 undated memoire and October 26, 1766. See also Luc Dhondt, "Plattelandslijnwaad en stadskatoen tegen en even na 1800. De organisatie van een oude en van een nieuwe industrie. Een memorie uit 1808 en haar relevantie," *Handelingen van de Geschied-en Oudheidkundige Kring van Oudenaarde*, XXXII (1995), pp. 89–149, (122); Van der Wee and D'Haeseleer, "Ville et campagne," p. 765.

113. Dhondt, "Plattelandslijnwaad en stadskatoen," 122; J. De Brouwer, *Geschiedenis van Lede. Het dorpsleven, het parochieleven, het volksleven* (Lede, 1963), p. 275.

114. Geert Leenders, "De beroepsstructuur op het platteland tussen Antwerpen en Brussel (1702–1846)," in Jan Craeybeckx and Frank Daelemans (eds.), *Bijdragen tot de Geschiedenis van Vlaanderen en Brabant. Sociaal en economisch* (Brussels, 1983), pp. 167–228.

115. Bruno Blondé, Hilde Greefs and Ilja Van Damme, "Consumers and Commercial circuits: Mapping the Retail Sector in Early Modern Antwerp," unpublished paper for the Fourth European Social Science History Conference, Session: Material Culture and Commercialsation: Shopping, Second-hand Market, Theft, 28 February 2002. See also Ilja Van Damme, "Changing Consumer Preferences and Evolution in Retailing. Buying and Selling Consumer Durables in Antwerp (c. 1648–c. 1748)," Bruno Blondé, Peter Stabel, Jon Stobart & Ilja Van Damme (eds.), *Buyers & Sellers. Retail Circuits and Practices in Medieval and Early Modern Europe* (Turnhout, 2006), pp. 199–223.

116. Carole Shammas, "Changes in English and Anglo-American Consumption from 1550 to 1800," in Brewer and Porter, *Consumption and the World of Goods*, pp. 177–205.

117. In 1652, the former dean of the second-hand dealers guild Hendrik Tessers expressed his doubts whether a painting by Brueghel was an original, Elisabeth Alice Honig, *Painting and the Market in Early Modern Antwerp* (New Haven and London, 1998), pp. 194–95. The dean of the second-hand dealers Johannes Aertsen gave two paintings by Van Dijck in pledge to the alderman Theodoor Andries van Kessel, Bert Timmermans, "Een elite als actor op de kunstscène. Patronen van mecenaat in het zeventiende–eeuwse Antwerpen," *Bijdragen tot de Geschiedenis*, 83 (2000), p. 33.

118. John Styles, "Manufacturing, Consumption and Design in Eighteenth-Century England," in Brewer and Porter, *Consumption and the World of Goods*, pp. 529–535; Maxine Berg, "New Commodities, Luxuries and their Consumers in Eighteenth-Century England" in Maxine Berg and Hellen Clifford (eds.), *Consumers and Luxury. Consumer Culture in Europe, 1650–1850* (Manchester and New York, 1999), pp. 63–85; Maxine Berg, "From

Imitation to Invention: Creating Commodities in Eighteenth-Century Britain," *Economic History Review*, LV (2002), pp. 2–3.

119. Roche, *La Culture des apparences*, pp. 340–342.
120. Nenadic, "Middle Rank Consumers," pp. 128–135.
121. "La boutique du fripier enregistre le mouvement de circulation des modes… ils vendent à une clientèle plus étendue les articles de la mode avec un léger décalage," Roche, *La Culture des apparences*, p. 349.
122. "… old styles and used objects could also be sold down at competitive prices at the end of the fashion cycle and fierce disputes between the corporations of mercers, upholsterers and second-hand dealers over the rights to trade in old goods bear witness to the lucrative nature of this market," Carolyn Sargentson, "The Manufacture and Marketing of Luxury Goods: the Marchands Merciers of Late Seventeenth- and Eighteenth-Century Paris," in: Robert Fox and Anthony Turner (eds.), *Luxury Trades and Consumerism in Ancien Régime Paris. Studies in the History of a Skilled Workforce* (Aldershot, 1998), p. 137.

2

USING THINGS AS MONEY

AN EXAMPLE FROM LATE RENAISSANCE ROME

Renata Ago

The aim of this chapter is to show the other side of the market of second-hand goods, focusing on the signification and meaning of the objects themselves, rather than investigating the parties involved in the trade. The idea is to reconstruct the sorts of feelings and emotions that connect things to their owners, rather than analyzing the economic strategies that lie behind the exchange of goods and the social relationships that make them possible. The approach I intend to adopt will therefore consider arrangements that are not related to the need of overcoming meagerness, of making ends meet, or of making the best out of one's resources. What I want to examine is not an "economy of scarcity," at least not in the usual sense of the expression, but rather an *ancien régime* economy, marked by insufficient circulation of cash more than lack of resources, and by a double status of consumer goods: some to resell, some others to keep.

Therefore, the issue here is not whether the market of second-hand goods is or is not a symptom of a backward economy or of the inadequacy of the resources of a certain group of people. The point is not to assess if it is or is not a bad copy of the market of first hand goods, a second choice market. The aim is rather to show that an active market of second-hand goods can be correlated to a different way of looking at things, using them as means to obtain other things, rather than as ends, i.e., objects to acquire, use and keep.

The Functions of Goods

Goods are used to communicate, to give meaning to the world, argues Mary Douglas.[1] But goods, even consumer goods, can be exchanged, thus serving a different purpose, which is not to fix meanings, but to make exchange possible.

The status of goods varies according to their function:

1a. As exchangeable objects, goods are purely a means. They are but a way to obtain other goods. Their value is essentially economic and is exchange value: these are cash-equivalent goods.

1b. As exchangeable objects, though, goods can be a method to obtain something other than more or different goods, i.e., to obtain services, using them as a remuneration for services offered by other people. Their value will still be essentially economic, but it will often be disguised as relational value – its purpose being to create a relation between two trading parties – born in the exchange.

2. As objects "temporarily or definitively kept outside the sphere of economical activity, under a special protection,"[2] goods are an end in themselves. The purpose of their acquisition is not exchange, but rather its opposite, their keeping. Their value is essentially symbolic and differs completely from their exchange value.

It is well known that these plural functions of goods coexisted throughout history, and that they still do. The relative weight of one or the other varied from time to time, along with the changes of other parts of the social and economical context. The clearest link is, I think, that between the status of goods and the development of the monetary system. Indeed, the diffusion of cash and widespread circulation of currency may well have allowed goods to be liberated from their function as mediums of exchange, thus attracting the attention of the social agents to the characteristics that better reflect their second function, i.e., putting "in communication the visible and the invisible," thus objectifying the identity of those who possess them.[3]

Lack of cash, especially of small change, and all the problems derived from a limited circulation of money are a distinctive feature of all pre-industrial Europe. Throughout the modern age Italy is full of complaints concerning "the lack of currency and the existence of patches (both geographical and/or social) where the lack of cash is a chronic problem."[4] When money was issued in a state, quite often just a small proportion of the coins were made of copper–silver alloy or copper. That is to say there was very little small change, so that most of the population was excluded from the circulation of money.[5] Despite this the lack of cash did not stop the market, which on the contrary had developed thanks to the ability of the actors to conceive several different strategies to get round the problem, the most common and important probably being to resort to credit. From the important international bankers, to the modest local artisans, everybody in the mercantile world had learnt how to sidestep the flaws of the monetary system creating an adequate network of debt and credit, where debits and credits were dealt with on paper, through a complex system of compensation.[6]

Considering the social practices, the little information available confirms what theorists say: where little cash is available, we notice extensive use of credit. For example, a study on the mercantile community in late seventeenth-century London – that is to say, on the social group that could more easily be in possession of cash – showed that cash transactions only counted for one-fifth of the whole trade.[7] Further evidence comes from documents specifically related to the "world of goods." The analysis of a great number of post-mortem inventories from different regions of seventeenth-century England shed light on the scarcity of cash kept in houses and, above all, its rarity: only one-half of the inventories, and in some areas only one-third, mention coins of some kind.[8] Similar information emerges from a collection of seventy-five inventories from Rome I am working on: in only three of the cases is cash mentioned, while at least one piece of silverware can be found in thirty-two lists.

Moreover, cash was not the only possible means of payment. Two decades ago, Ruggiero Romano and Ugo Tucci invalidated the idea of a sharp contrast between a direct exchange of things and one employing money. The natural economy and the monetary economy do not exclude each other: on the contrary, they coexisted and still coexist in different and complex forms. For example, it is well known that not only in the countryside but also in the cities wages were paid partly in money, partly in kind. The analysis of the actual methods of payment in early modern cities shows that the same was true for many kinds of goods.[9] Even a high-finance transaction could be based, at least in part, on objects as well as money. Federico Chabod reminds us that a contract stipulated in 1559 between the *duca* of Sessa and the Genoese banker Leonardo Spinola mentioned the loan of 180,000 liras cash and 70,000 liras in silk drapes.[10]

This last example demonstrates how objects can have a monetary function. Furthermore, in many circumstances they can actually be a reserve of wealth to be used as they are, or quickly converted into cash in case of need. This means that the disposal, sale or pawning of an object must be easy operations, that a second-hand goods market that will absorb these goods quite rapidly must also exist, and that people can get rid of these objects without hesitation. Anthropological studies, such as Jane Schneider's "Trousseau as Treasure: Some Contradictions in Late Nineteenth Century Change in Sicily,"[11] and more recent research on northwestern India, revealed how this happens with women's possessions.[12] In Sicily and India the trousseaux and dowry jewels are the most common forms of savings because they can be quickly converted in money, especially through pawning.[13] The little we know about the circulation of women's goods in pre-industrial European societies completely validates this piece of information.[14]

It was possible, then, to avoid shortage of cash through credit and through the monetary use of things: agricultural produce or man-made objects. In these cases, it was easy to change the meaning of the transaction, transforming it from the due remuneration of a service into an act of liberality. Renaissance authors themselves were well aware that the gift of an object could represent, most of the time, a payment. In his "five short treatises on the use of money,"[15] for example, Pontano carefully examines all the possible manners of giving, and warns us that the virtue of liberality "consists in the right measure in donating money, and cannot be without discernment in the choice [that is] to accurately judge what is given, the quantity that is given, when, how and why it is given."[16] After this, showing Alexander the Great's nobility as an example, he regards equally the donations in money distributed to the soldiers and those in food supplies distributed to the people, making clear not to distinguish between donation and payment.[17] And in his "De Splendore" he explicitly hints at a "remunerative" use of objects, where he tells us that "the furnishings must be bought by a gentleman with a view to an honest usage, because he will use them when he has need and will donate them when reason suggests, even in great quantity."[18]

The Monetary Function of Goods

Objects can then be used to buy other objects, or to pay for services, or to obtain money in credit. The evidence we have shows us that in Renaissance and Baroque Rome all these possible functions were largely utilized. Private correspondence, inventories and account books all demonstrate that payments in kind were very common, and that many objects were basically used solely to get money.

This can be seen in wills and testaments. The testator often commands that all his most precious things – furniture, silverware, jewels and so on – be promptly sold, and the proceeds invested buying public debt bonds or other credit bills. The owner then used these objects essentially to give body to an economic holding. If they have been a "treasure" for future generations to inherit, this has not happened because they have been objects with a symbolic and emotional value, but as a materialization of a financial equivalent.

These kinds of wills are left by people of different conditions and qualities: respectable women and courtesans, artisans and merchants, lawyers and public officers, plebeians and aristocrats, fathers and childless men. All of these mean to provide for the future of their heirs, converting objects that on the whole are superfluous into a financial income.[19] At the beginning of the seventeenth-century, even the *marchese* Vincenzo Giustiniani, a collector and Maecenas with a special reverence for art – paintings, sculptures, tapestries etc. – discards all the furniture, silverware and jewels he has accumulated throughout his life. In his will of 1631 he declares that immediately after his death be sold "all my silverware ... in my quarters, and in lady Eugenia's, my consort, and in the other rooms of my palace." To be sold are also "all my furniture, and fittings, and decorative furnishings ... both tapestries and silk drapes, and golden ones, and so baldachins, bed hangings, canopies, blankets, carpets and drapes ... of gold, silk, wool, linen and cotton-wool, and mattresses, and also leather, and hangings, and needleworks and stuff of any kind, and quality." And finally "all my jewels and fine vases."[20]

These precious clothes and furnishings did not acquire any special value for having been used by the master and having been under his eye for so many years.[21] If there is an exception, this only happens when the family palace must not be left completely empty. Contrary to its contents, it has a value that is not only economic. Excluded from the sale will be "all the hangings made of silk, or leather, or others, which will be used, and will be attached to the walls of the rooms of the palace … and all the leather chairs, and other things of leather, and the walnut tables … so that my palace will not at all be left empty and deserted."[22]

Nearly one century afterwards, another aristocrat, as educated and art-loving as Giustiniani, did not hesitate to pawn or sell most of the jewels of his young and elegant daughter-in-law. A list of "different jewels in the keeping of the *Ill.ma Signora Marchesa* Maria Isabella Vecchiarelli Santacroce,"[23] where necklaces, pendants, rings, diamond brooches, pearls and other precious stones given to the young woman as her dowry are enumerated, explains what happened to these in the few years between the wedding (1699) and the death of the father-in-law, Antonio Santacroce (1707). We learn that a diamond cross worth 300 scudi[24] "has been broken up, and six big diamonds and ten small ones have been taken to put them in a bracelet given to the *Marchesa* Davia, the daughter of Marquis Filippo Bentivoglio, when she got married;" that a pair of pendants made of two diamonds each was pawned at the *Monte di Pietà*, and that a "rosette made of nine diamonds was sold and it was bought by the broker of the *Monte di Pietà* where it was pawned." Many more jewels had been sold, donated or were pawned at the *Monte*, so that only eight out of the twenty-seven pieces in the list were still in possession of their original keeper. The same fate awaited two chandeliers, an ink-pot, some objects for the *toilette* and many more pieces of silverware that were also in the dowry.[25]

At the beginning of the eighteenth century the Santacroce family is definitely not in decline. An uncle has just been nominated cardinal and governor of the city of Viterbo, and the heir of the family has been nominated *Consigliere intimo di Stato* of the Emperor,[26] spending three years in Vienna, where he actively joins in the court life.[27] The sale of some of Maria Isabella's dowry goods is not the grievous consequence of serious financial difficulty. Rather than this, the point is that, as I said, dowry goods have a key function: they can be quickly converted into money, thus allowing the payment of debt or new investment. Clearly this is also true for personal objects that are not laden with emotional value that would lead to keeping them as long as possible, excluding them from the exchange. In the case of the Santacroce family, this distance from one's own personal belongings, this indifference for their value "as objects," is not general, being a characteristic of the older generation, represented by the father-in-law who took the jewels in consignment. The young daughter-in-law, on the contrary, is one of the first examples of a different attitude. I will return to this in detail later.

If family jewels can be disposed of without any hesitation, even more so with one's clothes, especially when the age or the circumstances of life made them inadequate to be worn. In this case too, Pontano's readers could feel justified in doing so. In one of his treatises on social virtue, he writes "It is not suitable for a gentleman to let his clothes wear out while he is using them, because old things cannot have splendour. So, before they lose their brilliance, he shall turn them into liberal deeds: he will donate them, then, to his friends, his acquaintances, to those who deserve thankfulness."[28] In 1634 a mature widow from Orvieto asked a Jewish second-hand dealer from Rome to sell some clothes for her, and at the same time recommended to her son, also living in Rome, that he should keep an eye on the entire operation. "If for that white dress he is not getting twenty scudi," she writes in a first letter, "he can sell it for eighteen, because I have to pay for what you know ... and I also remind you to try and sell the brocade robe."[29] "Tell me if the white dress has been sold" and check that "it is not lent to anyone," she insists some time afterward.[30]

In Rome, as elsewhere, it is very easy to find reference to the sale and purchase of both new and second-hand clothes, also by well-off people,[31] and, more frequently, to their hire, particularly when a special outfit was required. The post-mortem inventories, or those drawn up at the beginning of a guardianship, often include an estimate on the items of clothing made by a professional specialized in the buying and selling of second-hand things, with a view to selling them. Moreover, the account books we have, nearly all from noble families, confirm this habit. A receipt informs us that in 1659 the *principe* Giustiniani sold 40 *canne* of cloth "moth-eaten and ripped in several places." In spite of their bad condition, the *principe* managed to make 20 scudi out of them, not so little if we think that young *marchesa* Santacroce's diamond rosette had been sold for 56.60 scudi. Similarly, from an entry in the account books of the Spada household, we learn that the *marchese* Orazio gained 21 scudi from the sale of a damask canopy.[32]

All objects, then, not only precious ones, can be easily sold. They retain a financial value even when they are used directly, i.e., without having previously been transformed into money, as a means of payment, replacing the still too rare cash. Furthermore, the orders for payment of *marchese* Santacroce demonstrate how much it was possible to reduce the accounts with the household suppliers by giving back some old goods for new ones. Thanks to the "sale" of thirty-nine pairs of used and worn-out trousers and of seven heavy coats, the account with Israele di Tivoli "for tailor work ... that is repairing the used black livery with velvet laces" is reduced by 20 per cent, from 33.12 to 26.52 scudi. The same happens for the account with the coach-maker: in payment for a "new frame ... for the red leather-covered coach," he accepts the "used frame of the six-seater leather-covered coach." Consequently, he reduces the price from 52 to 40 scudi. The same is true for the accounts with the locksmith, the coppersmith, the saddler and so on.[33]

Agricultural produce and food in general may well be used with a monetary function, even more than clothes and objects. The widow from Orvieto who was selling her clothes is a landowner, and as such is constantly dealing with the problem of selling her produce. Her willingness to send money to her son, who is a practicing lawyer in Rome, is linked to the money she manages to get for the corn, oil and hemp from her farms. "As for now I cannot send you money," she writes in a letter, "because everything here is getting so cheap that I do not manage to sell a thing;"[34] "you are waiting for the bill of exchange to have money – she comments in another letter – and today I have indeed sold 296 pounds of hemp [...] and there came into my hands 10 scudi and 95 *baiocchi*, and of these tomorrow up to seven scudi are to be given to the Treasurer;"[35] "Today I have sold four jugs of oil for 34 *giulii* each,"[36] she announces in a third one; "and the money I am sending you I got from the wine I have sold and a part I have got from the pigs that were sold,"[37] she declares again in a fourth. Behind the scudos the woman has managed to scrape up, we have a clear image of the agricultural produce she has exchanged them with. It is therefore normal that, when this is possible, both she and her son prefer to resort directly to their produce when they want to pay for a debt or to make a gift. Her son in Rome writes that his mother should not complain for her lack of money and any expenses that she may have to face,[38] with reference to the low pay of an attorney in Orvieto: "with a bushel of corn one can quarrel for twenty years."[39] He also asks her to pay the carrier for his services, since she can "give him wine, or hemp, or oil."[40]

Several decades afterward the account books of the duchess Sforza Cesarini demonstrate that the custom of paying with agricultural produce is still common. In fact, the duchess is happy to pay in corn, especially in bread, and in coal. Several kinds of suppliers receive payments in kind. Records involve a second-hand dealer and a tailor, both Jewish, a locksmith, a carpenter, a shoemaker, a blacksmith and even a painter who regularly accepts coal in payment for his floral pictures. We can also add to the list a silversmith, an apothecary, a bookseller and the French seamstress who works for the duchess.[41] Payments in kind are not just for the humblest or the weaker supplier: they are used for respectable members of the middle class, such as silversmiths, apothecaries and booksellers.

Along with personal objects and agricultural products, the aim of domestic produce itself can be the exchange, rather than personal consumption. Inventories and account books show that domestic spinning and weaving are widely practiced throughout the seventeenth century. This does not mean that homespun linen, or hemp and the "gross home-linen" are going to be used as cloth for the family. On the contrary, it is quite evident that there is a market for such products, and that they can be exchanged for money or, most of the time, for better fabric. For example, at the beginning of the summer, when the widow from Orvieto feels the need of a fresher dress, being always very careful with her expenses she decides to dispose of 6 scudi worth of gross homespun cloth, to get a discount on some "lighter stuff" for a long vest and a petticoat. The expense goes down from 11.25 to only 5 scudi.[42] Other account books and receipts show how common this custom was: the *marchesa* Vittoria Patrizi Spada, for example, asks her housemaids to make and weave some silk, and then she sells it to the same draper she usually buys from.[43] Judicial documents tell us that women of a lower status do the same. This allows us to see the reels of flax or silk that appear in nearly all the women's inventories in a new way.[44]

The Gifts

Besides making payments, produce from one's farms can also be useful to make gifts. "His Lordship [the Pope] is expected from *Castello* on Sunday," writes Carlo Cartari to his mother, "and I would think appropriate if your Ladyship sent a basketful of wine to present him with."[45] Then, when the wine eventually arrives in Rome, together with all of the woman's recommendations on the matter of its distribution, he does not fail to carefully report all to her. He writes "I gave twenty flasks to His Lordship, twenty to our *sig. Cardinal Padrone*, twelve to *monsignor* Fausto, twelve to *monsignor* Boccabella, eight to the lawyer with whom I used to study last August, six to *father* Cherubino, eight to *cavalier* Giuseppino as a reward for the colours for the picture of *signor Zio*."[46] What these gifts are aimed at is clearly shown. The young man writes:

> On Wednesday, I went to present His Lordship with the wine, and he was so good as to accept it with his usual kindness ... He asked me how my sister was, I answered that she is well, and that she recommended to His Holiness her husband *sig.* Horatio; to this His Holiness answered that he was to be provided for; and he said this three or four times, with unusual affection and manner.[47]

Payments and gifts in kind are not only common among landlords, the practice being widely familiar in the urban ranks. At least, this is what emerges in the "Memoirs of the marriage between Aurelio Antonio Bandini and *Madonna* Laura Sarda," where we find a description, day by day, of all the stages of an engagement, of all the ceremonies involved and of the gifts that the groom presented the bride with nearly every day. The diary starts on a Thursday, May 6, 1593, when "at 7 in the evening ... we made the promise to take each other as husband and wife ... and I touched her hand and a contract was drawn for the dowry ... and I had her give to me a ring to make one marry her." On Friday and Saturday the witnesses are questioned to check the free condition of the intended couple and on Sunday Aurelio sends "*Madonna* Laura 4 quails and a piece of veal that altogether cost four *giulij*." Next Thursday, May 13, the young man takes to the girl's house the boy from the draper's shop "with a lot of rolls of velvet and *messer* Geronimo the tailor and they were happy with one roll and we got five *canne*, 40 *giulij* per *canna* it's 20 scudi altogether." On Friday the 14th he brings "*Madonna* Laura some fish which cost 18 *baiocchi*" and on Saturday the 16th "a quarter of a baby goat and mutton 16 *baiocchi*." In the meantime he has made an order for the ring: "I bought the ruby and I had it mounted and enamelled and it cost me 14 *giulij* for the making, two to work on the stone, one for the leaf, one for the six more beads of gold he has put." The next Friday again he gives her some fish, "a piece of pike which cost 19 *baiocchi*," and in the next days several "pounds of fruit," "a *mostacciolo* and a heart of marzipan," "two roasted turtle-doves," a pair of slippers and a pair of shoes. On May 24, at last, Aurelio sends to the bride's house a boy:

with the carriage and *Madonna* Laura and her sister her maid and the nun of *messer* Montiero went to *S. Maria del Popolo*, I and *messer* Iacomo and *messer* Montiero went there, we received the Holy Communion at the high altar and then *fra* Ioannino married us ... then we mounted on the carriage ... and returned home ... I had lunch and dinner and came home to sleep and there I brought my silver glass and a silver fork and two corals and a glass cup and another made of glass and a big knife and a big fork to carve on the table, I do not mention the fruit, veal and peas and other things brought to eat.[48]

As we can see, during the short engagement gifts in form of foodstuffs prevail, even if Aurelio, who comes from an urban environment, is not taking them from his own land. He had to buy every single thing, and for each of them he has noted the price.

In 1593's middle class, the gift of a fish or of a quarter of a small goat are not considered common or inelegant. Food gifts are equally common in 1628, in the Curial environment, although marzipan, candied fruit and similar delicacies are preferred.[49] But a man as refined as Cassiano dal Pozzo is aware that "it is a good rule" not to present important people with "edible stuff," so that he avoids sending "to the Palace" the "big box, or I should say case, of the excellent and delicious plums" from the "beautiful garden" of Giovan Battista Doni.[50] In 1702–3, among great aristocrats, although such gifts are exchanged, delicious and rare foods are chosen, such as pheasants,[51] melons,[52] bass,[53] tuna from Terracina,[54] jam,[55] candied fruit,[56] rosolio,[57] and even a turtle.[58] All these things are also decoratively presented. In the account books of *marchese* Santacroce's butler, the entries regarding the expenses for food gifts are completed by those concerning the cost of presenting them, arranging them as centerpieces, or decorating them with flowers.[59]

The wedding between Aurelio and Laura takes place in 1593. The practical and not really gallant nature of the gifts the man presents her with may well be explained by the lack of more sophisticated objects on the market, and at the same affordability of a fish or a quarter of a small goat, to give to his fiancée. At the beginning of the eighteenth century, an explanation based on the lack in the market would be much less convincing. The persistence of these old-fashioned habits must be explained differently. In any case, food gifts are not at all out of fashion. This is confirmed in the diary kept by Francesco Maria Febei during his term as *Conservatore* in Rome. The manuscript is really enlightening. Febei's interest is focused on the ceremonies of appointment, the following visits paid to the papal authorities and, of course, the gifts exchanged during all these occasions. Immediately after their election, the three new *Conservatori* are received by the *Cardinal Camerlengo*, who welcomes them from his bed and has them sitting on his right-hand side, to stress his superiority in hierarchy but, at the same time, to show them signs of respect (for example, his right hand). The next day, High Mass is celebrated in the church of Aracoeli and "a priest wearing a cotta gives each of us a silken flower." More ceremonies occur in the following days. As a sign of homage the *Conservatori* receive several fish heads decorated with rosemary and carnations. When the *Congregazione di Campidoglio*, which is composed of

several officials, is assembled, "when the meeting is halfway through fresh
water is given and chocolate and Savoia biscuits, to the four of us *Conservatori*
and prior they bring the silver plate with a silken handkerchief the colour of
coffee with a silver teaspoon, to the others ... the saucer with a similar
teaspoon but with no silken handkerchief." When the nuns from S. Lorenzo
in Panisperna want to express their devotion to the high Roman officers, they
send a basket with ten jars of conserve and a silken flower. The entries
concerning the ceremonies and the gifts are the true center of the short diary.
In fact, the conclusion is a disappointing thought:

> The profit has been quite small, not getting, subtracting the expenses for tips and
> others, to 50 scudi, being as far as 6.40 from this. The fish heads which I believed
> I would have had in good quantity were but 21 on my part that is

tuna heads	n° 17
sea bass heads	n° 03
sturgeon heads	n° 01
	21
beautiful silken flowers	n° 6
baskets of pastries	n° 2
basket of conserve	n° 1
holy images made of silk and paper	n° 6
a measure of S. Domenico	
a habit of the Carmine	
bread loaves in five places.[60]	

In other cases the remunerative function of gifts is even more evident. For
example Lavinia Cartari, who plainly does not trust her son's domestic
competence, choses a nun from her family as the keeper of the family
furnishings in Rome. But she knows too well that every service calls for a
remuneration: "remember to send something to sister Alessandra for Carnival,"
she writes in February, "so that she will take more care of our things."[61] Go and
say hello to sister Alessandra, she insists in August, so you can mention to her
"the clothes that can be ruined by moths, and also the other things."[62]

Personal objects can be sold without regret in order to make money; on the
other hand, money retains the mark of the agricultural produce it has been
exchanged with (oil, wine, corn, hemp, pigs etc.). Finally, agricultural produce
and foodstuffs that are bought at the market are immediately linked to their
monetary equivalent. There seems to be a well-shaped continuity between
goods and money, something strongly connecting the two and blurring the
boundaries between their respective functions.

Goods Excluded from the Exchange

If some goods and objects can be exchanged without regret, others are
jealously guarded, so that we may well say that they are willingly excluded

from "the common sphere of economical activity."[63] The most obvious example is the family palace, followed by collections with a particular artistic or scientific value.[64] But the exclusion of some objects from their usual utilitarian function, the reluctance to exchange them and the subsequent choice of keeping them do not concern these kinds of goods only. Even a single very common object can have its status changed, passing from a money-equivalent commodity to a protected possession. Moreover, the same people who do not hesitate to exchange some of their goods can be very jealous keepers of others. The correspondence between Carlo Cartari, his mother and her secretary, for example, not only reveals careful comments on the state of the agricultural market or on the exchange value of agricultural produce and objects, but also information about sowing, bulbs and the availability of pot plants, etc., and jokes on the shared passion for gardening. In the autumn of 1633, for example, Carlo sends some bulbs to Orvieto:

> The bulbs here included are three hundred and fifty, and more, all of them of very beautiful tulips as I have already written to *sig*. Angelo. Your Ladyship will do me the favour of bringing them to him, and to recommend them to him as much as possible, because these are the best ones I have. Please, do not let *sig*. Girolamo see them, or he would want some for himself.[65]

Lavinia, who is a practical woman, writes to him in reply that "today the secretary has sown them all," and she appears to be much more worried for the price of paper than impressed by the new fascination for bulbs. "When you write," she recommends, "make sure your handwriting is smaller so that everything can fit in a sheet, because I am spending too much."[66] Still, when in spring the bulbs begin to bloom, she allows herself space for a joke:

> The gardener [nickname for the secretary] says that now he has a great quantity of flowers, that is white double and single narcissuses and also yellow single ones, and white hyacinths and deep blue ones, and that he is enjoying them as I am and that he is so jealous that he always has the garden key in his pocket, but he says that your Lordship must not pride yourself calling them your flowers, because he claims that he is the master of this garden, and nobody else.[67]

"Now the invaluable bulbs will blossom"[68] says the son who is in Rome. "The gardener takes care of the flowers," replies his mother, "but he says that you can keep the invaluable ones for yourself," because they have not produced anything so far.[69] He rather "begs your Lordship to be so kind as to send him up to six orange trees and if among these there are one or two lemon trees he would be very happy."[70] In mid-April, seemingly, a surprise, the tulips start to bloom. They write from Orvieto:

> Here we are enjoying these beautiful flowers from your bulbs, I always have a pot of these in my room, and yesterday and today two of them bloomed with six petals each, one red and white and the other red and yellow, and in truth beautiful, and more and more people asked the secretary for some bulbs, but he excuses himself saying they are not his, even if they are.[71]

Even a matron as meticulous as Lavinia, who always pays attention to the practical aspect of any matter, allows herself to be fascinated by the beauty of these new flowers from Holland. She is only too happy to forget that her son invested money to buy them. She herself is ready to spend for the sheer pleasure of the eye: she writes: "Today sister Modesta sent me two beautiful branches of silken flowers with birds and fruit, to keep in the study, and they really are beautiful things, and I still do not know how much I will pay for them."[72] This ability to enjoy the beauty of things is probably favored by the great affection Lavinia exhibits for objects, something she shows on several occasions. Her attention for their intrinsic value, not only their exchange value, is shown by the care she has for the parcels she is sending to Rome, by the extreme accuracy she uses to describe every item she has included in every parcel and the tags she has prepared to recognize each item: flasks of wine of a certain kind "are marked with a red cloth," those of another kind "with a white cloth."[73] "A basket with two pieces of cured pork loin, thirteen pieces of sausage and the same number of liver sausages" is wrapped in some paper with "a big C on," and so on.[74]

The instructions left by Giovanni Maria Contelori, a gentleman from Cesi, to his wife and his housemaids are just as careful. When he leaves the family house to move to Rome, where he will be appointed associate judge at the court of the *Auditor Camerae*, Contelori writes on several loose papers careful instructions on how to wrap up the objects to take away and how to put away safely all that will be left in the empty house. The clothes, sheets, mattresses, blankets, linen and tow for spinning, dishes, pans, leather, and also

> all the saffron, spices and candies … and the pear trees we keep inside or apple trees … All the books of the children which can be put in a bag or a satchel on top of the pile so that it might be taken off … and look in the little cupboard over the marble table where can be found some printed dictionaries and other elegant books written with my own hand and others which can be useful for students, moreover between my law books there is a dictionary for students *in quarto folio* and the *vocabulario juris* and send them for the children with two or three lines [… and put the books for the children aside], so that they can be left wherever I want without disarranging the pile.

He also recommends to the women that, when preparing the baggage, the new clothes should be hidden inside old sheets, and linen and tow for spinning must be kept in separate satchels. "Do not forget the raisins" and the "little bag full of dried roses" or "those clothes inside the basket in the big cupboard which can be used here for mending and for the inner lining of *ciambellotto* and *moccaiale* as well as of wool." At the end, "Make an inventory of all the books remaining and send it to me with the other one with all the things in the house. Then make an inventory of all that is left in the boxes and lock them. Carefully close cupboard and wardrobes and lock doors and windows of my study …"[75]

With Contelori, the care for the objects themselves goes with the zeal of a careful administrator for the preservation of his own *masseritia* – furnishings.

Years afterwards, Carlo Cartari will show how the concern with aesthetic values and the passion for the objects themselves can reach higher levels. I will come back to this later. Here I intend to draw some more examples of an attitude which is halfway between the utilitarian and the "contemplative," where the status of goods wavers between the equivalence with money and intrinsic value. At least it is with this meaning that I think the testamentary dispositions of Dorotea Antolini must be interpreted.[76] Dying with no heirs, this well-off bourgeois, daughter and granddaughter of lawyers, does not request that all her goods be sold and all the money used for charity: she wants the objects themselves to become bequests. Some of her dresses made of velvet and brocade, with gold and silver laces, will become frontals for churches in Rome. The most interesting donation, though, is that of her jewels:

> I leave to the *Chiesa del Giesù* a jewel, which is pawned for seventy scudi, and a diamond necklace which is pawned for fifty scudi and a diamond ring for a hundred scudi, and I want all these three to be given by my heir to the *fathers* for the Virgin of Trapani … to put on the neck of the Blessed Virgin.

Just like the jewels, all the dresses are pawned and the heir is requested to redeem them. These personal belongings, which during her life have purely been money-equivalent, and which she clearly never made use of by wearing them, with her death become goods with an intrinsic value, which are to be preserved as such, to decorate altars and icons: their status as goods has completely changed.

The bequests for friends and servants confirm the woman's intentions. To each of them she leaves quite conspicuous amounts of money and also one object especially: a silver round basket for the testamentary executor, an ebony writing desk to the attorney, her precious dresses for her child's godmother and the home ones for the washerwoman, the shirts for the beggars and so on. Some of these goods, the silver basket for example, are also pawned. Therefore the object that has been left does not make up for a shortage of cash. It is explicitly intended as the bequest of one selected good, which gains a particular value because it has been the deceased woman's property.[77] On the other hand, when she wants her possessions to lose their relevance as things and to get their money equivalent-object status, Dorotea plainly says so: "Sell all my books, the spiritual and the secular ones, and give the proceeds to the poor."

Halfway between the utilitarian use of goods for their exchange value and the admiration for their intrinsic quality is the habit of giving ever more sophisticated gifts, according to what Pontano had already suggested. This is well illustrated by the account books of the Santacroce family, where, along with all the other objects that were to be donated as we have already seen, we find a "sideboard with crystals,"[78] a wig "*à la dauphine*,"[79] and four pen-decorated fans with views of Naples, Palermo and other cities, sent to Venice.[80] Some decades before, an affectionate husband had showered his wife with a profusion of gallant gifts, such as branches full of fake flowers, figurines made of papier-mâché for the Nativity, and some other keepsakes to put on top of the furniture.[81] At the beginning of the previous century Cassiano dal Pozzo had presented his brother's wife with a "little writing desk in the Indian style" full of "silken and golden flowers" that looked "as natural as it was possible and all varied" from one another, along with some "pretty glass things, such as small pendants, necklaces and these kinds of things."[82] The fashionable gifts we know best from the sources are those offered by Virgilio Spada to his relatives, especially to the female ones.[83] His gifts are precious flowers, books, drawings, coral vases, crowns and reliquaries of semiprecious stones, also "a Geneva watch with a mountain-crystal case"[84] and, just like dal Pozzo, two "ebony writing-desks with decorations."[85]

The reasons for this evolution are not immediately evident. The little silver plates covered with a silken handkerchief the colour of coffee, where Savoia biscuits are laid when presented to the *Conservatori* of Rome, do not have a different function from the jam and the fish heads. All these are a way to remunerate the magistrates' work without an open offer of money. It is clear, though, that the addition of an aesthetic value is not at all irrelevant, and the gift of a collectable good is clearly different from that of a useful one. The research of the unheard, of the never seen, but also of the sophisticated and the elegant is an obligation and at the same time an expedient that the worldly-wise giver can use to his advantage, transforming, as Carlo Cartari says, even dried plums into "a peculiar thing ... by placing them on the table ... in a silver plate."[86] This does not mean that the exchange value is forgotten or that the beauty of things prevails over their money equivalence. On the contrary, the two ways of considering objects generally coexist. Carlo Cartari, to whom we owe the comment on the dried plums, more than once appears to be a deep admirer of the intrinsic value of objects. He does not seem at all inclined to consider them for their mere exchange value. Still, he is not so shocked when the winners of a lottery quickly busy themselves in selling their prizes: "a remarkable diamond ring"[87] and a "crystal mirror."[88]

Conclusion

In his seminal book on *La Culture des apparences*, Daniel Roche had already discovered a similar behavioral pattern in eighteenth-century Paris: noble families habitually sold their clothing and thus actively supplied a second-hand market in this area.[89] What can be added to his reconstruction is that the reason for this did not simply lie in the imperatives of fashion that forced a person to renew their wardrobe more and more frequently. Second-hand active markets also existed for goods not so exposed to the whims of fashion, such as furniture or books. The reason why these old things were sold was not to comply with fashion but to gain resources in order to acquire new and different objects.

This exchange could be direct, as we have seen, but professional brokers, such as second-hand dealers, could also mediate it. For my argument this point has no relevance, since what I want to stress is that, in both cases, the reason for this behavior is not to be found in an absolute lack of resources but in a relative shortage of cash. From this point of view, things are not sold or given away to gain money, rather they are exchanged for other things as if they were money. The second-hand market is a consequence of this monetary status of things, and is also an imperative prerequisite for this mechanism to work. If things are to be used as money equivalents, a general agreement on their nature and on their ability to play this role is required.

The monetary status of goods has another important consequence. As long as things must be used to make exchanges possible, they cannot be kept, collected or cherished. Their owner cannot feel "objectified" in them.[90] A world of money-equivalent things is a world of transient possessions: as Christiane Klapisch-Zuber has so brilliantly shown many years ago, beautiful dresses, jewels and other bride apparel were frequently borrowed or hired, and, if they were bought, they were soon sold back afterwards.[91] I found a similar behavioral pattern in the account books of a Roman patrician family, in which an entry registers the purchase of a velvet dress and a golden chain and a few months later, another registers the selling of both items.

To keep something, one must be free to withdraw it from the circuit of the exchange. This can not only happen if he or she is rich enough to afford this withdrawal, but also if a cash economy is developed enough to allow for a shift in the status of things. Thus a consumer society, intended as a society that indulges in an accumulation of objects, can only develop if a cash economy is sufficiently developed.

In his *Philosophy of Money*, Georg Simmel argued that the spread of money makes people free from mutual physical dependence. When the master can pay his servant in cash rather than feeding and housing him, he gets rid of most of his responsibilities toward him. And, when the servant receives a monetary salary, he is no longer obliged to live in his master's house. The same happens with things. Only when there is enough cash to buy new goods without selling the old ones can objects acquire a new and different value, deriving precisely from time, i.e., the fact that they have long belonged to their owner. Only time can load things with both sentimental values and identity values.[92]

To be convinced of this, one has just to think of family houses or palaces, which acquire greater and greater value as long as they pass from one generation to another. Being preserved from exchange, they gain new meaning and a new sort of value that has no connection with money, but rather a strong association with signification and identity. If certain goods are to be viewed as an objectification of the subject, i.e., as a materialization of his or her identity, it is the presence of cash that makes this possible. On the contrary, as long as goods cannot be kept, but must frequently be reintroduced in the circuit of exchange, no objectification through material culture is conceivable.

An active market of second-hand goods can thus be viewed as a precious resource, allowing people to make ends meet. But it can also represent an extreme form of deprivation, implying the impossibility to rely on a set of stable things to give a meaning to the world.[93]

Translated from the Italian by Simone Caffari and Lee Shelton

Notes

1. M. Douglas and B. Isherwood, *The World of Goods: Towards an Anthropology of Consumption* (Harmondsworth, 1980).
2. K. Pomian, "Collezione," in *Enciclopedia Einaudi*, vol. I (Turin: 1978), pp. 330–64.
3. Ibid., pp. 330–64, p. 334.
4. See the introduction to R. Romeno and U. Tucci (eds.), *Economia naturale, economia monetaria*, in *Storia d'Italia, Annali*, n°. 6 (Turin, 1983), pp. XIX–XXXIII, p. XXVI.
5. Ibid., pp. XIX–XXXIII, p. XXVII.
6. Ibid.; see also R. Ago, *Economia barocca. Mercato e istituzioni nella Rome del Seicento* (Rome, 1998), p. 59; C. Muldrew, "'Hard Food for Midas': Cash and its Social Value in Early Modern England." *Past and Present*, 170 (2001), pp. 78–120.
7. P. Earle, *The Making of the English Middle Class: Business, Society and Family Life in London, 1660–1730* (London, 1989).
8. Muldrew, "'Hard food for Midas'," pp. 78–120, pp. 91–2.
9. See Ago, *Economia barocca*.
10. "Stipendi nominali e busta paga effettiva dei funzionari dell'amministrazione milanese alla fine del Cinquecento," in *Miscellanea in onore di Roberto Cessi* (Rome, 1958), vol. 2, pp. 188–363.
11. J. Schneider, "Trousseau as Treasure: Some Contradictions of Late Nineteenth-Century Change in Sicily," in E.B. Ross (ed.), *Beyond the Myth of Culture: Essays in Cultural Materialism* (New York and London, 1980), pp. 323–55.
12. H. Ward, "Worth its Weight in Gold: Women and Value in North West India," PhD thesis, University of Cambridge, 1997.
13. See J. Schneider, "Of Vigilance and Virgins: Honor, Shame, and Access to Resources in Mediterranean Society," *Ethnology*, 9 (1971); Muldrew, "'Hard food for Midas'," p. 80. G. Calvi and I. Chabot (eds.), *Le ricchezze delle donne: diritti patrimoniali e poteri familiari in Italia: XIII–XIX secc.* (Turin, 1998).
14. R. Ago, "Oltre la dote: i beni femminili," in A. Groppi, *Il lavoro delle donne* (Rome and Bari, 1996), pp.164–82.
15. See F. Tateo's introduction to his edition of G. Pontano, *I libri delle virtù sociali* (Rome, 1999), p. 16.
16. Pontano, *I libri delle virtù sociali*, p. 73.
17. Ibid., p. 79.
18. Ibid., p.231.
19. Some examples of testamentary dispositions for the disposal of furniture, silverware and other things can be found in Rome State Archives (hereafter ASR), *Trenta notai capitolini* (TN), uff. 28, Testamenti, vol. 2, cc. 63, 790, 916; Ibid., Notai RCA, b. 1474, cc. 6, 7, 23, 221, 266; Ibid., b. 854, c. 849.
20. ASR, Giustiniani, b. 132, cc. 29–31.
21. On the function of time in the creation of a symbolic link between the objects and their owner see D. Miller, *A Theory of Shopping* (Cambridge, 1998).
22. ASR, Giustiniani, b. 132, cc. 30–1. Giustiniani is not the only one to exclude from the sale part of his goods. Camillo Moretti, a lawyer, requested his heirs to sell everything but "the books on humanities," which might be used by his nephew (ASR, Notai RCA, b. 1474, c. 6, 1597).
23. ASR, Santacroce, b. 969 and b. 747, f. 3.
24. To give an idea of the value of 300 scudi I may say that it is the equivalent of the annual rent paid for a small palace (see Ago, *Economia barocca*, p. 169) and that the salary of a living-in apprentice is 6–8 scudi a year (ibid., p. 137).
25. Ibid.,
26. Ibid., p. 286.
27. He is actually in exile because of a duel, but this does not prevent him from fully joining in the court's life, nor does it cause any inconvenience to his family in Rome.
28. Pontano, *I libri delle virtù sociali*, p. 239.
29. ASR, Cartari Febei, b. 22, November 1, 1633.

30. Ibid., January 17, 1634.
31. D. Roche, *La Culture des apparences. Une histoire du vêtement: 17e–18e siècle* (Paris, 1989); P. Allerston, "The Market in Second-Hand Clothes and Furnishings in Venice, c. 1500–1650," PhD thesis, European University Institute, Florence, 1996; M.G. Muzzarelli, *Guardaroba medievale: vesti e società dal XIII al XVI secolo* (Bologna, 1999); R. Ago, "Il linguaggio del corpo," in C. M. Belfanti and F. Giusberti (eds), *La Moda* (Turin, 2003), pp. 117–48.
32. ASR, Spada Veralli, b. 775, account n° 16, 1681.
33. ASR, Santacroce, bill nos. 174, 193, 207, 208 for 1702 and 35 for 1703.
34. ASR, Cartari Febei, b.22, December 6, 1633
35. Ibid., December 13, 1633
36. Ibid., December 20, 1633
37. Ibid., February 1634.
38. His mother had written to him: "I have already bought a fur coat for Father Gregorio and I spent two scudi on it but believe me we spend here and we have to send our payment to Facchini [the attorney] or he will not do any more for us:" ASR, Cartari Febei, b. 22, December 6, 1633.
39. Ibid., December 10, 1633.
40. Ibid.,
41. ASR, Sforza Cesarini, b. 249, 1689.
42. ASR, Cartari Febei, b. 22, June 20 and 27, 1634.
43. Ago, "Il linguaggio del corpo."
44. Ibid.
45. ASR, Cartari Febei, b. 22, October 29, 1633.
46. Ibid., Debember 24, 1633.
47. Ibid., November 12, 1633 (the *sig.* Horatio he speaks of is the governor of Amelia, a small village in Umbria).
48. ASR, S Giacomo, b. 172/10 (Fabiani).
49. Ibid., b. 172/8, (Gavotti). In 1657 Maria Veralli presents the lawyers who are assisting her in a case with wax from Venice and refined sugar; Spada Veralli, b. 1002.
50. Quoted by D.L. Sparti, *Le collezioni Dal Pozzo. Storia di una famiglia e del suo museo nella Roma seicentesca* (Modena, 1992), p. 169, September 13, 1642.
51. ASR, Santacroce, b. 286, January 1701.
52. Ibid., February 1702; melons too are considered a delicacy: in an account book they are recorded as a special expense for the feast of the Assumption. Ibid., b. 713 (August 1552).
53. Ibid., b. 286, March 1702.
54. Ibid., July 1702.
55. Ibid., March 1702.
56. Ibid., March 1704.
57. Ibid.,
58. Ibid., May 1703.
59. Ibid., March 1702, and March 1704.
60. ASR, Cartari Febei, b. 40.
61. Ibid., b. 22, February 14, 1634.
62. Ibid., August 8 1634.
63. See Pomian, "Collezione."
64. Both palaces and collections are protected by entails that are meant to prevent their dispersion, as several new studies on the issue demonstrate: see M.L. Madonna and M. Bevilacqua, "The Roman Families in Urban Development," in P. van Kessel and E. Schulte (eds.), *Rome and Amsterdam. Two Growing Cities in Seventeenth-Century Europe* (Amsterdam, 1997), pp. 115 ff. and P. Findlen, *Possessing Nature. Museums, Collecting, and Scientific Culture in Early Modern Italy* (Berkeley, 1994).
65. ASR, Cartari Febei, b.22, November 1, 1633.
66. Ibid., November 8, 1633.
67. Ibid., March 21, 1634.
68. Ibid., March 25, 1634.

69. Ibid., March 27, 1634.

70. Ibid., April 4, 1634.

71. Ibid., April 18, 1634.

72. Ibid., May 25, 1634.

73. Ibid., December 18, 1633.

74. Ibid., February 14, 1634.

75. ASR, Miscellanea famiglie, b. 61, fasc. 6.

76. ASR, S.Girolamo, b. 4, cc. 183 ff., 1656.

77. Many years before, Benedetto Giustiniani behaved like Dorotea, rather than like his nephew Vincenzo, leaving to some "relative" of his "all the Spanish leather things which are in the little room in front of my chapel, and a saucer and two big, smooth chandeliers, and the red damask bed [...] bought in Bologna;" to Cardinal Montalto, his "benefactor," "so that he might remember me, my round painting of the Virgin Mary painted by Parmesanino" and to his testamentary executor, "my round painting of Mary painted by Giulio Romano." ASR, Sma Annunziata, b. 44, cc. 277–8.

78. ASR, Santacroce, b. 286, October 1702.

79. Ibid., November 1702.

80. Ibid., b. 747, 1703.

81. ASR, Notai AC, vol. 4772, cc. 32 ff., 1667.

82. See the letter of October 1627 quoted by Sparti, *Le collezioni Dal Pozzo*, p. 173.

83. This prelate's love for tidiness guided him to keep his account books very carefully, separating his expenses for other people from those made for himself. ASR, Spada Veralli, b. 827, cc. 7, 9, 10, 13, 17, 33.

84. ASR, Spada Veralli, b. 827, c. 7.

85. Ibid., cc. 7 e 9.

86. ASR, Cartari Febei, b. 33, August 31, 1672.

87. Ibid., August 10, 1672.

88. Ibid., August 6, 1672.

89. Roche, *La culture des apparences*.

90. This idea of "objectification" is derived from D. Miller (ed.), *Acknowledging Consumption: a Review of New Studies* (London and New York, 1995).

91. C. Klapisch-Zuber, "Le complexe de Griselda. Dot et dons de mariage au Quattrocento," *Mélanges de l'Ecole française de Rome. Moyen Age–Temps Modernes*, vol. 94 (1982), pp. 7–43.

92. Georg Simmel, *The Philosophy of Money*. Transl. by Tom Bottomore and David Frisby (London, 1978).

93. See Douglas and Isherwood, *The World of Goods*.

PROSTITUTION AND THE CIRCULATION OF SECOND-HAND GOODS IN EARLY MODERN ROME

Tessa Storey

Prostitution was a common enough phenomenon in late medieval and early modern Italian society. Demographic analysis of the parish records for Rome, for example, shows that in the early decades of the seventeenth century the minimum number of women officially known as prostitutes oscillated at around 1,200. Contemporary responses to prostitution were fairly homogeneous, and whether one looks at sources ranging from canon law to civic legislation, from traveller's accounts to literary portrayals there are a number of recurring topoi. These included the problem of sexual promiscuity; the ever present threat of the "*mal francese*" or syphilis; the danger of the corrupting influence of prostitutes upon honest women; the squandering of young men's inheritances; and the public nuisance frequently associated with the profession. Over and above these, however, there was one issue of overriding concern to contemporaries, which in popular narratives frequently took precedence over the immorality of their lifestyle. This was the issue of the prostitute's complicated and intense relationship to wealth in the form of material goods.[1]

Awareness of the commercial basis of the relationship constructed between prostitute and client was always present in the terminology used to describe the profession. As Patricia Cibin has pointed out, the Latin root "*Mer-*" of the term for prostitute, *meretrix*, means to earn, acquire and have commerce.[2] Another term for prostitution commonly employed in legal and criminal sources was "*commercio carnale*," or carnal commerce, and as a great many prostitutes interrogated before criminal courts explained, they earned their living by "negotiating" and "bartering" with their bodies. This commercial focus was also emphatically reflected in a great deal of contemporary literature, which portrayed the attractions and dangers of prostitution within a framework of a narrative based around essentially "economic" concerns. The life of the prostitute was articulated in terms of her economic rise and downfall and focused particularly on the relationship between the prostitute and material goods, demonstrating an almost obsessive interest in their material wealth.

Whether one studies literature produced by and for an elite readership, or texts generated for a broader, more popular market, there is the implicit assumption that prostitutes aspired above all to acquire material possessions, even entering the profession for that reason.[3] Another popular topos was that they quickly amassed such a hoard of furnishings in their apartments that their home resembled a treasure trove. This theme was taken up by the Englishman Thomas Coryat when he recounted his visit to a Venetian courtesan in the early seventeenth century:

> For their fairest roomes are most glorious and glittering to behold. The walles round about being adorned with most sumptuouse tapistry and gilt leather. ...Shee will shew thee her chamber of recreation where thou shalt see all manner of pleasing objects, as many faire painted coffers wherewith it is garnished round about, a curious milke-white canopy of needle worke, a silke quilt embrodered with gold.[4]

This topos emerges equally in more popular literary forms, such as the verses and songs printed cheaply in small-format booklets (octavo) for the broader market.[5] In one of the most well-known and frequently republished of these, *The Boast and Lament of the Courtesan from Ferrara*, the heroine describes her well-appointed home. "I don't know anyone who can match me, who has the house so well supplied with bread, wood, wine, oil and salt. ... I have a cupboard full of silver, the tables, walls and chests full of carpets and tapestries."[6]

However, as texts and images also made clear, the courtesan's ability to obtain such possessions waxed and waned and these objects were vulnerable to dispersal and loss. Indeed, the vulnerability of her material possessions formed a crucial part of narratives about the life of the prostitute. The courtesan's subsequent downfall and loss of wealth and status are not only shown as an inevitable moment in the cycle of the wheel of fortune, but they stand as punishment both for her carnal sins and for her social ambition, material greed and pride. This was otherwise understood as the sin of *lussuria*.[7] This vulnerability was demonstrated in many ways. In a cycle of images from the late seventeenth century we see how the formerly glorious courtesan, having fallen from favor with her client, is forced, weeping, to sell her goods on to a second-hand dealer.[8] Alternatively, two early seventeenth-century laments describe how two very successful but naive courtesans were approached by men who posed as clients in order to gain access to their apartments. They then murdered the courtesans and fled with all their possessions.[9] It would seem that this was not merely a literary trope, for in 1635 the *Avvisi* from Rome (manuscript news reports that circulated between different cities and courts at the time) reported a spate of thefts from prostitutes in Rome. In one case two prostitutes "were killed miserably in their own beds and then robbed, by people who used the pretext of their libidinous desires and went to sleep with them."[10] The report went on to mention several other cases in which a pair of thieves posing as clients had selected prostitutes who lived alone, and having gained entry to their rooms one of them would produce a dagger and threaten to kill the prostitute, whilst the other: "Went to investigate what was in the house and in the chests, and effectively stripped them of rings, pendants, dresses and sheets, whilst the poor unhappy prostitute, for fear of her life not only kept quiet but was forced to hand over her jewels herself and give them the keys to her chests."[11]

Literature, we know, does not hold a mirror up to reality; traveller's accounts and news reports are liable to distortion and exaggeration. Nonetheless, taken together these many and varied sources reveal interesting perceptions about Italian prostitutes and their possessions. Firstly, there is the creation and consolidation of this topos concerning the distinctive relationship between the prostitute and her material goods, including the assumption that they were likely to acquire a wealth of objects. This is particularly clear in those texts describing men entering their apartments for the sake of these goods: whether licitly, to marvel at them, or illicitly, to steal them for the sake of their resale value. Secondly, most accounts are equally concerned with the transience of these objects in the courtesan's household: the ways she acquires them, and how she loses them. In turn these descriptions demonstrate how these goods situated the prostitute in wider networks of commercial activity and offer tantalizing hints about the life cycles of these objects as they circulate through the city economy. Thus Aretino gives a description of how a cunning prostitute tells her lover that she can no longer afford to stay in Rome. He gallantly offers to provide her with everything that she needs to furnish her apartment and turns up later with the goods, accompanied by porters and many Jews, who acted as second-hand dealers in the city. "And having leapt out of the house he returned at vespers with a key in his hand and with two porters laden with mattresses, blankets, bedsteads, another two with bed frames and boards, and I don't know how many Jews following behind, with carpets, sheets, pots and kitchenware."[12]

Likewise, in the *avvisi* accounts of the prostitutes who had been robbed, there was a description of how the courts had attempted to find the criminals and trace the stolen goods by issuing descriptions of the goods to all the "silversmiths, second-hand dealers and Jews," ordering them to inform the authorities if they came across any of the stolen items. Both kinds of narrative then, fact and fiction, illustrate the "embeddedness" of the prostitute at the heart of the city's economy of "used" goods, since their clients had first owned the goods they gave them, or purchased them second-hand, and later these clothes and furnishings were recirculated back into the economy by the prostitutes themselves, by thieves or by dealers.

Less apparent at first glance from literary sources are the uses to which the prostitute's material goods were put. Given the moral nature of most of these texts, the acquisition and loss of possessions were interpreted as signs of her greed and immorality and were certainly not contextualized in a discourse of economic survival. However, when we look at recent studies on the roles and activities of women in the early modern urban economy, it would appear that the ways in which prostitutes managed their material economy were similar to those adopted by other poor women. The role of women in informal chains of micro-credit, pawning and brokering has recently been highlighted by Beverly Lemire who stresses the centrality of household wares in a micro-economy in which "mutable items also functioned as a kind of currency."[13] Work on the second-hand clothes market in England and Venice has also drawn our attention to the use of clothing and linen in particular as material collateral for credit. The implication would seem to be that the acquisition of large quantities of household goods was not in fact a symptom of the prostitute's "greed" but a sign of her sensible housekeeping and economic foresight.[14]

In this chapter I shift the focus of attention away from moral issues, and on to the economic practicalities of prostitutes' lives, looking in particular at the circulation of goods into and out of the prostitutes' domestic interior. And, although prostitutes were in many senses an atypical social group, I suggest that, by studying the ways in which material commodities circulated into and out of the homes of prostitutes, we can gain considerable insight into the nature of the circulation of material goods amongst the poor within early modern Italian urban communities more generally. This in turn adds to our understanding of the centrality of the second-hand goods market to both the short-term and long-term economic survival of the poor female householders in particular.

Acquiring Material Goods

Like the studies mentioned above, Renata Ago has shown that the Roman economy was founded to a large extent on the circulation of objects rather than coinage, and people could trade with "absolutely everything, and above all everything had a certifiable price."[15] It seems as if this trade in objects may have been an even more important feature of prostitute's lives than it was for many other people. For example, what little we know of the women working in "honest professions" suggests that they would expect to be paid essentially in coin. Servants or wet nurses received a monthly wage in coin, plus bed and board, whilst women engaged in professions like collar-making or taking in laundry would be paid a certain amount per collar or wash.[16] By contrast, each prostitute had her own verbal contract with each client, and, whilst coins were often included in the transaction, carnal relationships were extensively negotiated in terms of objects, food and drink, depending on the woman's status and the social rank of the client. These objects and the transaction between prostitute and client were often described as "gifts" that were "given" to her rather than as "payment," but this should not blind us to the economic importance of these objects to the prostitute's domestic economy. Further-more, as Ferrante has pointed out, the legal and theological framework that underpinned medieval and early modern understandings of the nature of the commercial exchange between prostitute and client meant that, before church courts, clients were legally bound to recompense the prostitute for her labour and the gift she made of her body.[17] Thus, although these objects were termed "gifts," legally they were all considered to be the equivalent of payment, and as such, they represented the woman's earnings and possessions. Indeed, in certain long-term relationships the client would supply his courtesan with all or most of the clothes and furnishings necessary for her to live in the style that accorded with his social status.[18] As the courts made clear, these goods were a prostitute's earnings and savings, and that was why she had such relationships in the first place. It was to be expected that she could not only keep them, but subsequently dispose of them as she needed. This is clarified for us in a case from 1594 in which a former client of a prostitute took back the furniture he had given her during their relationship and sold it. She then took him to court and, as the courtroom summary made clear, he was expected to return the goods, or compensate her for their value, since:

> When one wants to keep such a woman *a sua posta* ... it is necessary for him to dress her, shoe her and pay her expenses and give her all that she needs ... and once a man has bought any things or furniture for a similar woman, or any woman with whom he has had carnal friendship several times, those things have been earned by that woman, and she can do whatever she likes with those things as her own. And when she breaks with that friend who has bought her those things, that man cannot have, or hope to have any expectations of those goods.[19]

It was this practice of paying prostitutes through objects that meant that some courtesans could acquire a relatively valuable stock of furnishings and clothes quite rapidly if they found a well-off client. As we will see, the importance of these objects lay not just in their immediate use as furnishings and to create a suitable ambience and to impress the other men who visited her rooms, but also for their longer-term value as objects to be resold and pawned when cash was needed. As a rule prostitutes probably received, owned and subsequently disposed of far more material goods than did the average poor woman, and perhaps it was observation of this social practice that formed the bedrock of the belief that prostitutes had a particularly privileged relationship with material objects. By the same token it also makes them a particularly interesting social group for the study of the circulation of objects, because without a doubt the majority of the goods that were given to them were not new at the time.

Patricia Allerston's work on Venice has already alerted us to the range and extent of the "second-hand market" in Italy and the fact that this was not just a trade in "old rags" for the very poor, but that it catered for all social classes.[20] To this I would add an observation on the rapidity with which objects could move from one social milieu to another, or one geographical area to another. Camillo Capilupi, a courtier and humanist living in Rome during the mid-sixteenth century, wrote a letter to a friend in which he described having given a gift to a Neapolitan courtesan in whose arms he had spent "a delightful night."[21] As a sign of his appreciation he "courteously gave her two beautiful shirts worked in white and two pairs of silk stockings." However, these were not shirts that he had purchased from a second-hand dealer or a tailor. They had in fact been given to him by his good friend the Duchess of Camerino, who had had them made especially for him. Thus the shirts had moved, in a relatively short space of time, from a Duchess in Camerino, to a humanist in Rome and thence to a Neapolitan courtesan.

Even though prostitutes were given objects, they would still have had to make a great many purchases in order to furnish their rooms and dress well and the majority of these transactions would have taken place outside official channels. This may have been because the object was too cheap to require a credit loan, or to merit the high cost of an official transaction, or because it was purchased from a friend.[22] Thus, when Orsolina Parmegiana, collar-maker and *cortigiana*, wanted to buy a large steaming iron for collars, she asked a friend and fellow collar-maker if she could purchase hers.[23] Furthermore, post-mortem inventories show that small essential household objects, *massaritie*, made from durable materials with no "fashion" or display value were relatively cheap and were probably easy to come by.[24] Nonetheless, there were certain more expensive items that were purchased through formal channels, and the most prominent kind of formal trade entered into by courtesans was in clothing purchased largely from Jews.[25] This can be seen from a sample of fifty-one sale and purchase agreements drawn up by courtesans in Rome between 1595 and 1609 from a single notary's office in Campo Marzio, the district in which the bulk of prostitutes resided.[26]

Although the men with whom the courtesans made these transactions were not actually described as *rigattieri* (second-hand dealers) in the documents, this was presumably their trade, since this was the principal occupation traditionally open to the Jews.[27] Of the fourteen Jewish dealers named in the documents, a partnership run by a certain David de Nola and Leonis de Pianellis dominated the trade, accounting for thirteen transactions. Two other dealers (Angelo de Laste Romano and Joseph i Sirena) accounted for five transactions per head and the remaining dealers accounted for between one and three transactions each. So, from this small sample, three businesses appear to have controlled the bulk of the second-hand commerce with courtesans. It would be interesting to know whether these three equally dominated the market with other social and professional groups, or whether they specialized in trading with prostitutes and courtesans, perhaps stocking the kind of showy and colourful clothes they preferred to wear.

Furthermore, of the fifty-one transactions studied, the majority record the purchase of clothing. Only eight documents record transactions involving items for interior furnishing (furniture, drapes or leather wall hangings) and only four record purchases of jewelry. I interpret this in two ways. On the one hand, perhaps clients tended to give prostitutes and courtesans much of the furniture and jewelry they owned. Jewelry in particular seems to have circulated within the community as an object used as collateral for loans, so perhaps prostitutes acquired jewels from other women as a result of unredeemed pledges. Furthermore, as a result of the flourishing trade in *bigiotteria* or fake jewelry, jewels were presumably very inexpensive to acquire. On the other hand, when the average prostitute did have some money to spare they presumably preferred to spend it on clothes, since this was the most immediate and visible way of attracting clients and of advertising their wealth and status as a courtesan.

The commerce between prostitutes and Jewish dealers in clothing was dominated by the purchase of items such as dresses and *zimmare* (*a zimarra* was a long-sleeved cloak-like outer garment), which were in fact the single most expensive items in a woman's wardrobe. The prices paid ranged from about two scudi to twenty-five scudi apiece, with the bulk of the items costing between two and ten scudi. If we compare these costs to the typical earnings of other city-dwellers, both "honest" women and male artisans, we find that they were not cheap by the standards of the city's working population. Although artisan's wages varied considerably according to their skills, it was common for them to earn between three and six scudi a month, whilst a servant girl (living in) could earn about one scudo a month if she were lucky and a wet nurse who lived out, might earn two scudi a month.[28] So even the cheapest of these dresses would have cost the average honest working woman two months' wage. The kind of *zimarra* worn by a reasonably well-off courtesan and costing fifteen scudi would have cost even a good artisan about three months' wages.

The fact that the dealers dominated the market in expensive items such as dresses also raises the question of where courtesans bought the many other clothing items found in their inventories, such as shirts, stockings, shawls, mules.[29] One answer is that since they frequently possessed rolls of cloth and scissors we can presume that they often made their own clothes. Otherwise they must have bought directly from the shirt-makers, from peddlers and from market stalls.[30]

The Dispersal and Recirculation of Goods

If material possessions were accumulated by courtesans as a savings strategy, when they needed to raise cash they had to pawn, sell or barter some of their possessions. Jewelry, linen and dresses or cloaks were often used as surety for loans amongst poor women, and their wills show that they often turned to one another for these loans, rather than to pawnbrokers.[31] However, on her death in July 1655, Caterina Chiavari still had twelve lots of unredeemed objects pawned with the Monte di Pietà in Rome, which had been deposited there over the previous twelve months. These included four pairs of sheets, towels, a tablecloth and napkins, three forks, two knives and one silver spoon. Although each deposit had earned her only a very small sum of money, amounting to less than half a scudo, the inventory showing her remaining possessions suggest that these objects must have been carefully chosen as being suitable for pawning. Overall she had material goods worth 114 scudi, including several comparatively luxurious items such as a bedspread of golden lace, worth nine scudi.[32] Nor was pawning exclusive to the very poor. The successful courtesan Amabilia Antongetta left some of her silver tableware as surety for a loan of 280 scudi from a nobleman, which raises interesting questions about what he intended to do with the goods if she was not able to pay her debt. Would he sell them on, or would he adorn his dining table with her unredeemed pledge of three silver goblet stands, four candlesticks, a salt cellar, a pepper grinder and a little sauce boat, four silver spoons and eight silver forks?[33]

Another way to dispose of one's possessions and raise some cash quickly was simply to sell them in bulk, as the poor prostitute Beatrice Gaultieri did in 1602 when she sold Joseph Sirena, one of the Jewish dealers, a large number of household goods for 10 scudi.

> Five walnut chairs covered in worn embossed red leather, an old sideboard, a small table with a striped cloth, two old and broken stools, a small chair a pair of fireirons with brass balls at the top, two chairs seated with straw, a buffet, four brass candlesticks, two small, two large; a copper cooler, a copper jug, a window blind, two pans, a griddle, a grater and many other things of little importance or value.[34]

As the document records, the items were already "old," "used," "broken," "worn," "of little importance or value," which also shows that there was always a market for objects, however old.

The courtesan's possessions also found their way back into circulation on her death. In one third of legacies prostitutes bequeathed furniture, bedding, linen and small household objects and in some cases perhaps they hoped that they would help someone else to set up home. Thus the courtesan Olimpia Novarese left her servant the following items: "A straw mattress, a mattress, a blanket, two pairs of sheets, a chest, two wicker-seated chairs, a frying pan, the frame and boards for a bed and all the testator's kitchenware."[35] Given the multiple ways in which bedding in particular could be re-used, as objects that could be both rented out and used as collateral, the only legacy made by Aurelia di Gaeta, though apparently paltry, may have been invaluable to the recipient. She left two pairs of sheets, a blanket and two mattresses "out of charity" to the daughter of a washerwoman.[36] The courtesan's possessions tended to be bequeathed to servants and friends, but, when they were handed down to relatives, it was daughters and sisters especially, rather than sons or brothers, who benefited.[37]

The Church was also responsible for recirculating the post-mortem property of courtesans, since the Church benefited directly from the wills of courtesans in two ways. All women who had engaged in prostitution at any time in their life were required to donate one-fifth of their estate to the *Monasterio delle Convertite* on death and, failing this, their entire estate would be confiscated.[38] The monastery had its own estimators who valued their property, and presumably had their own channels for reselling these goods, perhaps directly to second-hand dealers, perhaps through auctions. In addition it was not uncommon for courtesans to bequeath what appear to have been their best dresses to a specific church and these would then be resold to raise alms, or re-used to make altar cloths. Thus Giulia Veneta left her parish church, Santa Maria del Popolo, "a green velvet cloak trimmed with silver, and a ruby velvet dress with ribbon."[39] Likewise, Isabella Galeotti left a "green dress in Perpignan [a French woollen cloth], with red, white and turquoise bands" to San Lorenzo in Lucina, specifying that they must make an altar cloth from it.[40]

Another way in which a courtesan could be divested of her clothes or jewelry was through their appropriation by the police, known as *birri*. In Rome the fine for transgression of sumptuary regulations was the removal of all the jewels or finery that a courtesan was wearing when arrested, which was a simple and rapid way of relieving prostitutes of the offending item and of a good percentage of their wealth, since the forbidden clothing or jewelry was generally ostentatious and luxurious, and for that very reason they were forbidden to wear it.[41] As with post-mortem property taken by the Church, once possessions had been confiscated from courtesans by the courts they must also have been put back into circulation, perhaps through official auctions, then bought by the *rigattieri*, silversmiths and so on. However, we may suppose that the *birri* also recycled some of the nicer items, giving them as gifts to their own courtesans, thus putting these items directly back into the same social networks.

Courtesans as Investors and Brokers

Whilst all these ways in which a courtesan's goods re-entered the market suggest a rather gloomy picture of the gradual decline into poverty and death, punctuated by the ritual seizures of goods, it would be mistaken from this to draw the conclusion that the circulation of goods away from courtesans was entirely passive. As the transactions between successful courtesans and men of the nobility make clear, second-hand goods could have many trajectories; not just moving "down" a social chain, or circulating horizontally amongst social equals, but also "rising" from the dealer, to the courtesan, and then to the gentleman or nobleman.

Deciding what to resell or pawn was presumably part of the normal juggling of the household budget for poorer women, and over and above this there is interesting evidence that courtesans bought material goods as a saving and investment, not just in the sense that they stored them up until they should need to pawn them or until death, but actively using material objects as a way of investing. Indeed, they were perhaps even acting as brokers, purchasing, storing and then selling on high-quality goods, perhaps at a profit or perhaps as a way to continually renew their possessions. To illustrate this, let us look at the documents that record the financial activities of two courtesans named Orinthia Focari di Siena and another, Domenica Calvi di Siena. Between 1604 and 1607 Orinthia, who lived in the fashionable Via del Corso, drew up fifteen notarial documents in the office run by the notary Tranquillo Pizzuti. These included her will, loans, investments and rental agreements and by looking at the range of her transactions we can gain insight into her many different commercial links. In 1606 she presumably wanted some jewelry made, since she bought six pearls "for earrings" worth one scudo each, from a Christian, Marco Antonio di Marco.[42] However, her preferred dealer seemed to have been Joseph i Sirena, a Jew, from whom she bought good-quality, even luxury goods. In November 1604 she bought a good woolen cloak for fifteen and a half scudi. In December the same year she bought another two cloaks from him, also worth fifteen scudi each. (One was red, the other in green satin, embroidered with flowers in gold thread and trimmed with gold braid.)[43] Then, in October 1606 she bought two showy pearl necklaces and matching earrings from him for sixty-five scudi, each consisting of hundreds of pearls.[44] The same document also records the purchase, for one hundred scudi, of "two rooms of new *corame* (a fashionable embossed leather wall-covering), one enamelled in black, five skins high and the other enamelled in gold and silver, leather for a side table, and eight chairs of red *vaschetta*, printed with red fringes, and four similar smaller chairs."[45] These items would have constituted quite an elegant room in which to entertain her clients and their friends, although perhaps this was not her only or main intention. For Orinthia also sold on her goods, not necessarily to dealers, but on at least one occasion to a private buyer, so perhaps she herself was acting as a 'dealer' or broker. One document records the money owed her in November 1605 by Illus. Theodoro à Porta Romana, to whom she sold a range of rather banal household furnishings, such as a bowl, window shutter and fire-irons, but they were made of quite elegant materials, such as brass, or walnut.[46] She may of course have been ridding herself of unwanted objects, but less easy to explain without reference to the idea that she was acting as a broker is the fact that in September 1605 she also put a large number of her goods into storage, to be "kept and conserved" by a certain Isabella Antonij de Troiolo.[47] Since Orinthia had just moved into new apartments the previous month, it does not seem likely that she was going away and needed to put her furniture in safekeeping. Possibly this document records the way she stored her acquisition; perhaps whilst finding new buyers or perhaps until she could find another apartment, which she could then furnish and rent out. Certainly, the goods she had stored on Isabella's premises represent a collection of extremely fine furnishings, worth taking very good care of. They also represent far more furniture than a single woman would have had need of:

> Three rooms of gold and silver enamelled *corame*; that is, one of old *corame* and the other two of new *corame*. Three beds, all gilded, with columns, six big mattresses of good wool, two chests covered in leather full of linen and other used cloths. [And so on] Five second-hand chairs of red *corame* for men, four new women's chairs of *corame*, three wooden dining tables, one with its cover of *corame*, the others without, four stools painted green, six of wicker, two pairs of fire irons with brass knobs, and three new jalousies at the window.[48]

Another wealthy courtesan with interesting trading connections was Domenica Calvi di Siena. In January 1601 she went to the Jewish dealer David de Rignano when she purchased a bed hanging, blanket and bedspread to match made of turquoise embroidered silk for forty-four scudi.[49] Two months later, she called on the services of Joseph i Sirena Jew (to whom Orinthia would go several years later), when she bought two glamorous dresses, worth twenty-five scudi each.[50] Yet, like Orinthia, she also sold her goods on to noblemen. Fifteen years later, in January 1615, we find her selling a bedroom completely furnished in *"tapezzaria di broccatello venetiano"* (Venetian brocade cloth) with its *padiglione*, bedspread, *(tornaletto)* blanket, cushions and small table, for the princely sum of 300 scudi to the *Illustrissimo* Cassiano del Pozzo di Vercelli, a noted collector, patron of the arts, who was to be profoundly involved in the artistic and scientific milieu of Pope Urban VII's court some years later.[51] Whereas earlier we saw how prostitutes came into possession of goods "above their station," these examples suggest quite a different kind of circuit: upwards from the successful courtesan to the nobleman. What we do not know is how Cassiano del Pozzo knew Domenica Calvi. Perhaps he had been entertained in her apartments as a client, or had merely visited in the context of more general male sociability and admired her furnishings. Possibly they had been put in touch by mutual acquaintances who knew that Domenica had furnishings to sell, and that Cassiano was seeking to buy.

Another document records that in 1607 Flora Francisi purchased four gold necklaces worth the considerable sum of 118 scudi from a nobleman, the Illustrissimo Francesco Bellina Milanese.[52] Similar questions beg to be asked. How did Flora Francisi know that the Ill. Francesco had four gold necklaces to sell? And if he was her lover, why had he not given them to her? What is certain is that, whatever the relationships between individual courtesans and those men with whom they traded material objects, successful courtesans were in an ideal position to act as 'brokers' of luxury goods. They were at the center of much male sociability. They seem to have been viewed – and viewed themselves – as women of fashion; buying luxury goods which were then in essence on public display, since they were seen by the great many men who visited their apartments. And as long as they maintained their social position they could continually invest in new goods and sell some on, whilst the large numbers of men visiting their apartments ensured that they were in touch with extensive and perhaps varied networks of potential buyers and sellers. This kind of circulation of goods is something hypothesized by Peter Thornton in his study of the development of the Renaissance interior, in which he posits that courtesans were "fashion leaders," and that their goods were sought after or copied by high-status men.[53]

Conclusions

This chapter has focused on the circulation of second-hand objects amongst prostitutes who constitute a rather anomalous social group in many respects. Firstly, the nature of their commerce meant that prostitutes probably received and later disposed of far more material goods than did the average poor woman. Secondly, the financial instability and relatively short working life of the prostitute (most had given up or died by the age of thirty-five), meant that material objects were particularly important in their economy as a form of savings for their future, perhaps more so than for the woman who lived off a regular wage.[54] Furthermore, thanks to their "friendships" with large numbers of men from different social and geographical backgrounds, each with their own social and economic networks, prostitutes seem to have occupied a nodal position in the material economy of the city, at the crossroads and intersections of a great many pathways of goods.

In addition to these factors it must be recognized that prostitutes and courtesans were not a homogeneous economic group; some were extremely poor, many were considered to be "comfortably off" and amongst those, some were comparatively wealthy.[55] These women would have adopted different economic strategies according to their place in the economic hierarchy at any given time and their ambitions for the future, and they clearly participated in multiple systems of circulation. The poorest women relied on the resale and pawning of simple objects and presumably sought to obtain items that would hold their value over time: a strategy that was perhaps similar to that of other poor women in the city, for whom the circulation of material objects must also have played a central role in economic survival. Other prostitutes, those aspiring to or already mixing in elevated social circles and taking noblemen as their clients, were part of an economic system that depended on fashion and the need for the constant renewal of luxury objects: heavily worked and ornate furniture; elaborate textiles and wall coverings. Yet, bearing in mind the need to save for an uncertain future, they would also surely have needed to accumulate objects with a lasting resale value.

I opened with a discussion of the prominence attached to the relationship between the prostitute and material goods in early modern portrayals of prostitution and I have argued that this should not be passed over as an empty literary stereotype. Indeed, an exploration of the circulation of goods in the lives of prostitutes not only confirms that image, but actually makes sense of it, showing how and why they acquired those valuable objects and their importance in the daily lives and financial strategies of prostitutes. These objects were not merely symbols of vanity and greed, as moralizing discourse would suggest, but an indication of the extent to which such women relied upon the accumulation and circulation of goods, whether they were trying to survive from week to week, saving for their uncertain future, or even, as we have also seen, building up sufficient possessions for them to have a small trading empire of their own.

Notes

1. I am distinguishing here between the concerns of the Church as expressed in explicitly moralizing texts, and broader social concerns that are articulated through texts such as poems, dialogues, travellers' accounts and moralizing tales for the "popular" market.

2. Patricia Cibin, "Meretrici e Cortegiane a Venezia nel '500," *Donnawomanfemme: Quaderni Internazionale di Studi sulla Donna*, 25–26 (1985), pp. 79–102, 81.

3. These comments are based on an extensive study of Italian texts and images from the sixteenth and seventeenth centuries. For a more detailed discussion see Tessa Storey, *Carnal Commerce in Counter Reformation Rome* (Cambridge, 2008).

4. Thomas Coryat, *Crudities* (orig. 1611), Reprint (Glasgow, 1905), pp. 403–5.

5. My use of the term "popular" indicates that it was published in a cheap format, would have been circulated by peddlers to a broad section of the population, read in taverns and recited in piazzas. One assumes from this that the ideas contained within were generally well-known by the mass of the population, not that they necessarily agreed with them.

6. All translations are mine. *Il vanto e lamento della cortigiana ferrarese per esempio a tutte le donne di mala vita* (Siena, 1540), (*Il vanto*, lines 55–60). This was a text which was published and re-published in many variations throughout the sixteenth century.

7. For an illuminating discussion of the vice of lussuria see John Sekora, *Luxury: The Concept in Western Thought* (Baltimore, 1977).

8. *La vita et miseranda fine della puttana* (Venice, c.1650). This series is reprinted in David Kunzle's *The Early Comic Strip: Narrative Strips and Pictures in the European Broadsheet from c.1450 to 1825* (Berkeley, 1973), p. 275.

9. *La Veronese. Caso compassionevole* (Macerata, 1619). (Biblioteca Apostolica Vaticana (hereafter BAV), Capponi, Stampati v 683, int. 85) c 106. And Valentino Detio detto Colloredo, *Caso lacrimoso e lamentevole. Di Cecilia Bruni muranese cortegiana in Venetia à San Paterniano* (Macerata, 1621) (BAV Capponi Stampati, v 683, int. 32) c 358.

10. Archivio Segreto Vaticano (hereafter ASV), Barberini Latini 4975, c16r–v.

11. ASV, Barberini Latini 4975, c44r, 44v45r, 45v. In another version of a similar scam, men posing as *sbirri* (policemen) simply came to the women's house and took away their possessions, without bothering about having sex.

12. Pietro Aretino, *Ragionamento* (Milan, 1984), p. 147.

13. Beverly Lemire, Ruth Pearson and Gail Campbell (eds.), *Women and Credit: Researching the Past, Refiguring the Future* (Oxford, 2002) p. 5.

14. Beverly Lemire, "Consumerism in Pre-industrial and Early Industrial England: The Trade in Secondhand Clothes," *Journal of British Studies*, 27:1 (1998), pp. 1–24, and *Dress, Culture and Commerce: The English Clothing Trade before the Factory: 1660–1800* (Basingstoke, 1997). Patricia Allerston, "Reconstructing the Second-hand Clothes Trade in Sixteenth- and Seventeenth-century Venice," *Costume*, 33 (1999), pp. 4–56, and "Clothing and Early Modern Venetian Society," *Continuity and Change*, 15:3 (2000), pp. 367–90.

15. Renata Ago, "Di cosa di può fare commercio: Mercato e norme sociali nella Roma Barocca," *Quaderni Storici*, 91:1 (1996), pp. 113–33, 114.

16. Ibid., pp. 122, 123 especially.

17. This has been extensively discussed by Lucia Ferrante in her work on prostitution in Bologna. See particularly "Il valore del corpo: ovvero la gestione economica della sessualità femminile," in Angela Groppi (ed.), *Il Lavoro delle Donne* (Rome and Bari, 1996), pp. 206–28.

18. This was known as being "*tenuta a posta sua*" or being "*mantenuta.*" Such a client might be termed her "*amico fermo,*" yet this did not exclude her from having other relationships. Renata Ago describes an interesting example of this in her "Di cosa si può fare commercio," pp. 113–33.

19. Archivio di Stato di Roma (hereafter ASR), Archivio Sforza Cesarini, II°parte, seria SXII, vol I, filza AZ, cnn. Filza 3 (interna) 1594–5. May 26.

20. Allerston, "Clothing and Early Modern Venetian Society."

21. The letters are reproduced in L. Berra, "Cinque letter inedite," *Archivio Storico Lombardo*, 20 (1890), pp. 366–8. Berra explains that Capilupi was a courtier who served first the Estensi, and then passed to the Gonzaga family. The Duchess of Camerino was Giulia Varano, unhappily married to Guidobaldo della Rovere, Duke of Urbino.

22. Renata Ago discusses the costs of using a notary, and points out that the vast majority of commercial transactions in Rome would have been informal. Renata Ago, *Economia barocca: Mercato e istituzioni nella Roma del Seicento* (Rome, 1998), pp. 131–54.

23. ASR, Tribunale Criminale del Governatore (hereafter, TCG), Processi, XVII sec. Vol. 146, c7–79; Orsola Brunetta Veneta, September 12, 1618, c42rv.
24. A typical entry will list a few larger kitchen objects, such as trivets and fire irons, and then mention "many other things of little value."
25. Of fifty-one documents studied, the courtesans traded with fourteen Jews, two neophytes and seven Christians, with the bulk of the transactions (82 percent) taking place with Jews.
26. These are drawn from the archives of the Nineteenth Capitoline Notarial Office, which was based in Campo Marzio.
27. See Carlo M. Travaglini, "Rigattieri e Società Romana nel Settecento," *Quaderni Storici*, 22:2 (1992), pp. 415–48.
28. These references are drawn from observations from the criminal archives.
29. For example, a later inventory showed "Three pairs of stockings (one of lace) and five hankerchiefs valued at .30 *giulii* and six shirts valued at 2:50 scudi." ASR, TNC, v257, (1655), c607–609v. Flavia De Baronis, September 20, 1655. She was probably a courtesan, given that she was obliged to leave goods to the *convertite*.
30. Various sources lead me to suppose that prostitutes, like women generally, were often able and equipped to make their own clothes. Some had pairs of scissors in their possession and lengths of cloth to make into clothes.
31. I discuss this in "Fragments from the "life-histories" of jewelry belonging to prostitutes in early-modern Rome," *Renaissance Quarterly*, 19:5 (2005), pp. 647–657.
32. ASR, Trenta Notai Capitolini (TNC), U19, vol. 257, 1655. Caterina Chiavari, July 28, 1655, c233r–235v. She had probably been implicated in prostitution in some way since one third of her estate was due to the Monastery of the *Convertite*.
33. ASR, TNC, U19, vol. 72, Amabilia Antognetti Romana, January 19, 1607, c167.
34. ASR, TNC, U19, vol. 64, Beatrice Gualtieri, December 17, 1604, c888rv.
35. ASR, TNC, U19, vol. 35, Olimpia Novarese, June 11, 1595, c552.
36. ASR, TNC, U19, vol. 36, Aurelia Mattei Barbarrossa di Gaeta, September 1, 1595, c2rv. It was very common in Rome for people to rent out both linen and beds. Montaigne himself notes this in his *Voyage en Italie*, and Renata Ago mentions the sums to be made in "Di cosa si può fare commercio," 122.
37. Ninety-three people and seven institutions were beneficiaries of fifty wills drawn up by courtesans in the period 1594–1609. Thirty-five were family members, fifty-eight were not related to them. Twenty-six were female relatives, and nine were male relatives, six of whom were their sons. All this ties in with what we might expect to find, given the strongly female composition of the prostitute's households, the fact that women were economically more vulnerable, and that prostitutes were not likely to be linked to male relatives.
38. For a thorough discussion of this, see Alessandra Camerano, "Donne oneste o meretrici?" *Quaderni Storici*, 99:3 (1998), pp. 637–75.
39. ASR, TNC, U19, vol. 67 pt.1, August 14, 1605, Giulia Veneta, c827rv.
40. "Una veste di perpignano verde con le liste rosse bianche et turchina che se ne debba fare una parato per l'altare." ASR, TNC, U19, vol. 63, Isabetta Galleotti Graffignano, August 21, 1604, c804rv.
41. See for example ASV, Arm.IV, t60, p215, t80, p180.
42. ASR, TNC, U19, vol. 71, Orinthia Focari da Siena, October 6, 1606, c297rv.
43. ASR, TNC, U19, vol. 64, Orinthia Focari da Siena, November 4, 1604, c539r and U19, vol. 64, December 6, 1604, c825r.
44. One of the necklaces consisted of 226 large baroque pearls divided by 100 small *perlette migliarole* and the other of 100 baroque and 100 *migliarole* pearls. ASR, TNC, U19, vol. 71, Orinthia Focari di Siena, October 20, 1606, c181.
45. Ibid.
46. ASR, TNC, U19, vol. 68, Orinthia Focari da Siena, November 18, 1605, c514r–515r.
47. ASR, TNC, u19, vol. 68, Orinthia Focari da Siena, September 28, 1605, 232r.
48. "In primis tre stantie di corame de oro et argento smaltati cioè una stantia di corame vecchia et le altre due stantie di corame nove. Tre lettiere tutte indorate con le sue colonne, sei matarasse grandi di lana boni, doi forzierei coperti di pelle con il p{...}..usati pieni di biancharia et altri panni usati. Cinque sedie di corame rossi usate da homo, quattro sedi di

corame da donne nove, tre tavole di legno da magnare una con il suo tappetto di corame, et le altre senza, quattro scabelli dipinti di verde, sei sedie di paglia. Doi para di capofochi con le palle di ottone, et tre gelosie nove alle finestre." ASR, TNC, vol. 68, Orinthia Focari Senese e Isabella q. Antonij de Troiolo, September 28, 1605, c232r,

49. ASR, TNC, U19, vol. 53, Domenica Calvi da Siena, January 18, 1601, c122rv.

50. One of silver cloth, with gold trim, and the other of orange and purple wool with gold and silver decoration. ASR, TNC, U19, vol. 53, Domenica Calvi da Siena, March 1, 1601, c454.

51. "Una stantia tutta fornita di tapezzaria di broccatello venetiano con il suo padiglione, tornaletto coperta cuchini et tavolino, con molte altre biancarie." ASR, TNC, U19, vol. 96, Domenica Calvi Senese, September 1, 1615, c87rv. Whilst in 1615 Domenica Calvi would have been at the apex of her career, Del Pozzo had only just arrived in Rome, and would not become *consigliere* to the future Pope until 1623. Francesco Solinas (ed.), *Le Straodinarie raccolte di Cassiano dal Pozzo: 1588–1657* (Rome, 2000).

52. ASR, TNC, vol. 73, Flora Francisi, July 26, 1607, c753r.

53. Peter Thornton discusses the possible influence of women generally and courtesans in particular on the development of the Renaissance domestic interior in his book *The Italian Renaissance Interior, 1400–1600* (London, 1991). Since he relies exclusively on literary sources it is interesting that archival research helps to substantiate his thesis.

54. I have calculated this from census data collected for the first two decades of the century. Well over 60 percent were under thirty years old.

55. This emerges from my work on the economics of Roman prostitutes, in Storey, *Carnal Commerce*.

4

"The Magazine of All Their Pillaging"

Armies as Sites of Second-hand Exchanges during the French Wars of Religion

Brian Sandberg

The inhabitants of the southern French city of Montauban emerged from their city walls in mid-November 1621, as the army that had been besieging them for months retreated slowly out of sight.

> The besieged jumped down from the hornworks, pursuing from the river bank the last of those retreating … others went to the gabions, barricades, and trenches of the enemies to take all the spoils they could find, all those who were in the town notified of this retreat came there in a crowd – young and old men and women without distinction of sex ran up to have part of the spoils, even the sick remained strong and robust to take their portion – the quantity of barrels and gabions that were found was almost innumerable, for other than the spoils one found little because the enemies had retreated taking them by boat to Moyssac.[1]

This description hints at the massive second-hand market that accompanied early modern warfare, yet the hasty scramble for the left-over goods after the failed siege of Montauban represented only a final stage in the circulation of second-hand goods through the city and the army surrounding it at the time of the siege.

Months before, the residents of Montauban, a city "menaced with siege," had hurriedly prepared the community's defenses during the summer of 1621 for an imminent siege by Catholic troops. This southern French city had joined the Huguenot cause and become embroiled once again in the religious violence and civil warfare that had divided France periodically ever since 1562.

Montauban had long been known as a Huguenot stronghold because of its predominantly Protestant population of 17,000, and its bastioned fortifications, which had been enlarged in the 1580s and 1590s.[2] Masons, artisans and laborers worked furiously throughout 1621 to repair and extend the fortifications ringing the urban area. The city became a center for recycling stone and building materials, as the workers demolished outlying buildings near the walls and cleared lands around fortifications to allow clear fields of fire for the defensive artillery.[3] The defenders reportedly included at least a thousand soldiers from the surrounding countryside and three thousand of the city's inhabitants serving as soldiers and "all carrying arms."[4] One can imagine Montauban's armorers working long hours to repair and refit the city's supplies of arms and armor, and artisans in the city were also operating at least two gunpowder mills to feed the "hungry guns."[5] The urban population swelled as the powerful Protestant duc de Rohan brought troops and supplies to support the defenders, and refugees from nearby towns and villages sheltered within the walls. The residents of the nearby town of Realville heard of the approach of the duc de Mayenne's Catholic army and fled as refugees with their furniture, which could potentially be converted into cash if the refugee families became desperate.[6]

Montauban's inhabitants increasingly had to rely on hoarded supplies and a closed second-hand market as their enemies gradually constricted the flow of people and goods into the city. Catholics had long denounced Protestant troops for disrupting commerce and threatening Catholic communities in southern France, claiming that Montauban was the "magazine of all their pillaging."[7] Now, Catholic soldiers were disrupting Montauban's communications and the troops of the Catholic duc d'Épernon were blockading La Rochelle, another major Protestant city, to prevent its residents from aiding beleaguered Montauban.[8]

Encampments of Catholic troops sprang up around Montauban, transforming the surrounding countryside into a periphery of entrenched suburbs. Then, king Louis XIII arrived in August 1621, leading a royal army to complete the investment of the city.[9] The concentration of thousands of soldiers in the camps created temporary alternative trading networks between the besieging army and Catholic commercial centers in the provinces of Languedoc and Guyenne. The nearby Catholic city of Toulouse became the principal logistical center for the royal army, funneling troops and supplies to the troops besieging Montauban: "Fifteen pieces of cannon left Toulouse, with powder and ammunition to fire eight thousand shots, and three times more remain in the city's arsenal for the king's service," one source reported.[10] Catholic nobles, soldiers and workers from all over southern France came to participate in the siege. According to a Catholic observer in Vivarais, "the siege of Montauban had attracted almost everyone and especially the nobility."[11]

For the noble elites who served as military officers and commanders during the siege, the daily life in the encampments provided opportunities for sociability and exchange. Louis XIII took up residence in a château near Montauban and hosted many courtiers and regional nobles. Throughout the lengthy siege, the king encouraged his nobles by engaging in martial spectacles and ceremonies. Mounting his horse one day, for example, he toured the main camp and "carried his arms to the quarter of Monsieur de Montmorency."[12] Nobles, likewise, displayed their honor and status in camp by hosting lavish entertainments. Chefs, valets and servants must have bustled about to entertain the elites and to prepare the elaborate dinners that nobles at the siege described.[13] Soldiers' clothing, weapons, armor, and equipment exhibited the largesse of their noble commanders, who were expected to outfit their companies and regiments. When the duc de Montmorency arrived at the siege in mid-October, he led reinforcements that he had raised in the province of Languedoc – largely using his own financing and credit to arm and supply the troops.[14] The ostentatious display and conspicuous consumption that permeated noble culture ultimately relied on alternative financing through credit, pawnbroking and second-hand trade.

The siegeworks at Montauban resembled a massive construction worksite. As the siege wore on week after week, the besieging army's soldiers and civilian workers constructed trenches, mines and artillery platforms. Catholic artillery battered the city's fortifications, as the besieging gunners tried to breach the walls and demolish bastions. Sorties and countermining by the defenders slowed the besiegers' progress and casualties from disease and combat took an increasingly heavy toll on the besieging army. When Louis XIII and his advisers finally abandoned the siege and ordered the royal army to begin a withdrawal in mid-November 1621, the second-hand market at Montauban shifted to the disposal and reallocation of pillaged goods among the survivors of the siege.

Armies as Sites of Exchange

The preceding discussion of the siege of Montauban reveals that early modern armies were important sites of exchange and provided alternative markets for the circulation of second-hand goods. Building materials, military supplies, weapons, metals, leather goods, pillaged items, household belongings, luxury possessions, food products and clothing could all be bought and sold in the besieged city and in the surrounding encampments of the besiegers. The depiction of Montauban as the "magazine of all their pillaging" certainly suggests the potential for a garrisoned city to stockpile and redistribute goods. While this description referred specifically to the Protestant garrison, the phrase could have aptly described the Catholic army besieging the city in 1621 as well. The notion of an army as a magazine suggests the social and economic dimensions of the networks that allowed military forces to assemble. In early seventeenth-century French, *magasin* could refer to a military supply depot, an accumulation of goods or a place to sell merchandise – and these usages often overlapped.[15] Considering garrisoned cities and armies as magazines allows us to rethink the social and economic dimensions of early modern military organizations around the time of the siege of Montauban.

During the European wars of religion, each field army assembled as a unique combination of disparate military forces, which were rarely based on standing military forces. Warrior nobles and military entrepreneurs hastily raised companies and regiments, providing their troops with armor, weaponry and articles of clothing. Most troops did not have uniforms or standardized equipment, although some professional soldiers and specialist units, such as Swiss infantrymen who operated in mercenary companies, brought their own clothing and equipment with them.[16] Once these soldiers assembled into field armies, they relied on a steady flow of goods through their camps, especially since armies spent considerable portions of their campaign seasons in siege activities and sedentary encampments.[17] Besieging forces, garrisoned cities, large field armies and troops in winter camps all depended on extended networks to supply their needs over prolonged periods of time. Since no permanent military organizations provided regular logistical services, nobles and entrepreneurs instead arranged supplies using a wide variety of commercial networks and ad hoc arrangements to deliver new and second-hand goods to these patchwork assemblies of diverse soldiers.[18]

The field armies of the religious wars were often as large as some of the major cities of the period, frequently composed of ten to forty thousand soldiers and large numbers of camp followers – including bakers, butchers, launderers, valets, armorers, merchants, artisans and refugees – who provided informal logistical services to support the troops on campaign.[19] Armed communities not only consumed massive amounts of food, clothing and military supplies, but also engaged in a wide range of economic and commercial activities. Second-hand exchanges represented a crucial sector of the economic activity in these mobile marketplaces, especially for the soldiers and camp followers, who relied on second-hand trade for their livelihood, or even survival.

This chapter uses research on civil conflict during the French Wars of Religion of 1562–1629 to explore the dynamics of second-hand trade in and around armies in the early modern period.[20] While archives offer only limited information on the second-hand trade during the religious wars, documents dealing with the numerous conflicts in southern France during the latter stages of the religious wars do provide glimpses of the second-hand market in action as clothing, jewelry, art objects, furniture and other items passed through army encampments. While this chapter discusses the broad range of goods involved in second-hand trade, exchanges of weapons and war materials will emerge as important examples because they often remain the most visible aspects of the second-hand trade in surviving archival sources. Analyzing the relationships between the key actors involved in economic exchanges in military organizations allows us to consider the issues raised by the circulation of second-hand goods during the siege of Montauban.

Armorers, Merchants and the Circulation of Weapons

The armies of the French Wars of Religion created mobile marketplaces, providing loci for merchants buying and selling all types of second-hand goods. While it is impossible in a short chapter to explore the wide range of merchant activities around armies in this period, numerous surviving account books show that merchants supplied food, clothing, equipment and other goods to soldiers and officers in armies fighting in southern France during the French Wars of Religion.[21] Army encampments attracted merchants and peddlers who bought and sold all sorts of goods from soldiers and officers.

Merchants and armorers involved in the arms trade and the circulation of second-hand weapons were especially active in army camps. The growth in the sizes of military forces during the sixteenth and seventeenth centuries fueled a burgeoning European market in arms that is only now beginning to be studied comprehensively.[22] Studies of the "Military Revolution" often disagree about the chronology, mechanisms and dynamics of the dramatic changes that occurred in early modern warfare, but all point to a growing importance of firearms techniques and technologies, which reshaped military practices and influenced state development significantly in the sixteenth century.[23] Historians have focused on the links between military administration, war finance and the development of what John Brewer calls the "fiscal–military state," tending to ignore the circulation of arms outside of institutional control and state direction.[24] While the early modern European arms trade was linked in some ways to state investment and institutional development, the French monarchy could not cope with the demands of supplying large armies with the dizzying variety of arms and munitions required for thousands of soldiers, who were not equipped with standardized weapons or equipment. Much of the arms trade involved "private" manufacturers and merchants operating to produce arms, then to sell them when armies assembled, providing sites for the exchange of weapons.

Early modern European arms production involved numerous armorers working to keep up with demand in one of the most important early modern industries. Key centers of arms production during the sixteenth and seventeenth centuries included Milan, Venice, Nuremberg, Amsterdam and Paris.[25] Arms suppliers in these cities provided weapons and armor for diffusion throughout the European market and beyond. In addition, numerous other peripheral centers of arms manufacture fed regional markets and trading networks. Blacksmiths, cannon founders and other arms producers operated industrial workshops manufacturing a wide variety of weapons for diverse sectors of the arms market. Many of these arms producers not only manufactured weapons, but also acted as merchants, selling new and used weapons through open trading.[26]

Armies in France also attracted foreign arms merchants to provide additional weapons and supplies for their troops. Both Protestant and Catholic forces managed to purchase substantial quantities of weapons and munitions from Dutch merchants during the French Wars of Religion.[27] For example, a Dutch ship carrying "29 cannons, munitions and arms for 10,000 men" to aid French Protestants ran aground on the Languedoc coast and the shipment was seized by Catholic troops.[28] Some European governments tried to limit sales of arms into France by granting official licenses to legitimate certain arms sales, while prohibiting others.[29] Languedoc officials frequently worried about the problem of armed bandits operating in the Pyrenees mountains, and how to curtail the circulation of arms along the border with Spain.[30] Throughout the 1620s, regional administrative and judicial bodies in southern France tried to limit imports of arms into the region. However, foreign arms merchants seem to have traded freely regardless of official privileges or sanctions.[31]

Second-hand arms merchants and peddlers seem to have been part of the everyday life of early modern armies, buying and selling goods in armies' encampments. While it is difficult to trace the activities of these arms dealers, there are indications that colporteurs, hotel keepers and *merciers* (petty merchants) sold small arms, armor and equipment throughout the early modern period.[32] Camp followers and peddlers traded new and used weapons all across Europe, perhaps using techniques similar to the colporteurs studied by Laurence Fontaine.[33] Unfortunately, little research has been done on the expansive European second-hand arms market and the circulation of used weapons.[34] In early seventeenth-century southern France, evidence of the activities of colporteurs around armies comes from the attempts of the *parlement* of Toulouse to block sales of arms by issuing bans on trade with "rebels."[35] In 1628, for example, the *parlement* condemned those who "to sell better their grain, wine, oil, salt, gunpowder, lead and other [goods], carry them to rebel towns, despite the interdictions and prohibitions made in the edicts of this said court."[36] This document and others like it clearly show that small merchants and peddlers were operating around armies and garrison towns, selling arms and military supplies, as well as other goods that soldiers needed.[37] The circulation of used weapons through peddling and resale networks suggests that armies were involved in even broader aspects of re-use, such as recycling.

Artisans, Laborers and the Recycling of Arms and Ammunition

Artisans and laborers worked as independent contractors to provide a variety of logistical and transport services that supplied the armies of the French Wars of Religion. While some of their activities involved producing goods and distributing food, much of their labor involved recycling.[38] Many aspects of late sixteenth- and early seventeenth-century military practice relied heavily on used objects and on the second-hand trade in weapons. The forms of recycling performed by workers included conserving, preserving, collecting and re-using a wide variety of weapons, armor, ammunition, weapons components and scrap metal.

Early modern French armies depended on the recycling of bronze and iron to produce the large artillery pieces necessary for siege warfare.[39] Metal-workers routinely melted down objects such as church bells and statues, re-using them to found cannon during civil wars. At Montpellier, church bells and other metal objects were recycled into cannon in preparation for the defense of the city in 1622.[40] During the preparations for sieges throughout the religious wars, artillery pieces and artillery ammunition were often manufactured by recycling metal. Early modern artillery normally fired solid shot, but also could use recycled ammunition. At the siege of Mas d'Azil, one of the town's defenders reported that the enemy cannon "fired continually and after having fired their cannonballs, they fired dishes, musket balls and plates, which no doubt did as much harm to them as it did to us; but the *maréchal* [who commanded the besieging army] was so angry that he thought more of destroying than of conserving."[41] This comment suggests that military commanders in the French Wars of Religion were normally concerned with conserving and recycling metal because of its importance for artillery.

Early modern firearms had very long lives, since they could be essentially "recycled" through successive modifications and repairs. Arquebuses, muskets and pistols could be refitted, altered and adapted fairly easily. Such alterations had to be performed by artisans capable of fashioning individualized parts to fit weapons that had no standard designs or specifications.[42] This lack of standardization in firearms manufacture meant that replacement parts such as lock mechanisms and triggers often had to be fabricated on campaign. Because troops needed regular repairs of weapons and adjustments to armor, blacksmiths normally accompanied companies and regiments.[43]

Small arms ammunition depended on a continual supply of lead, which had to be collected, recycled, then distributed through the lead market.[44] Artisans manufactured lead projectiles to fit specific weapons, but soldiers probably did the work of recycling lead for their own weapons at times. As the town of Mas-d'Azil was gradually invested in 1625, the Protestant defenders manufactured grenades and musket balls on the spot, presumably from scrap metal.[45] During sieges and after battles, spent musket balls could be recycled and re-used. Roger Burt's deduction that lead projectiles were "too difficult or distasteful to recover," and thus "*non*-recyclable" is unconvincing, and some surviving evidence clearly demonstrates the practice of recycling arquebus and musket balls.[46]

The explosives used in firearms and artillery could also be recycled. We should perhaps even think of gunpowder production and maintenance as a recycling process, since black powder tended to degrade during transportation and storage. Gunpowder manufacturers and users had to use various techniques to maintain and renew powder mixtures to prevent its constituent ingredients from separating.[47] Towns and fortifications operated magazines to stockpile the saltpeter, sulphur and charcoal needed to manufacture gunpowder. As civil war loomed in March 1621, for example, the Estates of Languedoc requested that workers in the town of Narbonne "beat the powder and convert sixty *quintaux* of saltpeter from Narbonne's magazine into arquebus powder." In addition, Narbonne was to purchase twenty-five *quintaux* of match and fifty *quintaux* of balls and lead "all of which should be placed in the magazine of the said Narbonne to serve … when necessity demands."[48] Rarely could magazines provide enough gunpowder and supplies for warfare, though. The duc de Rohan gave Protestant captain Chambon wide latitude to prepare a new magazine at Montpellier for its defense precisely because the existing magazine proved inadequate.[49]

Occasionally armies were able to gather enough munitions to operate for short periods of time without seeking new supplies. The 1629 civil war in Languedoc represents a highly exceptional case in that a large royal army that was already assembled was able to rely on the transport of already existing munitions from the magazine at Lyon and other cities along its route, thus avoiding having to purchase or manufacture new gunpowder. "As for war munitions," one document records, "the king has more now than he needs, without making any new purchases. It suffices simply to transport them to the necessary places." The massive amounts of powder and supplies at Lyon – which included "twenty cannon, 300 *milliers* of powder, 20 *milliers* of lead, 100 *milliers* of matches," and other supplies – demonstrate the immense demands of seventeenth-century warfare.[50] Even in this exceptional case, workers probably had to reprocess and renew even these existing supplies so that the gunpowder would be reliable.

The formidable bastioned fortifications built during the sixteenth and seventeenth centuries according to the famous *trace italienne* style were often built by recycling building materials. Military engineers relied on used stone and bricks to construct the retaining walls for the earthen bastions which protected towns' defensive artillery. Religious reformers and iconoclasts pillaged and attacked religious sites during the French Wars of Religion, sometimes re-using stone from damaged churches and monasteries in new fortifications.[51] For example, Protestants improved and reconstructed the bastioned fortifications of Montpellier during 1621, using stone quarried from the city's cathedral, parish churches and monasteries. The Protestant-dominated city withstood a siege the next year, but, after a negotiated peace, the fortifications began to be dismantled and the cathedral rebuilt using the same stones again.[52] When communities tore down buildings to make room for new fortifications or extensions of defenses, as Montauban did in 1621, workers then recycled materials from the destroyed buildings.

In turn, unneeded or dilapidated fortifications could be demolished and their stones re-used in new buildings. Because of the recycling and resale potential of such operations, merchants were frequently involved in demolition enterprises. In June 1635, for example, a royal commissioner contracted with merchant Jean Escaig for the demolition of the fortifications of Mas-d'Azil and the merchant reportedly worked with such "diligence" that "the razing and demolition was completed down to the foundations by the month of August."[53] For the construction or demolition of fortifications to operate as recycling, though, large quantities of building materials had to be managed and transported by hundreds of workers, who were often soldiers.

Soldiers and the Pillaging of Goods

The soldiers who made up the backbone of armies during the French Wars of Religion also represented actors on the second-hand market. Pillaging became part of everyday life for communities in the path of warfare as troops plundered farmhouses and sacked towns, seizing massive amounts of goods.

The powerful images of early modern soldiers and deserters out of control remain etched in the historical memory of the religious wars throughout Europe.[54] Each conflict during the French Wars of Religion unleashed widespread looting and disorder. Throughout southern France, armies pillaged "friendly" communities as well as "enemy" towns, since the difficulties in defining enemies during periods of civil warfare left all communities highly vulnerable to widespread pillaging by troops on all sides of the conflict. Officials in the province of Languedoc frequently reported the "disorders, calamities, and extreme miseries of the said province." Rampaging troops performed "extortions, larcenies, pillages … ransoms, outrages, murders, burnings, and other enormous crimes," leaving the "sad marks of an entire desolation."[55] The Estates of Languedoc often deliberated on the problem of pillaging, but the assembly's attempts to limit the damage to the province had little success since noble officers frequently compensated their troops by allowing them to pillage when their pay was in arrears.

Soldiers preyed on civilians' valuables when ransacking homes and pillaging communities. They loaded their wagons with furniture and clothing seized from undefended villages and châteaux in the path of armies.[56] Besieged cities fell victim to soldiers who stormed their breached walls, as did many cites that surrendered, despite capitulation agreements intended to avoid looting. After Pamiers capitulated in 1628, soldiers entered the town, targeting civilian homes for booty. "The soldiers pillaged all the furniture," according to one account, since "it has never been possible to prevent them from doing so."[57] While troops seized furniture, clothing, and other belongings from townspeople and peasants, weapons were often specifically listed amongst civilians' losses. For example, residents of Souppets in Languedoc complained of losses they suffered when the duc de Montmorency's Catholic troops passed through their village, including a "halbard worth three livres" and "a sword worth three livres."[58]

Soldiers had to have ways of immediately reselling goods and converting their loot into easily transportable cash or jewelry, especially because infantrymen could only carry so much weight on their backs and in the encumbered carts that followed their units. Soldiers who made off with pillaged goods then sold them off, often to camp followers marching with the army or other noncombatants.[59] Scholar Geoff Mortimer argues that during the contemporaneous Thirty Years' War in Germany, "the principal beneficiaries of the plundering were often not the soldiers but the citizens of neighbouring towns, who bought up the stolen goods for a fraction of their value from looters mainly interested in cash, either as a more portable form of booty or as the price of the next meal."[60] Regardless of who profited most from such exchanges, clearly pillaging and the second-hand market for plunder were integral parts of early seventeenth-century warfare.

Army encampments provided resale opportunities for these disorderly soldiers, who needed to unload their looted goods as soon as possible. Furniture, art objects, clothing, and other heavy goods often had to be sold and converted into money or transportable valuables through exchanges or sales. It comes as no surprise, then, that artistic works depicting gambling proliferated during the religious wars.[61] Less visible in these camp scenes were the debt mechanisms and the bartering practices upon which soldiers depended to profit from their ill-gotten gains. Soldiers clearly made money from the goods they captured from their enemies by reselling them in encampments, but the scale of profits is unclear. After the battle of Les Ponts-de-Cé in 1620, one observer reported that the prince de Condé purchased a captured horse worth more than 300 scudi for a mere 40, and that "I saw lots of other goods go for miserable prices."[62] Coats and shoes would have presumably been some of the most important items used, traded or resold after battles, despite their relatively small monetary value. Ample evidence alludes to the stripping of valuables from the bodies of dead and wounded men after battlefield defeats or when troops retreated hastily. Used goods also circulated in large quantities during sieges, where work on approach trenches and defenders' sorties created frequent skirmishes.[63] The bodies of the victims of trench warfare could be easily pillaged, and their clothing and other belongings redistributed in camps that attracted merchants and camp followers over an extended period of time.

Random violence by marauding troops only represented one dimension of soldiers' pillaging activities, however.[64] Infantrymen and cavalrymen were also involved in broader forms of second-hand exchange through their companies' coordinated plundering practices. Military units engaged in raiding warfare, launching small-scale directed operations to forage, burn crops, harass enemies or seize weapons and supplies. Such raids involved targeting specific communities and engaging in a more controlled form of pillaging. For example, Protestant troops from Languedoc raided in the province of Dauphiné in 1628, "bringing back some pillage, including two hundred muskets that they transported to Bagnols."[65] Armies used raiding operations against the logistical support of opposing armies, especially by attacking wagons and boats that were transporting weapons to ongoing sieges.[66] Military units used coercion to seize goods from "enemy" communities and to plunder the châteaux of nobles in opposing armies. Although negotiated agreements for the capitulation of towns and fortresses often stipulated that the exiting troops could retain their weapons, furniture and other belongings, such agreements were not always honored.[67] When the Protestant garrison of the town of Lunel capitulated in 1622, a signed "written composition" allegedly stipulated "that the soldiers would exit with their arms, specifically the captains with pikes and the soldiers with swords, the other arms and baggage on wagons." However, "their faith was violated, the arms were pillaged, the captains and soldiers were killed, massacred, robbed or wounded." The Protestant author who recorded this incident deplored the fact that the Catholic troops took "no care to amend the injury nor to restore the arms and other belongings pillaged."[68] Yet military units routinely confiscated goods and sold them off for the profit of the troops and their officers.

Early modern armies also engaged in "regulated plundering" through elaborate contributions systems that extracted resources and goods from communities by threatening utter devastation.[69] Towns and villages along supply routes and in war-torn areas were expected to provide lodging, food and supplies for troops – and the penalty for failing to do so often involved burning and pillaging on a massive scale. For civilians in such communities, warfare was ever present and burdensome. In late sixteenth-century and early seventeenth-century prints portraying the plunder of villages, "war and soldiers are not seen to be at the root of this torment and desolation, but instead they are depicted as actors punishing a sinful world."[70] Soldiers could be seen as agents of God's wrath because they enforced a system of extraction that was accepted by elites as necessary. While armies exacting contributions often focused on seizing grain, food products and domesticated animals, soldiers could also extort money and goods for resale.

In their economic activities, soldiers had to engage in negotiations with their captains in order to carry out resale exchanges. Captains operated as redistributors during military operations by managing the second-hand pillage market, since much of each company's plunder tended to pass through captains' hands. When military units confiscated weapons and goods, noble officers took the best of the pillage and redistributed the rest – apparently often established by appraising goods and distributing them based on a percentage agreed to by troops and their officers.[71] Jacques Callot's depiction of supervised soldiers looting a convent shows how closely noble officers were involved in directing pillaging activities. The organization of stolen objects outside the church and the careful loading of plunder into a wagon in this Callot print suggest how nobles managed the redistribution of goods pillaged by their subordinates.[72]

Military Entrepreneurs and Informal War Finance

Nobles were the principal organizers of warfare during the French Wars of Religion of the sixteenth and seventeenth centuries, employing their military offices, clientage networks and wealth to mobilize armies and wage warfare.[73] Early seventeenth-century French military systems relied on local and regional nobles to mobilize rapidly to deal with border threats and civil conflicts, especially when religious conflicts broke out in southern France, where many Protestants and Catholics lived in mixed confessional communities or in neighboring towns. These noble commanders and captains acted as military entrepreneurs, equipping their troops with arms, ammunition, clothing and supplies largely at their own expense when they raised troops.[74] Nobles and their clients pursued complex exchanges and purchases to equip their troops with the broad array of leather goods, metal products, clothing, shoes and food products that they needed to operate effectively.[75] Armies could only assemble in their encampments with the funding and organization supplied by nobles using a complicated system of informal war finance.[76]

Because early seventeenth-century French armies largely relied on localized recruitment and mobilization, the second-hand arms market was essential for weapons procurement. Powerful French nobles were sometimes able to draw on patronage connections and broad trading networks to procure weapons from distant sources. For example, nobles arranged for arms transfers from

Flanders during the 1615 civil war in France.[77] The seigneur de Châtillon coordinated arms shipments for his troops, recording that, in February 1622, "ships arrived from Marseilles charged with war munitions and various provisions."[78] Usually, however, nobles engaging in civil warfare simply could not wait for arms shipments from major arms production centers to ready their troops to fight.

Instead, nobles' châteaux acted as centers of production, repair, storage, and redistribution of arms and armor. Early seventeenth-century nobles normally lived in fortified châteaux or modified medieval castles that could potentially withstand attacks by rival nobles during civil wars.[79] A surviving inventory of a château owned by the Protestant seigneur de Cabrières near Nîmes shows that the château had "all sorts of munitions like musket balls, cords and gunpowder."[80] Another inventory gives us a glimpse of the armory of a château belonging to François de la Jugie, comte de Rieux, immediately following his death in battle during the 1632 civil war in Languedoc. This inventory, which was drawn up by a royal notary, shows that the comte maintained more than one hundred muskets, dozens of polearms, one hundred fifty infantry corselets, several pieces of artillery and a variety of other weapons in his château.[81] To maintain such large armories in their châteaux, nobles engaged in purchases of arms and munitions to supply a small garrison and to stockpile reserves.[82] These southern French nobles must have been regular customers of armorers and merchants, but insufficient documents have surfaced to demonstrate the dimensions of arms merchants' networks in this period.

Captains had to invest in arms, armor, clothing and military supplies, using their own credit, then redistribute these goods to the soldiers in their companies.[83] When a Languedoc noble purchased muskets in the remote town of Mende to arm his Catholic troops to fight in the surrounding Cévennes mountains in 1629, he presumably bought used weapons. As a consul in the town, he would have been a privileged buyer with substantial monetary resources.[84] Raising forces locally lessened the monetary burdens on nobles somewhat, allowing them to finance substantial military forces for shorter periods of time and to use short supply lines. For example, when the duc de Montmorency's army threatened the Protestant town of Nîmes in 1621, it used the nearby town of Beaucaire as its supply base, or "place of arms."[85]

Despite the vast wealth of many early modern French nobles, military entrepreneurship relied heavily on credit and alternative financing to pay the costs of mobilization and warfare.[86] Nobles seem to have used pawnbrokers as creditors to raise money for warfare and armies drew on broad financial networks to maintain themselves in the field. When nobles needed to raise money through alternative financing, one of the easiest forms of credit involved pawning pieces of jewelry, weapons and luxury armor for cash. In one spectacular case, Marie de Médicis reportedly pawned her "beautiful string of diamonds" for 400,000 livres in order to raise troops during the 1619 civil war.[87] Expensive weapons such as jewel-encrusted pistols and arquebuses with ivory inlays represented valuable art objects that were attractive to pawnbrokers. Historian Kristen B. Neuschel observes that "there is much evidence that nobles frequently sold or pawned their precious jewels and dishes in order to get cash for war-making, for ransoms, or more routine purposes. The value of several pieces could equal a month's average living expenses for the entire household."[88] Luxury arms seem to have routinely passed in and out of armorers' workshops and pawnbroker's hands, and must also have circulated in armies.[89]

Nobles sought cost-sharing arrangements with local and regional financiers and institutions to reimburse – or at least to ease – their financial burdens in equipping their troops. For example, when captain Conseil raised troops near Lavaur in 1622, the diocese of Lavaur paid for purchasing the weapons for his company.[90] Similarly, the diocese of Toulouse covered the costs of purchasing weapons and powder for one hundred cavalry and a thousand infantry in 1621.[91] Such reimbursements were often delayed by months or years, however. The comte de Bioule raised a company of *chevaux-légers* and "engaged several of his friends" to raise five or six companies of infantry to aid in the Catholic cause in Languedoc during 1621. The comte had to "advance huge sums" in recruiting these troops and in the "purchase of arms and munitions." The Estates of Languedoc provided for the comte de Bioule to be reimbursed only in December 1621 as his troops were being disbanded or put into winter quarters.[92] Huguenot nobles used similar methods of alternative financing and reimbursement to arm their troops, but relied on different clientage networks in funding warfare. The powerful Protestant duc de Rohan provided for his armies in Languedoc during the 1620s through his own spectacular wealth and his direction of war financing by Protestant communities. Rohan arranged for a purchase of powder, match and musket balls for Protestant troops in Languedoc in 1622.[93] During the siege of Montpellier the same year, the nearby Protestant town of Nîmes gave the captain of the duc de Rohan's bodyguard twelve pounds of powder, six pounds of lead musket balls, and twelve bales of match to distribute to his guards.[94] The same town of Nîmes purchased muskets from at least one merchant to provide for Huguenot soldiers in this period, presumably at Rohan's instigation.[95]

These systems of alternative financing placed the enormous burdens of the costs of warfare on the entire French society. When military entrepreneurs were unable to obtain reimbursements quickly enough, they resorted to what historian John A. Lynn calls a "tax of violence" to feed and supply their troops.[96] Contributions and forced requisitions often replaced financial credit and purchases during periods of serious civil warfare. In the context of religious warfare, Catholic noble officers could often obtain royal approval for their confiscations of Protestant properties and belongings. Although some of this confiscated property may have been restituted after peace agreements, furniture and other belongings were probably often resold.[97] Noble officers routinely requisitioned weapons and supplies when launching military operations during the French Wars of Religion. For example, the duc de Montmorency attempted to borrow weapons and supplies from Lyon and the province of Dauphiné as he assembled troops in Languedoc in 1627.[98] Armies frequently borrowed arms and supplies when passing through friendly or neutral communities during civil wars. Members of the Estates of Languedoc associated the financial burdens of purchasing weapons and military supplies with the ravages of warfare, lamenting that "a great part of [the province of Languedoc] finds itself occupied by rebel enemies and the rest is entirely ruined."[99]

In this context, noble military commanders played key roles not only in supplying their troops, but in mobilizing broad local and regional economic networks of production, credit and exchange. Warrior nobles' ability to use the informal financial instruments of credit, reimbursement and pillage redistribution in raising military forces allowed them to exercise significant power in French society. The armed communities that warrior nobles directed provided key mobile centers around which important financial networks and second-hand markets coalesced during the French Wars of Religion.

Conclusion

This chapter has sketched the outlines of the second-hand trade of goods through army encampments during the French Wars of Religion. Artisans, merchants, officers and soldiers actively exchanged used goods in the immense second-hand markets that grew up around field armies in this period. Clothing, furniture, jewelry, weapons, war materials and other objects circulated through these "magazines" in ways in which we are only beginning to understand. This study of the actors and commodities involved in the second-hand trade of the religious wars has partially revealed the dynamics of these complex exchanges, but only a thorough investigation of the trading networks around armies can fully assess the complex relationships between violence and the informal economy in the early modern period.

Arms and armor emerge as highly visible objects in the second-hand exchanges in army encampments of the religious wars. Weapons could be treated as commodities, as sources for mechanical parts, as resources for raw materials, as credit instruments or as art objects. The second-hand trade in arms was thus as integral to the political culture and the system of war finance as it was to the practice of warfare. The armies of the French Wars of Religion represented vitally important but ephemeral sites of second-hand exchanges for these weapons. At the end of each campaigning season or following peace agreements, armies quickly demobilized. The processes of demobilization might have ideally involved beating swords into plowshares – an ultimate re-use of weapons that destroyed them by recycling metal and other materials for nonmilitary uses.[100] However, when conflicts subsided during this period of serious but intermittent warfare, military demobilization rarely brought any comprehensive attempt to dispose of weaponry.[101] Fortifications were sometimes razed, but arquebuses, muskets, pistols, pikes, swords, suits of armor and other weapons were retained by nobles and soldiers. Weapons were then stored in châteaux, stocked in city arsenals, stashed in homes, or sold off to second-hand merchants – until another conflict again accelerated the arms market. In this context of protracted civil conflict, the meanings of weapons remained highly ambiguous and the circulation of second-hand weapons operated in distinct modes particular to the culture and society of late sixteenth-century and early seventeenth-century France.

Encampments filled with soldiers, merchants, armorers, peddlers and pillaged goods were hardly confined to France in this period, however. The exchanges of used goods that intersected in the armies in the French Wars of Religion suggest some of the patterns of the broader European second-hand market during the period of the wars of religion. Used goods were so vital to early modern military practices that the second-hand trade in many ways created and sustained the very armies that served as "magazines" for the trade in plunder throughout Europe.

Notes

I would like to thank Laurence Fontaine for the opportunity to contribute to this volume and for her helpful comments on previous drafts of this chapter. I enjoyed immensely our collaboration during the *Echanges Alternatifs* conference at the European University Institute, where I spent an intellectually rewarding year researching and writing in 2002–3. I would also like to thank Pernille Arenfeldt and the peer reviewers for their careful readings of a previous draft of this piece.

1. "Tableau du siege de Montaulban," Bibliothèque Nationale de France, Paris [hereafter, BNF], Mss. fr. 18756, f° 65–66.
2. Philip Benedict, "The Huguenot Population of France, 1600–85," in *The Faith and Fortunes of France's Huguenots, 1600–85* (Aldershot, 2001), pp. 75–9. Philip Conner, *Huguenot Heartland: Montauban and Southern French Calvinism during the Wars of Religion* (Aldershot, 2002), pp. 16, 151. Janine Garrisson and Paul Duchein, *Louis XIII et les 400 coups* (Toulouse, 2002).
3. BNF, Mss. fr. 18756, f° 3–7. *Recit veritable de ce qui s'est passé aux trois nouvelles sorties de ceux de Montauban. Furieusement repoussés, chassés, & battus par messieurs les duc de Mayenne & comte de Bassompierre* (Paris, 1621), BNF, 8° Lb36 1742. Michael Wolfe, "Walled Towns during the French Wars of Religion," chapter 11 in James D. Tracy (ed.), *City Walls: The Urban Enceinte in Global Perspective* (Cambridge, 2000), pp. 317–48. Hélène Guicharnaud, *Montauban au XVIIe 1560/1685. Urbanisme et architecture* (Toulouse: Picard, 1991), chapter 1.
4. *Recit veritable de ce qui s'est passé aux trois nouvelles sorties de ceux de Montauban.*
5. Presumably, the Huguenot defenders of Montauban were running additional gunpowder mills, since an account describes the accidental burning of two mills during the siege, yet the city continued to consume copious amounts of gunpowder in its defense. BNF, Mss. fr. 18756, f° 28–29. The phrase "hungry guns" was employed in the early modern period and is used in historical literature. For example, see Thomas F. Arnold, *Renaissance at War* (London, 2001), pp. 24–34. Early seventeenth-century French language alluded to this metaphor of feeding artillery by using the term *munition* to refer to supplies for artillery and *pain de munition* to refer to soldiers' food rations.
6. Involved in a complex civil war that had already resulted in the fall of several Protestant towns, Huguenot refugees were numerous. *L'Estat du siege contre Montauban par l'armée Royale de sa Majesté contre ceux de la Rebellion. Avec les remarques des fortifications de la Place,*

& scituation d'icelle. Et generalement ce qui s'est passé par Mr. le Duc de Mayenne, jusqu'à present. Le tout extraict des Memoires escriptes au Camp Royal, le 12. Aoust 1621 (Paris, 1621), BNF, 8° Lb36 1730. See also, BNF, Mss. fr. 18756, f° 19–20.

7. *L'Estat du siege contre Montauban par l'armée Royale de sa Majesté contre ceux de la Rebellion*.

8. *La prise et transport des bleds; et autres provisions des habitans de la Rochelle. Par Monsieur le duc d'Espernon ensemble l'empeeschement des eaux douces en ladite ville, & l'incommodité qu'elles apportent aux Habitans. Les preparatifs des Vendages. Les deffaictes qui se sont faictes és lieux circonvoisins. Et generalement tout ce qui s'est passé à ce subject jusques à present* (Paris: Isaac Mesnier, 1621), BNF, 8° Lb36 1740. Another source claimed that "M. d'Espernon tient maintenant bloquee du costee de la terre en sorte que personne ne peut y entrer ny en sortir," BNF, Mss. fr. 3810, f° 44. However, some communications did continue between La Rochelle and Montauban, since messengers were occasionally able to make it through the siege lines. See: BNF, Mss. fr. 18756, f° 54; Guillaume Girard, *Histoire de la vie du duc d'Espernon* (Paris, 1730), pp. 363–68.

9. *L'Estat du siege contre Montauban par l'armée Royale de sa Majesté contre ceux de la Rebellion*.

10. *L'arrive de l'armee du roy, devant la ville de Montauban, avec trente mille hommes. Et les furieux escarmouches faictes entre monsieur le duc de Mayenne & les assiegez* (Paris, 1621), BNF, 8° Lb36 1741.

11. *Les Commentaires du soldat du Vivarais* (1908; reprint, Valence, 1991), pp. 41–2.

12. Jean Héroard, *Journal de Jean Héroard*, ed. Madeleine Foisil, 2 vols. (Paris, 1989), p. 2786.

13. François de Bassompierre, *Journal de ma vie: Mémoires du maréchal de Bassompierre* (Paris, 1870–7), vol. 2, pp. 325–8, 336–40.

14. Simon Du Cros, *Histoire de la vie de Henry dernier duc de Montmorency. Contenant tout ce qu'il a fait de plus remarquable depuis sa naissance jusques à sa mort* (Paris, 1643), pp. 41–2.

15. Alain Rey (ed.), *Dictionnaire historique de la langue française* (Paris, 1992), vol. 2, p. 1163.

16. Most European military systems adopted uniforms only in the late seventeenth century. For a discussion of military life before armies had uniforms, see: Jean Chagniot, *Guerre et société à l'époque moderne* (Paris, 2001), pp. 63–7.

17. James B. Wood considers this issue in a section on an army's "division of time." James B. Wood, *The King's Army: Warfare, Soldiers, and Society during the Wars of Religion in France, 1562–1576* (Cambridge, 1996), pp. 237–45. For a discussion of the normalcy of siege warfare in the seventeenth century, see: John A. Lynn, "Food, Funds, and Fortresses: Resource Mobilization and Positional Warfare in the Campaigns of Louis XIV," in John A. Lynn (ed.), *Feeding Mars: Logistics in Western Warfare from the Middle Ages to the Present* (Boulder, 1993), pp. 137–59.

18. For excellent overviews of warfare during the European wars of religion, see Andrew Cunningham and Ole Peter Grell, *The Four Horsemen of the Apocalypse: Religion, War, Famine and Death in Reformation Europe* (Cambridge, 2000); Chagniot, *Guerre et société à l'époque moderne*; J.R. Hale, *War and Society in Renaissance Europe, 1450–1620* (Baltimore, 1985).

19. On the notion of an army as a "walking city" and the problems of supplying one, see Hale, *War and Society in Renaissance Europe, 1450–1620*, p. 159. On camp followers, see: Barton C. Hacker, "Women and Military Institutions in Early Modern Europe: A Reconnaissance," *Signs: Journal of Women in Culture and Society* 6 (1981), pp. 643–71; André Corvisier and Jean Jacquart (eds.), *Les malheurs de la guerre. I: De la guerre à l'ancienne à la guerre réglée* (Paris, 1996); George Forty, *They Also Served: A Pictorial Anthology of Camp Followers through the Ages* (London, 1979); Myron P. Gutman, *War and Rural Life in the Early Modern Low Countries* (Princeton, 1980); Herbert Langer, *The Thirty Years' War*, trans. C.S.V. Salt (New York, 1990), pp. 97–102.

20. The most important recent works on religious violence and warfare during the French Wars of Religion are: Wolfe, "Walled Towns during the French Wars of Religion," pp. 317–48; Stuart Carroll, *Noble Power during the French Wars of Religion: The Guise Affinity and the Catholic Cause in Normandy* (Cambridge, 1998); Wood, *The King's Army*; Barbara B. Diefendorf, *Beneath the Cross: Catholics and Huguenots in Sixteenth-Century Paris* (Oxford, 1991); Denis Crouzet, *Les Guerriers de Dieu. La violence au temps des troubles de religion, vers 1525–vers 1610* (Paris, 1990); Arlette Jouanna, *Le Devoir de révolte. La noblesse française et la*

gestation de l'État moderne, 1559–1661 (Paris, 1989). My own archival research focuses on religious and civil violence in France between 1598 and 1635.

21. For several examples, see Archives Départementales [hereafter, AD] Hérault, B 22590 and B 22746.

22. Peter Edwards, *Dealing in Death: The Arms Trade and the British Civil Wars, 1638–52* (Stroud, 2000); Harald Kleinschmidt, "Using the Gun: Manual Drill and the Proliferation of Portable Firearms," *Journal of Military History* 63 (July 1999), pp. 601–29; Jan Piet Puype and Marco van der Hoeven (eds.), *The Arsenal of the World: The Dutch Arms Trade in the Seventeenth Century* (Amsterdam, 1996); Keith Krause, *Arms and the State: Patterns of Military Production and Trade* (Cambridge, 1992); Langer, *The Thirty Years' War*, pp. 158–186.

23. For key works in the Military Revolution debate, see: Bert S. Hall, *Weapons and Warfare in Renaissance Europe: Gunpowder, Technology, and Tactics* (Baltimore, 1997); Geoffrey Parker, *The Military Revolution: Military Innovation and the Rise of the West, 1500–1800*, 2nd ed. (Cambridge, 1996); Clifford J. Rogers (ed.), *The Military Revolution Debate: Readings on the Military Transformation of Early Modern Europe* (Boulder, 1995); David Eltis, *The Military Revolution in Sixteenth-Century Europe* (New York, 1995); Jeremy Black, *A Military Revolution? Military Change and European Society, 1550–1800* (Atlantic Highlands, 1991); Michael Roberts, "The Military Revolution, 1560–1660," in Clifford J. Rogers (ed.), *The Military Revolution Debate: Readings on the Military Transformation of Early Modern Europe* (Boulder, 1995), pp. 13–35 [originally published in 1956].

24. John Brewer, *The Sinews of Power: War, Money and the English State, 1688–1783* (Cambridge, 1988).

25. On key early modern arms centers, see: Silvio Leydi, "Milan and the Arms Industry in the Sixteenth Century," in Stuart W. Pyhrr and José-A. Godoy (eds.), *Heroic Armor of the Italian Renaissance: Filippo Negroli and His Contemporaries* (New York, 1998), pp. 25–33; Peter Krenn and Walter J. Karcheski, Jr., *Imperial Austria: Treasures of Art, Arms and Armour from the State of Styria* (Perth, 1998), pp. 38–44. On armorers and founders as protoindustrial workers see: Robert C. Davis, *Shipbuilders of the Venetian Arsenal: Workers and Workplace in the Preindustrial City* (Baltimore, 1991); Frederic Chapin Lane, *Venetian Ships and Shipbuilders of the Renaissance* (Baltimore, 1934).

26. Silvio Leydi makes a distinction between grand *armuriers-marchands* and small armorers on this point. Silvio Leydi, "Les armuriers milanais dans la seconde moitié du XVIe siècle. Familles, ateliers et clients à la lumière des documents d'archives," in José-A. Godoy and Silvio Leydi (eds.), *Parures triomphales. Le maniérisme dans l'art de l'armure italienne* (Milan, 2003), pp. 36–7.

27. H.P. Vogel, "The Republic as Exporter of Arms 1600–1650," in Jan Piet Puype and Marco van der Hoeven (eds.), *The Arsenal of the World: The Dutch Arms Trade in the Seventeenth Century* (Amsterdam, 1996), pp. 16–17; G. Beks, "Dutch Arms for France 1635–1640," in Jan Piet Puype and Marco van der Hoeven (eds.), *The Arsenal of the World: The Dutch Arms Trade in the Seventeenth Century* (Amsterdam, 1996), pp. 36–41. On the Dutch illicit trade in arms, see Pauline Croft, "Trading with the Enemy, 1585–1604," *Historical Journal* 32 (June 1989), pp. 281–302.

28. Du Cros, *Histoire de la vie de Henry dernier duc de Montmorency*, pp. 40–1. Another source reported that "des armes que M. de Chastillon parsoit venir des pays bas en Languedoc sont heureusement tombée entres les mains de M. de Montmorency," BNF, Mss. fr. 3810, fº 44.

29. Leydi, "Les armuriers milanais dans la seconde moitié du XVIe siècle," p. 44.

30. AD Hérault, G 1835. On arms and frontier zones or borderlands, see: R.B. Ferguson and N.L. Whitehead (eds.), *War in the Tribal Zone: Expanding States and Indigenous Warfare* (Santa Fe, 1992).

31. Jenny West argues that, even in eighteenth-century Britain, "the legislation to prohibit or severely restrict the private trade in gunpowder proved to be largely, if not entirely, ineffective." Jenny West, *Gunpowder, Government and War in the Mid-Eighteenth Century* (Woodbridge, 1991), p. 129.

32. Claude Gaier, *L'Industrie et le commerce des armes dans les anciennes principautés belges du XIIIme à la fin du XVme siècle* (Paris, 1973), pp. 159–60.

33. Laurence Fontaine, *History of Pedlars in Europe*, trans. Vicki Whittaker (Durham, 1996).

34. Art historian Evelyn Welch is one of the few scholars currently working on acquisitions of second-hand weapons and armor, but her study of second-hand markets during the Renaissance is not yet published.

35. "Arrêt," AD Tarn, C 207. "Prohibition a touts marchans et autres personnes daporter ou faire porter aucunes armes ou munitions de guere sans passeport signé de sa M. et contresigné par un des secretaires d'Estat sur peine damende arbitraire et confiscãon desd. armes & munitions," AD Haute-Garonne, B 1913, f° 16–17.

36. *Arrest de la cour de parlement contre les rebelles* (Toulouse: Raymond Colomiez, 1628), AD Tarn, C 207.

37. Laurence Fontaine argues that for peddlers, "armies and war always created places where there were excellent profits to be had ... A fondness for military routes was one of the constants of the profession." Fontaine, *History of Pedlars in Europe*, pp. 32–3.

38. This chapter avoids focusing on the many bakers, butchers, cooks and other food providers in army encampments, since they were not primarily involved in second-hand trade.

39. The best introduction to early modern European gun-founding techniques is Carel de Beer, *The Art of Gunfounding: The Casting of Bronze Cannon in the Eighteenth Century* (Rotherford, 1991).

40. André Delort, *Mémoires inédits d'André Delort sur la ville de Montpellier au XVIIe siècle (1621–1693)* (Marseille, 1980), pp. 2–3; Jean Baumel, *Montpellier au cours des XVIe et XVIIe siècles. Les guerres de religion (1510–1685)* (Montpellier, 1976), p. 179. The metal from the church bells at Lunel may have been re-used in the same way. See: AD Hérault, 34 H 4.

41. Jacques de Saint-Blancard, *Journal du siège de Mas-d'Azil en 1625 écrit par J. de Saint-Blancard, défenseur de la place, contré le maréchal de Thémines*, ed. C. Barrière-Flavy (Foix, 1894) [extrait du *Bulletin de la Société Ariégeoise des Sciences, Lettres et Arts* 4 (1894).], pp. 28–9.

42. Not until the development of techniques of mechanical drawing and machine tooling in the eighteenth century would weapons manufacture begin to be standardized. Ken Alder, "Making Things the Same: Representation, Tolerance and the End of the Ancien Regime in France," *Social Studies of Science* 28 (August 1998): pp. 499–545.

43. AD Hérault, B 22772.

44. On early modern lead collecting and the lead market, see Donald Woodward, "'Swords into Ploughshares': Recycling in Pre-Industrial England," *Economic History Review*, 2nd series, 38 (1985), pp. 175–91.

45. Saint-Blancard, *Journal du siège du Mas-d'Azil en 1625 écrit par J. de Saint-Blancard, défenseur de la place, contré le maréchal de Thémines*, pp. 25–26.

46. Roger Burt, "The Transformation of the Non-Ferrous Metals Industries in the Seventeenth and Eighteenth Centuries," *Economic History Review*, New Series, 48 (February 1995), pp. 32–3.

47. Hall, *Weapons and Warfare in Renaissance Europe: Gunpowder, Technology, and Tactics*, chapter 3. See also: Sarah Barter Bailey, "The Royal Armouries 'Firework Book'," chapter 5 in Brenda Buchanan (ed.), *Gunpowder: The History of an International Technology* (Bath, 1996), pp. 57–86; Bert S. Hall, "The Corning of Gunpowder and the Development of Firearms in the Renaissance," chapter 6 in Brenda Buchanan (ed.), *Gunpowder: The History of an International Technology* (Bath, 1996), pp. 87–120; Kelley DeVries, "Gunpowder and Early Gunpowder Weapons," chapter 7 in Brenda Buchanan (ed.), *Gunpowder: The History of an International Technology* (Bath, 1996), pp. 121–35; and John Francis Guilmartin, Jr., *Gunpowder and Galleys: Changing Technology and Mediterranean Warfare at Sea in the Sixteenth Century* (Cambridge, 1974).

48. Deliberations of the Estates of Languedoc held at Carcassonne, 1621, AD Hérault, C 7059, f° 78–9.

49. Archives Municipales [hereafter, AM] Montpellier, EE 929.

50. "Conseil Général, en 1629, en Languedoc," July 14[?], 1629, Archives de la Ministère des Affaires Étrangères, Paris [hereafter, AAE], 1629, f° 52.

51. For precedents of re-using building materials from fortifications, see Philippe Bernardi, "Récupération et transformations: les produits dérivés de la brique et de la tuile dans le bâtiment au Moyen Age," in *La Brique antique et médiévale. Production et commercialisation d'un matériau* (Rome, 2000), pp. 401–9. I would like to thank Laurence Fontaine for introducing me to Bernardi's work.

52. AD Hérault, G 1835. AD Hérault, G 1418, f° 19. Ghilsaine Fabre and Thierry Lochard, "L'impact urbain de la contre-réforme à Montpellier (1600–1706)," in Anne Blanchard, Henri Michel, and Elie Pélaquier (eds.), *La Vie religieuse dans la France méridionale à l'époque moderne* (Montpellier, 1992), pp. 55–78. Jean Nougaret, "La contre-réforme à Montpellier: la traduction architecturale," in Anne Blanchard, Henri Michel, and Elie Pélaquier (eds.), *La vie religieuse dans la France méridionale à l'époque moderne* (Montpellier, 1992), pp. 79–134. "Arrêt du parlement de Toulouse contenant les noms des séditieux accusés du pillage des églises de Montpellier en décembre 1621," June 20, 1622, in Charles Aigrefeuille, *Histoire de la ville de Montpellier depuis son origine jusqu'a notre temps* (1882; reprint, Marseille, 1976), vol. 4, pp. 680–1.

53. Jean-Jacques de Lescazes, *Le memorial historique, contenant la narration des troubles, et ce qui est arrivé diversement de plus remarquable dans le païs de Foix et diocèse de Pamiés, depuis l'an de grâce 1490 jusques à 1640* (1644; reprint, Pamiers: Imprimerie Soula, 1989), p. 167.

54. Colin Jones, "The Military Revolution and the Professionalisation of the French Army Under the Ancien Régime," in Clifford J. Rogers (ed.), *The Military Revolution Debate: Readings on the Military Transformation of Early Modern Europe* (Boulder, 1995), pp. 152–155; David Parrott, *Richelieu's Army: War, Government, and Society in France, 1624–1642* (Cambridge, 2001), chapter 10.

55. "Commission du roy," AD Hérault, A 47, f° 201–3. Brian Sandberg, "Bonds of Nobility and the Culture of Revolt: Provincial Nobles and Civil Conflict in Early Modern France, 1610–1635," (Ph.D. Dissertation: University of Illinois at Urbana-Champaign, 2001), pp. 295–6.

56. Soldiers pillaged furniture and other goods at a château in Languedoc. AD Hérault, G 1418, f° 28.

57. "Les soldatz ont pillé tous les meubles; jamais il n'a esté possible de les en empescher." BNF, Dupuy 100, f° 298–301.

58. "Estat des foules que le lieu de Souppets a souffert sur la passaige et logement de gens de guerre des troupes de monseigneur de Montmoranci," AD Hérault, B 22712.

59. Hale, *War and Society in Renaissance Europe, 1450–1620*, pp. 117–118.

60. Mortimer cites a contemporary account of the Swedish army's occupation of Munich: "At this time much robbing and plundering took place, particularly in the countryside, and all kinds of things were brought in here. There was no scarcity of buyers, and in the mornings when the Swedes brought in a number of loaded wagons everything was sold out in a few hours, so then they went back out to get more booty …. Thus you could get a horse or a cow for ten kreuzer, or for up to a gulden or a taler you could buy a really magnificent beast, if you could get fodder for it and if they didn't steal it back from you." Geoff Mortimer, *Eyewitness Accounts of the Thirty Years War 1618–48* (New York, 2002), pp. 82–3.

61. Langer, *The Thirty Years' War*, pp. 71, 75–6, 82, 83–4. Gail Feigenbaum, "Gamblers, Cheats, and Fortune-Tellers," in Philip Conisbee (ed.), *Georges de La Tour and His World* (New Haven, 1996), pp. 149–81.

62. "Il Bottino per alcuni soldati e stato buono, et hieri io veddi vendere un cavallo che comperò il P.e di Condè 40 scudi, che valeva più di 300 et ho veduto dar via molt'altra robba a viliss.mo prezzo; ma lasciarmo queste bagatelle." Presumably scudi here refers to French écus. Anonymous letter entitled, "Dal Pont de Scè li 8 Agosto 1620," in "Copie di lettere scritte al Residente Bartolini," Archivio di Stato di Firenze, Mediceo del Principato 4635, unpaginated.

63. One account mentions weapons that were stripped from the dead at the siege of Montpellier. "Memoire ou journal du siege de Montpellier," BNF, Mss. fr. 23339, f° 174.

64. Peter Paret illustrates the contrasts between disorderly plundering and well-coordinated pillaging activities of military units using Jacques Callot's prints from the 1630s. Peter Paret, *Imagined Battles: Reflections of War in European Art* (Chapel Hill, 1997), pp. 31–9.

65. *Voyage de M. le duc de Rohan en Vivarais, in Les Commentaires du soldat du Vivarais* (1908; reprint, Valence, 1991).

66. "Memoire ou journal du siege de Montpellier," BNF, Mss. fr. 23339, f° 167.

67. For an analysis of early modern conventions of siege capitulations and the 'law of the siege', see Geoffrey Parker, "Early Modern Europe," in Michael Howard, George J. Andreopoulos, and Mark R. Shulman (eds.), *The Laws of War: Constraints on Warfare in the Western World* (New Haven, 1994), pp. 40–58.

68. "Memoire ou journal du siege de Montpellier," Mss. fr. 23339, f° 164–5.

69. Cunningham and Grell, *The Four Horsemen of the Apocalypse*, pp. 110–11.

70. Ibid., pp. 107–8.

71. Hale, *War and Society in Renaissance Europe, 1450–1620*, pp. 117–18, 149–50.

72. Jacques Callot, "Destruction of a Convent," no. 6 of *The Large Miseries of War* (1633); Paret, *Imagined Battles*, pp. 33–4; Paulette Choné, "Les Misères de la guerre ou 'la vie du soldat': la force et le droit," in Paulette Choné, Daniel Ternois, Jean-Marc Depluvrez, and Brigitte Heckel (eds.), *Jacques Callot, 1592–1635* (Paris, 1992), pp. 396–410.

73. See Brian Sandberg, *Heroic Souls: French Nobles and Religious Conflict after the Edict of Nantes, 1598–1635* (forthcoming).

74. David Parrott's study of the French Army during the Thirty Years' War provides an excellent description of the entrepreneurial "way of warfare" in early seventeenth-century Europe. I disagree, however, with his portrayal of French military practice in this period as a deviation from the broader European pattern. Parrott, *Richelieu's Army*, chapters 5–6. The classic study of military entrepreneurship in the first half of the seventeenth century remains Fritz Redlich, *The German Military Enterpriser and his Work Force: A Study in European Economic and Social History*, 2 vols. [*Vierteljahrschrift für Sozial- und Wirtschaftgeschichte*. Beihefte 48.] (Wiesbaden, 1964–5).

75. In the early seventeenth century, nobles organized their own military units and managed the arms procurement processes. John A. Lynn shows that "before the personal reign of Louis XIV, the army passed on the primary responsibility for the purchase of weapons to the captains." John A. Lynn, *Giant of the Grand Siècle: The French Army, 1610–1715* (Cambridge, 1997), pp. 180–1. Early modern military entrepreneurship also extended to "private" arming of naval forces. See Carla Rahn Philips, *Six Galleons for the King of Spain: Imperial Defense in the Early Seventeenth Century* (Baltimore, 1986). For contrasts between seventeenth-century arms procurement practices and later systems, see Alder, "Making Things the Same," pp. 499–545.

76. For examples of purchases of arms, gunpowder and munitions, see AD Hérault, B 22590, AD Hérault, B 22610, and AD Hérault, C 8406.

77. M. Gurson de Foy to Marie de Médicis, Gurson, November 17, 1615, BNF, Clairambault 366, f° 48–9.

78. BNF, Mss. fr. 23246, f° 5–8.

79. Anne Touzery-Salager, *Les Châteaux du Bas-Languedoc: Architecture et décor de la Renaissance à la Révolution* (Montpellier: Espace Sud, 1996), chapter 1. For a discussion of early seventeenth-century thought on châteaux, see Georges Poisson, "Des châteaux à visiter au début du XVIIe siècle," *XVIIe siècle*, 118–19 (1978), pp. 3–23.

80. AD Gard, 1 E 374, f° 67.

81. Inventaire, AD Aude, 2 E 17, f° 12. Sandberg, "Bonds of Nobility and the Culture of Revolt: Provincial Nobles and Civil Conflict in Early Modern France, 1610–1635," pp. 222–8.

82. AD Hérault, G 1418, f° 28.

83. Geoffrey Parker suggests the ways in which credit was used in procuring arms for the soldiers of the Spanish Army of Flanders during the Dutch Revolt of the late sixteenth and early seventeenth centuries. Geoffrey Parker, *The Army of Flanders and the Spanish Road, 1567–1659: The Logistics of Spanish Victory and Defeat in the Low Countries' Wars* (Cambridge, 1972), pp. 48–9. See also: Lynn, *Giant of the Grand Siècle*, pp. 24–30, 180–3; Parrott, *Richelieu's Army*, pp. 225–46.

84. AD Lozère, C 820, f° 76.

85. "Le duc de Mon-morency y fut quelques jours; mais comme il vit que ce n'estoit pas un lieu qu'on peust garder, il l'abandonna pour s'en retourner à Beaucaire, qui estoit pour lors sa place d'armes." Du Cros, *Histoire de la vie de Henry dernier duc de Montmorency*, p. 39. Laurence Fontaine points out that Beaucaire's important trade links through fairs held in the town would have facilitated its role as a supply base. The fair of Beaucaire, first held in 1464, would become the most important in all of France by the late seventeenth century. Emmanuel Le Roy Ladurie, "Difficulté d'être et douceur de vivre: le XVIe siècle," in Philippe Wolff (ed.), *Histoire du Languedoc*, 2nd ed. (Toulouse, 2000), pp. 247–8, L. Dermigny, "De la Révocation à la Révolution," in Philippe Wolff (ed.), *Histoire du Languedoc*, 2nd ed. (Toulouse, 2000), pp. 357, 375–6.

86. I have explored war finance in a conference paper entitled, "'He had no difficulty in serving himself to money': Warrior Nobles, Civil Violence, and State Development in the French Wars of Religion," presented at the Annual Meeting of the Society for French Historical Studies in 2001.

87. BNF, Cinq Cens de Colbert 97, f° 121.

88. Kristen B. Neuschel, "Noble Households in the Sixteenth Century: Material Settings and Human Communities," *French Historical Studies*, 15 (Autumn 1988), pp. 611–12.

89. Leydi, "Les armuriers milanais dans la seconde moitié du XVIᵉ siècle," pp. 36–37.

90. AD Tarn, C 1167, f° 268. AD Tarn, C 1167, f° 284.

91. AD Haute Garonne, C 708.

92. This incident refers to Antoine de Cardaillac de Lévis, comte de Bioule. Deliberations of the Estates of Languedoc held at Béziers and Carcassonne, 1621, AD Hérault, C 7059, f° 119.

93. AD Hérault, B 22659.

94. AD Hérault, B 22660.

95. "Regre des desliberaõns politiques de la maison consulaire de Nymes 1621," BNF, Languedoc-Doat 258, f° 4–6.

96. John A. Lynn, "How War Fed War: The Tax of Violence and Contributions during the grand siècle," *Journal of Modern History* 65 (June 1993), pp. 286–310.

97. For an example, see: AD Haute-Garonne, B 1913, f° 321–2.

98. Du Cros, *Histoire de la vie de Henry dernier duc de Montmorency*, pp. 154–6.

99. Deliberations of the Estates of Languedoc held at Béziers and Carcassonne, 1621, AD Hérault, C 7059, f° 20–1.

100. Woodward, "'Swords into Ploughshares': Recycling in Pre-Industrial England," pp. 175–91.

101. Article 13 of the peace of Montpellier in 1622 referenced articles 58–60 of the Edict of Nantes in discussing demobilization, but failed to produce mechanisms for a permanent disarmament. *Articles de la paix generale, accordee par le roy à ses subjects de la religion pretenduë reformee. Sur la supplication faicte à sa Majesté par leurs deputez au camp devant Montpelier, le 19. octobre 1622*, BNF, 8° Lb36 2069. The orderly demobilization of troops typically became a major political and social concern after peace agreements. See: AD Haute-Garonne, B 1913, f° 22–3.

5

The Exchange of Second-hand Goods between Survival Strategies and "Business" in Eighteenth-century Paris

Laurence Fontaine

Le chiffonnier
Je l'ai prononcé, ce mot ignoble? me le pardonnera-t-on? Le voyez-vous cet homme qui, à l'aide de son croc, ramasse ce qu'il trouve dans la fange, et le jette dans sa hotte? Ne détournez pas la tête; point d'orgueil, point de fausse délicatesse. Ce vil chiffon est la matière première, qui deviendra l'ornement de nos bibliothèques, et le trésor précieux de l'esprit humain. Ce chiffonnier précède Montesquieu, Buffon et Rousseau.
Honneur au chiffonnier.[1]

[*The Ragman*
Did I utter that ignoble word? Will you excuse me? Do you see that man, collecting, with the aid of his crook, what he can find from the mire, and throwing it in his sack? Don't turn your head; it is a matter of pride, a matter of false delicacy. This vile rag is the raw material, which will become the ornament of our libraries, and the precious treasure of the human spirit. This ragman comes before Montesquieu, Buffon and Rousseau.]

Apart from the seminal work of Daniel Roche, studies of the town under the *ancien régime* have scarcely touched upon the ways in which money circulated on a daily basis. However, the economy at that time was hardly controlled by institutions at all. While the majority of families had to juggle with irregular incomes to meet their daily needs and to prepare for the hard knocks of life, sudden contingencies, sickness and unemployment, many countries such as France did not have, prior to the nineteenth century, institutions specializing in banking, insurance or financial planning. Added to the lack of financial institutions was the shortage of legal tender, and, because of this, not only were the majority of transactions based upon credit, but also, for the most part, money circulated in the form of goods. Finally, everywhere in Europe, an aristocratic economy with its values and restrictions coexisted with a capitalist economy that was more or less vigorous and dominant, depending upon the country. Salaries, pensions and loans were routinely paid, at least partially, in kind. This exchange of goods in lieu of money has also received scant attention in the literature of the *ancien régime* economy. It is these circulations, the forms they took and the professions they generated that are the focus of this chapter.

To gain a clearer impression of how second-hand goods were used as an alternative form of currency, an initial exploration of certain features of the economy of the *ancien régime* will be helpful. Though the European economy was largely founded on credit at that time, this was, however, still to a very great extent interpersonal, and it took very specific forms, depending upon the standing of whoever was borrowing and who was lending. Everything hinged upon the "period of credit" granted or declined and not everyone had the same amount of time at his or her disposal. It lessened according to social status: the higher the status, the more time acted in favor of the debtor and against the creditor. Only gambling debts escaped this schema and had to be paid without delay as to gamble was, above all else, to consume money. Gambling debts were debts of honor.

This unequal availability of time meant that those without status (the vast majority), and all those without property to set against their borrowing, had access only – if one excludes credits given by family members when they could – to credit that was in fact only a deferred sale: pawning (the loaning of money in exchange for a pledged item) was the financial instrument, par excellence, of the economies of the poor. This was the usual practice among social groups with budgets too impoverished to support an economy involving risk that could be spread over time; the violent social impact of the economy and the vulnerability of their position obliged them to survive within an uncertain economy stretching no further than the immediate present. The practice of pawning was thus the main financial instrument available to them and, in fact, when there was a shortage of work in the working-class urban milieu, objects were pawned incessantly.

These different characteristics explain why the market in second-hand clothes, and the entire range of other products, was one of the most important markets in pre-Revolutionary Europe, even if the places and the actors involved are still largely unknown. To explore this economy in more detail, this chapter will focus upon one example, Paris in the eighteenth century, because it is only at the micro level that one can hope to rediscover the modalities and the agents of these transactions which arose more from informal practices than from official markets.

An investigation into this underground economy is very difficult since it has largely escaped the archives. Two major sources do, however, enable us to gain access to it: judicial archives, which provide evidence of small- and large-scale frauds, and which give an indication of how criminal practices were concealed behind more acceptable and legal activities; and contemporary writers, who described the realities that they encountered. The *Tableau de Paris* by Louis Sébastien Mercier, the prolific eighteenth-century journalist and writer, is thus an irreplaceable source. Certainly, his pen becomes deliberately moralizing as soon as he turns to the question of praising family values, but his eye is extremely acute in observing economic micro-networks, the social and cultural practices linked to them, and the small trades that they generate. Moreover, whenever they exist, other sources always corroborate what he says.

After briefly describing the main figures of the official second-hand markets, this chapter will set out, in the first instance, to indicate the role played by these transactions in aristocratic circles, secondly, to explore the role played by women in this economy and, thirdly, it will endeavour to trace the creation of the first official *mont de piété* (pawnshop) in France, set up in 1778 by the state to regulate secured loans in response to the proliferation and excesses of private lenders.

The Importance of Official Second-hand Commerce

Before this informal economy is described, the place occupied by the official trade in second-hand clothing in the Paris of the eighteenth century will be outlined. Clothing was at the heart of this economy because very often these were the only goods that the poor possessed.

The figures indicate that the second-hand trade was by far the most important of the clothing markets. In 1725, those making new clothes numbered 3500 tailors and dressmakers. These figures are, however, very rough, since the separation between new and old was still, at that time, far from watertight. Against them, Paris numbered around 700 second-hand clothes dealers and as many female linen merchants, and above all between 6,000 and 7,000 women dealing in second-hand goods.[2] Like the used-clothing merchants, the second-hand goods dealers covered a vast spectrum of trading fortunes, from rich merchants to very modest second-hand dealers, close to beggary.[3] The Auvergnats and the Jews were the principal actors in these second-hand markets. The former specialized in crockery and the latter in second-hand clothing. They all relied on migration to cover the different locations and the different sectors of the market. Thus the humble itinerant ragmen who collected old rags, and who exchanged clothes and objects for a little money or some goods, worked for the big well-established merchants, who were, themselves, tied to the export markets and the paper-pulp factories.[4]

Louis-Sébastien Mercier described at length the business in second-hand clothing then established at Les Halles. He also referred to the existence of a Monday market at the Place de Grève, the site where state executions normally took place. This temporary market was run solely by women. Finally he showed that, in the eighteenth century, buying clothes from someone else carried no stigma. In the nineteenth century, everything would be very different.[5]

> Under the pillars of Les Halles, ... stretches a long line of clothing shops, selling old outfits in poorly-lit premises, where stains and colours disappear.
>
> ...Squat idle stallholders call out to you quite rudely; and once one of them has invited you in, all these shopkeepers repeat the same tedious invitation as you go on your way. The wife, the daughter, the maidservant, the dog, all bark at your ears; it's a squealing that will deafen you until you are outside the pillars.
>
> ...You will find there just about everything to furnish a house from the cellar to the attic, beds, wardrobes, chairs, tables, desks, etc. Fifty thousand men have only to arrive in Paris, and they will supply them the next day with fifty thousand beds.
>
> The wives of these second-hand clothes dealers [*fripiers*], or their sisters, or their aunts, or their cousins, go every Monday to a sort of fair, known as the *Saint-Esprit*, which is held in the Place de Grève. There is no execution on this day: there they spread out everything to do with clothes for women and children.
>
> Lower middle-class ladies [*Petites-bourgeoises*], brothel keepers, or excessively austere housewives go there to buy, everything from bonnets, dresses, blouses, and sheets to shoes. Police informants wait there for crooks, who come to sell stolen handkerchiefs, napkins and other stolen goods...
>
> One could say that this fair is the female undressing [la défroque] of an entire province...
>
> This, here, is the dress of the president's dead wife which the "madam" will buy, the poor working girl adorns herself with the bonnet of the marchioness's chambermaid. They dress themselves in public, and soon they will even change their shirts there.
>
> The purchaser does not know, and does not care to know, from where the corset she barters over has come. The poor, innocent young girl, under her mother's very eye, reclothes the one with whom a lustful girl from the Opéra was dancing on the previous evening. Everything seems purified by the sale or by the inventory after death.
>
> ... In the evening, this whole heap of rags is carried away as if by magic; not a *mantelet* remains, and this inexhaustible store will reappear without fail on the following Monday.[6]

The last official actors in the second-hand market were the auctioneer-bailiffs (*huissiers-priseurs*). They bought their wares through royalty and were in charge of the public sales. It was through them that most second-hand items were placed on the market. Four types of event helped to sustain them: the settlement of inheritances; the bankruptcy of shopkeepers; debt seizures; and the sale of uncollected pawned items.

> Losses, bankruptcies, deaths, all are favorable to the auctioneer-bailiffs: reversals, variations in fortune, changes of place and of status always culminate in forced or voluntary sales.
>
> The auctioneer-bailiffs thus profit from all events that perturb human life. The immense range of the needs that afflict the capital oblige it to perpetually trade in any merchandise whatsoever against money; money thus becomes merchandise like everything else, and the auctioneer-bailiff always knows this...

When you have attended one of these tumultuous sales, you will have the monotonous cries and the buzzing in your ears for a fortnight.

In this way everything, from a Rubens painting to an old jerkin threadbare at the elbows, is auctioned. Thus one sees philosophical proof of the intrinsic value of objects...

The auctioneer-bailiffs are subject to puffed-up chests; the stuffy air of the hall full of coppersmiths, resellers, saleswomen etc., infects their lungs.

They are happier when, with harsh austerity, in the open air of the Place Saint-Michel, they sell the confiscated furniture of a poor debtor, who stares and sighs at the bed upon which he will lie no more. The unflinching bailiff auctions off for the benefit of the creditors in the same tone that, the day before, he auctioned the bronzes, the diamonds, the fine wines of the tax-farmer, the bishop and the duchess, who died of too much opulence.[7]

Public sales were one of the main venues for competition between professionals and private individuals. Louis Sébastien Mercier denounced the grasping conduct of the shopkeepers, who did everything in their power to force out private individuals. These sales, he declared, were in the control of the professional cartels (*grafinade*).

These are a group of merchants who do not outbid each other at sales because all those who are there when an object is purchased have a share in it; however, when they see that an individual desires a particular object they force up the price of it and bear the loss, which, although significant for a person acting alone, becomes slight when divided between all the members of the league. These leagues exist for jewelry, diamonds, clocks and watches: they prevent the public from taking advantage of inexpensive goods.

These understandings between merchants occurred not only among those trading in luxury goods but also among milliners (*crieuses de vieux chapeau*) and second-hand dealers,[8] and documents relating to the most successful merchants on the rue du faubourg Saint-Honoré confirm that they were in the habit of getting part of their stock from the public sales.[9] According to Mercier, the merchants' success in controlling these sales meant that *Les Petites Affiches*, one of the first French newspapers to announce the auctions that took place after a death, "are only of service to upholsterers, jewelers, merchants in the fashion business, and the young men who trade in horses, pictures and diamonds,"[10] whereas, by making the information about these sales easily accessible, the paper should have been helping individuals to break into this type of business.

Alongside, and very often linked to, these official means of exchanging second-hand goods, the informal sector proliferated. It had two major sources: the needs of the aristocracy and those of the people for whom the acquisition and sale of an object, and the secured loan that went with it, were at the heart of survival strategies, and mechanisms for saving and financial security that they tried to put into effect. Let us begin with the part played by these transactions among the nobility.

A Commercial Arena for Aristocrats: "Business" and "Curio Collectors"

Between the seventeenth and eighteenth centuries, the nobility successfully slipped into the trading relationship quite openly. They knew how to appropriate and exploit that major form of exchange, sale by auction, at the same time that they entered the market more directly via the building up of collections that, under the guise of a passion, enabled purchase, exchange and resale. The world of the collection, the first of which were constituted in the European courts and developed, in the seventeenth century, in parallel with the salons, represented another economy – that of "taste" and an evolution in the presentation of self that put moral qualities to the fore, and signaled an entrance into new worlds of excellence, which developed with travels and science, and with which it was fitting to show one's familiarity.[11]

With regard to curios, the nobility entered the commercial world by making use of the very old practice of sale by auction.[12] Thus developed a parallel second-hand market in which nobles operated without intermediaries.

Mercier – and the entries for *curieux* (collectors of curios) and *brocanteur* (second-hand dealers) in *l'Encyclopédie* support Mercier in this assertion – suspected them of hiding behind the pleasure of collecting, and the obsession that it excited, to openly succumb to the pleasures and profits of commerce.[13] Mercier writes:

> Our Lords, under the name of *curieux* [curio collectors], are often wonderful *brocanteurs* [second-hand dealers], who buy without need, without passion, and only to have bargains, jewels, horses, pictures, old prints, and so forth cheaply. They set up stud farms or cabinets of wonders, which soon become shops: one would think them to have a passion for *beaux-arts* [fine arts]; they love money. These vases, these bronzes, these works of art, to which they seem attached, and which they worship, could belong to anyone who will take them for gold.[14]

He also dedicated a chapter to the jewelry trade: "[There is an] enormous trade in jewelry: among rich men items of jewelry are constantly being resold. Certain individuals have in their homes stocks of jewelery to rival the shops of the jewelers themselves: they are jealous and proud of this honorable reputation."[15]

The resale of fashion items is the other important activity that concerned the elites. It was engendered by the need to keep up to date with fashion, the cycles of which were continually shortening. Moreover, paying for new objects by getting rid of older ones was common practice between the aristocrats and their suppliers.[16] This activity was simply called 'business':

> This is the generic term to describe any form of trading in second-hand goods. Rings, cases, jewelery and watches circulate in place of money. If someone needs money, he starts out with the contents of a shop. He will lose, it is true, more than half his investment when he wants to turn it into cash; but this is what is called *affaires* (business).

Young people are often involved in this type of business. Dresses, skirts, negligees, cloth, lace, hats, silk stockings are all traded. They know that they will be tricked, yet need pushes them onwards and they take on all sorts of merchandise. A mass of men are engaged in this destructive industry, and the upper classes are among the most skillful of them.[17]

Whether these exchanges were generated both by the continual need for fashion to be renewed or by a basic need for money, whether to facilitate the acquisition of the latest stylish objects or for other reasons entirely, the fact remains that jewelery and fashion items circulated as though they were paper money, except that their depreciation in value was significant and rapid. This depreciation was to the delight of intermediaries who scoured the town in search of money and customers.

The *courtiers* (brokers), who featured here most prominently, attracted Mercier's attention:

The man who offers you money looks gaunt and half-starved; he wears old clothes. He is always tired; he sits down when he comes in, for in a day he covers all parts of the city in order to match sales and purchases and to link the frequent exchanges of various goods.

First you place in his hands your bills of exchange. He leaves: within the hour they will have been scrutinized by the entire clique of *courtiers*. Then he comes back to offer you cheap stockings, hats, braid, cloth, raw silk, books – he will even offer you horses. It is up to you to turn these objects into money. Suddenly you are a hatter, a hosier, a bookseller or a horse dealer.

Your bill of exchange has been paid in merchandise; sometimes you will get a quarter of it as cash. And the same *courtier*, whom you are obliged to turn to again, is also the man to take this merchandise off your hands: a new piece of sharp practice which soon reduces your bill of exchange to a third of its original value.[18]

The lack of cash, then, was both cause and pretext for a parallel exchange of goods, but this parallel exchange always generated a great loss on the resale prices.

An Informal, Largely Female World

Women were at the heart of this micro economy, where clothing circulated as a form of currency, and where it was rented out and pawned according to need, because they were confronted by the following challenge. On the one hand, they had a reduced political, administrative and legal capacity, which constrained them to manage their business without sparkle or imagination. But, on the other hand, in spite of restrictive supervision and regulations, they had to manage the family finances and perpetually juggle their regular financial needs and irregular income. And they had to do it with budgets that they rarely controlled. Thus, their social roles, in an incompletely monetarized economy and in a legal environment that marginalized them, explains why, from the Middle Ages on, they animated the networks for the sale and resale of used clothes.

However, it is extremely difficult to pick up the trail of the women who were active in pawn broking and the second-hand markets since they were of no interest to the state and its various records. Some post-death inventories allow us to guess at the role of women, like Marguerite Lambert, laundress from Lyons, who left furniture and effects to the value of 153 livres in the room where she lodged but had credits of 2,162 livres. She had lent to different people, including on one occasion more than 1000 livres.[19] Only the legal archives, in which particular women and the excesses of the trade were from time to time severely criticized, allow us to guess at the most ordinary practices. The Bastille archives contain details of a number of these working-class women in eighteenth-century Paris, arrested because their demands exceeded the amount they lent out, because they charged exorbitant rates of interest, or because they sold articles pawned, or used them to yield further profit by renting them out.

Some examples of such women show us different aspects of this small-scale female financial delinquency: excess usury by a woman named Lestrade who lent £36 on two silk robes and three petticoats worth £150, earning her more than £3 12s per month in interest;[20] sale of secured items by Marie Magdeleine Le Fort, the wife of a pit sawyer, who had sold a baker's coat and smock that she had accepted as security from him for a loan of £22,[21] or a woman named Roger and her daughter who had not given back the outfit of gray cloth braided with gold with which a gentleman had secured a loan of £120.[22]

These women worked in collaboration with other lenders. They took on responsibility for a loan and made it pay, like la Demoiselle Benoist, who charged 2 sols per livre in interest and served as *courtière* (broker) to pawnbrokers, although she could not resist reselling the securities when she herself did business.[23] To stand surety, however, was not without its risks. Thus the widow La Tour found herself threatened with prison when the grocer's son that she had invited to the house of the Demoiselle Prunier stole from her. Prunier then claimed against the intermediary.[24]

The file on Dame Bertrand, a pawnbroker arrested in 1735, contains all of these elements. She worked for herself, in association with Dame Noret, and Lord (*Sieur*) Lafosse, who acted as a lender. Through these women's inter-mediary, Lord Malbay pawned an outfit with Lafosse, against 3 louis and 12 livres interest for four months. When he retrieved the item, he found "in the pockets love letters and a note for 444 livres in favour of a certain Dasarsis." Malbay went to see Dasarsis who confirmed that he had rented the outfit from the women Bertrand and Noret. Once arrested, the complaints came flooding in: Bouin, a laundry worker, said that the Dame Bertrand charged her 12 livres interest for a dress and petticoat that she had bought for 68 livres with her savings and pawned to help her parents secure a loan of 21 livres given by M. Desmaret through the intermediary of Dame Bertrand. Others complained of her propensity to keep the securities entrusted to her: a certain Régnier, captain in the Nanterre regiment, described all the clothes and objects that he had had the imprudence of pawning to borrow 84 livres, and that the usuress refused to give back to him: an outfit with a silver fabric waistcoat worth 550 livres, a damask chamber robe worth 100 livres, two embroidered shirts worth 60 livres, a pair of silvered candlesticks worth 24 livres and two tortoiseshell snuffboxes worth 30 livres. Luckily for her, Dame Bertrand had a sister who had caught the eye of an aristocrat, who therefore rapidly signed her release papers.[25]

Maidservants were at the center of this redistribution, since they often received clothing as a bonus, and the world of prostitution was also very much tied to pawn broking, both because prostitutes had to invest in their appearance and because they also received in payment from their clients gifts of clothing. The archives of the Bastille reveal borrowers such as La Dubuisson, a *fille du monde*, who borrowed 40 livres, with 4 livres interest for the first month, on a blue silk waistcoat embroidered in silver from La Leloup. She gave it to La Sagest to find a lender, but the two go-betweens doubtless sold the item.[26] And lenders such as Marie Anne de Lostaing, the widow of a footman, who had been banished to Dijon, his home town, for public debauchery: Elisabeth Le Tellier, employed by a female linen merchant, feared getting nothing back of the 350 livres of cloth and lace that she had entrusted to de Lostaing.[27] Friendships were formed: Marie Catherine Bellemont, a sixty-year-old prostitute and lender on security, had fallen into the company of a guardsman's wife and his sister, a prostitute, madam and brothel-keeper. All three caused quite a stir in the street.[28]

Along with the female pawnbrokers (*prêteuses sur gage*), the police would also arrest the fine clothes reseller (*revendeuses à la toilette*). In fact, the activities of the latter would be hard to distinguish from the former, if not for the fact that they dealt with a more up-market clientele in the urgent need to find money. It was to these women that the aristocrats turned when they had to pay their gambling debts.

> The *revendeuse à la toilette* [fine clothes reseller] is welcome anywhere. She brings you fabrics, lace and jewelery that belonged to someone who needed cash to pay gambling debts. She is in the confidence of the finest ladies, who ask her opinions and arrange several matters on the basis of her advice...
>
> It has been said that a *revendeuse à la toilette* must prattle endlessly but nonetheless maintain unfailing discretion, must possess boundless agility, a memory for objects, unflagging patience and a strong constitution.
>
> Women such as this only exist in Paris. They make their fortune in a very short time.[29]

Trévoux's dictionary mentions their existence too, while Savary, in his dictionary of commerce, also insists on the uniquely Parisian aspect of the profession whilst further underlining their role in the diffusion of contraband goods:

> In Paris those women who go to people's houses to sell second-hand clothes and jewelry that others wish to get rid of are called *revendeuses à la toilette*. They are also often involved in the clandestine sale of smuggled or illegally imported goods, such as fabrics from the Indies, painted canvases, Flanders lace, and so forth..., either on their own account or acting on behalf of someone else.[30]

They were also linked with second-hand clothes dealers and constituted the profession of *courtier au feminin* (female broker); like the woman Leonard, *courtière* (broker) and *revendeuse à la toilette*, who owed five creditors, including two haberdashers, nearly 30,000 livres for "merchandise entrusted to her," and who dealt in all kinds of goods: Persian rugs, fabrics from the Indies, satins, dresses, jewelery, watches.[31]

They found themselves at the Bastille for the same reasons: usurious loans, resale of securities or handling stolen goods. Resale was tempting inasmuch as these *prêts sur gage* (secured loans) were made with a very great disproportion between the value of the security and the money lent. So we come across one woman from Grassy, a *revendeuse à la toilette*, who was arrested on the complaint of a priest who had entrusted to her a necklace to sell, which she had passed on to her husband, a prisoner at the Petit Châtelet;[32] or Marie Ursule Mazerine, a widow, *revendeuse à la toilette*, and *prêteuse sur gage* (pawnbroker), who refused to return two watches to a watch-dealer who had given them to her, together with a satin gown lined with flamed taffeta belonging to the wife of a Parisian bourgeois who had left them against a loan of 25 livres for a month with interest paid in advance, even though the dress was worth 150 livres;[33] Marie Suzanne Peret alias Germain alias Richard, who kept the securities of a master enameller;[34] and Jeanne Françoise Lefèvre, *revendeuse à la toilette* and shopkeeper's wife, accused of being "an untrustworthy pawnbroker who kept an item entrusted to her."[35]

All of these women, whatever the scope of their business, also worked together. They represented one of the links in the financial business of resale which was a particular force in the city, and in which money, goods, clothes and other objects changed hands via a long chain of intermediaries. These women knew to whom to go to borrow money, or to sell second-hand goods, and the shopkeepers came to them when one of their female customers needed money. It was not unusual for there to be three or four intermediaries involved in a transaction. Thus, Madeleine le Dagre used a dealer, Hérissier, to dispose of two pieces of cloth for 355 livres. Hérissier gave them, with other items, to Delaunay, the widow of a ship's lieutenant, associated with a man "without wealth or profession," who paid only half of the value of the pieces of cloth and owed him 1,500 livres for other items.[36] The female broker (*courtière*), Deshayes, who remitted the engraved gold watch of the assistant to a major of the battalion of the Mantes militia to a second broker, who placed it with a third, who disappeared with it.[37] A tailor approached Javotte Gouillon to lend 10 *écus* to one of his clients against a dress that the *revendeuse à la toilette* sold three months later.[38] Catherine Villers, wife of a cork-maker's assistant (*garçon bouchonnier*), gave two outfits placed by Lerson as security for a loan of 60 livres to a lackey of the Bishop of Autun and the poor borrower could not recover his clothes.[39]

Lending money for day-to-day survival or acting as an intermediary for a more important lender, providing them with information on potential lenders and borrowers and serving as intermediaries and sometimes as guarantors were part of the activity that women undertook, thanks to their position at the heart of communities and their capacity for soaking up information about the families all around them.[40] These stories also bear witness to the ingenuity of women and of their spirit of enterprise, since they knew how to extract a double profit from these transactions when the occasion arose, a first one by procuring a little extra money, which they could increase by acquiring and reselling a few small objects or foodstuffs, and a second one by actuating a thriving parallel rental business.

But not all women sank voluntarily into petty theft. A number of them survived using their savoir-faire as couturières to rework second-hand clothes on demand for second-hand clothes dealers, and some specialized in making children's clothes. Here, too, the frontier between new and second-hand was effaced, as used clothing was transformed into raw material from which tailors and couturiers, usually women, took the best parts to turn into clothes termed new.[41] Thanks to the judgment issued against Marie-Denise Toutain, wife of the carpenter, Simon Moreau, and against her sister, Antoinette Toutain, inculpated in having sold clothes at the Meaux Fair on Monday, May 16, 1796, we build up a picture of the diverse aspects of their modest activities as well as the link that these women maintained with official commerce. During the trial, the widow, Françoise-Geneviève Maréchal, a second-hand clothes dealer in Paris, declared that "Moreau's wife is his worker" and "that in the package containing the goods… the trousers and the coat belonged to her, having herself given them to the Wife Moreau, who did not have much merchandise, to sell them." Thus half of the eighty-two pieces that she sold belonged to the dealer and consisted "of 44 pieces of different stuffs, whether for the use of men, women and children, whether old or new or coloured consisting of jackets, waistcoats, blouses and petticoats, all these pieces were packed together in a piece of tapestry tied with a cord;" hers, packed "in a ballot tied with a cord" consisted of "women's pouches, skirts, petticoats, blouses, *culottes* and waistcoats, jackets, handkerchiefs, the remainders of painted Jouy fabrics, wrapped in canvas and swaddling clothes, a collection of painted wool cloth, twill and other fabrics, all old with the exception of the Jouy piece for the use of men, women and children, the said stockings of cotton thread and wool also old." In her defense, the woman invoked the smallness of her trade, "of such little consequence that she had not been constrained to take a trading licence." The two women's defense lawyer, le C. Perrot, revealed that the two sisters had no other way of surviving: "Moreau's wife, mother of a family with nothing, put up for sale just the few effects originating from her husband and herself as well as goods entrusted to her for sale by a licensed trader … that she was obliged to sell to feed her family." As for her sister, the lawyer explained that, "indigent and crippled, she is incapable of earning her living other than by hand-making children's clothes … that she was in the habit of going to the markets of Paris and its vicinity and that no one had ever asked her if she had [licenses]." He concluded by stressing the extent to which these practices were commonplace: "the Moreau women and the Toutain girl are like many citizens in every commune of the Republic who similarly make children's clothes with old linen that they procure for themselves, without being able to purchase a license; the proceeds of trading in most cases did not amount to the price of the smallest license."[42]

These women were also victims of the determination of official merchants, who strove to maintain a monopoly for themselves in the trade. Mercier too denounced these seizures of goods on the grounds that women such as these two were themselves the victims, without properly understanding what was happening to them.

> There is nothing more frequent, and nothing more dishonorable to our legislation. One often sees a commissioner with his bailiffs, running after a clothes vendor, or after a small-time hardware-seller, pushing around a portable stall…
>
> They publicly strip of her goods a woman who carries on her back and on her head forty pairs of *culottes*. They seize her togs in the name of the majestic community of second-hand clothes dealers … they arrest a jacketed man who carries something wrapped under his coat. What is seized? New shoes that the unfortunate man hid in a rag. The shoes are confiscated by ordinance, this sale becoming detrimental to the Paris cobblers.[43]

Living at the margins of legality, within an informal economy, numerous ordinary women developed their own economic cultures, based on guile and secrecy, which served to mask and disguise their illicit, or barely legal, economic practices, as well as cultures of solidarity to compensate for their lack of legal protection. These ruses took two forms. They would exploit all the possibilities of the institutions by, for example, renting out clothes that had been pawned. But they also showed their capacity to turn on its head the image that society assigned to them. This is very apparent in the criminal economy where they used, beyond their savoir-faire in matters of couture, the fact that they were less heavily punished by the justice system to become the principal handlers and dealers in stolen goods. In the Paris of the eighteenth century, the celebrated bandit Cartouche was thus accused of using women of humble stock on a large scale.[44]

The Institutionalization of the Secured Loan

The need to institutionalize this economy made itself felt in response to the needs of the population. But, because this private sector of the economy was extremely active and powerful, and more often than not was controlled by the biggest merchants and financiers, it was very difficult for official pawnshops to become established in France. After a fruitless attempt in 1637, a *mont-de-piété* (pawnshop) was created in 1777 in Paris in a period of great impoverishment, on the initiative of a group of bankers and politicians who believed that affordable credit was more effective than charity in saving the poor.[45] The project, inspired by the organization of six establishments in French Flanders, aimed to "assure money aid under the least onerous terms and turn the benefit to the relief of the poor." A quotation from Necker delineates all the social strata targeted: "The *mont-de-piété* was established," he wrote,[46] "with the aim of assistance to subjects so that they can be relieved in their domestic affairs; assistance to shopkeepers so that they can avoid the shame and harm of seizures."[47]

In spite of Necker's support, the cause of the *monts-de-piété* was not won in the rest of France; for, whilst encouraging the creation of such a body in Paris, Necker was not disposed to curb the systems of private loans:

> I do not believe, however, that it is convenient to extend these establishments into the provincial towns: one must consider such precautions as a way of softening abuses that cannot be prevented; but in those places where the police are not overburdened, it is easy to destroy the usurers' profession, or at least to contain the traffic within known bounds. It is only in the commotion of a great capital that moral depravation needs accommodating, and a sort of conciliation needs to be made with vice that cannot practically be wiped out: elsewhere the remedy would only spread evil ideas.[48]

The Parisian *mont-de-piété* was finally set up on December 9, 1777 and, from January 5, 1778, an internal regulation completed its constitutive charter. Although placed under the control of the Lieutenant of Police, this institution possessed an autonomous regime and its own accounts were checked each year by a commission, composed of four councillors of the *Grand Chambre* of the *Parlement* and of a representative of the Procurator General. The pawnbroking monopoly was given to them.

The success of the Parisian *mont-de-piété* was immediate and, from the first months, more staff had to be recruited. On February 12, 1778, a cashier-controller, an assessor and a chief clerk (*premier commis*) managed the establishment with seven assistants (*commis*) to which five extras were very soon added. On March 2, a further three assistants (*commis*) were recruited. From March 30, the flow of business was such that the shops had to be expanded and several divisions created. By the end of the year, the *mont-de-piété* comprised no fewer than twenty-seven employees and twenty-six pawnbrokers.[49]

Let us turn once again to Louis Sébastien Mercier, who was present at the opening of this pawnshop:[50]

> A *mont-de-piété* has finally just been established, known elsewhere as a *lombard*; and the administration, by this wise, long-desired, establishment, has issued a mortal blow to the barbarous and harsh fury of voracious usurers, always ready to despoil the needy...
> Nothing better demonstrates how much the capital needed this *lombard* than the endless flow of applicants. Such peculiar and incredible tales are told that I dare not set them down here without first having sought more precise information, which will allow me to guarantee their veracity. There is talk of *forty barrels filled with gold watches*, doubtless to express the prodigious quantities that have been deposited. What I know for sure is that I have seen between 60 and 80 people waiting their turn there, each one come to borrow not more than *six livres*. One was carrying his shirts, another a piece of furniture, another what remained of a wardrobe, and another his shoe buckles, an old picture, some poor clothes, and so forth. They say that there is a new crowd there almost every day, and this gives a very clear idea of the extreme shortage of money from which most of the city is suffering ...

Rich people borrow as well as the poor. One woman gets out of her carriage, wrapped up in her coat, and deposits 25,000 francs' worth of diamonds so that she can go gambling in the evening. Another takes off her petticoat and asks for the price of a loaf of bread...

We are assured that a third of the effects are not collected: a further proof of the strange shortage of cash. The sales that take place offer many luxury goods at low prices, which may harm the smaller merchants somewhat. But besides this it is no bad thing that these goods, which were excessively highly priced, should now experience a drop in their exorbitant rates.

It is said that the system is already being abused. The poor are bullied, and the objects offered by the destitute are estimated at too low a price, which means that they are being offered virtually no help. Charity should be the driving force and should be more important than other superficial and vain considerations. It would not be hard to turn this establishment into a *temple of mercy*, generous, active and compassionate. The good work has begun: why should it not be completed in a way that will satisfy the poorest people most?

On opening, the *mont-de-piété* had in its tills a sum of 558,200 livres, thanks to the discounting of notes to the bearer under the guarantee of the Hôpital général. After one month, it had already lent 101,154 livres. At the inaugural meeting on December 22, the director was authorized to borrow at 5 percent. The funds were drawn in several ways. On November 14, 1778, exchange agents were invited to procure funds at six months, averaging a commission of 1/8 percent: that is 25 sols per 1000 livres. The establishment, which sought long-term deposits, offered premiums for two-year deposits. From December 3, 1778, the Hôpital Général, which had already contributed to the constitution of the initial capital, had to guarantee further sums up to 4 million. At the same time, the number of administrators was increased from four to six. It offered 4.5 percent for deposits of one year and 3.5 percent on loans of six months. Funds grew, and, after a year, the accounts were healthy: on December 31, 1778, there were 128,508 items pawned for 8,309,384 livres and 60,551 items had been redeemed for 3,179,523 livres and in the shop 67,957 items for 5,129,861 livres.

The following year, a Genoan company offered 4 million livres at 5 percent reimbursable in fourteen years, on condition of being exempted from tax, which the King accepted by conceding the *vingtième* tax. In February 1789, the pawnshop had received so many deposits that it decided to give only 5 percent interest on deposits of a year, up to a limit of 6 million. Beyond this sum, it would be given only at 4.5 percent. On December 31, 1789, the operating capital reached more than 13 million livres, of which close to 5 million were placed at 4.5 percent and the rest at 5 percent.

As for the loans, the letters patent of December 9, 1777 fixed for Paris the quota of loans at four-fifths of the value by weight for gold or silver and two-thirds of the estimated value for other objects. The valuers, chosen from amongst the attendant auctioneers (*huissiers-commissaires priseurs*) of the Châtelet, had a commission rate (*droit de prisée*) of one denier per livre. The rate of loans had an implicit upper limit of 10 percent to the extent that the administration was authorized to retain only two deniers per livre and per month for the administration costs (making two sous per livre per year). The loan could not be less than three livres.[51]

An immediate subject of fascination for the Parisians, the Paris *mont-de-piété* came to play the role of a veritable bank for Parisian artisans, as indicated by the nature of the objects pawned and the modest sums loaned. Five divisions of the establishment, each receiving close to 80,000 articles for a value of around a million livres in 1789, were reserved for clothes, linen, sheets and remnants of fabrics. In two other divisions, the most precious objects were pawned. In the first were deposited diamonds, jewels, lace and new goods. In 1789, the sum total of the 52,221 pawned items of this order reached 7,630,667 livres. Such figures corroborate Mercier's assertions: "The opulent borrow as much as the poor. One woman gets out of her carriage, wrapped up in her coat, and deposits 25,000 francs worth of diamonds so that she can go gambling in the evening." The second division took silver, watches, bronzes, buckles, swords and pictures, and was well supplied: records show 89,461 articles to a value of 5,420,145 livres.

Mercier was struck by the quantity of watches in or among the objects pawned, which he reports as rumoured to be in tonnes. They were indeed numerous and, for instance, in a single day, August 26, 1783, 139 gold watches were deposited. A glance at the columns of clients in the registers shows that Mercier had accurately understood the diversity of this clientele. On the same morning in 1788, two midwives, a wine merchant and a tailor, amongst others, passed before the estimators at the pawnshop and had their gold watch valued at 84 livres; then a cobbler with silver buckles, for which he got 32 livres; a jeweler with a clock for 252 livres; and a middle-class woman from the Rue d'Argenteuil, who deposited 150 livres worth of silverware. A carpenter brought a seven-volume set of Voltaire's works; a dancer from the Comedy Entertainments (Délassements-Comiques) pawned his theatre costumes; someone else deposited four pictures estimated at 260 livres, and so forth.[52]

Soon, customer practices showed that clients knew how to use the market, not only to contend with immediate economic difficulties and to attempt to allay those of the future, but also to maximize the profits from the valuable objects that passed through their hands.

Secured loans had become part of the culture of the people, who knew how to exploit all means to earn a few sous. Apprentices, servants and day labourers employed in the jewelery trade brought the precious metals they worked; and, in the professions that enabled speculation upon the time lag between receipt of raw materials or merchandise and the delivery of the finished products, they knew equally well how to make full use of the pawn office to deposit their merchandise or tools that they were not using, and to enable the money they had gained from it to bear fruit, before withdrawing these particular kinds of deposit.[53]

If one takes the average transactions – objects pawned, withdrawals, renewals and sales – per year, from 1785 to 1789, one notices that of 490,000 articles deposited (around 14 million livres), barely 25,000 were sold (making 1,200,000 livres), which shows that the great majority of the clients were solvent.[54] Of the 1,500,000 livres brought by sales of pawned items in 1788, 600,000 livres came from the sale of clothes previously belonging to the needy, 300,000 livres from silverware, 200,000 livres from watches, 200,000 livres from jewels, and only 200,000 livres from other goods.[55] In relation to the overall activity of the pawnshop, these figures indicate, on the one hand, that the majority of clients used this option to pass through a difficult patch, and that the proportion of merchandise deposited was modest. It follows from this that the fears of merchants that the establishment would serve as a refuge for fraudulent bankruptcies were largely unfounded, and Mercier was wrong when he wrote that a third of objects were not withdrawn, but he had warned that he was only reporting this from hearsay. In spite of everything, either with the desired purpose or deliberate intention of harming a competitor, the support that the pawn office brought to artisans and small traders kept being regularly criticized.[56]

It remains the case that the success of this institutionalization of the secured loan in Paris bears witness to the vitality of informal financial circulation and of the prevailing need to officially control and develop it. The analysis of pawned items invites reflection upon the fascination that people had for the gold watches and jewels so frequently mentioned in the inventories after death:[57] beyond their own utility or a desire to imitate the aristocracy, watches were also objects of easily realizable value. The purchase of luxury items and the use that town-dwellers of early modern Europe made of them were perhaps signs that they already had a "preference for nonliquid assets": money thus invested beyond the sole pleasure of consumption immobilized capital, which thereby escaped the solicitations of those close by and allowed cash to be borrowed. The rise in popular consumption can also be read – and perhaps first and foremost – as an accumulation of savings. More generally, the importance of precious metal objects and luxury articles in these financial exchanges adds another dimension to urban consumption: it reflects the precariousness of work in the economies of the *ancien régime* and the lack of monetary currencies and of financial institutions. In return, it plays a by no means negligible role in the city economy by giving it an indispensable element of suppleness.

Finally, the study of how used objects circulated in Paris shows that the principal agents in this commerce were positioned at the margins of the commercial world: migrants and women make up the majority. Migrants because they found two advantages in this commerce: a way into the market without needing to make huge investments, and products that were well adapted to the organization of these migrants within hierarchical networks; which enabled them to trade in different places and with diverse clienteles. Women made a living in large numbers from this commerce because they possessed the culture of clothing and because they were the best agents of information about the life of the districts. The presence of aristocrats is only an apparent contrast, since they too were theoretically excluded from the trading sphere and since the exchange of objects, before being part of the culture of collection, was part of the culture of gift giving.

Translated by James Turpin and Sheila Oakley

Notes

1. Louis Sébastien Mercier, *Tableau de Paris*, ed. Jean-Claude Bonnet, 2 vols, (Paris, 1994) (original edition published between 1781 and 1789), vol. 1, chap. CLXXXIV, pp. 452–3.
2. Daniel Roche, *La Culture des apparences. Une histoire du vêtement XVIIe–XVIIIe siècle* (Paris, 1989), pp. 328 and 344.
3. Roche, *La Culture des apparences*, pp. 313–45. On the *fripières* specializing in the resale of court robes, see Carolyn Sargentson, *Merchants and Luxury Markets. The Marchants Merciers of Eighteenth-century Paris* (London, 1996), pp. 106–7.
4. Françoise Raison-Jourde, *La Colonie auvergnate de Paris au XIXe siècle* (Paris, 1973); Laurence Fontaine, *History of Pedlars in Europe* (Cambridge, 1996).
5. See chapter 7.
6. Mercier, *Tableau de Paris*, vol. 1, chap. CLXXXII, pp. 448–50.
7. Ibid., vol. 1, chap. CLXXXII
8. Ibid., vol. 2, chap. DLXVI, pp. 109–11.
9. Sargentson, *Merchants and Luxury Markets*, p. 32.
10. Mercier, *Tableau de Paris*, vol. 2, chap. DCXX, p. 312.
11. Krystof Pomian, *Collectionneurs, amateurs et curieux. Paris, Venise XVIe–XVIIIe siècle* (Paris, 1996), p. 52; John Brewer, *The Pleasures of the Imagination: English Culture in the Eighteenth Century* (London, 1997).
12. Antoine Schnapper, "Probate Inventories, Public Sales and the Parisian art market in the Seventeenth Century," in M. North and D. Omrod (eds.), *Art Markets in Europe, 1500–1900* (Aldershot, 1998), pp. 131–41.
13. See also Annie Becq, "Artistes et marché," in Jean-Claude Bonnet (ed.), *La Carmagnole des Muses. L'homme de lettres et l'artiste dans la Révolution* (Paris, 1988), pp. 81–95.
14. Mercier, *Tableau de Paris*, vol. 1, chap. CCCIX, pp. 808–9.
15. Ibid., vol. 1, chap. CLXXV, p. 415.
16. Sargentson, *Merchants and Luxury Markets*, pp. 32–3.
17. Mercier, *Tableau de Paris*, vol. 1, chap. CLI, pp. 365–6.
18. Mercier, Ibid., vol. 1, chap. DLIII, *Courtiers*, vol. 2, pp. 57–60.
19. Jean-Pierre Gutton, *La Société et les pauvres. L'exemple de la généralité de Lyon (1534–1789)* (Paris, 1971) p. 63.
20. Archives de la Bastille, dossier 11573, year 1745, June 7, 1745. It is difficult to determine precise salary levels because portions of wages were generally given in kind. However, records show that wages tended to oscillate between 8 and 12 sols. For a synthesis and a reflection upon their variations over the eighteenth century, see Gérard Béaur, *Histoire agraire de la France au XVIIIe siècle* (Paris, 2000). There are 20 sols in one livre.
21. Archives de la Bastille, dossier 10697, year 1720.
22. Ibid., dossier 10899, year 1725, July 26, 1725.
23. Ibid., dossier 11885, year 1755, December 21, 1755.
24. Ibid., dossier 11891, year 1755.
25. Ibid., dossier 11273, year 1735, January 24 1735. For examples in Venice, see Patricia Allerston, "Clothing and Early Modern Venetian Society," *Continuity and Change*, 15:3 (2000), pp. 367–90, pp. 377–9.
26. Archives de la Bastille, dossier 11904, year 1755, August 19, 1755.
27. Ibid., dossier 10706, year 1720.
28. Ibid., dossier 10868, year 1725.
29. Mercier, *Tableau de Paris*, vol. 1, chap. CLXVI, p. 392.
30. Jacques Savary des Bruslons, *Dictionnaire universel de commerce, d'histoire naturelle et des Arts et Métiers*, 5 vols. (Copenhagen, 1759), article: revendeur, revendeuse.
31. Roche, *La Culture des apparences*, p. 336.
32. Archives de la Bastille, dossier 10884, year 1725, March 12, 1725.
33. Ibid., dossier 11580, year 1745, October 3, 1745.
34. Ibid., dossier 11898, year 1755, Agust 31, 1755.
35. Ibid., dossier 11911, year 1755, March 31, 1755.
36. Ibid., dossier 11282, year 1735, November 26, 1735.

37. Ibid., dossier 11916, year 1755, June 22, 1755.
38. Ibid., dossier 11899, year 1755, November 16, 1755.
39. Ibid., dossier 11915, year 1755, November 30, 1755.
40. See for England Beverly Lemire, "Peddling Fashion: Salesmen, Pawnbrokers, Tailors, Thieves and the Second-hand Clothes Trade in England, c. 1700–1800," *Textile History*, 22:1 (1991) pp. 67–82, and *Dress, Culture and Commerce: The English Clothing Trade before the Factory, 1660–1800* (London, 1997); also Jeremy Boulton, *Neighbourhood and Society: A London Suburb in the Seventeenth Century* (Cambridge, 1987), pp. 88–90.
41. See Harald Deceulaer, who has provided evidence for this activity in Holland, "Entrepreneurs in the Guilds: Ready-to-wear Clothing and Subcontracting in late Sixteenth- and early Seventeenth-century Antwerp," *Textile History*, 31:2 (2000), pp. 133–149.
42. A.N. BB 18822 Justice Seine et Marne quoted by Richard Cobb, *La Mort est dans Paris* (Paris, 1985) pp. 170–1. I thank Françoise Bayard who drew my attention to this reference.
43. Mercier, *Tableau de Paris*, vol. 2, chap. DLXXVI, pp. 143–4.
44. Patrice Peveri, "Techniques et pratiques du vol dans la pègre du Paris de la Régence d'après les archives du procès de Louis-Dominique Cartouche et de ses complices," Thesis for the École des Hautes Études en Sciences Sociales, 1994.
45. Yvon Marec, *Le "Clou" rouennais des origines à nos jours (1778–1982) du Mont de piété au Crédit municipal. Contribution à l'histoire de la pauvreté en province* (Rouen, 1983), p. 70.
46. J. Necker, *Oeuvres*, vol. II, p. 454, quoted by R. Bigo, p. 117.
47. Bigo, "Aux origines du Mont de Piété parisien," pp. 116–17.
48. J. Necker, *De l'administration des finances de la France* (Paris, 1784), vol. 3, p. 293, quoted by Marec, *Le "Clou" rouennais*, p. 70.
49. Bigo, "Aux origines du Mont de Piété parisien," p. 118.
50. Mercier, *Tableau de Paris*, vol. 1 p. 662–4, chap. CCLXII, article: *Mont-de-piété*.
51. Bigo, "Aux origines du Mont de Piété parisien," p. 121
52. Ibid., p. 124.
53. For England, see the examples in Mélanie Tebutt, *Making Ends Meet. Pawnbroking and Working-class Credit* (London, 1984).
54. Bigo, "Aux origines du Mont de Piété parisien," p. 125.
55. Ibid.
56. Ibid., pp. 122–3.
57. Around 1700, in Paris, 13 percent of domestic servants and 5 percent of wage earners already possessed a watch. This expanded rapidly throughout the eighteenth century and, in the 1780s, 70 percent of inventories of domestics list them and 32 percent of salaried employees (*salariés*). Daniel Roche, *Le Peuple de Paris* (Paris, 1981), p. 226. At one time, it was cheap watches that were being acquired (27.1 percent in 1725 and 17.2 percent in 1785) but the major phenomenon was the lightning growth of gold watches (7.1 percent in 1725 against 54.7 percent in 1785). Jewels follow the same trend and the frequency in the inventories pass from 49.2 percent in 1725 to 78.1 percent in 1785. Cissy Fairchild, "The Production and Marketing of Populuxe Goods in Eighteenth-century Paris," in John Brewer and Roy Porter (eds.), *Consumption and the World of Goods* (London, 1993), pp. 228–48 (230). The drop in the figures for cheaper watches should be taken with a pinch of salt: it could signify simply that they were no longer considered worth entering in the inventories.

6

Uses of the Used

The Conventions of Renewing and Exchanging Goods in French Provincial Aristocracy

Valérie Pietri

In the French *ancien régime* period, resales and exchanges of second-hand goods were vital to economic life. Eighteenth-century economic structures revolved around the circulation and exchange of rare consumer goods (more so, in any case, than in the later industrial and post-industrial consumer cultures). However, this notion of rareness must be thoroughly explored, since evidence of accelerated consumption and renewal of consumer goods, above all during the second half of the eighteenth century, contradicts the hypothesis of a slowdown in productivity. This new mobility was first adopted by the elite, from the court aristocracy to the rural elites, before reaching lower social strata. This pattern continued throughout the early modern period, becoming more conspicuous and extensive over time. It was a movement deeply linked with the evolution of the sociability of the elite, but also determined by the structures of a luxury economy (understood in the broad sense of this term) and the social life of the court. These new practices raised intense debates over the moral value and the consequences of wanting a luxurious life.[1] But even more intense was its influence over the chain of production that depended on luxury-item production and the consumer habits of this trade. The emergence of luxury culture introduced a new kind of relationship to consumer goods. One was supposed not only to buy expensive and distinguishing items, but also to change one's clothes, jewelry and even furniture in order to follow the fashion. So, one had to dispose of not only enough income to incur such expenses, but also the means of sustaining and renewing one's luxury belongings. The mechanisms of this commercial machine have already been explained by Fernand Braudel[2] and Norbert Elias[3] and others have since extended and deepened their analysis.

Our task in this chapter will be to approach these aspects of second-hand commerce from two perspectives. First, we will investigate to what extent this commerce aimed to reduce the cost of distinguishing oneself through consumer habits. Second, we will explore how second-hand trade allowed greater flexibility in responding to the stringent demands of fashion. This approach has been already skillfully elaborated by Daniel Roche in an exemplary study of the culture of appearances – a phenomenon that permeates the history of clothing. But this study has only shed light on the Parisian situation, and the provincial consumption behaviours are still to be explored. In order to develop a comparison with the Parisian case, it is important to remember Roche's main conclusions about the Parisian second-hand economy.

The Parisian second-hand dealers formed a tight network that was under permanent police scrutiny, due to their obvious (and often necessary) ties with criminal groups (clothes thieves were prosperous during the century of the Enlightenment). Yet these same merchants were at the very heart of this archaic but evolving market. It appears that the aristocrats would freely sell and even buy second-hand apparel and clothing. Indeed, Roche found that 12 percent of creditors to the Parisian second-hand dealers market were of aristocratic or clerical background. This figure indicates a heavy involvement of aristocrats in the second-hand trade, although we should note that the second-hand dealers would also sell new items. The Parisian market was unique, due to its sheer size, the range of merchandise available, and the fantastic array of choices it offered buyers and merchants alike.

Research into the roles the aristocratic class played in economic networks has improved steadily, exploring issues such as aristocrats' use of credit and their dealings with merchants involved in the luxury trade.[4] In such a study, it is equally important to establish how much of the domestic budget of aristocratic families was committed to luxury spending. We have therefore chosen to focus on a particular group of aristocratic families from medium and low nobility in the Provence area, selected because of the availability of sources documenting their economic activities.

Aristocratic Consumption and Participation in Second-hand Trade

Studying the second-hand market is made easier by referring to the records of second-hand dealers and retail merchants, even though the use of these records can also be problematic. Such merchants were required to keep account books and *livres de police*,[5] in order for the authorities to keep a close eye on the origin and provision of their coveted merchandise. Yet it must be acknowledged that a large part of this market escaped the attention of the authorities and is thus invisible to historians.[6]

Another approach relies on written evidence recorded in the account books of customers who bought and sold second-hand belongings, and this will be the starting point for our study. Such account books are more haphazard and less consistent than the merchants' ones, but nevertheless provide fresh insights into the second-hand trade. First, we can see how this social group understood and used everyday objects. Second, the accounts reveal the social demands that made second-hand goods necessary. Finally, these documents allow a consideration of the terms "new," "old," and "second-hand" (even though the latter did not appear as such in any records). The most valuable of these sources, for the purposes of this chapter, are the *livres de raison*,[7] which record the income and expenses of households. These books were often incomplete and therefore did not record finances exhaustively. Furthermore, the provision and the quality of the goods in question are often omitted (making it unclear as to whether they are first- or second-hand). Thus, to take the example of clothing, one cannot tell whether different prices for similar items are due to, say the quality of fabric, or rather due to one of the items being second-hand. While such details were seldom recorded for purchases such as furniture and ordinary items of clothing, expensive clothing was often recorded in detail. An elaborate piece, such as a dress or a particular costume, required records indicating which tailor they had been ordered from. Thus we have taken into account only such explicitly documented items in our study, either from the aforementioned sources, or from others such as wills (inheritances composed of this sort of item), post-mortem inventories, or correspondence referring to transactions and/or the destination of family belongings after important events.

Before considering how second-hand items fitted into the domestic economics of the Provence aristocracy, we need to give some indication of the dimensions of aristocratic family fortunes and to point out that the second-hand trade was not the only way to reduce expenses. Despite the fact that the families chosen for the study all belonged to the "small" and "medium" aristocracy, the finances of these families varied greatly. The financial situation of Madame Castellane La Valette, whose fortune as a widow amounted to a mere 4,000 *l*[8] per annum, contrasts sharply with the impressive 100,000 *l* dowry of sir Ricard de Brégançon's daughter. Between these extremes were relatively well-off families such as the Villeneuve de Bargemon family boasting an annual income of 20,000 *l*, or the Chanteraine family with 14,000 *l* per annum, or even the Madeleine de Raimondis family, averaging 11,000 *l* per annum. Despite differences in their revenues, these families all managed their properties stably and remained unafflicted by serious financial problems.

In order to reduce luxury expenses, the provincial aristocrats would resort to an array of *trucs*, or ways of making money.[9] The use of credit was but one of these. They would organize domestic economics to ensure, as far as possible, self-sufficiency and the re-use of goods. The two key areas that were most self-sufficient were food preparation and clothing. Domestic (and therefore female) labor allowed such families to limit their expenses on repairing and styling clothes. Indeed, recorded purchases of low-cost materials are not always followed by a tailor's charge, as these were only incurred when making elaborate clothing from expensive or delicate material. This sort of work complemented the widespread practice of mending and repairing everyday items – which prolonged the life of one's wardrobe – as well as handing down items to younger siblings or servants. Such practices were not limited to clothing; they also allowed families to preserve furniture and various useful items, as well as to restore them to suit the fashion of the day. Saddles belonging to servants, for instance, were often "mended," but so were those of their masters. Also, mattresses were "repaired" and "restuffed" as well as chairs, sofas, settees and other pieces of furniture. The costs of renewing domestic items never equalled that of buying new ones, even though it required the services of specialist craftsmen.[10] Yet these costs were often listed under "mending." For instance, Antoine de Robert[11] successfully limited his clothing expenses by making good use of domestic and professional handcraft.

A close look at Robert's 1718 accounts reveals that his greatest total expense was for raw and semi-finished material, such as string and fabrics (71 *l* 11 *s*). Then came the charges from his tailor (44 *l* 14 *s*), whom he called upon only twice; once for the material of a piece of clothing and the labor cost it incurred (42 *l* 14 *s*), and once for the labour cost of another item (2 *l*). The only finished products in his expenses were shoes (25 *l* 12 *s* total that year) and a handful of items that required highly specialized skills such as buttons (1 *l* 18 *s*), canes (8 *s*), corset stays for his sister (3 *l*), decorative lace (2 *l* 2 *s*), ladies' gloves (14 *s*) and a hat (4 *l* 3 *s*). These last accessories appear as the only ornamental items in the family wardrobe, which was otherwise largely produced and maintained in the home. The rest of the material purchased was largely cloth, such as cotton (9 *s*), wool (6 *l* 12 *s*), silk (1 *l*), *baptiste*[12] (13 *l* 7 *s*) and *toile de Cambrai*[13] (15 *l* 6 *s*). The family was apparently concerned with appearances, but within reason. Furthermore, although it is impossible to determine the precise quantity, much of the material used was actually produced within the house itself. Records contain several mentions of wages paid for wool and hemp spinning (15 *l* 7 *s*, spread into nineteen separate payments), dyeing (6 *l* 5 *s*, in two payments), and even silk preparation (3 *l* 12 *s* "for silk spinning"). Antoine de Robert owned herds of sheep that were bred for wool, but also cultivated hemp (hence the appearance of a 4 *l* 2 *s* payment for hemp seed), and even farmed silkworm.[14] Finally, the accounts mention four payments, during the course of 1718, for shoe repairs.

In addition to using labor in the domestic sphere to improve the family's self-sufficiency, aristocrats would retrieve or reprocess valuable items, which meant participating in a commercial exchange. Thus the "second-hand" market allowed investments in consumer goods to be recycled. Aristocratic families engaged in the second-hand trade with two key concerns: to limit their expenses (and thereby reduce debt), and to respond to the increasing demands of a distinguished consumer culture. Most *livres de raison* omit any mention of such expenses, since few aristocrats recorded them. Out of twenty of these books, only four contain such records, and only two of these were updated daily: Monsieur de Chanteraine's and Madame de Raimondis's (although the latter does not contain her personal expenses). The contents of these books are surprising, as they reveal only ten sales and two purchases of "second-hand" items in fourteen years for Monsieur de Chanteraine,[15] against twelve sales and one purchase over nineteen years for Madame de Raimondis[16] (this book continues until 1789). Our surprise at how infrequently these aristocrats incurred heavy expenses in second-hand goods is outweighed only by that of finding many more sales than purchases. In their dealings with the second-hand market, the Provence aristocrats would apparently sell their belongings freely, but hesitated to purchase, and therefore became suppliers to the second-hand market rather than its customers. This could be explained by any number of factors, notably the concern for displaying new items in one's home to keep up appearances. The Chanteraine family, for instance, bought new items or, when they felt the need to limit their expenses, produced them themselves, as they did their servants' clothing. In fact, receiving clothing from one's employer's family often counted as part of the agreed wages of a servant. Yet shrewdly selling old or used goods was also a way of ensuring one's success in the competitive culture of ostentation, as it allowed a noble house to renew its wardrobes or interior décor. One could exchange old items for new ones by paying the price difference, although this was done more to lower the cost of expensive items rather than to obtain ordinary items cheaply.

However, buying second-hand goods had its limits, as crafted items often had identifiable characteristics, and a fairly closed circle of peers were likely to recognize them. Some second-hand transactions remained unrecorded, as we have already noted. Existing documents suggest that these families quite systematically sold the personal belongings of deceased relatives and occasionally also purchased second-hand items from heirs.

The Belongings of the Deceased

From the point of view of an heir, inherited goods fell into two categories of use, depending on material circumstances (such as the heir's living far away). Some objects were retrieved for personal use, but many chose to sell some or all of these items. The following criteria would strongly influence this choice in favour of sale:

- If the items were deemed useless to the heir.
- If the heir was in financial difficulty and needed to provide for funeral expenses or personal expenses.
- If the heir lived too far away from the deceased for the value of the belongings to make up for the cost of shipping them.

We will look at a set of examples that illustrate these choices, and show that a compromise between selling and retrieving the belongings was most often found.

Most inheritances consisted of material property, which might be described in documents loosely as belongings (*effets*), or more specifically as old clothing (*hardes*), or particular items. However, certain inheritances were specifically bequeathed in view of sale. For instance, monsieur de Raphaelis, a former prior, died on June 17th 1764, leaving his main heir, François de Brun, the responsibility of writing to the senior administration of the Seillans[17] hospital "to take into charge certain belongings, including kitchenware, books, furniture and the old clothing of the deceased, in view of selling them for a total value of 111 *l*."[18] The sale of these items was intended to make up a donation for the poor.

As we have seen, the beneficiaries of wills would sometimes part with their newly inherited items because of their insufficient value, or logistical problems, or financial hardships, or a combination of these difficulties. This was the case in the de Bargemon family. Henri-Pierre-Joseph de Bargemon died in November 1745 in a shipwreck, during a trip from Brest to Toulon. Although his family was by no means struggling financially, his mother, Elizabeth de Flotte d'Agoult, was not opposed to her cousin, Chevalier de Sartoux, selling her son's belongings. She wrote to one of her sons about her decision:" Tell Sartoux to sell your brother's service uniform and any other belongings if he believes it would be profitable to do so."[19] Clearly, the belongings of the deceased relatives were kept only insofar as they were needed, to be used by either family members or other benefactors. Thus aristocratic families were a constant source of merchandise for the second-hand trade, which it is worth noticing, did not always go through professionals. For instance, even though law strictly forbade it, military uniforms were most likely redistributed, sold or handed down within the army.

Although in a different context, the same flexibility of second-hand sales can be seen in Madeleine De Raimondis's willingness to sell her husband's belongings after his death. In a series of different transactions, she sold some of his shirts (142 *l*), his watch (120 *l*), his snuffbox (483 *l*) and even a silver sword hilt (53 *l*), as well as some furniture and horses.[20] As these possessions were of no use to her, their sale allowed her to alleviate financial pressures[21] and, later, even to buy similar items for her son.

In some cases, financial pressures were such that an heir would sell all of the inherited belongings immediately, particularly when the deceased was the family breadwinner or a soldier whose family relied heavily on his pay. Thus in Fréjus, Madame de Flotte d'Agoult, a nun of the Ursuline Sisters, wrote to the bishop of her diocese, on behalf of the widow and daughter of Monsieur de Lisle, requesting that they should receive compensation for the sale of his belongings – particularly his uniform – as he had died serving his king and country : "It would be a great act of generosity for his widow and daughter if your Excellency could have his clothing and personal belongings sold, and the ensuing money safely kept for their benefit."[22] Nevertheless, those who had access to the necessary transport, or who could ask a friend or family member to retrieve inherited goods, often chose to keep them. The belongings of deceased soldiers were frequently returned to their families by close friends or relatives who were in the army themselves.

François de Brun was a wealthy family man, who lived off his private income. In 1736, he received an inheritance from his uncle, Joseph de Brun de Boades, who was an army officer. This consisted of various income-generating investments, but also of some personal items, returned by the beneficiary's brother Dominique, who was also in the army and had been assigned to a post only twenty leagues from their uncle. Dominique brought the following belongings: "An embossed [*gaufrée*] carpet tapestry, ten chairs, an armchair, six pieces of solid silver cutlery, two torches, a salt cellar, two vermilion tankers, two dozen shirts, a salt cellar, over eight dozen sets of table linen, and thirteen table cloths, some of which [were] particularly handsome."[23] Not surprisingly, Dominique chose some small but valuable items, but curiously also selected large, cumbersome valuables (linen, furniture, the tapestry) for their quality. It is worth noticing that François gave his brother a gift of the uncle's "small watch"[24] for his troubles. Indeed, Dominique's own belongings were distributed in like manner after he died of "malignant fever" in 1742. However, the geographical distance from his heir complicated matters. But, once again, a family member took on the responsibility of transporting the goods. This time it was François's brother-in-law, Etienne Dominique de Raimondis, who made the journey. However, he lost a number of Dominique de Brun's possessions to Captain de Savignac, his companion. Savignac claimed the deceased soldier's equipment – including his horse, his mules, his tent and some "small items" – on grounds "that each had promised the other these items, should he survive."[25]

Other beneficiaries were reluctant to sell, despite their distance from the deceased, for fear of losing out in the exchange. This was the case in the de Berghes family. After moving to Provence, a branch of the family stayed in touch with their relatives via the canoness of the Maubeuge Chapter, who was part of the family herself. Upon the death of the canoness's brother, baron Claude-François de Berghes, his belongings went to his nephews, as he had no children of his own. Thus the canoness offered their mother to sell the newly acquired belongings – which she claimed were of little worth.[26] As her nephews were undecided as to what to do with them, she wrote once again to the Provence branch of the family, to give some details of the post-mortem inventory and ask once again for a decision. She added: "My nephews are to make arrangements with you, should they want to keep it.[27] If so, I shall have to find a mean of sending it to them, along with any other important furniture, notwithstanding the large distance that separates us."[28] Madame de Berghes conveyed the children's wish to have the objects sent to them, in spite of the canoness's reservations regarding the cost and complications of doing this ("be aware that you will have to pay for transport from here to Dunkerque, and also the boat shipment"[29]). But the de Berghes family was well-versed in disputes over inheritances, and went ahead with the shipment all the same. Thus the canoness made an initial shipment of those objects that were valuable but not cumbersome. But, wary of Madame de Berghes's determination, she added, "should you decide to sell [the remaining items], be sure to inform me, and I will supervise their sale and send you detailed accounts of any profits made."[30]

While our records indicate many sales and shipments of the belongings of deceased relatives, traces of their purchase are less frequent and rarely indicate the name or the title of the buyer. However, the following two transactions allow us to trace the buyers' names. The first was the purchase of a dress belonging to Madame Ricard de Brécançon, after her death in 1731. It was in

1733 that her husband, Louis Hercule de Ricard, recorded the proceeds of this sale under his father's name. The buyer was the Marquise de Boutassy de Chateaulard. It was a singular item described as: "A cherry-red velvet costume, entirely new, which madame de Brégançon had fashioned for her own use, and never wore. It had even [remained] in the care of her seamstress."[31] The marquise recorded that Monsieur de Ricard (the father) had stated (at his son's request) "that the suit had cost 212 *l* and he would not settle for a penny less." Without dwelling upon the reasons for this statement, we focus our attention on the exceptional circumstances of this transaction, as it was a second-hand sale of a new item, priced on a par with commercial, new-item sales. Assuming the marquise's statements are reliable, the only credible explanation would be that – as she suggests – she had seen and taken a liking to the piece on a visit to her tailor and decided to purchase it at its original price, when she found out who had ordered it. Thus she treated it as if she had placed the order herself, and knew it was safe to do so as it had never been worn (this was clearly a decisive factor).

In another example drawn from our documents, the purchase of the used belongings of a deceased aristocrat involved women's clothing, but also some furniture. A 1781 transaction appears in a *livre de raison* belonging to Elizabeth de Castellane La Valette. She notes that she bought a number of items belonging to a certain Madame du Fresnay, notably seven dresses and their matching aprons. This was done through an impoverished relative, referred to as "la demoiselle Marianne." In contrast to the ambiguity in some of our previous examples, these objects are clearly second-hand, having both belonged to and been used by another person (such as the "old black dress" bought for 42 *l*). This is confirmed by their low price when compared to new items, as many dresses went for approx 45 *l* and settees for 20 *l*. Madame de Castellane La Valette was in need of such a bargain and, as can be seen through her resourceful management of family finances, it was necessary to maintain her social status under the conditions. We can assume that she intended to display these items publicly, without fearing for her reputation, as Madame du Fresnay was (according to our research) apparently not Provençal, and thus her belongings were not identifiable. In addition, Madame de Castellane La Valette was a widow and probably had a limited social life.

The Many Lives of Valuable Items

Luxury goods such as jewelry and silverware were created, and therefore exchanged, differently from other belongings. This specifically can be explained by their use as reserves of capital, but also by the relative ease of making the old appear new.

Selling one's silverware was not exclusively a case of using a financial backup to meet a pressing need for cash. Such sales also involved exchanging one's used silverware for new pieces, to renew one's collection. This was facilitated by the nature of valuable metals, as they were measured by weight rather than by the quality of each individual piece. One example appears in the *livre de raison* of Elisabeth de Castellane La Valette. She mentions a sale of silver pieces:

> I was left silver cutlery from my mother-in-law's collection, which was very old indeed, and out of use. This I sold at 50 *l* per mark, totaling 222 *l* 10 *s*. I used the money to replace the candle-rings of the chandeliers, some candleholders and snuffers, as well as two soup spoons. This amounted to 225 *l* and 10 *s*, and I paid a further 3 *l* to have the items engraved.[32]

A second illustration of replacing silverware is mentioned in the *livre de raison* of Monsieur de Chanteraine, who noted in 1787: "Receipt from Aubert the goldsmith, for selling kitchenware and a gold chain, amounting to ten *naves*[33] three ounces of silver for 522 *l*, plus 648 *l* for the gold chain. With this I bought a dozen silver-handled knives at 156 *l*. The net amount left over was 492 *l*."[34]

Jewelry was also frequently exchanged, since stones could be retrieved and re-used in different settings when necessary. But this practice contained risks, as their ostentatious role meant that jewels could be recognized and thus could ridicule their second owner. The risk was even bigger when exposed to the higher strata of society for it was a very demanding background regarding appearances. There was no room for approximation in Parisian high society, which had its own rules on that peculiar matter, as the provincial aristocracy often learned at its expenses. Parisian and provincial were not separate worlds and any aristocrat would be concerned about his reputation in both places as one interferes deeply with the other. The following example suggests that the compromise solutions accepted in provincial aristocracy were not so easily tolerated in Paris, and one would have to increase drastically one's ostentatious spending to enter Parisian society without incurring mockery and despite. However, the mechanism remains the same : one could use second-hand items as long as nobody was able to notice.

One of the most *apparent* families in Aix, the de Brégançon, made its mark in the eighteenth century by marrying a daughter to the Vicomte de Narbonne-Pellet.[35] The new bride was presented to the Parisian court, and made her debut in Parisian high society shortly after her marriage. An embarrassing episode of this new social life illustrates the intense scrutiny and the vital social function of jewelry in family affairs, but also how heavily it depended on inheritance. From this point of view, even dowries could be seen as a form of second-hand trade.

Madame de Ricard De Bérulle, an outstanding Parisian aristocrat, wrote to her cousin Madame de Ricard De Brégançon in March 1761 to give news of her daughter, the new Vicomtesse de Narbonne. But this letter also contained critical undertones, sparking off what became known as the "diamond affair":

> As all other wives own precious diamonds and are well able to recognize their value, I thought it best to lend your daughter some of my own for her visits to such houses, and keep her own to adorn her hair, as I feared she would be mocked should their real value be noticed ... For having shown them to various jewelers ... all estimated their value between 1,300 and 1,500 *l*, and Lempereur[36] advised me

that their sale would reach nothing exceeding 1,200 *l*. The jeweler himself could not sell them for more than 1,500 *l* as the larger diamonds are roses, the others are semi-brilliant (some of them are not even of this quality), and concluded that the stones of the earrings were forged out of diamonds from Maltese crosses or the like."[37]

The concerns expressed by Madame de Ricard de Bérulle, over what she regarded as a threat to the good reputation of her family in an astute and unforgiving Parisian high society, ultimately cost Madame de Brégançon dearly. Adding insult to injury, the letter betrays a certain smugness regarding the Parisian eye for quality jewels, clearly more discerning than that of aristocratic counterparts in provincial France. Madame de Brégançon had little choice but to send a stinging 3,000 *l* in cash to compensate for her blunder, for the in-laws to order some "pretty earrings" from a jeweler for her daughter. In that case, the problem was not the fact that Madame de Brégançon had given second-hand jewelry for her daughter's dowry, even though her cousin perfidiously noticed it. The problem was that the diamonds had been over estimated at the expense of the Vicomte de Narbonne, and surely Madame de Ricard de Bérulle had set up an agreement with the young couple to get some money from the thrifty Madame de Brégançon. However, the letter of Madame de Ricard de Bérulle demonstrates that jewelry could easily be renewed to supply the second-hand trade, since precious stones could easily get new settings and precious metal could always be turned into other shapes or sold to be melted down.

Valuable second-hand goods probably were exchanged regularly in the contents of dowries, even though most marriage contracts do not include details of the contents of "everyday clothing (*hardes*), chests, and jewelry," and therefore prevent any definitive conclusions regarding the handing down of a family's valuables.

Conclusion

French aristocrats were heavily involved in the second-hand market because it provided valuable resources with which to face the challenges of increasing social pressures, both from competition within the aristocracy, but also from aristocrats' increasing need to distinguish themselves from members of other classes. Expectations that one would renew one's clothing and interior décor became stronger during the eighteenth century due to the ruthless demands of fashion. This forced certain provincial aristocratic families to be more resourceful in their financial management, and thus explains why they turned to the second-hand trade. But, even though this market became an important means for them to sell their used goods, these families rarely bought second-hand goods. This is especially clear in a context of widespread use of credit in aristocratic purchasing habits. Second-hand sales represented an indirect financial resource that allowed aristocrats to get rid of items that had become redundant, and thus to acquire new belongings that suited newer tastes and fashions. Buying second-hand, however, meant risking one's prestige, as it might be possible for visitors to identify the items.

This analysis has also revealed some surprises as to how Provençal aristocrats viewed their luxury belongings, beyond their actual value. Many had no qualms about getting rid of family possessions, even when there was no pressing financial need to do so. The main criterion that determined what would be kept and what would be sold was apparently the utility of the items or, rather, their usefulness. Thus, despite a climate of abundance, the *ancien régime* was little different from earlier periods of French history, in which deprivation was a much greater decision factor than nostalgia in such matters. The almost total absence of signs of sentimental attachment to objects only confirms this view. Indeed, practical concerns often determined the fate even of an aristocratic family's emblazoned valuables, such as silverware, despite the romantic picture painted by nineteenth-century aristocrats. Although silverware played a vital role in the ostentatious *mise en scène* of a family's prestige, wealth, power and tradition, it was readily sold by weight to provide newer items, which would be emblazoned in turn. It was therefore not their authenticity that determined their value, but rather their usefulness in the midst of an unforgiving competition to display ostentation and to keep up appearances.

Translated from the French by David Kelly

Notes

1   Beginning toward the end of the seventeenth century, intense debates arose over luxury in France. On one side, some thought that luxury was corrupting French society (Boulainvilliers, Beauvillier, Saint-Simon and Fénelon). On another side, some claimed that luxury stimulated productivity and creativity (Boisguilbert, Mandeville, Cantillon and Voltaire).

2   Fernand Braudel, *Civilisation matérielle, économie et capitalisme, XVe–XVIIIe siècle*, 3 vols. (Paris, 1979), vol. I, pp. 229–90.

3   Norbet Elias, *La Société de cour* (Paris, 1985), pp. 47–61.

4   Natacha Coquery, *L'Hôtel aristocratique: le marché du luxe à Paris au XVIIIe siècle* (Paris, 1998).

5   Second-hand dealers had to note down in a special register, referred to as a *livre de police*, the price of items they bought and sold, the name, condition and adress of sellers in order to prevent traffic of stolen goods. These registers were controlled by the police.

6   Daniel Roche, *La Culture des apparences. Une histoire du vêtement, XVIIe–XVIIIe siècle* (Paris, 1989), pp. 313–45.

7   *Livres de raison* are account books (in latin *liber rationum*) held by the head of the family. Some of them only register expenses, some are much more detailed and register family events like birth, wedding, death, trials, etc.

8   Note on the translation: the currency at this time was split into "livres" and "sols," which we have indicated on amounts quoted here as *l* and *s* (e.g., 12 *l* 4 *s* = 12 livres and 4 sols).

1 livre = 20 sols; 1 sol = 12 deniers. As a comparison for prices of items mentioned in this chapter, the current price for 1,5 pound of bread is 3 sols.

9   This term is used in a precise sense by Michel de Certeau in his different writings, such as *L'Invention du quotidien* (Paris, 1980).

10 Draguignan Municipal Library [hereafter BMD], M 213. A saddle that was bought for 50 *l* was "mended" for 5 *l*.

11 Archives Départementales des Alpes-Maritimes [hereafter ADAM], 1 E 24/3, *Livre de raison*.

12 Very thin linen cloth.

13 Kind of cloth made in Cambrai.

14 ADAM, 1 E 24/3. Correspondence regarding his business.

15 ADAM, 9 J 2.

16 BMD, M 213.

17 Seillans is a small village in Provence, near by Fayence and Cannes.

18 BMD, M 142, François de Brun's *livre de raison*, f°127.

19 Archives Départementales du Var [hereafter ADV], 23 J 16, letter on December 2, 1745.

20 BMD, M 213.

21 Much of her income was unpredictable, certain sources being vulnerable to a sudden crisis, such as her farming business. This explains why the sale of the wheat of Canaux was exceptionally bad in 1783 and 1786, and brought in fairly low profits in 1777 and 1779. Thus Madame de Raimondis sold her husband's watch and some of his belongings in 1781, and the sword hilt and the snuffbox, later in 1783.

22 ADV, 23 J 15, letter on December 14, 1714.

23 BMD, M 142.

24 Ibid., f°3.

25 Ibid., f°25.

26 ADV, 2 J 79, letter on June 25, 1768.

27 This refers to a piece of cloth the baron had ordered just before his death. The Canoness equally mentions silverware the baron had entrusted to a certain Madame de Gersy, which was to be added to the inventory.

28 ADV, 2 J 79. Undated letter.

29 Ibid. Letter on March 30, 1769.

30 Ibid.

31 ADV, 1 J 190, *Réquisition* [request for payment] from Louis Hercule de Ricard and *Declaration* of Marchioness of Boutassy de Chateaulard, June 5, 1743.

32 ADV, 1 J 236, Elisabeth-Antoinette de Gravier's *livre de raison* (widow of François de Castellane-la-Valette).

33 Measure for precious metals.

34 ADAM, 9 J 2, Monsieur de Chanteraine's *livre de raison*.

35 Mademoiselle de Ricard received a dowry of 100,000 *l*, which is an indication of the family's fortune and its importance in Provençal high society.

36 Lempereur was the name of a Parisian jeweler.

37 ADV, 1 J 190, letter on March 10, 1761.

7

The Scope and Structure of the Nineteenth-century Second-hand Trade in the Parisian Clothes Market

Manuel Charpy

Although the second-hand market affects all other areas of nineteenth-century trade, and appears frequently in analyses of consumption of this period,[1] a study of this market has not been conducted to date. The absence of research in this area comes as a surprise considering it allows valuable reading of consumer habits which can (a) go beyond the usual questions of what was fashionable and unfashionable, and (b) avoid conflating consumption with production in this area. Among the many sub-areas of trade, the clothes market is a choice category for such a study because it thrived in the very heart of nineteenth century commercial and social life, but also because it is valuable in documenting nineteenth-century trade more generally. Beneath the romantic picture of the second-hand market as a lower-price alternative trade that nestled amongst the branches of mainstream commerce, a number of questions remain regarding the different roles of the used-goods market. Its relationship with mainstream commerce and its innovations remain unexplored. Also, considering the supply routes available to distributors at the time, studying this market helps a wider understanding of the conventions of purchase, sale and use of consumer goods. And, lastly, casting light upon the specific nineteenth-century boundaries between first- and second-hand goods yields valuable insights on how the production of material goods was experienced and understood during this century.

It is beyond the scope of this chapter to trace the evolution of such production and how it was perceived at the time. However, reconstructing a model of the flows, displacements and changes in the destinations of its merchandise is an achievable and worthwhile project, even if it is only to single out and study these three threads from amongst the intricate sinews of consumer culture.

An Outline of Second-hand Trade

A Mixed Trade

The peddler is a crucial figure in any picture of nineteenth-century Parisian streets. He is always shown laden with old and tattered clothing, pieces left over from military uniforms and a selection of random curios. A series of wooden engravings called *Cris de Paris* represented well the archaic and obsolete nature of this profession. Such salesmen were later perceived as romantic figures of a bygone era, or even emblems of the political and social instability of the end of the century, and thus highlight the hiatus between this trade and mainstream commerce.[2]

Despite the renewal of literary interest in the iconographic figure of the peddler in recent years, it is difficult to get an accurate picture of the structure of this market. Indeed, their business took place outside of shops and they dealt in negligible sums of money. Also, they were unable to work in the same place for any length of time, due to legal constraints. Only a small number of them were awarded the status of *brocanteur d'habits ambulant*.[3] The main reason for engaging in this unrewarding trade was probably the low cost of setting it up. Commercial and legal archives record surprisingly few of them as professionals. Just as Jean-Clément Martin said of the second-hand salespersons of Niort, these Parisian merchants appeared to be "below bankruptcy." They were almost never bankrupt, and even more rarely in credit.[4] Their relative absence from archives suggests it was an informal and precarious trade, cast out to the fringes of mainstream commerce.

Women also participated in second-hand trade, as *marchandes à la toilette*[5] and – as distinct from the men – were sometimes the object of administrative procedures. For instance, a widow named Mme Fernel who traded on Rue Fontaines-du-Temple went bankrupt in 1850 because of a mere 299 francs debt, which was not covered by the 191 francs' worth of merchandise seized.[6] This consisted of a random selection of old clothes and accessories, indistinguishable from her own belongings. Indeed, it is even more difficult to draw conclusions from such examples because of this closeness between personal and professional life; this situation can be seen in many such professionals. In 1850 there were at least fifteen such merchants within the Paris city walls, constituting a tight web of small markets. Despite the fact that their trade appeared less haphazard, stocks were low quality and poorly organized. The second-hand market in Carreau Beauveau-Saint-Antoine was described as a "collection of haphazard rags and old clothes."[7] At the beginning of the July Monarchy the Notre-Dame market was compared to a "sale of old laundry and ragbags."[8] In 1837, the Carmes market was said to consist of "piles of old rags," and forty years on was still known as an "accumulation of used rags and bric-a-brac too despicable to be named."[9] However, in 1835 the Temple market had 1550 merchants and was considered quaintly attractive for its dishevelled charm, which fascinates historians still today.[10] An article in *L'Illustration* portrays filthy, rodent-ridden market stalls of incongruous second-hand items.[11] This portrayal was to contribute strongly to nineteenth-century literature, engraving it into posterity. Such observers of the second-hand market describe it as a closed community of back-stabbing swindlers and conmen. Associated with impressions of the merchandise available at these markets, these representations of the trade foreshadowed its generally unstable and untenable nature.

But, while the literature suggests that contemporaries already appreciated the quaint charm of door-to-door sales, the reality of a key network of second-hand commerce remains under a cloud. Indeed, a web of small second-hand shops – as portrayed in Atget's *fin-de-siècle* collection[12] – constituted a peculiar trade indeed. Records of merchandise seized by legal institutions suggest that these shops often dealt in second-hand trade as an alternative to their main trade, often intermingled with their stated activity. To give a few examples of this, Mr. Mazuit's shop in Gros-Caillou boasted "fifty kilogrammes of old laundry," but also "brass pottery" and ironwork of sorts, and even "odd tools and kitchenware."[13] Another such example can be found in the rooms that Mr. Chamalet rented to builders on Rue de la Croix-Nivert, from which he sold clothes ranging from long coats to skirts, but also shoes and some tailor-made items including used shoes.[14] This recipe of stocking haphazard merchandise in shops offering other services – mostly yielding poor results – was used by many shopkeepers in working-class areas of Paris.

The nature of this commerce, together with the conditions it thrived in, made it a useful fallback trade, which was convenient as it went mostly unheeded and unhindered by administration, avoiding unwanted formalities.

The Common Structure(s) of a Disparate Trade

Yet, despite the relative lack of control over second-hand trade, photographic investigation by the Union Photographique Française[15] shows what appears as an entirely different facet of the trade. One photograph shows a certain Mr. Blancard's shop sign, bearing the following inscription: "This shop was founded in 1855. Best deals, wide selection of merchandise, and low prices." Further investigation reveals a more up-market commerce. These photographs show tidily presented racks and stacked items, a picture that hardly fits those of the bric-a-brac of street sales, as mentioned above. This intriguing new picture is best illustrated in the École-de-Médecine area. This neighborhood boasted fifty shops by 1860, and is thus a good starting point to further investigate this facet of the second-hand clothes market. As distinct from the rough-and-ready *friperies* (second-hand clothes shops) mentioned earlier, we find records of shops such as Mme Leroy's in Rue Monsieur le Prince, where the clothes on sale include "woolen trousers, ordinary or pressed," "ladies' pressed-wool jackets, and light summer cloth" and "tunics of the National Guard." After her death in 1849 her stock was evaluated at 2,142 francs, as the clothes were in good condition. Added to this, her shop contained "an oak counter," "four chairs made of cherry wood and stuffed with straw, each bearing a small mirror in its painted woodwork," as well as the "shelves and woodwork" all along the walls of the shop, which composed the working furniture necessary to her trade.[16] Mr. and Mrs. Leroy took out a commercial lease "of significant worth" which, at the time of the legal inventory had "still several years to run." They also invested substantially to set up and decorate their shop. Records of stocks in the shop at the point of Mme Leroy's death cast light on two key aspects of the shop-based second-hand trade.

Firstly, this type of commerce was aimed at specific markets, notably the local builders and craftspeople. The phenomenon of specialization explains both the narrow range of merchandise found in these shops, and the widely diffused advertisements and prospectuses such as appeared during the July Monarchy. Thus, in the Temple neighborhood, Mr. Giroult began to specialize in "uniforms for the National Guard and firemen" in 1840.[17] Neighboring this shop were others that specialized in children's clothing, ladies' wear or funeral dress. Mme Duval's case is even more representative of this phenomenon. She was a widow whose shop was saved from bankruptcy through such specialization. At the end of the 1840s, she was still struggling to get by with a jumble of random items, but then reorganized the shop to focus on children's clothing and funeral garments at the beginning of Napoleon's Second Empire. It grew substantially from this point onwards, and became an increasingly successful commerce. Thus specialization became a necessary path for any shop that aspired to financial success and aimed to secure its survival.

The second key factor in this new type of trade was the choice of merchandise. The Leroys' thorough accounts reveal that their stocks were carefully and coherently selected, composed of consecutive sets of identical items. Peddlers, street merchants and less organized second-hand retail outlets did, however, stock single pieces of clothing, depending on what they happened to come by. This unplanned composition of stocks contrasted strongly with the series of identical items into which more prosperous shops organized their commerce.

As well as specialization of trade and choice of stocks, investment in facilities and property value is key to a thorough understanding of this branch of the trade. Once again, the descriptions of the Leroys' shop arouse our attention. Records indicate that while some neighboring shops were set up in run-down buildings, often rented without a lease, others were well established in respectable properties, and built up a solid reputation with local inhabitants. Mr. Lesoudier was another one of these merchants, who by 1852 owned seven outlets, three of which were rented to other shopkeepers. His own residence was an opulent apartment with several bedrooms, a living room, a dining hall and a boudoir, which he then left for a more modern residence on Place Saint-Michel. The closeness of this residence to his shops clearly shows that he was well established amongst entrepreneurs and managers. His well-run shops all gave on to Rue de l'École-de-Médecine,[18] which again confirms his reputable status, notably for the students. At number 23 on the same street, Mr. Leroussel contracted an eighteen year lease and was paying 3,000 francs rent, as well as 1,150 francs in licensing fees; more than most new-item retailers had to pay for their shops. Some second-hand shop owners would even take out substantial loans from banks or legal offices in order to finance a new shop,[19] such as Legrain who borrowed from the Sinet[20] bank in 1854. Descriptions of property claimed by legal offices, taken from post-mortem inventories, contain items such as mahogany desks, gas-powered appliances and tall-framed mirrors, which suggests that the quality of furniture and decoration demanded substantial investment.

The second-hand clothing trade was threatened by social and professional pressures, as can be seen in the variety of illustrations mentioned earlier, to the point that it hardly even rates as a professional category. Even those merchants whose revenue was fairly stable were increasingly under the threat of bankruptcy. While some were due to minor problems, economic crisis was the main cause, just as it was for other trades. Second-hand commerce did not feed off the closure of powerful industry, but actually suffered as a result, notably during the mid-nineteenth-century period.[21] They even fed into mainstream trade, providing substantial employment such as Lesoudier (mentioned above) did, employing ten workers. Of the 1,150 employees on record in Temple in 1847, 864 were non family members. Only sixty-five of these shops were run by the owner only, while 112 had a single employee, and ninetythree hired between two and ten personnel. One second-hand business is recorded to have had ten legally declared workers,[22] showing it was possible to establish oneself in a comfortable social position from within this trade. Thus, within second-hand commerce, the combination of specialization, stock management, investment in property, furniture and decoration, and workforce management challenges our earlier picture of a frail profession, thriving on the borders of mainstream commerce.

Provisioning the Market

If qualifying the exchange of goods is generally a risky business, it is all the more so here, even if one is to work with general estimates. We can, however, find clues as to the frequency of sales. The legal clerk who drew up the inventory for Mrs. Leroy's stocks after her death in 1849 noted that "as her husband took over ... sales increased and stocks were entirely renewed."[23] These sales totaled approximately 350 pieces sold within a month. Mr. Vachon in Belleville, in the same situation, declared having sold one-third of his stock for over 1,000 francs in only three weeks.[24] The clothing appearing on records of legal appraisals varied according to the season. The evidence suggests that stocks were renewed all the more quickly as merchandise was inexpensive. Quite resistant therefore to the whims of market forces, the second-hand market had a safety net of regular and substantial supply. The sheer bulk of merchandise required to supply 300 to 400 shops as well as thousands of market stalls, leads to the question as to how such supply was possible. Indeed, the explanations given by moralists of the day (and even upheld by some of today's historians) – i.e. theft, smuggling and bootlegging – leave much to be desired.[25]

The importance given to the uniform in legal records and advertisements, and more generally in nineteenth-century social life calls for further investigation of supply routes. Posters advertising uniform auctions appeared from the early Restoration period. These were supervised and organized by military officials, and offered mostly reworked military clothing and the belongings of deceased patients, retrieved from military hospitals. To name but some of these items: "Hungarian-style shako caps" [*Coëffe de Schako*], cloaks, robes, jackets, woolen and pressed-wool trousers, shirts, boots, clogs, gaiters, policemen's hats, shoulder pads, knapsacks, etc.,"[26] as well as reworked military clothing, and belongings of deceased military hospital patients. The records of the Administration of Military Property (les Domaines Militaires) give the names Lamouroux, Verdreau, Brière, Legot and Fauché as second-hand bulk retailers owning large stocks of military clothing. Although his was only a medium-sized commerce, Lamouroux swept up 2,000 francs' worth of merchandise in a single transaction. Furthermore, his business totaled 15,000 items bought between 1825 and 1831.[27] All of the above shop managers had enough disposable capital to raise funds to the same level as their counterparts in new-item commerce would. They could also pay suppliers in cash upon delivery. And, finally, they were all wholesale dealers; none of them dealt in single-item retail. Sales to single-item retailers were conducted in open auctions.

Only a small number of uniforms were resold as they were initially used; most were altered for civilian use. In 1850 the quartermaster issued the following statement: "Disused uniforms and items therefrom may be sold by the appointed auctioneer [*le commissaire-priseur*], on condition that the following alterations are made to tunics: rows of buttons must be removed from all corsets, and sleeves cut to clothing-level."[28] Such uniforms could be found on the market to be worn as ordinary jackets, often dyed or otherwise altered according to fashion. Unlike street merchants selling chance items of uniform, shop owners such as Giroult would offer full sets of National Guard dress or firemen's uniforms. Others would recycle them as everyday wear, or for work purposes, such as "stagecoach-drivers' headwear."[29] Some used them for ceremonial dress,[30] or, imitating those of prestigious military figures, used them as stage costumes. Some shop owners provided theaters, history players and circuses with military uniforms "to represent any European army,"[31] as Fortin and later Garnier did. Thus the military ensured a constant supply of uniforms to second-hand clothes sales. But of course uniforms were not the only type of clothing that fueled this trade.

Bulk retailers found they could come by large quantities of clothing for civilian use in voluntary and legal auctions, conducted by small shopkeepers who had declared bankruptcy or needed to liquidate stock. These sales were held in hotels or private residences and took place weekly following advertisements in posters and in *Petites Affiches*[32] and wholesale dealers were the main buyers.[33] The next most important sales after these were in the Mont-de-Piété district, where stocks mostly came from warranty that had been secured by legal offices. Indeed, second-hand wholesale dealers were dominant buyers, to the point that they were complained of for taking over the auctions.[34] From shawls to smocks, and even full wardrobes of clothing, selling one's clothes became common practice, totaling 60 percent of deposed items.[35] In 1883 – which was a bad year for clothes sales – over 110,000 items were sold. Again, the military provided the bulk of second-hand wear, but hospitals also organized sales at the end of each season of the year, providing huge quantities of dead people's clothes unclaimed by their families.[36] During the July Monarchy these sales gathered huge numbers of clothes merchants, bulk and retail dealers alike.[37] Substantial sales were also organized by customs offices and hospices.[38]

Lastly, from the early 1830s the new-item trade and production industry also provided a share of merchandise, composed mostly of outmoded clothing, items damaged after floods or fires, and faulty pieces. Thousands of items also came on to the second-hand market after a department store (*Grand Magasin*) shut down or went bankrupt. In such cases, "Messrs wholesale clothes retailers and salespersons" were given first choice.[39] Given the quantities the organizers hoped to sell, these retailers were the only customers who could buy such large quantities, and thus ensure a complete sell out. However, the stocks provided in such sales in Paris alone did not satisfy Parisian demand. If the second-hand market began to run dry, retailers would have to "scour every neighbourhood in the capital," and even "attend public sales within or without the capital" in order to come by "second-hand merchandise," as twenty-seven shop owners in Temple noted in an 1842 petition to the *Préfet de Paris* (Parisian police central authority).[40]

The categorization of merchants into bulk, semi-bulk and single-item sale, enabled specialization amongst second-hand merchants. With each transaction, quality merchandise would be filtered out, which explains the mediocrity of goods at the bottom of the scale. This gradual discrimination of merchandise also meant that the stocks of the wealthiest retailers only required minor finishings in preparation for sale. Rather than doing it themselves, they subcontracted it to seamstresses and dry cleaners. This we know from their financial records, but it also shows in the concentration of these subcontracted trades in the vicinity of second-hand shops. Shopkeepers kept repairs to a minimum, as distinct from peddlers or *fripiers ravaudeurs*,[41] and thus their trade was much closer to that of the mainstream shopkeeper than the craftsman.

Scale and Scope of Second-hand Commerce

At first glance, second-hand trade appears to operate on a small scale, providing salespersons with hardly enough income to get by, thriving in any available space, and mostly relying on regular customers. So it is unsurprising to note that it was "a widespread habit amongst second-hand salesmen to do business at the local wine merchant's or tavern."[42] The police were issued with several requests to ban such commerce, "in wine merchants' houses and other such establishments."[43] Thus it becomes clear that clothes sales were commonplace in centers of sociability.

Marchandes à la toilette, whom we know better from literature, also worked in such limited spaces. A widow by the name of Delparte, whose commercial debts were almost all accrued within the street she worked from, is a good example of this. Her clientele was "composed only of customers from within the neighborhood."[44] Similarly to local market stallholders and small shop owners all around Paris, they did not dispose of the sort of income that advertisement or transport required. Their trade was therefore tightly woven into the social fabric of everyday economic life (in local markets and small shops).

However, this reading passes over some of the complexities that need to be addressed here. Reputable centers of second-hand trade attracted customers from all over Paris. Several of these could be found in Temple and École-de-Médecine. For instance, in 1832 Mr. Nadaud was looking for a set of clothes to be presentable for his return to his country home. He naturally went looking for them in the Temple area,[45] just as others would cross the city to École-de-Médecine for their clothes. Second-hand commerce was thus a landscape of small shops over which a handful of key shopping areas towered conspicuously. A journalist from *Le Figaro* noted in an 1857 report on shops in Temple that "nearly all shops carry the sign: Shipments Outside Paris and Abroad Available."[46] True enough, these merchants maintained close ties with their countrywide clientele. Mr. Giroult, for instance, held work papers[47] stating he "trades with the local administration offices of small communes across France, providing inexpensive uniforms for their National Guard."[48] Many others held a similar status, and some wealthier merchants even owned transportation facilities such as Mr. Garnier's "two oxen," "four chests" and "three white wooden weather protection hoods," all of which allowed him to deliver to customers inside and outside Paris.[49] Thus surplus stocks in the capital could be sold across the country, or clothes brought into the Paris market, according to where demand was strong. Furthermore, Paris was a key marketplace for international trade in clothing. Indeed, the aforementioned shop signs for sales across France and abroad require that we look beyond French borders for an adequate understanding of the second-hand Parisian trade.

In 1849, Faustin I of Haiti was made emperor and thus decided to put together a national guard. However, the funds available to him were insufficient to provide this new force with uniforms, so he sought the necessary clothing in the Parisian second-hand clothing market. This provided many a story for newspapers, which relished the caricature of "Negroes in regimental pomp," dressed in French uniforms.[50] Less concerned about these unusual appearances, Guillaumin saw it as a sign of the economic importance of this trade, in his *Dictionary of Commerce and Navigation*, writing that "Export allows the sale of a great many used uniforms, some of which are in pristine condition; this explains how 200,000 National Guard tunics – made available after the tragic events of December 2 – were sold in Brazil and Saint-Domingue [the Dominican Republic]. These provided Emperor Soulouque

[Faustin]'s guard of honour with our light infantry uniform."[51] Accountancy books retrieved from shops that stocked these uniforms record the 1848 reform whereby many uniforms were introduced into the second-hand circuit.[52] French exports of all types of old clothing were commonplace and regular, and therefore cannot be explained; hence these sudden releases of large quantities of clothing on to the markets cannot be explained by military events alone. For the newly founded South American countries, an impressive number of second-hand clothes came from France; the *Tableau général du commerce*[53] (a study conducted by customs administration) gives a clear overview of this international exchange. In order to issue the documents necessary for administrative and tax purposes, the category of "old or worn clothing" was created in 1834. It disappeared only in the late 1870s, when international exchange had suffered overall and frontier control administration was undergoing heavy reform. Going by the official figures – which were most likely grossly underestimated as second-hand and new merchandise were difficult to distinguish from one another – total export of second-hand clothing is shown to have increased from 50 tonnes in 1834 to 500 tonnes in 1848. The later figures match those of the new-item export in the same year. Export figures reached 1,260 tonnes in 1854, reaching a record 1,838 tonnes in 1867, and then dropped steadily afterwards. In 1877 figures were still reaching 1,109 tonnes, which suggests the trade still thrived during the *fin-de-siècle* period, despite its inextricability from the tailor-made clothing trade. The sheer bulk of merchandise available, as well as the high profitability of second-hand clothes commerce, suggests that it was ideally suited to international trade. Paris – as a marketplace for used clothing from all across Europe – was a stronghold of this international commerce.

Export was mostly geared toward industrialized or industrializing markets. These ranged from Western European countries to Sardinian States to Hanseatic cities, and not least, countries neighboring France, which absorbed over 60 percent of all clothing exported. Only 10 percent went to other European countries (including Russia), Latin America and the Atlantic coast of the USA. North Africa and Senegal only appeared as buyers during the early July Monarchy. Whereas the quantities exported were near-negligible in 1839, they increased steadily thanks of to new markets opening, such as Algeria, which alone absorbed 5 percent of total trade in 1860. India appears as the smallest of these markets in the 1830s, to be replaced only in this position by China and Japan thirty years later, all of which imported negligible quantities of clothing. This international dimension of used-clothes sales highlights the ability of Parisian merchants to build a widespread reputation and organize long-distance transport of merchandise. Although it consisted of both civilian and military clothing, it is near impossible to determine with any certainty which customers these clothes were meant for, or their uses in each country. However, Latin American populations appeared to have a strong demand for uniforms, so by contrast it can be inferred that Sardinian States, Belgium and Switzerland imported only civilian wear. Either way, the second-hand economy developed by approximately 90 percent, mirroring a similar increase in the imports of manufactured and tailor-made new items. Both clothes trades shared the same channels for transportation and sales, and were more generally interwoven in international commerce.[54]

From our earlier study of the trade of reworked uniforms, we have uncovered a market that extended and organized itself as an intra-national and international sales network. This gives a clear indication of the scale of transformations in nineteenth-century society and economic life.

Advertisement

Innovations in nineteenth-century commerce – such as fixed pricing, *grands magasins* and advertisement contrast with the outward appearance of the second-hand market, which evoked obsolescence and a quaint but archaic trade. The circumstances seem almost to have conspired to confirm this belief. Indeed, advertisement consisted mostly of hailing passers-by or market-goers. Street merchants and stall owners sold mainly by means of gestures and verbal communication. They themselves accepted the label *marchands à la main*.[55] In 1885, in its concern to modernize the city, the *Préfecture de Police* issued a ban on "announcing the nature and price of one's articles for sale by way of shouts and cries, stopping passers-by to offer them merchandise, and barring their way, or pulling them by their arm or clothing."[56] These merchants seemed to dispose only of words and gestures to ensure the advertisement of their goods. However, the archives reveal that, in fact, prospectuses, billboards and newspaper advertisements were used by second-hand dealers for publicity purposes. These written forms did not replace oral advertisement, but rather complemented the merchants' activity. From the early stages of the July Monarchy, they began to produce prospectuses and business cards, following the general commercial trend to seek out and maintain one's clientele.[57] In the early 1840s, a number of second-hand merchants began to use headed notepaper for their professional mail correspondence. They also printed ornate receipts, especially at the end of a season, when renewing stocks called for urgent liquidation. Some advertised in local newspapers and some rare merchants even signed on to the *Bottin-Didot* commercial directory. Literacy was a must, as administrators required them to keep financial records, which

Figure 7.1. Lebreton, "narchand [*sic*] de bric à brac," *circa* 1835. Cabinet des Estampes du Musée Carnavalet, Mœurs 34/Tailleurs

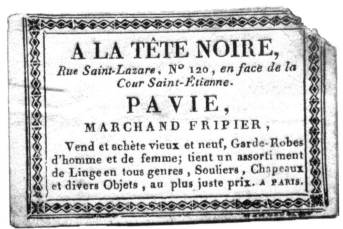

Figure 7.2. "À la tête Noire," Mr. Pavie, *circa* 1850. Cabinet des Estampes du Musée Carnavalet, Mœurs 17/Fripiers

helps us understand how they adapted so quickly to these new forms of advertisement. The integration of advances in advertisement techniques went together with increased specialization of shops. This indeed led a number of second-hand retailers to give new names to their conventionally homonymous shops. Thus *Chez Beaumont* became *À la Grâce de Dieu* ("God's Grace"); Mr. Damard took on the name *À la Redingote Grise*[58] for his shop sign, and Mr. Giroult's outlet was christened *Au Petit Bénéfice*.[59] As these signs were not regulated they appeared profusively. Disputes between the *Préfecture* and shopkeepers ensued during the winter of 1842 over "standing shop signs made of hats, umbrellas and pieces of clothing that clutter public spaces, from squares to alleyways."[60] These confirm that second-hand merchants valued visual advertisement as crucial to their business.

Shop owners in Paris city center began to set up overhead shelters for window-shoppers and pay special attention to window displays, from the

Figure 7.3. "Aux quatres mousquetaires gris," Mrs. Benoist, *circa* 1860. Cabinet des Estampes du Musée Carnavalet, Mœurs 34/Tailleurs

Figure 7.4. Mrs. Duval, "Modes pour dames et enfants," 1885. Archives de la Préfecture de Police, DA723. She pins her card on her request sent to the Préfecture de Police (October 14, 1885)

early 1830s. Petitions to the Emperor regarding the plans for a new covered market indicate that these merchants showed concern for the appearance of their shops. The petitions complain of the poor layout of the market hall on the plans, describing it as "a tangle of passageways cluttered with shops, which the distracted customer [would be] loath to fully discover." They claimed

Figure 7.5. Mr. Blin, "Marchand fripier, spécialités d'effets civils et militaires," *circa* 1890. Archives de Paris, Série AZ

that, although second-hand clothes sale "is an experience of pleasant, casual surprises of the everyday wanderer," it is nonetheless important to "attract buyers with goods they had not originally planned to buy."[61] In markets and shops alike, second-hand clothes merchants seem to have lived up to the professional demands and the call for change to the same level as the new-item trade. In the 1880s some of them would freely use electricity, that is surprising for a trade which, according to stereotypes, would prefer darkness in order to hide signs of repair. But it is all the more surprising when we consider that most merchants were hardly discovering the role electricity could play in advertisement. In her shop in the Temple neighborhood,[62] Mrs. Duval is known to have "made use of the electric lamp." Thus the commercial practices of second-hand trade were not only based on models predating the industrial revolution, but for the most part embraced the commercial innovations of the age. Following the example of new-item commerce, second-hand merchants sought to attract a type of customer whose buying habits were rapidly changing. No effort was made to hide the nature of this commerce in its many forms of advertisement. Thus the term "second-hand" was not necessarily understood pejoratively at this time.

Consumption

Adapting to New Consumer Habits

Until the 1860s, customers would evaluate merchandise in the same way, regardless of the first/second-hand distinction. Professional nomenclature was used and understood loosely, allowing the same merchant to be in turn "a clothes merchant," a "dealer of second-hand clothes" or a "tailor and second-hand salesman," or just a "tailor." This flexibility in the trade indicates that the boundaries between new- and old-clothes trades were very blurry indeed.

Touching, handling and inspecting clothing was common practice before buying in any second-hand shop. A mirror or cheval glass allowed customers to test clothes for size, as – with the exception of military clothing – sizes were not marked on the items themselves. At a time when price tags and labels were reserved for luxury items one would have to assess the quality and condition of each piece individually. That an item was second-hand was not an issue in the buying process, or at least did not remove from the item's value, in the buyer's view. Shopkeepers – even new-item retailers – displayed new and used clothing together; clothing was thus rarely identified as second-hand or new, so this did not influence prices. In an article for *Le Figaro*, a journalist named Monnier elaborates on "the art of buying in the Temple district [which] demands a certain learning and acquired know-how,"[63] as haggling was then all the rage. He explains that it was common knowledge that merchants in the area used an "arithmetic system" to determine the minimum sale price of an item, and these were set for sales assistants. But for these 'mysterious' pricing laws, a figure was agreed upon using words and gestures. Bargaining was the rule for second-hand market sales. Although by the end of the century, a handful of shops fixed prices on each item,[64] this did not put an end to bargaining. Rather it shows that shop owners wanted to fit into the commercial scene set by department stores and leading new-item outlets. Conversely, the *grands magasins* (department stores) drew upon the quaint attractiveness of the second-hand by staging fake bazaars inside their shops, where prices of oriental carpets were negotiated at length with an assistant dressed in a turban.[65] Finally, in their effort to adopt commercial innovation, many second-hand shopkeepers even accepted payment in instalments, according to their receipts.[66]

The Diversity of the Trade

Although wholesale dealers supplied most merchandise, shops would also buy from individual customers. To give some examples of this phenomenon, a student in Paris named Vingtras-Vallès wore a yellow jacket that was a damning sign of his provincial origins. He hailed a street merchant, who gave him "forty shillings [*sous*] for this artefact."[67] Five years later, another countryman named Déguignet was joining the army, and sold his useless civilian clothes to a tailor–second-hand dealer in Quimper for fifty francs, even though "they [were] worth more than double."[68] But outside of such unfair transactions, these examples show that the combined use of purchase and sales was a key aspect of second-hand trade. Indeed, once people had the possibility of selling their clothes at any given time, one's wardrobe became a form of savings. This can be seen by the widespread appearance of clothing and household laundry in dowries, and the institution of the *trousseau*.[69] Quite the opposite of today's conception of clothes as perishable goods, they were then seen as a long-term investment, which explains why items dating back to the 1830s could still be found in auctions during the Second Empire.[70] Clothing was commonly included in inheritance and wills. Trade in Mont-de-Piété was intense and pawning was common amongst moneylenders, who called out for "all clothes new and old, men's and women's wear alike."[71] Thus clothing played a key role in credit and capital management in nineteenth-century economic life.

Parisians would resort to the second-hand trade when money became scarce. Poverty but also a change of financial circumstances would force them to sell clothing. But we have to ask who would buy clothes during economic downturns, who the buyers were. Indeed, customers and sellers were apparently distinctly separate. Literary works refer to this trade as "charity for those recently fallen out of fortune;"[72] a stereotype confirmed by the low prices of sale. In the aforementioned *Figaro* article, Monnier estimates the value of a complete set of worker's clothes at forty shillings [*quarante sous*].[73] The high standards of dress amongst Parisian churchgoers suggests that such low prices on clothing of reasonable quality satisfied an otherwise untouched market niche. Just as National Guard uniforms became available to a wider social group through their sale on the second-hand market, this also allowed more precarious groups within the Parisian population to buy clothes on the common market. It is worth noting, however, that second-hand clothes appeared at all levels of commercial prosperity. Extreme poverty effectively provided second-hand salespersons with cheap clothing delivered right to their shop door. According to advertised prices and records from legal experts after seizing a shop's stocks, used clothing was sold between 30 and 50 percent more cheaply than new items. But a comparison between specific items – such as petticoats, evening trousers or dresses, and children's clothing – reveals that these differences in pricing were often far less significant. Similarly, the prices of items sold in military jumble sales, as well as clothes that came back into fashion, were close to those of equivalent new items. This again shows that the distinction between new and old clothing was at best hazy. Whereas nowadays a used item is automatically priced lower than a new one, the nineteenth-century buyer would judge each piece of clothing for its own worth and, if it was in good condition, nothing would distinguish it from a new item.

Writers played upon the fears and apprehensions of customers to sell it as a dark, decadent but attractive commerce. In 1834 a moralist by the name of D'Antonnelle depicts it as a space in which social hierarchy becomes confused. In Temple, he writes, "the rags of a pauper might rub off the dainty shawl of a duchess … and rough boots scrape against satin shoes." The second-hand clothes market became a safety net for the aspiring middle class, otherwise described as "parasites, knights of industrial fame, upstarts whose credibility and social existence rest only upon a decent set of clothing."[74] But, outside of the moral arena, these descriptions give the historian an insight into the social diversity of the clientele of this trade. Some of its merchandise was clearly not destined for customers who were in financial difficulty. The type of clothing, the designs and choice of materials suggest that customers did not only come to second-hand shops out of necessity. Mr. Fribourg's shop on Rue de Paradis, for instance, sold "summer jackets," "long, black woollen frock coats," "ladies' footwear" and even "striped shoulder wraps" or "tartan dressing gowns." Clearly these were clothes intended for people whose concern for their appearances carried into their private rooms, thus providing used-clothes dealers with a more up-market clientele. During the July Monarchy a new trade appeared, which lay somewhere between the tailor and the second-hand clothes merchant, i.e., that of the *tailleur-brocanteur* (tailor–second-hand dealer), which involved "repairing and restoring clothes to suit the fashion of the day." Mr. Schindler on Rue de Valois-Batave boasted he could "restore all men's and women's wear to its original condition, making your tired and worn clothing as good as new." With "decorative buttons, silk, taffeta or strapwork," Schindler's trade consisted of what was euphemistically known as *le raccord* (joinery).[75] In a chapter in Roret's 1828 *Manual of Elegance and Hygiene*, he reserves this "notorious skill" for the robes of legal clerks, to which "they must add a velvet collar" by means of this so-called joinery, but otherwise warns against such *demi-nouveautés* (half-novelties).[76] Although these voices gradually succeeded in limiting these renovations to the domestic sphere, their very clamour suggests that many customers did not distinguish between tailors and *tailleurs-fripiers*.

Just as we saw earlier that there were many shades of prosperity and wealth in second-hand shops, equally the used-clothes market attracted a wide variety of customers. Parisians, for the most part, did not associate this trade with poverty or obsolete goods. Though it did indeed give the less wealthy access to mainstream clothing, it especially gave buyers a choice of clothing they would not otherwise have had, and also the opportunity to change and renew their wardrobe more often.

A Multiplicity of Appropriation

As we have been arguing so far, second-hand commerce blended into mainstream economic life during the first half of the nineteenth century, for consumers and traders alike. Since there were no means of assessing the value of new and old items displayed indiscriminately, the boundaries between these categories are blurred. Second-hand trade facilitated access not only to clothes, but also to a wider range of items. This allowed certain people not only to imitate their social superiors, but also to borrow or even appropriate a new social identity with the clothes they could now wear.

The concentration of shops around the École-de-Médecine area was largely due to this phenomenon; second-hand merchants noted the concentration of students in this neighborhood, and thus set up in their hundreds. The consumer habits of these students give us a new take on the traditional mechanisms of nineteenth-century clothes purchase. Second-hand trade allowed them to start their own fashions, often a patchwork of mainstream trends and fanciful nostalgia. Quick turnover of used clothing allowed them to keep up with a fast-moving fashion market. The clothes on offer reflected the particularly flighty fashions that blossomed in this neighborhood. Long frock coats remained steadily fashionable but different types of top hats and high hats came in and out of fashion successively. The second-hand trade also provided a wide range of accessories, which, for instance, satisfied the demand for the 1830s "middle ages" look, but also allowed militant supporters of the Republic to show their political colours with "moderate Republican clothes."[77] A student could wear or subvert a military uniform, seek out curios and find a rare item to wear proudly, outshining peers. The process was therefore one of borrowing rather than imitating another's image or persona. However, this outline of the student clientele is not representative of all buyers of second-hand clothing, which shopkeepers' records suggest were a largely working-class population, mostly composed of builders and manual workers.

It is safe to assume that used clothing was mostly purchased by those whose income was low. The trade allowed a less wealthy clientele much greater freedom in its choice of clothing, which new-item shops did not. But this does not preclude the fact that the wider choice available was also a strong incentive to buy second-hand. The beginning of the July Monarchy saw a rise in the numbers of workers and craftspeople buying their clothes second-hand. A few shops, such as Mr. Legrain's on Rue Phélippeaux, sold woolen shirts, jackets and waistcoats to a clientele of manual workers and business employers wishing to dress sophisticatedly.[78] But, for the majority, everyday clothing dominated sales. The clothes on offer in Mr. Delanoé's shops typified the everyday dress of the Parisian laborer. On offer was a mixture of various smocks, linen trousers, gaiters, nightshirts and headscarves. There were also more specialised items, such as long-sleeved bustiers for wine merchants, coachdrivers' wear, and even second-hand tools.[79] Once again, these examples point towards a process of building what Pat Hudson labels "singular identities,"[80] rather than mere imitation or even borrowing an image or a role. The aspiration toward an upper-middle class lifestyle is in itself an insufficient explanation of the shift toward the second-hand trade. Rather, an outline of the shifts in working-class identity begins to appear from our investigation of this market. This is confirmed by Nadaud's 1832 account of the "red-and-blue-collared smock, worn with a belt bearing the Republican colours [which was] the fashion of the day."[81] These shifts of identity became all the more apparent under the Third Republic. In 1893 a journalist shed light on this phenomenon, writing that:

> the Temple clientele is mostly composed of manual workers who wanted a more upmarket set of clothes for their Sunday best. Working jackets and trench coats were preferred, and these were mostly bought second-hand. More sophisticated jackets or frock coats were considered appropriate only for office workers and were therefore more scarce at the Temple market. The working jacket [*veston*] was best accepted by the working population. Indeed, the same worker who would be mocked for coming to work in a frock coat would be seen as sly and resourceful if he had come by a more modest but respectable set of clothes at Temple market.[82]

As items would move more freely down the chain of social hierarchies, the creation and reinforcement of group identities were easier, and not just for students and manual workers. The middle classes and bourgeoisie also discovered and created fashions via second-hand sales, notably in auctions.

From Notre-Dame to the Suburbs: Upheaval and Downgrading

Accounts of the end of second-hand commerce appeared frequently in *fin-de-siècle* literature and press, either as nostalgic reminiscences or as portrayals of the underworld of Parisian commerce. The July Monarchy sparked off a deep change in this trade and its space in the Parisian economic landscape.

The Modern Spirit

In the winter of 1834 a group of shop owners and local personalities from the Cité area sent a petition to the Paris prefecture requesting an end to the clothes and jumble sales on their parish grounds. This outdoor market at the south end of Notre-Dame was composed of over 200 stalls. Early in the following year the police announced that it was to be moved to the Halle aux Veaux, on Quai de la Tournelle, on grounds that "the bric-a-brac and clothing market adjacent to Notre-Dame mars and clutters the outside of one of our greatest monuments."[83] Aesthetics and presentation were the prime causes for concern given by the authorities. As a city pioneering the modern age and thus aiming to attract tourists, Paris could no longer afford to harbor uncontrolled and unclean commerce in its very center. Prints from the famous 1828 guide *Le Véritable Conducteur Parisien* (The Real Paris Explorer) only confirmed the suspicion that the cathedral was to be cleansed of this parasitic commerce. Once it was stripped of its role in everyday economic life, it was to resume its full historic grandeur. Thus the project was riding on the double strength of Parisian history and tourism. Although for the most part the police tolerated and even helped second-hand tradespeople, the disorganized and uninstitutional character of the trade soon made it appear as a vestige of the poverty and primitive lifestyle of medieval Paris. The institutionalization of many second-hand shops was partly due to the need to overcome such fears in customers, and thus signals the fact that perceptions had begun to turn against the trade. Measures requesting the display of official documents on shop signs, effective roofing over stalls, and a ban on "harassing and disturbing window-shoppers" were brought in, in an attempt to contain the trade, but also to help it find a place in the makings of the ideal city of the modern era. Merchants themselves took steps to meet the joint demands of council administration and inhabitants.

But these last felt that the proximity of such activities was a threat to their property value. The criminal and hygienic problems associated with second-hand trade became a recurrent concern. Hygiene was particularly an issue, with the 1832 epidemic, as second-hand commerce was singled out as a cause for contagion. "Peddling" was banned, stocks of used items were quarantined or subjected to impressive "chlorine fumigations," and the police kept a close eye on the markets.[84] But still the Temple market and its allegedly Oriental merchandise were held as one of the main causes for the epidemic. Little by little, undesirable second-hand shops or jumble stalls were closed or evicted from the city. The Halle aux Veaux market was thus moved six times and in 1853 several attempts were made to remove the Fesq-Beauveau-Saint-Antoine bazaar.[85] This drive to cleanse the city of anything resembling second-hand commerce also led the city council to replace the Place Monge market with rows of tree plantations,[86] and to evict clothes dealers from the Aligre market. In buildings and domestic spaces, second-hand dealers were equally rejected or refused entrance when people caught on to these administrative measures. Thus by the Second Empire, inhabitants had adopted the council's ethos of improving the sanitary conditions and aesthetics of the city, thus furthering the interests of speculators.

From Clothes to Spoils

By the turn of the century, the number of second-hand shops had fallen sharply in spite of their efforts to adapt to the changing commercial scene. Even the hundred remaining shops – against five times this figure in 1860 – were struggling to get by. Advertisers were increasingly disparaging of this ailing trade. In 1888 Maisondour captured a growing disappointment with second-hand commerce in an article for *Le Courrier des Halles*. He holds that:

> In the new department store bazaars ... one has at least the reassurance of not being taken for a ride; prices are clearly labelled, items are brand new and one doesn't expose oneself to the parasites of a former owner! Finally, one can trust that one won't be hailed unpleasantly by salespersons who see customers as prey to their hunt for profit; as buyers to take advantage of.[87]

In the 1870s, fixed pricing was used in all outlets although the July Monarchy generation still had not shaken the habit of haggling with sales assistants. Nonetheless, the absence of a fixed price was construed as a potential swindle or bad deal, as prices varied strongly depending on the customer. Second-hand shops suffered heavily as a result, despite their efforts to integrate fixed pricing, since the very nature of the trade depended upon the possibility to drop or negotiate prices. In less than half a century, haggling and bartering had become archaic practice, and were increasingly frowned upon.

This gradual detachment from used-item commerce, despite its being an integral part of nineteenth century economic life, can be explained by a change of customers' approach to merchandise itself. Previously, one would only refer to the item's previous owner to evoke the instability of social hierarchies. But from 1870 the former owner's body came back to haunt second-hand clothes. Maisondour spoke of remnants of smells, parasites, blood and illness, which could stay with an item after sale. According to him, buying second-hand was equivalent to wearing another's clothes. Analysts talked of used items as plunder of belongings retrieved from the dead. Customers were shocked and disgusted by the smallest trace of bodily fluids or odours. This fear was fueled by an increased awareness of the dangers of contagion. In 1898 Dr. Brunel wrote of the clothes on sale in Temple, that "old rags, laundry, clothes and carpets festering in ragpickers' bags and old tattered frocks which are often sold after their wearers died of illness, are neither disinfected nor cleansed of soil and tuberculous spittle, where the most morbid of bacteria proliferate."[88]

These health hazards were known or at least suspected since the late eighteenth century. But, whereas buyers had once aimed their suspicion at the merchants themselves, the late nineteenth century began to focus on the merchandise and the "abundant dust and dirt emanating from such clothing."[89] In order to maintain a useful and worthwhile trade, but also due to a general ignorance of health risks, the authorities did not interfere with second-hand trade until the scare began. Louis Pasteur's theories contributed strongly to turning the tables. Thus in 1881 the Mont-de-Piété was equipped with a sterilizing device, but only in 1894 did the council legislate on public sales of "laundry, used clothing and bedclothes."[90] But, from the moment Parisians began to see a bodily threat in second-hand clothes, no measure of legislation or sanitation could save the trade.

Earlier in the century, between the July Monarchy and the Second Empire, a number of second-hand shops set up in the city center, usually after several previous moves. Mrs. Leconte, for instance, although she was arrested in 1830 for "illicit second-hand dealing," later established her trade successfully on Rue de la Montagne Sainte Geneviève. Used-clothes merchants could thus find a market niche in shops in the city center and, by the middle of the century, they could even aspire to financial success. But by the 1870s this was no longer possible. Mr. Oudard had, like others, turned to second-hand trade in 1870 after his debts as a tailor had become unmanageable, but eventually went bankrupt in 1881, unable to repay his debts as a tailor for men's clothing.[91] Indeed, the trade plummeted in 1870 and shopkeepers slowly deserted even the best of commercial locations, near schools or in highly frequented areas such as train stations. In 1862 a second-hand shop was still running next to a luxury hotel, in the heart of a very cosmopolitan area. This was the Grand Hotel on Rue Scribe and Boulevard des Capucines, which still rented out one of its floor spaces to a second-hand clothes dealer (*brocanteur d'habit*).[92] But it disappeared in 1872, as it was surely seen as a deterrent for hotel customers, and could no longer afford the expensive rent. On top of these problems, second-hand dealers could no longer compete with the arrival of specialized tailors producing ready-made items, and were thus constantly forced to lower their prices. Gradually as used clothes were disregarded by the general public, much of their former clientele was taken over by these "renewals" shops. Thus in 1898 Brunel declared that "credit repayment stores, grand bazaars and department stores, selling all kinds of new items in conditions which our [second-hand] shops cannot match, as well as the public's new-found reserve with regard to its purchasing habits foreshadow the certain death" of the trade.[93]

The few shops remaining inside Paris city walls survived only thanks to their proximity to a very faithful clientele, such as in Rue de l'École-de-Médecine or Belleville. Others recycled their trade as antique clothing shops, such as Mr. Fortin, who retrieved used opera costumes.[94] Most of those that survived until 1890 kept going; the antique clothing trade was indeed quite successful, offering military uniforms from earlier in the century, eighteenth-century suits and even dresses formerly owned by countesses. In this trade, as opposed to that of *friperies*, signs of age on merchandise such as scratches and reworking of materials (especially shawls) were considered a stamp of authenticity.[95] Gradually the term "second-hand" with its connotations of age, became synonymous with poor-quality merchandise, and antique clothing retailers began to separate themselves from this trade. Whereas administrations could hardly distinguish between new and used merchandise earlier in the century, the end of the nineteenth century saw a distinct cleavage between these two categories, because of both identifiable criteria in the outward forms of the trade and also a shift of perception in customers themselves.

The Birth of Flea Markets

Although second-hand commerce was on the wane inside Paris, this did not put a stop to it altogether. In fact, it thrived in certain communities on the outskirts of the capital, at first in Belleville, Ménilmontant and La Villette, and by the turn of the century in other suburbs closer to the city center. Saint-Ouen and Montreuil thus provided large spaces for second-hand markets.[96] Merchants could also set up in the slums (*zone*) surrounding the capital, where they could also avoid unwelcome legislation. This was a phenomenon that began to take shape in many large cities. The merchandise sold in these flourishing markets was uncannily similar to that of the earlier jumble sales of the city center. They became a refuge for those shop owners fleeing debtors, and customers were mostly from the poorer suburbs. But among this new clientele there was a new type of consumer, who came in the hope of finding clothing to suit the fashion of the day.

This exodus of second-hand trade toward the more working-class areas on the outskirts of Paris continued slowly until, at the turn of the century, a handful of shops that had remained in the center became destinations for the Sunday outings of the bourgeoisie. As these shops were scarce in the city center their "otherness," became attractive and recreational. This difference from mainstream commerce even became a stamp of authenticity. Shoppers began to make their way to second-hand shops and markets in the hope of finding a rare or peculiar object. Marcelle Tinayre's accounts of her outings around Paris which took her to "antique shops all morning" and "second-hand shops all afternoon" are convincing clues to the recreational role of these markets. In her diary she describes such a day, where she and a friend finish up "in dark and pungent bric-a-brac shops in Plaisance, inhabited by rough, unkempt Auvergnats and touchy Polish Jews." But "despite the crumbling plaster, the spiders and bad smells in the shops, and the money-grubbing merchants," she continues, "I had a wonderful time … rediscovering the pleasure of shoppers' fever; enjoying the hunt for a precious item and the feeling of discovery, which many collectors share" as they browse through these shops. Such curious shoppers go scouting far outside Paris for "genuine" items, as far as finding provincial merchants who are "attached to their old trinkets, and sometimes won't even sell them, they have grown to love them so much," and who "unfold old silks as if they were undressing a ghost of an old mistress, and where nothing is cheap but everything is genuine."[97] The antique shops on Boulevard Haussmann and Quai Voltaire soon became aware of the newfound interest in such trade, and thus began to stock old silks and veils and costumes of yore, from Brittany or China.[98] The new pleasure of decorating one's apartment with historical relics took precedence over hygiene concerns. The upper middle class began to fill its interiors and its fancy dress parties with historical costumes from antique shops, sometimes even "authentic uniforms from Napoleon's guard."[99] At this stage, second-hand commerce was beginning to resemble what we now know, alongside antique trade. The used-goods trade, now foreign to most Parisians dwelling in the center, thus became an experience of authentic and exotic items, considered more attractive and respectable for their age.

Conclusion

Although today second-hand commerce is clearly separate from antique and new-item trade, in the nineteenth-century it was extremely widespread and melted into almost every other area of economic life. It was written into the new pages of nineteenth century commerce, not scribbled in the margins of mainstream trade. Because consumers' purchasing habits did not distinguish second-hand goods from new ones, it was both familiar and unrecognizable. "Second-hand" or "old" clothes appeared as categories only once public opinion began to look down upon the trade in its shapelessness and disorderly appearance, creating a marked difference between new and old goods. To understand the triumph of new-item trade in the nineteenth century, one must see how it was set in contrast with the second-hand trade, through a new concern for hygiene.

From this point onwards, an object would come into the second-hand circuit if it was outmoded, useless or worn-out. At the same time, we find that the patterns of consumption of these goods reveal more than the imitation of one's social superiors. Indeed, these patterns are complex processes of choice which allowed customers to appropriate and create identities. In the light of today's assessment of the complexity[100] of consumer goods, the history of second-hand commerce has yet to be written. In an era where history and the thirst for novelty were equally defining, this is a choice area to explore the different forms of nineteenth-century consumption.

Notes

1. See Jean-Paul Aron, "Débris," in *Le Mangeur du XIXe Siècle* (Paris, 1973); or Frederic Barbier, "Bouquinistes, Libraires Spécialisés," in Roger Chartier and Henri-Jean Martin (eds), *Histoire de l'édition française*, vol. 3 *Le Temps des éditeurs, du romantisme à la Belle Époque* (Paris, 1990), and Dominique Poulot, "Une nouvelle histoire de la culture matérielle?" *Revue d'Histoire Moderne et Contemporaine*, April–June (1997), pp. 344–357.

2. A song by P.J. Béranger, a clothes salesman from the First Restoration period, goes "Les modes et la politique/ Ont cent fois rempli ma boutique," which translates as "Politics and fashionable ways/have filled the air in my shop always." Extract from "Vieux Habits! Vieux Galons! Réflexions Morales et Politiques d'un Marchand d'Habits de la Capitale," in *Chansons de P.-J. Béranger, 1814–1835* (Paris, 1861). This is a theme also found in many caricatures of the day, such as Daumier's *Le Marchand d'Habits* (1840).

3. See Archives de Préfecture de Police (APP), Certificates of privation. One could translate it as "peddlers in second-hand clothes."

4. Jean-Clément Martin, "Le commerçant, la faillite et l'historien," *Annales ESC*, 6, (1980), pp. 1258 ff.

5. See chap. 5 in this volume.

6. Archives de Paris (AP), D11U3/126. Judicial liquidation report, April 11 1850.

7. APP, DA 178 report, 1837.

8. APP, DA 307.

9. *La France*, 23 March 1877.

10. Philippe Perrot, *Les Dessus et les dessous de la bourgeoisie, une histoire du vêtement au XIXe siècle* (Paris , 1981), pp. 69–92.

11. *L'Illustration*, n° 233, August 14, 1847.

12. Notably photographs of Rue des Prêtres Saint-Séverin (1899) and Rue des Anglais (1902).

13. Archives Nationales (AN), ET/XXIX/1107. Inventaire après décès (post-mortem inventory), November 11 1845.

14. AP, D11U3/137. Dossier de faillite (Bankruptcy report) no. 9954, June 19, 1851.

15. AP, Fond U.P.F., One photograph on Rue de l'École-de-Médecine (3Fi11436) shows the shop sign for Mr. Blancard's shop, wiche reads: "Maison fondée en 1855. Réelles occasions, grand choix de Marchandise à très bas prix" (Establishment founded in 1855. Genuine deals and a wide choice of merchandise at low prices).

16. AN, ET/XLIII/880, Inventaire après décès (post-mortem inventory), September 11, 1849.

17. AP, 10 AZ 328.

18. AP, D1P4, Calepin du cadastre (cadastral survey of) rue de l'École-de-Médecine, 1852.

19. On this practice: Philip T. Hoffmann, Gilles Postel-Vinay, and Jean-Laurent Rosenthal, *Des marchés sans prix. Une économie politique du crédit à Paris, 1660–1870* (Paris, 2001), pp. 295 ff.

20. AP, D11U3/171, Dossier de faillite (Bankruptcy report) no. 11342, November 17, 1854.

21. AP, D14U3/1, Dossier de liquidation judiciaire (Judicial liquidation report) n° 539, March 23, 1849.

22. Chambre de commerce de Paris, *Statistique de l'Industrie à Paris résultant de l'enquête faite par la chambre de commerce pour les années 1847–48* (Paris, 1851), "Vêtement."

23. AN, ET/XLIII/880, Inventaire après décès (post-mortem inventory), September 17, 1849.

24. AN, ET/XXXVII/612, Inventaire après décès (post-mortem inventory), July 13, 1850.

25. See: Daniel Roche, "Du vol à la revente: un autre aspect de la diffusion des vêtements," in *La Culture des apparences. Une histoire du vêtement XVIIe–XVIIIe siècle* (Paris, 1989) or Perrot, "Ravitaillement traditionnel et essor de la confection," in Perrot, *Les dessus et les dessous*, to see how the nineteenth-century press omitted any descriptions of supply circuits, bar these prescriptive hypotheses.

26. AP, DQ10/369 and 370.

27. Ibid.

28. AP, D3R4/20, Letter no. 39.

29. See Monnier in *Le Figaro*, no. 217, March 15 1857: stagecoach-drivers' hats were made with "débris de capote de la troupe de ligne" (the remains of squadron hats) by Mr. Bienfait, as this was his specialty.

30. Norbert Truquin, *Les Aventures d'un prolétaire à travers les Révolutions* (Paris, 1977), p. 47 ff. recalls: "Un tailleur prit nos mesures et nous tailla des vêtements de cérémonie dans des habits de réforme de la troupe … mon habillement se trouva être en beau drap noir," translated: "A tailor took our waist measurements, and designed ceremonial costume for us, out of used military clothing … my costume was made of wonderful black pressed wool."

31. Bibliothèque Historique de la Ville de Paris (BHVP), Actualité/120, Habillement, Publicité du marchand Fortin, vers 1845. Cabinet des Estampes du Musée Carnavalet, publ. Jallais, 20, rue de Bruxelles, "Curiosité, antiquité, spécialité d'armes, coiffures, costumes militaires de toutes les époques. Location pour MM. les artistes," (transl: "Curiosities, specialist weaponry, wigs and military costumes of all periods to rent for players and artists"), circa 1870.

32. This was an advertisements newspaper.

33. AP, D1E/93-115, Archives des commissaires-priseurs (Police Auctioneers' Archives).

34. Archives du Mont-de-Piété, Carton 58, Liasse 1.

35. Ibid., Cartons 13 et 60.

36. Archives de l'AP-HP, Comptes généraux des hôpitaux et hospices civils, 2M/1-30.

37. APP, DB371, Note du Préfet Delessert, October 24, 1845.

38. BHVP, Actualité/120, Comptoirs des ventes.

39. Ibid., Habillement. Liquidations diverses (Miscellaneous liquidations).

40. APP, DB371, Petition, March 12, 1842.

41. This refers to second-hand salespersons whose trade also involved mending and working clothing.

42. Société Internationale des études pratiques d'économie politique, *Ouvriers des deux mondes* (Paris, 1856–62), "Enquête no. 34. Auvergnat Brocanteur en Boutique à Paris."

43. APP, DB371, Courrier de 1853 et ordonnance no. 35, December 1865.

44. AP, D11U3/610, Dossier de faillite (Bankruptcy report) no. 10276, September 23, 1868.

45. Martin Nadaud, *Léonard, Maçon de la Creuse* (Paris, 1998), p. 71.

46. Monnier in *Le Figaro*, no. 217, March 15, 1857.

47. AP, 10 AZ 328.
48. Ibid.
49. Inventaire après décès de (post-mortem inventory of) M. et Mme Garnier, April 22, 1833. AN, ET/XXXII/336. The value of the merchandise and working furniture of Mr. Garnier's shop was estimated at the impressive sum of 8,185 francs.
50. Monnier in *Le Figaro*, no. 217, March 15, 1857.
51. Gilbert-Urbain Guillaumin, *Dictionnaire universel théorique et pratique du commerce et de la navigation* (Paris, 1859–61), "Vêtements confectionnés," pp. 1759 ff.
52. AP, D3R4/21, Lettres de l'intendant no. 2510 ff.
53. *Tableau général du commerce de la France avec ses colonies et les puissances étrangères, Direction générale des douanes et des contributions indirectes, 1837 à 1846* (Paris, 1848).
54. Ibid. and see Guillaumin, *Dictionnaire universel théorique et pratique du commerce et de la navigation*, "Vêtements confectionné," "Marseille" and "Le Havre."
55. AP, DB371, petition, April 16, 1866.
56. Ibid., December 1865.
57. APP, DB371, "Contre la distribution d'imprimés indiquant magasins et boutiques au Marché du Temple," statement on November 17, 1842.
58. Translates as "The Grey Frock Coat."
59. This name is a word-play, meaning both "Where Profits are Small" and "A Small Advantage" (implying, that purchase in this shop provides the customer with this).
60. AP, DB371, Letter on January 24, 1842.
61. AP, DB371, petition, April 16, 1866.
62. AP, DA723, Mme Duval, Letter on October 14, 1885.
63. Monnier in *Le Figaro*, no. 217, March 15, 1857.
64. See ibid: ed. U.P.F., Mr. Blancard, who had a shop on Rue de l'École-de-Médecine, used this in the early twentieth century.
65. Cabinet des Estampes du Musée Carnavalet, Mœurs/Grands magasins.
66. AP, 10 AZ 328. Mr. Giroult's invoices for the Mayor of Hesdin (Pas-de-Calais).
67. Jules Vallès, *Le Bachelier* (Paris, 1970 (1881)), p. 64.
68. Jean-Marie Déguignet, *Mémoires d'un Paysan Bas-Breton* (Le Relecq-Kerhuon, 2000), pp. 122 ff.
69. This was a set of outfits that children were given as part of their inherited property, upon leaving home.
70. AP, see D42E3-D60E3, judicial auction archives.
71. The *Crédit Municipal* administration was constantly trying to get rid of such merchants practicing usury, and regularly compiled lists of thie names. Archives du Mont-de-Piété, Carton 13, Liasse 2.
72. Monnier in *Le Figaro*, no. 217, March 15, 1857.
73. Ibid.
74. D'Antonelle, *Nouveau Tableau de Paris au XIXe siècle* (Paris, 1834) "Le marché aux vieux linges," pp. 352 ff.
75. BHVP, Actualité/120, Tailors, 1800–50.
76. *Code de la toilette, Manuel complet d'élégance et d'hygiène, contenant les lois, règles, applications et exemples, de l'art de soigner sa personne, et de s'habiller avec goût et méthode* (Paris, 1828), chap. IV, "Des raccords."
77. Vallès, *Le Bachelier*, pp. 208 ff; see also Jean-Claude Caron, *Générations romantiques. Les étudiants de Paris et le Quartier Latin (1814–1851)* (Paris, 1991), "Uniforme(s) étudiant(s)?," pp. 169 ff. and Stana Nenadic, "Romanticism and the Urge to Consume in the First Half of the 19th Century," in Maxine Berg and Helen Clifford, *Consumers and Luxury. Consumer Culture in Europe 1650–1850* (Manchester, 1999).
78. AP, D11U3/171, Dossier de faillite (Bankruptcy report) no. 11342, November 17, 1854.
79. AP, D11U3/392, Dossier de faillite (Bankruptcy report) no. 324, July 1862.
80. Pat Hudson, *The Industrial Revolution* (London, New York, Melbourne, Auckland, 1992).
81. Nadaud, *Léonard, Maçon de la Creuse*, pp. 71–2.
82. "Paris vécu. Le carreau du Temple," *La Paix*, January 4, 1893.
83. APP, DA718.

84. Préfecture de Police, *Journal des Commissions Sanitaires Établies dans le Département de la Seine*, 1832, no. 2.

85. APP, DB373.

86. *La France*, March 23, 1877.

87. "Les Marchands du Temple," *Le Courrier des Halles*, August 5, 1888.

88. Dr Bunel, *Rapport au Préfet, Projet de Réorganisation du Temple*, April 29, 1898.

89. APP, DA718, Letter on April 30, 1866.

90. Préfecture de Police, *Conseil d'hygiène publique et de salubrité du département de la Seine, Rapport sur les ventes de linges, hardes et objets de literie à l'Hôtel des Commissaires-priseurs*, Paris, December 7, 1894.

91. AP, D11U3/1020, Dossier no. 10761, September 6, 1881. Faillite de Oudard (Oudard's bankruptcy), 141, boulevard Magenta.

92. AP, D1P4, Rue Scribe, 1862.

93. Dr Bunel, *Rapport au Préfet*, p. 2.

94. AN. The carton AJ/13/567, amongst others, contains leaflets and records of sales organized in 1856 and 1860 "par suite de réforme, d'environ 10 000 costumes en coton, soie, laine et velours" [which, after reworking, total approximately 10,000 cotton, silk, wool and corduroy costumes]. AP, Me Chapentier's registers list the buyers' names.

95. *Rapport de l'Exposition Universelle de 1867 à Paris*, 35ᵉ classe, *Habillement* (Paris, 1868).

96. Archives Communales de St-Ouen, AR/2706; Archives Départementales St-Denis, DM6 3/3.

97. Marcelle Tinayre, *Madeleine au miroir. Journal d'une femme* (Paris, 1912), "L'antiquaille" pp. 91 ff.

98. The Bottin-Didot shop directory contains over fifteen antique shops that specialized in purchase and sales of materials, tapestries or antique costumes, from the early 1890s.

99. BHVP, Actualité/120, Habillement, Advertisement by Mr. Fortin, op. cit. See also the sales of "costumes historiques de l'époque Louis XV et Louis XVI" (historical costumes dating back to the Louis XV and Louis XVI periods) officiated by Mᶜ Ridel. AP, D42E3/30-50.

100. This refers to a study by Jean-Luc Marais, *Histoire du don en France de 1800 à 1939. Dons et legs charitables, pieux et philanthropiques* (Rennes, 1999).

8

"What Goes 'Round Comes 'Round"

Second-hand Clothing, Furniture and Tools in Working-class Lives in the Interwar USA

Susan Porter Benson

Working-class family economies in the interwar USA depended heavily on second-hand goods as one of many expedients to stretch insufficient resources.[1] Used items could offer an indirect entry to consumer culture, stretch a tight budget to supply comforts not otherwise available, provide both investment and use value, and enhance wage-earning possibilities. I examine here three main streams of circulation of second-hand goods: of clothing, which was primarily for its direct use; of household goods such as furniture, which served as investment goods; and of tools, which helped in making a living.

The United States entered what is usually regarded as the era of mass consumption in the interwar period, but the working-class majority tasted the joys of consumption in a very limited way. My forthcoming book, *Household Accounts: Working-class Family Economies in the Interwar USA*, centers on this contention. I originally set out to write a history of working-class consumption, hoping to find both evidence of working-class immersion in a national culture of abundance and documentation of distinct racial–ethnic patterns of consumption. I found neither. My book argues that, at least in the interwar USA, the glass of consumption was half empty rather than half full. Underemployment and unemployment ate significantly into working-class families' standard of living; insufficient and irregular income made life a difficult and often defeating struggle to supply the basic necessities and the occasional luxury. Far from finding the 1920s a time of prosperity and plenty for working-class families, I found strong threads of continuity between the 1920s and the 1930s. The difference between the two periods was one of degree rather than of kind: the wolf may have howled at the door more persistently and loudly in the 1930s, but that howl was heard through the 1920s as well.[2] Second, I have found very limited evidence of group-specific patterns of household economy; some groups, in some places, turned more to one strategy than to another, but again the difference was more one of degree than of kind, and all drew on a common array of strategies. This finding goes against the grain of recent studies that have emphasized the specificity of the cultures and experiences of different groups, and indeed it confounds my own expectations. But the sources are clear on this point, and I have had to con-clude that urban-industrial families throughout the country – at that moment in capitalist development – chose from a similar set of options and framed a similar array of responses. That said, I want to be very clear that I am not arguing that racial–ethnic differences do not matter. Race, especially, matters deeply in the USA, and in my sources I hear some condemn the racism of which they were targets and others spout racist abuse. To leap, however, from an understanding of racism to an assumption that race must shape every aspect of life is to essentialize what is in fact a socially constructed category. African American families, for example, do not forge family strategies based only on their African Americanness, but on the simultaneity of circumstances of race, gender, class, age, place and time that confront them. During the 1920s and 1930s, proletarianization appears to have embedded European American and African American native-born and European- and Mexican-born immigrant families in material circumstances more similar than they had been in the past or would be again. As a result, they drew on a common and flexible range of strategies in meeting their material needs and wants.[3]

Working-class consumption was but one aspect of a complicated array of working-class economic activities, including wage-earning, household production, market replacement, reciprocity and market activity. I thus use the broader notion of the working-class family economy, a term that includes the range of decisions families made about earning and spending money as well as their efforts to avoid the money economy through a whole range of non market activities. My concern is neither with absolute levels of consumption nor with quantitative aspects of the family budget; rather, I seek to understand how working-class families negotiated the use of family funds, how they made qualitative judgments about what they wanted and what they didn't, how they framed family strategies, and how these strategies articulated with individual goals and desires. These families were not swept up by the economy of abund-ance, but lived in a complex economy in which scarcity conditioned daily life and plans for the future. By no means peculiarly American, it had much in common with other economies distant in time and in space: the economy of makeshifts evoked by Judith Bennett for medieval Britain, the struggle to achieve subsistence identified by Steve Stern in late colonial Mexico, and the resourceful exploitation of market possibilities depicted by Gracia Clark in contemporary Kumasi, to cite only a few examples. Working-class families in the interwar USA may well have shared more with these distant groups than with middle-class household economies deeply drawn into the culture of abundance.[4]

My view of working-class household economies is not the only possible one and is powerfully shaped by the sources on which I rely. I use two main types of sources: first, reports on home-visit interviews with woman wage earners conducted by field agents for the Women's Bureau of the US Department of Labor during the 1920s and early 1930s and, second, studies of families confronting unemployment produced by settlement workers and academic social scientists during the late 1920s and the 1930s. The use of second-hand goods was not unique to these decades, but the lack of comparable documentary sources for earlier and later periods makes it difficult to develop a longer chronological perspective on their use. Both bodies of evidence were compiled almost exclusively by woman researchers and were – always in the Women's Bureau studies, and often in the other studies – presented from a woman-centered point of view. The accounts are, as a whole, vivid and compelling, as close as we are likely to get to the voices of working-class women themselves. The middle-class and elite people who tell us what their working-class informants said were arguably the most sympathetic interpreters of working-class life from the outside; their goal was less to reform working-class people than to mobilize state aid and public opinion on their behalf. A gender dynamic, especially in the Women's Bureau data, often led the investigators to tell us more than the interview schedules asked them to. Although distinctly different in education, class, ethnicity, and race, the Women's Bureau agents and the wage-earning women whom they visited in their homes shared a pleasure in a good story about daily life, and when the agents recorded those stories we are the richer for it.[5]

By far the broadest and deepest of the circulating streams of used items was that of clothing, which appeared universally in all times, places and sources and and was segmented by gender and generation. Second-hand clothing was both a finished product and a raw material, with women diligently repairing and refashioning used clothing into garments that fitted the wearer and the current fashion. Used clothing came from myriad sources: second-hand clothing dealers, family, friends, employers, teachers, non profit organizations' rummage sales and, in one intriguing case, a woman received from a friend "a coat that had been left at her house and never called for."[6] Even the poorest, eager to help kin or friends, might be able to offer a bit of used clothing when they could afford no other assistance.[7] My sources privilege transactions outside the commercial market; dealers in used clothing make no more than a cameo appearance. But, even in the non commercial circulation of used clothing, provenance might matter very much. E. Wight Bakke, investigating the lives of unemployed families in New Haven, Connecticut, during the Great Depression, learned from an indignant mother about the social costs of accepting clothes from charitable organizations: "Secondhand clothes from the rest of family are all right. But the other day a neighbor's child had it flung into her face by a schoolmate, 'That looks like the coat I gave to the Red Cross.' I'll not let that happen to [my daughter]."[8]

Second-hand clothing stretched tight budgets a crucial bit further. A study of electricians and longshoremen in Houston revealed that "the depression-era economy seems to have cut most deeply into the expenditure for clothing." Among their replies to questions about clothing expenditure were: "Damn little this year," and "Furnished by someone else."[9] The desperate family might simply stop spending anything at all on clothing and depend, as did a New York family, "on chance windfalls from anywhere."[10] The value of clothing rested almost entirely in its use rather than in its potential to raise cash. A Utah family supported by a laborer father found when they desperately sold off clothing that "they have little of value;"[11] clothing depreciated quickly and dramatically. That same family, by contrast, reaped enormous benefit from the used clothes they received as gifts and bought at rummage sales: such were the economies of buying second-hand garments that this family of eight, including six children aged two through seventeen, spent a total of $10 per year on clothing and relied on the mother of the family to make over what little they bought. Families in dire straits made used goods do very hard work indeed; one Rhode Island woman was still wearing second-hand shoes a year after they had been given to her.[12] But, even for those doing relatively well, second-hand clothing freed up scarce cash for things that mattered most; one African American family bought most of their clothes at Goodwill (a non-profit outlet similar to the Salvation Army) except for "Sunday best" and shoes.[13] In a study of San Diego Mexicans, two of the three families who spent the most (between two and three times the median expenditure) on clothing also received gifts of used clothing. These families ranked in the top income quintile of those interviewed; the example defies easy assumptions that used clothing always flowed to the poorest.[14] Other considerations may have included family membership (with larger families handing down used clothing from older to younger members and childless families passing garments to those with children) as well as family and friendship connections.

The circulation of used clothing intersected with sewing, a persistently important aspect of domestic production. Second-hand clothing was rarely usable as it came to the recipient: it had to be altered, updated in style, buttons and other fasteners replaced, worn spots mended. Clothing was often cut down for smaller wearers, allowing the use of the best of the fabric. Making over clothes was a skill of enormous value during hard times; those who didn't have it hastened to learn, as did the schoolgirl daughter of an unemployed Chicago ironworker, who "had become very resourceful in making over hats and clothes."[15] Making used clothing look new and fashionable required great skill; a settlement worker observed that the wife of an unemployed machinist was able to do a decent job of making over clothes for her children, but did less well for herself: "It was evident that she was wearing her unmarried sister's cast-off clothing, blouses that had been dyed."[16] Successful tailoring could avoid the shame of having shabby or unfashionable clothing. A Columbus, Ohio, woman "dressed herself and her family well by cleverly planning and sewing;" her "daughter's fear of having her clothes ridiculed by her class mates urges the mother to continually struggle for as much as they can get in the way of clothing and to make it over."[17]

Women responded differently to their place in the circulation of second-hand clothing. For some it was a way of life, such as the Fall River, Massachusetts, mother of seven children under the age of thirteen who boasted that "We have spent hardly a nickel for clothes ever since we were married [fifteen years ago]. Friends have given me things and in this way I have always kept the children clothed."[18] Others saw it as a sign of their disadvantaged class position; a New Orleans woman, for example, told a settlement worker that "she has never had to do this before but now 'she must forget her pride' in order to manage."[19] And for some saw the effort as futile and shameful, as did Czechoslovak immigrant mother of nine who said, "I cannot patch the clothes any more, – they are all patches." When a local settlement house gathered some used clothes, she went "over late in the evening to carry the things to her home. The neighbors did not see her, and the children did not know how the things all got there."[20] But some rose to the challenge and took great pride in their resourceful efforts, as this account of another New Orleans woman shows:

> When one of the workers at the settlement took over some things where the material was good and suggested that Mrs. Broussard make them over for the children, she was overjoyed. "Now," she said, "that will give me a little more money to spend for food. I won't have to buy the dress for sister that she needs so badly and I can make a coat out of this skirt for Susanne. I will dye some of these things and you must come and see what I make of them."[21]

Clothes donated by employers, which might be seen as badges of humiliation and were enitrely unacceptable as a substitute for wages, might be eagerly received when they were of high quality and in near-new condition.[22] One young woman wrote about her happy relationship with an employer's wife: "His wife became interested in me and gave me her daughter's cast-off clothes which, made over, made me some of the prettiest clothes that I have ever had."[23] A complicated path of circulation is suggested by the comment of a Connecticut woman frantic to outfit her daughter for school: "Finally in desperation I wrote to a friend who used to work for a 'rich lady.' This friend used to send pretty things to Virginia but has not done so recently. I don't know whether she is still working for that lady, but if she is, I guess she won't mind my writing."[24] This incident is one of the few in which we know who initiated the exchange, the giver or the recipient.

The vast majority of second-hand garments were women's and children's; adult men's clothing appears infrequently.[25] This was partly for material reasons: men's work clothing and suits were likely to be worn until threadbare, with the best clothing moving into everyday use as it wore out. Cultural factors probably figured in as well. Men's fashions changed little during these decades, and so men had little incentive to replace serviceable clothing with new versions of the same styles. Husbands' clothing seemed to be off the radar of most women interviewed; women typically mention that they purchased their own and their children's clothing, omitting mention of men's, or that men purchased their own clothing out of spending money they withheld from the family fund.[26] As a result, women apparently had limited opportunities to contribute their husbands' clothing to the second-hand stream and they and their children reaped most of the benefits from used clothing. One young man of twenty-two resented the shabbiness of his clothes, envying his eighteen- and nineteen-year-old sisters "because they can make their clothes over."[27] In another family, the mother and her daughter managed to "keep up [their] former standards in appearance" by wearing shoes and clothing given to them by friends, but such hand-me-downs apparently did not come the father's way and he felt "that his somewhat shabby appearance prevent[ed] him from getting work."[28] Only rarely did men receive second-hand clothes, and those they did were usually more formal attire rather than workaday garments. A typical example was the Minneapolis man to whom a social agency gave a "fairly presentable suit of clothes" to wear as he hunted for a job; as he told a settlement-house worker, "a guy hasta make a good impression nowadays."[29]

A generational dimension was involved as well. In most cases, siblings or parents gave the clothing to the woman householder, who distributed it within the family and remodeled and repaired it as her skills, time, resources, and inclination allowed. A few intriguing cases, however, show how second-hand clothing could become implicated in intergenerational conflict. A young woman whom we know only as Mary struggled with her very traditional Polish-immigrant parents over her use of makeup, her interest in clothing (Her mother felt that "clothes … was a sin."), and her disobedience; she finally quit school and took a job as a domestic servant. As a YWCA worker reported, "The woman who employs her gave her some of her pretty dresses and this convinced Mrs. M. [her mother] that Mary was working for a person who was leading her astray."[30] In this case, the parents' fears about their daughter were justified: she became an occasional prostitute. In many families, young women could look only to hand-me-downs for the clothing they craved; the ways in which these goods could become entangled in complicated family dynamics is shown by the tale of a fourteen-year-old Chicagoan, the daughter of Polish immigrants, who were tolerant of her aspirations even though they could not afford them.

> Friction between the mother and child has arisen because the mother is unable to give the girl money for the little things she wants and should have. Many irritating and distressing incidents have occurred because of the shortage of money. For instance, the child's shoes were worn out and beyond repair. For several week she wore galoshes until they too gave out. Desperate, Mrs. Topolski walked several miles to the home of a relative for aid and this sister gathered up all the shoes of her 16-year-old daughter that she could spare. The visitor found Mrs. Topolski at home, surrounded by twenty-five worn-out, high-heeled slippers, figuring on how to get one pair of shoes out of the mess for Angeline. The girl came running in full of hope, and burst into tears at the sight.[31]

A mother's frustrations and hopes, a daughter's resentments and desires, all come into sharp focus around that pile of second-hand shoes. The peer cultures of the high schools that more and more working-class children were attending during the interwar years placed a high value on fashionable clothing, and young women felt this pressure especially keenly. In one touching case, the peer group helped out one of its own to meet group standards: when a Minneapolis high-school girl wanted "to dress up better her friends give her clothes; one girl gives her a coat and another a dress and so on."[32]

Gender and generation figured less prominently in the circulation of second-hand furniture. As might be imagined, adults made the decisions about the disposition of household goods, and husbands and wives seem to have done so together as part of joint economic strategizing. Although working-class families gained almost entirely as the recipients of second-hand clothing, they benefited from being on both the demand and the supply sides of the circulation of second-hand furniture. Consider the case of the Faileys, a Louisville, Kentucky, family with five school-age children and a father skilled both in carpentry and plumbing who had been fortunate enough to secure year-round employment. At their most prosperous, they had a home "better furnished even than one would expect in the circumstances," but during Mr. Failey's second winter of unemployment they finally had to sell the furniture "bit by bit to purchase food." After a series of crises, Mrs. Failey began to refurbish the smaller quarters to which they had moved with second-hand furniture from Goodwill Industries.[33] As the Faileys' fortunes plummeted, they first contributed to and then purchased from the stream of second-hand furniture, in both cases doing better than they would otherwise have done.

Unlike clothing, which kin and friends exchanged without the mediation of cash, most furniture circulated in the cash market. Household goods figured but rarely in exchanges among friends and kin. Among the few examples was a Mexican family that moved from California to San Antonio and received a houseful of furniture except for their beds from friends.[34] In Depression-era Connecticut, investigators found that more families sold furniture than added to their stock, but those who did mostly did so through gifts from friends or kin.[35] In most cases, however, furniture was bought and sold for cash, as families rarely had enough extra furniture to share or the financial security to forgo the money they could gain from its sale. My sources are mute about whether furniture was being sold to dealers or to other families, but they do show that the purchase of second-hand furniture, especially on installment payments, was an important money-saving strategy. One Kansas City meatpacker, for example, paid off her used furniture at the rate of two or three dollars a month, whereas those who bought new furniture usually paid more than that every week.[36] Buying second-hand furniture did not necessarily mean buying second-rate furniture, for furniture loomed large in a family's investments and was often well cared for, moving into the used-furniture market in good condition.

As an investment, furniture was likely to be sold when times were hard or when the capital tied up in it could be better used elsewhere. The use of household goods in this fashion suggests the tenuousness of ownership of valuable goods such as furniture, jewelry, and automobiles; the working-class acquisition of such items was not a steady process of accretion but a cyclical one in which goods acquired during good times had to be sold or pawned in bad times. In some cases, the second-hand market offered the primary entry into higher-end consumption. The emergence of a market in used automobiles during the 1920s, for example, gave many working-class families their only access to this icon of mass consumption; twenty-four of twenty-six San Diego Mexican families owning cars, for example, had bought them second-hand.[37]

Selling household goods met many different types of family emergencies. Proceeds from the sale of $500 worth of furniture, for example, cushioned the slide of a Mexican immigrant from skilled auto painting to chronic unemployment, providing cash to feed his family as debt mounted for rent, medicine and utilities.[38] Thrown out of work by technology, a Pittsburgh pipe cutter and his family struck out in a new direction by opening a grocery business financed in part by the sale of their living-room furniture. The business failed and they lost their remaining furniture; the bare necessities of furniture that they then bought on the installment plan were later repossessed, "leaving only mattresses, broken chairs, and a hot plate."[39] Three times this family entered the trade in second-hand furniture, but only once from a position of comparative power. A Wisconsin Quebecois family sold its $1,100 (about half a year's pay for the carpenter father) worth of furniture to finance its move to Minneapolis for a new start.[40] When another family's only wage earner was injured on a foot press, the family sold its furniture to get along until she had recovered.[41] A Massachusetts family was able to keep its house only because the bank that held its mortgage allowed them to suspend payments in exchange for a lien on their furniture.[42] Even when a family moved before destitution set in, they might have to contribute their furniture to the second-hand market if they were buying it on installments, as dealers often refused to allow debtors to move their purchases any distance.[43]

The sale of furniture certainly involved heavy economic costs, since families sold as used what they had bought as new, but it also involved psychic costs. When pushed, families tended to sell the more luxurious – and often most expensive – pieces first; pianos and Victrolas were often the first household items to go, followed by parlor furniture.[44] Far from a simple matter of selling off non essentials, the sale of these items often cut deeply into the family's sense of itself. One New Haven, Connecticut, man ruefully told an interviewer: "You didn't buy a piano and victrola just to have them, you know. Now us – we bought them to keep the children happy and at home. When you sell – you sell those things that are a part of you."[45] Selling furniture as part of breaking up housekeeping was an unsettling ordeal: a Kentucky woman confided to a settlement-house worker "I hated to part with my furniture; I didn't know when I'd ever get as nice again, but we had to sell it all, even my folding bed." She and her family first lived with her parents but soon "wore out [their] welcome" and ended up in furnished rooms, a sorry comedown from the snug little cottage they had once owned.[46] Adding to the distress was the fact that families, once having made the painful decision to sell, sometimes had difficulty in finding a buyer at a reasonable price; the Vanzettis, a Philadelphia family, had given up their flat and gone to live with Mrs. Vanzetti's mother, but failed to sell their dining-room furniture.[47]

Furniture bridged the gap between those second-hand items that had use and investment value and those that might be used in wage earning. An Oklahoma widow filled a rented house with furniture and built up a thriving business taking in boarders, but when the house was sold she had to sell her sizable stock of furniture "at a loss."[48] On the other side of the fence was a Rochester, New York, woman whose husband was chronically employed; they had had to sell their furniture but were saving to buy more, presumably second-hand, so that the woman could "take roomers."[49] Evidence about the role of furniture in wage earning is anecdotal, but one source offers remarkable detail about the use of used sewing machines, a common household item that could easily do double duty in making over second-hand clothing and earning cash. In 1933, Women's Bureau agents visited 305 upstate New York women doing industrial homework on leather gloves.[50] Their interview notes tell us that forty-one women, or nearly one in eight, used second-hand tools in their work; an additional woman had sold her old machine to another homeworker. The interview schedule did not specifically ask about second-hand equipment, and so these machines were probably only the tip of the iceberg of a flourishing market in used capital equipment. About six in ten of the women had purchased their used machines, although it is impossible to know if they did so from other workers, from manufacturers selling off old-model machines, or from commercial dealers. The other four in ten reported that they had received their equipment as gifts or had borrowed it. The cash market in used equipment, then, accounted for only 60 percent of the transactions; as with hand-me-down clothing, although to a less dramatic degree, a substantial stream of second-hand items circulated outside the cash market.

In all, fifty used items were mentioned: thirty-three machines, fifteen motors and two tables. The predominance of machines over motors can probably be attributed to the durability of the basic sewing machine; carefully maintained, as these interviews testify that they were, a machine could last many decades. Motors, on the other hand, were less readily tinkered with by the homeworkers and more prone to burning out. Tables probably figured relatively little in the second-hand trade because they could be re-used with new machines or turned to entirely different purposes if the owner ceased to work at sewing. These items figured differently in the different sectors of the market – cash purchases, gifts and loans. Machines were most likely to be conveyed definitively: all but four were bought or received as gifts. About half (seven) of the motors and both of the tables, on the other hand, were borrowed, presumably with the idea that they would someday be returned to the lender. Presumably, motors were regarded as too valuable and tables as too enduringly useful to be given as readily as machines. The non cash transactions in used sewing equipment were largely among kin (eleven of the sixteen exchanges involved family members, three were among friends, and two were unspecified), among women (nine of the donors or loaners were women, and the sex of five was unspecified), and intergenerational (the nine female kin donors or loaners included four mothers-in-law, three mothers and an aunt, but only one sister).

These transactions were embedded in larger networks of reciprocity and exchange, another aspect of the pattern of mutual assistance among women that we observed in the case of hand-me-down clothing and that has been more broadly found in a wide variety of times and places. The inter-generational aspect is especially intriguing, suggesting a familial culture of industrial homework in which older women either gave their used equipment to younger kin when they bought new machinery or passed along their equipment when they retired from the trade. One mother, for example, was buying herself a new machine on installments for $158.50 and turned her old one over to her eighteen-year-old daughter, passing along not just the machine but also training her in the skills of glove making.[51]

Although the Women's Bureau agents did not record homeworkers' comments on the meaning of this second-hand equipment to them, their dire circumstances suggest that it was crucially important. One woman who worked with a second-hand machine and motor supported herself and her two children entirely on industrial homework after her husband died; the availability of used equipment surely eased her transition to a very different life.[52] Another woman working with a second-hand machine and a borrowed motor had a similarly difficult situation: her husband had been unemployed for nine months, her two working children were unable to support the family, and she had to turn to glove making even though she was "sick and [it was] hard for her to work."[53] Even for those in less desperate straits, used equipment served a variety of pressing needs. The mother of an eighteenth-month-old daughter was working on a machine and motor loaned by her mother-in-law until her child was old enough for her to return to the factory.[54] The daughter of a blind woman who could not be left alone worked at home on a second-hand machine and motor.[55] Unlike many varieties of women's wage earning, industrial homework on gloves required a capital investment, and second-hand equipment dramatically lowered the cost of entry.

Men, too, took advantage of second-hand tools in their wage-earning efforts, but because my sources privilege the female perspective I can offer only a few tantalizing examples of men both drawing on and contributing to the circulation of used goods. In Depression-era New Haven, Connecticut, a man laid off from a lucrative job as a munitions worker bought a used truck for $15.00, overhauled it, and replaced its body and cab, and set out on a successful new career as a hauler.[56] A Philadelphia man who used his truck to moonlight on hauling jobs had to sell it, adding to the second-hand stream, when he lost his principal job and could no longer afford the $10 monthly garage rent.[57] Other sources might well illuminate men's participation in the circulation of capital goods: we can imagine some men purchasing the tools of their trade from those leaving the field or from elderly retiring workers, and other men inheriting both tools and skills from their fathers.

The importance of second-hand goods in all three streams of circulation – clothing, furniture and tools – suggests that we cannot fully understand working-class family economies without taking such practices into account. Nor, for that matter, can we understand the culture of consumption and its continuing connections to home production. The dense circulation of second-hand clothing allowed women to use their domestic skills to fashion clothing that they could never have afforded new and to outfit themselves and their children in current styles. Clothing had long been a badge of status, but became even more so in the interwar period when the mass production of fashionable goods raised the bar for public appearances; access to second-hand clothing made it possible for those who could not buy directly into this world to participate in it nonetheless. The flourishing market in used furniture allowed working-class families to play both sides of the street as sellers and buyers. Furniture provided an investment that paid dividends in its use and in the enjoyment of it, and it could also be sold to realize needed cash. Families could enjoy, even if only briefly, the pleasures of an overstuffed parlor set or a piano or a Victrola and hope, once they had to be sold, to acquire similar items again when things looked up. Their contributions to the market in used household goods provided opportunities for other families to buy needed and desired items at less than full retail prices. The third stream of circulation, that of goods that could be used in wage earning, was a key element in helping working-class families to expand their slender budgets by allowing them to acquire low-cost capital goods to enter a variety of pursuits either as wage earners, in the case of the industrial homeworkers, or as independent entrepreneurs, like the women who took in boarders and the men who engaged in hauling. And, finally, the circulation of used clothing and of used capital goods shows the continued importance of ties of mutuality outside the cash market and of the ways in which those ties could be used to open small doors into the world of mass consumption for working-class families in the interwar USA.

Notes

Thanks to Edward Benson, Kate Dunnigan, Charles McGraw, Catherine Page, Margaret Robinson, Christina Simmons and Sherry Zane and to the participants in the Colloque EUI Florence on *Les Circulations des objets d'occasion*, October 2002, for very helpful comments on earlier versions of this article. The research on which it was based received generous support from the National Endowment for the Humanities, the National Humanities Center, the University of Connecticut Humanities Institute and the University of Connecticut Research Foundation.

1. I define as working-class those families in which the wage earners engaged in blue- or white-collar nonsupervisory jobs or ran small one- or two-person businesses such as fishmongering or draying.
2. Susan Porter Benson, *Household Accounts: Working-class Family Economies in the Interwar USA* (Ithaca, NY, 2007). See also my essays: Susan Porter Benson, "Living on the Margin: Working-class Marriages and Family Survival Strategies in the United States, 1919–1941," in Victoria de Grazia (ed.) with Ellen Furlough, *The Sex of Things: Gender and Consumption in Historical Perspective* (Berkeley, CA, 1996), pp. 212–43, and "Gender, Generation, and Consumption in the United States: Working-class Families in the Interwar Period," in Susan Strasser, Charles McGovern and Matthias Judt (eds.), *Getting and Spending:*

European and American Consumer Societies in the Twentieth Century (Cambridge, UK, 1998), pp. 223–40.

3. On African American proletarianization, see Joe William Trotter, Jr., *Black Milwaukee: The Making of an Industrial Proletariat, 1915–1945* (Urbana, IL, 1985). These may also be the day-to-day commonalities that led to the multi-racial unionism of the Congress of Industrial Organizations; see Lizabeth Cohen, *Making a New Deal: Industrial Workers in Chicago, 1919–1939* (Cambridge, UK, 1990).

4. Judith M. Bennett, *Ale, Beer, and Brewsters in England: Women's Work in a Changing World, 1300–1600* (New York, 1996); Steve J. Stern, *The Secret History of Gender: Women, Men, and Power in Late Colonial Mexico* (Chapel Hill, NC, 1995); and Gracia Clark, *Onions Are My Husband: Survival and Accumulation by West African Market Women* (Chicago, 1994).

5. On the importance of shared stories, see the Personal Narratives Group (ed.), *Interpreting Women's Lives: Feminist Theory and Personal Narratives* (Bloomington, IN, 1989), especially pp. 261–4.

6. Ruth Shonle Cavan and Katherine Howland Ranck, *The Family and the Depression: A Study of One Hundred Chicago Families* (Chicago, 1938), p. 119. On teachers, see Marion Elderton (ed.), *Case Studies of Unemployment Compiled by the Unemployment Committee of the National Federation of Settlements* (Philadelphia, 1931), pp. 117, 98.

7. National Archives, Records of the Women's Bureau, Record Group 86.3.3, Records of the Division of Research and Manpower Program Development, Series Unpublished Studies and Materials, 1919–72, Box 3, Folder "Mothers' Pensions 1925–26," 5. Note that Women's Bureau interview schedules are cited either by number or by an abbreviation of the interviewee's name.

8. E. Wight Bakke, *The Unemployed Worker: A Study of the Task of Making a Living without a Job* (New Haven, CT, 1940), p. 272.

9. Ruth Alice Allen and Sam B. Barton, *Wage Earners Meet the Depression* (Austin, TX, 1935), p. 21.

10. Elderton, *Case Studies*, p. 211.

11. Ibid., p. 321.

12. National Archives, Records of the Women's Bureau, Record Group 86.3.4, Records of the Division of Special Services and Publications, Bulletin 131, Box 297, 5-2-11.

13. Social Welfare History Archives, University of Minnesota, Helen Hall Papers, Box 48, Folder 9, Perrywinkle Family.

14. Heller Committee for Research in Social Economics of the University of California and Constantine Panunzio, *How Mexicans Earn and Live: A Study of the Incomes and Expenditures of One Hundred Mexican Families in San Diego, California* (Berkeley, CA, 1933), pp. 14, 36.

15. Cavan and Ranck, *The Family*, p. 119.

16. Elderton, *Case Studies*, p. 316; see also pp. 173, 348, and National Archives, Records of the Women's Bureau, Record Group 86.3.4, Records of the Division of Special Services and Publications, Bulletin 124, Box 219, Mrs. Bessie L.

17. Helen Hall Papers, Box 43, Folder 2, Price.

18. Elderton, *Case Studies*, p. 58.

19. Ibid., p. 145.

20. Ibid., p. 287.

21. Ibid., p. 62

22. Elizabeth Clark-Lewis, *Living In, Living Out: African American Domestics and the Great Migration* (Washington, DC, 1994), p. 157.

23. Sophia Smith Collection, Smith College, YWCA Papers, Box 31, Folder 5, "The Autobiography of a First Generation American Girl."

24. Bakke, *Unemployed Worker*, pp. 272–3.

25. See, for example, Elderton, *Case Studies*, pp. 173, 145, 148.

26. See, for example, National Archives, Records of the Women's Bureau, Record Group 86.3.4, Records of the Division of Special Services and Publications, Bulletin 74, Box 97, 90 and Box 102, 957 and 960; Bulletin 88, Box 122, Folder "Kansas City, Kansas, 2-Cudahy," 32–20.

27. Robert Cooley Angell, *The Family Encounters the Depression* (New York, 1936), p. 144.

28. Elderton, *Case Studies*, p. 145; see also Helen Hall Papers, Box 45, Folder 11, Chesnough, p. 3a.
29. Helen Hall Papers, Chesnough, p. 9.
30. YWCA Papers, Box 31, Folder 5, "Second Generation Girl."
31. Elderton, *Case Studies*, pp. 261–2.
32. Ibid., p. 287.
33. Ibid., pp. 180–1.
34. National Archives, Records of the Women's Bureau, Record Group 86.3.4, Records of the Division of Special Services and Publications, Bulletin 126, Box 226, 76.
35. Bakke, *Unemployed Worker*, p. 278.
36. Records of the Women's Bureau, Record Group 86.3.4, Bulletin 88, Box 122, 37–9.
37. Heller Commitee and Panunzio, *How Mexicans Earn and Live*, p. 53.
38. Elderton, *Case Studies*, pp. 242–4.
39. Ibid., pp. 38–41; quotation from p. 41.
40. Ibid., pp. 121–2.
41. National Archives, Records of the Women's Bureau, Record Group 86.3.4, Records of the Division of Special Services and Publications, Bulletin 60, Box 33, Folder "survey materials – New Jersey #2-1147," 45.
42. Elderton, *Case Studies*, pp. 127–8.
43. Ibid., p. 151.
44. Ibid., pp.17, 43, 51–2.
45. Bakke, *Unemployed Worker*, p. 260.
46. Elderton, *Case Studies*, pp. 92–3.
47. Ibid., pp. 296–7.
48. National Archives, Records of the Women's Bureau, Record Group 86.3.4, Records of the Division of Special Services and Publications, Bulletin 48, Box 25, Folder "#48 survey materials – home visit schedules," 38.
49. Elderton, *Case Studies*, p. 364.
50. National Archives, Records of the Women's Bureau, Record Group 86.3.4, Records of the Division of Special Services and Publications, Box 207, Bulletin 119, Box 207, Folders "#119 Schedules – Home Visits (Gloversville, NY)" and "#119 Schedules – Home Visits (Johnstown, NY)."
51. Bulletin 119, Folder "#119 Schedules – Home Visits (Johnstown, NY)," Box 207, 199.
52. Bulletin 119, Folder "#119 Schedules – Home Visits (Gloversville, NY)," Box 207, 211.
53. Ibid., 206.
54. Ibid., 126.
55. Ibid., 160.
56. Bakke, *Unemployed Worker*, p. 229.
57. Elderton, *Case Studies*, p. 215.

9

MOVING ON

OVERLOOKED ASPECTS OF MODERN COLLECTING

Jackie Goode

More than sixty paintings by major artists, including Breughel, Boucher and Watteau have been torn up and thrown out with the rubbish by an art thief's mother, French police said yesterday. The destruction of the £1 billion collection amassed by Stephen Breitweiser, 31, from 172 European museums, has shocked the art world.[1]

In the spring of 2001 in the vacant C&A building on Oxford Street in London, the Exhibition "Breakdown" opened, in which the artist Michael Landy placed every one of his 7,226 possessions on a production line conveyor belt which then carried them into sacks destined for landfill. The exhibition (which consisted, after the initial cataloguing and destruction, of an inventory) attracted huge media attention, as well as 45,000 visitors.[2]

We don't necessarily need to know a great deal about painting to share the shock of the art world reported above. Similarly, the extent to which Michael Landy's act of disposal constituted the breaking of a taboo is evidenced by the fact that "he became the subject of sermons on the morality of consumerism; his work was attacked for its wanton destruction; and a priest and psychiatrist offered counseling." Such responses to acts of destruction of material objects are indicative of the strength of relatively unexplored feelings surrounding the goods each of us acquires in our lives, and, in particular, the sense of shock and outrage when such goods are intentionally disposed of so finally. This is especially so when the goods in question constitute some of our most important relationships with the world, whether these relationships are represented by Dutch Masters, or shabby "hand-me-downs." The hardest possession for Landy to get rid of in his exhibition, for example, was a sheepskin coat that had belonged to his father. It had assumed a totemic significance. "I really felt I was jinxing my dad by destroying it," he commented.

This chapter explores the issue of disposal through an investigation of modern popular collecting. The ways in which collecting has been studied as a particular form of consumption has neglected some important issues. For example, there has been an overemphasis on acquisition, and a failure to recognize the significance of second-hand goods and their circulation. Disposal of collected items and the problems this presents illuminate the social and economic relations of consumption, our relationships with material culture and systems of circulation. This overlooked aspect of modern collecting is explored via participant and nonparticipant observation at a variety of auctions and antiques and collectables fairs and centers in England over the last three to four years, plus in-depth interviews with collectors. The interviews were tape-recorded, transcribed and analyzed with the support of a qualitative data analysis program.

My starting point in relation to contemporary forms of popular collecting was participants' own perspectives on their activities. Despite "pathologizing" overtones that tend to characterize them as obsessives or denigrate them as "trainspotters" or "anoraks," my interviewees' talk about themselves, their objects and the processes and practices of collecting revealed much more positive and appealing qualities, including: having retained a childlike wonder in a cynical world; displaying an aesthetic appreciation of beauty and craftsmanship; capturing the exotic even in a shrinking world; pleasure in serendipity, and, lest we forget that commercial transactions are involved, the astute deployment of knowledge required to scoop the legendary "bargain." The following extracts from interviews are introduced to support my analysis of collecting as the circulation of second-hand goods located in a network of social relationships, a circulation that is stimulated by a variety of triggers:

> The thing I like best that it says about me is that I'm passionate about something. 'Cos I'm pleased that I have a passion, you know, that I really care about something. 'Cos in some ways I've grown up as a fairly cynical world-weary sort of person, and that's not very – I don't find that very attractive somehow. I'm pleased to think that I have a wide-eyed side to me, you know? [Paul, music]

> I saw a couple of pots in the window of an antique shop and thought they were beautiful. The guy who sold them to us said, "Did you know there's just been an exhibition at the V&A, and there's just been a book published?" So we got the book. And everything in it was just gorgeous, and it went from there. I just couldn't believe that such lovely stuff existed … it's first of all the gorgeous glowing colors, erm, I suppose to a lesser extent, it's the knowledge that it is all done by hand and by skilled craftspeople, but most of all, as well as the color, it's when the design fits the shape of the pot … There's a real pleasure in seeing something beautiful and buying it, certainly. And there's a real pleasure in looking at them. I sit every day and drink my morning cuppa and I look at the mantelpiece, and I was looking at them this morning thinking "that is just beautiful." [Liz, Moorcroft pottery]

I think it's a combination of, they are miniature works of art in terms of the stamps themselves, and that they have been produced to act as messenger bearers from lands far across the sea. I know we live today in a very shrinking sort of world where people go on holidays to places you would think you would never get to in times past. But there is still that element of "that's quite a romantic sounding place," or it has certain interest about it. It's a way of acquiring a culture, combined with the fact of these letters and cards. You think, "They've traveled miles, gone all over the place.' [Barry, stamps]

I was in this little junk shop, with really dirty, filthy windows ... I peered through the door and I saw a bunch of objects, some of which were swords, stacked in this like large umbrella stand ... very first one I picked up was what's called a Shamshir, Persian sword. Pulled it out the scabbard and only got it what, about six inches out of the scabbard, and thought "My god, look at that!" There was a watered steel blade, made in a certain way to give this appearance, and they'd kept the gold cartouche on, so: chiseled, inlaid with gold. And I pulled it out and I thought "My god!" Had it back: "How much d'you want for that?" I got it for six pounds fifty! [laughs] This was 1970. And I couldn't wait to get out the shop with it, looked at it and thought, "Oh god, yeah, it's really really high quality, this one," took it down to the Victoria and Albert ... can't remember who it was who identified it now, but it was made by a chap called Asadullah of Ispahan in 1620, and he said, in their opinion, it was genuine, 'cos this erm Asadullah was quite often copied ... but this was too genuine. It's got the gold cartouche on saying "Asadullah of Ispahan, servant of god" and, even more interesting, the quillons, the cross pieces on the hilt which protect the hand, were chiseled steel, and he suggested that the sword had been owned by a chap called Lutf Ali Kahn Zand, who ruled most of Persia, and he was assassinated in 1795, in the last of the Zand dynasty. ["Amazing! What did you do with it when you'd heard all of that?"] I took it home and treasured it [laughs]. I thought, I felt really really really chuffed. You know – fantastic! It's, again, it's not the value of it, because obviously, I sold it at Sotheby's, erm, again that went with a lot of the other swords to pay the bloody solicitor. But it wasn't the value that really pleases you. You see something and you think, "That's really really good." You purchase it, and it's a bit of a chance, isn't it, that you were right. You get it dirt cheap, and then you find that it's really really excellent quality, and you got it right, and you've got something there which is unique. Certainly that sword was. [Gordon, swords]

If, as the quotations at the beginning of this chapter indicate, disposal of objects highly valued by society is so counter-intuitive and shocking, and if singular items acquired as part of an individual collection have the transformative powers on the person and their social worlds suggested by the above speakers, it seems fitting to inquire why they were disposed of, what practices were involved, and how easy or difficult it was to accomplish. The *Circulation des objets d'occasion* Conference encouraged me to go back to my data on collecting in order to move beyond acquisition and the early stages of the collecting career, and to see what collectors had to say about disposal, that point at which items so lovingly acquired enter into circulation once more.

Here then, I too am "moving on," from an emphasis on the acquisition, maintenance, and completion of a collection, to examine the "moving on" of this special category of "things." Contrary to expectations, perhaps, disposal does not necessarily signal the end of the collecting career. It does, however, present the collector with a number of dilemmas, which I will examine in some detail. First of all, however, reasons for the neglect of these important aspects of collecting are briefly considered, before turning to an examination of the moment of disposal as a crucial aspect of a collecting career.

Collections as Second-hand Circulation

I should like to go beyond traditional definitions of collecting that are elite and gendered. I conceptualize collecting as: a set of practices in which objects are acquired and exchanged over time; not only in a systematic, but also in an interrupted ad hoc way; according to a variety of social, economic and cultural constraints; and in which they are brought for a time into a symbolic relationship with other objects and with the collector. Further, these practices may be implicated in the construction and maintenance of identities, as well as in sets of wider social and economic relations and systems of circulation.

Popular interest in markets for collectables has been expanding rapidly. At any given moment in the contemporary Western world, around a quarter to a third of all adults are willing to identify themselves as collectors.[3] In the UK, specialist publications and television programs have raised the profile of this trade, contributed to continuing expansion in the range of goods constituting "collectables," and encouraged increased levels of trading. Definitions of collecting, however, have traditionally rested on what we might call a "connoisseur" model of collecting, that is, an elite activity engaged in primarily by or on behalf of rich and powerful men, with an emphasis on the knowledge, expertise and taste demonstrated in the acquisition.[4] The relationship between the collector and the objects collected is seen as evidence of the status of the collector, and motivations may also be addressed. In this elite form, the implicit demonstration of wealth and power by the collector may be glossed over by a portrayal of performing an altruistic duty on behalf of the nation, by preserving its heritage for future generations.

A classificatory system of some kind that removes objects from use and brings them into a special relationship with each other as components of a preconceived whole is usually seen as crucial,[5] with objects (or experiences) constituting a set, systematically and passionately acquired according to predetermined conceptual boundaries (such as the *artificialia* or *naturalia* of cabinets of curiosity), or perceptual boundaries (such as the subject of the images depicted on postage stamps); further, the relationship between the collector and the objects acquired is seen as an intimate and irrational one.[6]

Definitions of more democratized contemporary forms of collecting categorize it as a special form of consumption, in which acquisition is seen as the key process. There may also be rituals such as "orienting, identifying, arranging, and cataloguing"[7] or post-purchase "possession rituals" (of examining, holding, admiring, and displaying items), as the owner transforms the purchase into part of the collection.[8] Much writing is also informed by a "completionist" model, which suggests that the collection will at some point be finished and require no further acquisitions.

While most writers stress the relationship between the objects themselves, as part of what is referred to as "seriation,"[9] more recent studies favor a broader definition which includes an accumulation of objects whose sequence is largely a subjective creation of the collector,[10] this subjectivity being reflected in references to desire: "The pure collector's interest is not bounded by the intrinsic worth of the objects of his [*sic*] desire; whatever they cost, he must have them."[11] Finally, some authors note a temporal aspect, which adds a longitudinal element to the acquisition.[12] In relation to the temporal aspect, I would add that there may be variation in the regularity and consistency of collecting, and, indeed, in whether or not it includes a preconceived notion of the final product in the form of the "complete collection." For example, women's studies have shown how, in relation to work, a linear, uninterrupted model of "career" that progresses in a systematic way towards a preconceived end has functioned to "count women out" of the picture. The sociology of consumption has developed along similarly gendered lines: efforts by male workers to increase income have been characterized as a heroic opposition to employers, while women's practices as consumers in "saving the household the same few pounds a week by the development of the requisite abilities" have been trivialized.[13] Applied to collecting, these insights suggest that women's collecting, constrained by access to time and disposable income, may follow a much more interrupted path than men's.

Recognizing an element of constraint in consumption practices is in any case important in a field that has tended to be dominated by cultural studies rather than political economy. The "must have, whatever the cost" notion smacks strongly of the elite model of collecting, although this is not made explicit. The "popular" collectors in my study to some extent felt bounded by both economic and moral constraints which they dealt with in quasi-magical ways. There are frequent accounts, for example, of wavering over a potential purchase at an antiques fair. The decision is made by default: if the desired object is still there when they have gone around the fair one more time, they will buy it; if not, they will decide that they were not "meant" to have it. At the same time, collectors and dealers alike make moral judgments about pricing, labeling some traders "fair" and others "greedy."

In contrast to studies of collecting, a noticeable aspect of the study of consumption has been that trade in second-hand goods has been largely ignored. This is an important omission: "By value alone, this market is massive, most especially because of the contribution of second-hand cars, yet, even now, it is remarkably little studied. Perhaps this is because second-hand goods are seen as historically more important than now. If so, this judgment is incorrect."[14]

The fact that some people place a premium on newness over and above considerations of cost, while others value second-hand goods (also, in some cases, for reasons other than cost), invites further investigation. In his historical study of the roots of modern consumption, McCracken describes the decline of the patina system, which he suggests came to an end in the nineteenth century. A shift in values attached to commodities and consumption took place, whereby inherited goods lost much of their personal value, in favor of a perceived increase in the worth of newness in itself. It has been suggested that a continuation of this development accounts for the tawdriness associated with second-hand commodities that continues today. But attention is also drawn to the paradox that wealth remains an inherited rather than an achieved asset, and since household items in particular are often passed from parents to children, on death at least, these particular second-hand goods are often still valued in deeply personal ways. What is clear, though, is that the "contemporary valorization of newness" has expanded from an elite practice to a mass culture.[15] Collecting, however, on the whole stands outside this analysis, in its continued valorization of certain categories of second-hand goods, for example, in relation to the consumption of "heritage."[16]

The publication in the UK of Miller's Guides to Antiques and Collectables, and the many trade newspapers, together with the enduring success of television programs such as the *Antiques Road Show* and its numerous variants, appear to have both raised the profile of trade in second-hand goods of all kinds, and encouraged the population to become involved in trading, or at least to search their attics for something of contemporary cultural interest. Media coverage of such activities amplifies trading and vice versa, and the media represent one mechanism in a predatory relationship between alternative kinds of trading and the mainstream retail sector. This aspect of the counterculture has been illustrated in relation to second-hand clothing, in a study that draws attention to the entrepreneurial opportunities offered by second-hand goods: "the presence of this particular entrepreneurial dynamic [of buying and selling] has rarely been acknowledged in most subcultural analysis. Those points at which subcultures offered the prospect of a career through the magical exchange of the commodity have warranted as little attention as the network of small scale entrepreneurial activities which financed the counterculture."[17]

Of course, modern collecting is not confined exclusively to second-hand goods. There are huge markets in "instant" collectables, the kind of ceramics and figurines that appear every week in newspaper color supplements, as well as Beanie Babies, Pokemon cards, etc.[18] Further, the predatory relationship between "alternative" and "mainstream" trading identified with reference to second-hand clothing can also be seen in relation to the collecting of these. The Moorcroft factory in Staffordshire is just one example of pottery manufacturers who own and run collectors' clubs, and who regularly announce the launch of new lines only available to members, and only for a short time, before they are discontinued. But this creation of markets in "new collectables" via the introduction of manufactured scarcity is a phenomenon I shall look at in greater detail elsewhere. This chapter is confined to the collection and disposal of second-hand goods acquired in a variety of arenas, from junk shops, antiques fairs and antiques centers, to charity shops, car boot sales and as gifts.

A further omission in consumption studies, and in studies of collecting, has been a focus on acquisition at the expense of disposal. Theorizing of modern consumption as having its origins in a commitment to romanticism, for example,[19] examines what has been called the "desire-acquisition-use-disillusionment-renewed desire" cycle.[20] What happens to earlier acquisitions between disillusionment and renewed desire goes unexamined. In relation to collecting in particular, the neglect may arise from the fact that theorizing has once again rested on the connoisseur model, and has been characterized by a rather static approach: descriptions of individual collections,[21] and explorations of the status, personality and motivations of the collector.[22] Although there has recently been a conceptual shift toward collecting as a process, current studies have not moved far beyond mapping the incidence of contemporary collecting, cataloging the variety and value of objects collected and "kept"[23] and examinations of the sites at which purchases take place.[24]

Recent developments in the broader study of consumption have rectified these omissions to some extent. There has been a renewed interest in production and distribution; an awareness of the power of retailers over producers, and of the impact of consumer choice on retailers; a move away from overdetermined categories like class and status, toward questions of how consumer objects produce subjects, or "singularity;" a conception of the meaning of objects not being ascribed but worked out perfomatively; and a history of consumption that challenges the "standard" history, and traces modern consumption practices back to the early eighteenth, and even late seventeenth centuries, with apparently novel practices shown to have deep historical roots.[25] Most recently, there have been attempts to refocus a "largely disembodied and socially disembedded account of consumption" by foregrounding the place of emotion, and to show how the issue of "disposability" as an integral part of consumption, has historically been caught between two moral discourses of the household, those of thrift and hygiene.[26]

Despite these developments, there has been a continuing lack of academic attention paid to entrepreneurial activity. The focus remains primarily on consumption and acquisition, as opposed to trading or disposal. It has been noted, for example, that Douglas and Isherwood's classic *World of Goods*[27] has chapters on why people want goods, why they save and how they use goods, but "there is no chapter that says why (or how) people make dirt or waste goods, nor how dirt and waste enter and/or exit the cybernetic system."[28] Studies using "rubbish theory"[29] have sought to rectify this to some extent.[30] But, even within the sociology of food, the accent has been on gendered divisions of labor in the planning, provision and preparation of meals,[31] as opposed to practices surrounding its disposal. Exceptions come from historical studies, including a social history of trash,[32] and a study of intra-familial transfers of clothing.[33] Nevertheless, studies of present-day circulations of second-hand goods are hard to find. Locating my own study of collecting within a conceptual framework that focuses on the circulation of second-hand goods is particularly helpful therefore, since it provides an opportunity to rectify some of these omissions and to build upon my earlier research.[34] This examined issues of identity – both the meaning for the collector of the goods themselves, and the ways in which objects mediated collectors' own identity construction. At the same time, in order to recognize the dynamic aspects of this area of social and economic life – the rites of passage, the staging posts, the acquisition of expertise – it introduced the notion of the "collecting career." It is time to move this analysis on.

Many areas of social life can be conceptualized at a number of levels, and as performing a number of functions. The postwar rise of DIY (do-it-yourself), for example, has been conceptualized not simply as a function of economic considerations, but also as a way of "doing gender," that is, of creating a specifically male regime within the home, resulting from a decline in time spent at work or in pubs. In this analysis, the husband's "doing up" the kitchen is a gift to his wife as much as a way of saving money.[35] In the same way, the notion of "the bargain" motivates much consumption of second-hand goods, rather than any altruistic desire to minimize waste.[36] This multi-faceted approach can be applied to collecting. The surge of public interest in "retrochic" in the UK in the 1960s, for example, which, in its flea-market and car-boot aspects, "helped to form Britain into a nation of collectors," has been seen as "an alternative consumerism, pandering to the nostalgia for a simpler life."[37] But it was as much about creating second-hand style as it was about taking up a political stance towards consumption per se.

Similarly, the circulation of second-hand goods as a process that sustains economic and social relations, and which can be seen as one of the ways in which social integration is maintained, broken or reinforced, is variously experienced by participants at different points in the process. As I have argued, disposal has been a neglected aspect of this process. The following interview extracts, illustrating collectors' experiences of the moment of disposal, are used to further support my analysis of collecting as the circulation of second-hand goods. Extracts come from interviews with: Paul, a music collector; Barry, a philatelic historian; Dennis, a collector of money boxes and a host of other ceramic goods; Lydia, a collector of teapots; June, a collector of antique linen and textiles; Liz, a collector of Moorcroft pottery; Gordon, a collector of Japanese swords and art; and Ellen, who became responsible for the disposal of another's collection.

The Problematics of Disposal

Many collectors had stories of what might be termed "unintentional disposal," that is, they had lost items through breakages. One couple whom I met at an antiques fair told stories of a number of losses from their collection of eighteenth-century ceramics, mostly as a result of shelves falling down, which the husband had inexpertly put up. One such disaster had occurred when the wife placed a figurine on the mantelpiece so that she could enjoy looking at it "when there was nothing on the television." But the string on a mirror her husband had put up above the mantelpiece broke, and it fell and smashed the figure. The wife told how she kept the biggest pieces, a head and a piece of an arm, as a reminder of the original. Even in such extreme circumstances, it appears, there can be an active resistance to disposal.

A second category might be termed "temporary disposal," a way of dealing with items their owners were in fact keen to dispose of, but were inhibited from doing so. Lydia exemplified this. Her collection of teapots had begun with a treasured Japanese tea set given to her by her mother for her seventh birthday, and it had been added to by further gifts from well-meaning friends, who passed on items which they themselves had inherited or had spotted in antiques or bric-a-brac shops, to enhance her collection. The literature on gifts[38] makes clear the obligations involved, and Lydia felt able only to dispose temporarily of some of what she described as the worst "monstrosities" – by hiding them away in a cupboard until such time as she might need to display them.

These two categories do not, of course, lead to the circulation of second-hand goods: in the first case, disposal was more or less final and, in the second, items were removed from and restored to the collection, rather than "moved on." Disposal does not necessarily lead to reentry to systems of circulation. Items did enter into circulation, however, via "rational disposal," that is, when disposal took place as a means of moving on to the next stage in the collecting career. Dennis and Gordon had each got rid of whole stamp collections when they were younger. Disposing of their collections at that stage, by giving them away or selling them to fellow enthusiasts, represented their own "moving on" in the sense of having acquired new collecting interests. Dennis moved on in stages through a number of interests before specializing in money boxes, while Gordon became interested in swords through his professional involvement in metallurgy. He then progressed to Japanese prints when swords became too expensive. For these collectors, disposal as a byproduct of changing interests was an integral part of a continuing career.

The same was true for other interviewees, but they illustrated a category that might be called "enforced disposal." One reason for this was lack of space. Amateur collectors have been seen as in many ways equaling professional curators in their knowledge of and care for their collections.[39] But even relatively small "popular" collections take up room, whether they are "publicly" displayed in the home, or stored away. For some of my interviewees, having "no room to move" in the house meant moving on some items from their collection. This applied particularly to Dennis. A self-employed building contractor, he owned a number of properties. When he moved his most important collections into his current house, it took his new partner four or five months to sort them into boxes to store in the garage:

["So what has brought you to the point of saying I want to get rid of stuff now?"] Basically space. I can't see anything ... Doreen started living with me six month ago and I says "Right, I need to sort out the garage, it's floor-to-ceiling, collections of everything just in boxes" ... that garage is full of collectables, my other garage is full of collectables, the roof is full ... If I tried to put them out I'd want a place of horrendous proportions.

Figure 9.1. Two photographs showing one end of Dennis's loft

The photograph Dennis took of Doreen at the time shows how she felt about the task ahead (see Figure 9.2).

June's collecting of Victorian linens and household textiles was motivated in part by a desire to preserve a disappearing way of life, and this meant that

Figure 9.2. The photograph Dennis took of Doreen at the time, showing how she felt about the task ahead

she too was actively resistant to disposal. But she was forced to let the goods reenter circulation, after much heart-searching. Not having room to move in the house led her to sort through her collections. This had made her realize just how much she'd got, and she decided the time had come to start selling some of it. Constraints of space had turned "conservation" into "hoarding:"

> I'm hoarding, I know I am. And there's a point where it will get damaged in the end if I'm not careful. Or you end up getting moths in. They get stains ... all sorts of things can go wrong ... I'm starting to think perhaps I should be selling it ... I'd like to display them more at home but it's not really feasible. You see these people on television ... they have these collecting programs, and they have these tailor's dummies with wonderful dresses. And I think, "I don't know how you can do that," because our house isn't small, but you've got to live in it – and how do you get round?

Yet another set of tensions around disposal arose for other couples. Dennis, Paul, Liz and Gordon also illustrated "enforced disposal" but for them it had been necessitated by divorce. Exactly how they went about parting with items varied. Dennis had taken disposal in his stride, partly because he had retained sole possession of his most treasured collection (his 8,000 money boxes), and partly because he enjoys the hunt more than the possession:

> ["You parted from your first wife?"] I've parted from my second one, and parted from my third one. ["Did the collections come into any settlement?"] No, I always give them the house, and the car, and everything in it, and I have to go out and buy it all again. They took all what they wanted. It don't mean nowt to me. ["You just let them choose what they wanted?"] Yes. The joy is hunting it, finding it. Finding it is the buzz.

Liz's collecting career had begun as a joint venture with her husband, and as they loved Moorcroft equally, they tried to be fair and systematic about how they shared it out between them when they parted, so that she too felt quite happy about the outcome:

> We made a list and we drew lots for everything, and we stuck by it. We agreed in advance – well, no, we made some lists of things that were roughly equivalent in value and size and attractiveness, and then we just drew lots for which of us got each one ... Because it was all antique-y stuff, we kept a record of what we'd paid for it, and what it was, when we bought it, and where, so we knew what we'd got, we knew who liked what bits best, and therefore – some I must admit, we just said "Yeah, I like that, I'll have that – you like that, you have that," and we agreed on those kind of things – but when it came to we both liked it, then we drew lots and just took our chances.

Paul's difficulties in disposing of items in his collection revealed how the sometimes ambiguous and ambivalent nature of gifting between partners can lead to shifting categorizations of objects and ownership. While he was definitely the collector in the family, "enforced disposal" demonstrated that "his" collection also appeared to contain records ostensibly purchased as gifts for his wife. Splitting the collection was hard for him, he explained, because he had only ever bought music for her that he himself also liked. Guilt about having initiated the divorce led him to give his wife some choice about what she would keep:

> I'd always been the buyer, but I'd often bought things for her that I knew she'd like, 'cos I'd got the mentality that wanted to go and look for them, and she's – I don't want to say this in a disparaging way of women – but typically women don't go out looking for things like that ... and I would do that on her behalf – partly to satisfy my own thrill of the chase, but also to give her something she liked. So there were things that she wouldn't have if it weren't for me. ["Did you give her a choice, then, when you parted?"] Yes. Out of a sense of guilt to some extent, yes.

There was no question for Gordon of splitting his collection, but he had had to dispose of part of it in order to pay for his divorce. In the case of the Persian sword, what hurt most was the knowledge that he would never acquire its like again:

> I sold it at Sotheby's – again, that went with a lot of the other swords to pay the bloody solicitor. Selling something like that Persian sword, that really hurt because it's the one really good high-quality thing that I'd got in the collection, which I knew was excellent quality – the genuine thing – really really really good quality, and something that I'll never be able to afford to buy again.

These interviewees illustrate the way household and marriage can provide a context for variable resistance to disposal, and for disposal as part of the dynamics of marital relationships, as opposed to being "merely" the subject of market-driven or commercial decisions. Perhaps the most difficult kind of disposal of all to contemplate, however, is the "final disposal" of one's collections. My interviewees had all thought about this issue, with various degrees of discomfort. In one study of bequeathing, women had frequently spoken of informal bequests, where property is passed on during the giver's lifetime, as a symbolic way of acknowledging relationships. The authors characterized this as "a logical extension of women's kin-keeping role." Men appeared to engage in these informal distribution activities much more rarely. Their talk about the disposal and division of property centered around the problems that could occur if these were not organized through a will. The authors concluded: "Men see it as an economic issue concerning the disposal of financial resources and material property; women tend to see inheritance in the context of close relationships, and use it as a means of consolidating these ... For men, bequeathing is about control of assets ... for women it is much more about managing relationships."[40]

The accounts of my interviewees did not unequivocally support this gendered division, as both men and women had given some thought to the implications for the recipients of being left collections that were unlikely to hold such meaning for them as they had done for their creators. Barry explained:

I haven't any illusions that any members of my family are really going to go on in the same specialized sort of way. They have got plenty of interests of their own. I have got some grandchildren who are interested in stamps, but being the age they are it's difficult to sort of foretell how that will develop ... Collections in big stately homes, where they seem to go on forever, or they remain frozen – "great grandfather made a collection of elephants' tusks and we've still got them all" – I think in our sort of families they might well say "Yes, these stamps look all very pretty *but –*!"

His reference to "our sort of families" reinforcing the contrast, highlighted at the beginning of this chapter, between elite and popular collecting, Barry planned to sell his collection eventually at a specialist stamp auction, to make "a little extra nest egg." The same concerns not to burden her family with what she recognized as an interest peculiar to her were also part of June's decision to "start trying to move some of them on to people who really are as interested as I am." Paul, on the other hand, did express concern about the ultimate fate of his collection, and had "tested out" in advance the reception his records might receive, by giving some to his partner's daughter as a gift:

["What will happen to it all in the end?"] Mmmm! Mmmm! I don't know. I think about this occasionally. And Carole has sort of reassured me that if anything happened to me, that she wouldn't, that she would treat it with respect. Which is quite reassuring, because at times when we've disagreed, she's shown a real lack of respect for it ... I have thought of where I would want it to go ... I'd like to think that Gina might want them, Carole's daughter ... I gave her something from my sale box – a set of early ska and reggae things I had in a box – a set of three LPs that I've since bought as a double CD, and that was gonna go out and be sold. And I gave it her for Christmas and she really liked it, and I was quite pleased with that. And there's a lot of other things that she'd quite like, but there'll be lots of other things that she'd have no interest in, so I don't know, I don't know. It's a difficult one.

It wasn't so much respecting the collection as respecting its owner that exercised Ellen, when she found herself in the position of disposing posthumously of another's collection. She had unexpectedly come across a collection of spoons embellished with crests of towns, when preparing her father's house for sale after his death. She had got rid of most things, using a hierarchical system of categorization and disposal, from "really useful" items given to adult nieces and their family and friends, who were still in the process of setting up homes; through "good stuff," such as better-quality glassware, also kept for distribution within the family; household goods and clothing passed to a neighbor, who organized jumble sales on behalf of the British Legion ("In a way that was blurring the lines between charity shop and jumble"); to the remainder, which was bagged up as rubbish. The spoons came as a great surprise, however, and trying to solve the puzzle they represented was integral to the decision-making around their disposal. Part of the surprise was to do with how uncharacteristic of her parents their acquisition seemed: her parents were not normally "organized or systematic," they did not favor display or ornamentation in the house, and any explanation about a sentimental marker of a pleasurable day out also seemed unlikely. With no reliable interpretation of their symbolic meaning to guide their disposal, and the category of *memento mori* having been filled already, Ellen pondered their fate. She explained that the ideal solution to the problem of disposal would have been if one of her nieces had said, "Oh, I'd like to have those, they'd make a good display, and they would be a nice reminder." And a "runner-up good home," she went on, would have been if she'd known another collector of spoons: "That would have been excellent, and I would have thought, 'Oh, Dad's spoons are incorporated into that. That's very nice.'" The difficulty was the prospect that they would simply be converted back to their commodity value. With hopes that they would either be incorporated into another's collection, or at least achieve a use value, they were put into a hospice sale. But disposal of "another person's life" into this unpredictable system of circulation was painful for Ellen:

> Even if we were to understand [the collection of spoons], it has no value anymore, it's so difficult … Apart from useful practical things like microwaves, the disposal in one sense is very sad because nobody does want this. You are so aware of how personal all these things are, because nobody wants them because they were my mother's or because they were Dad's, they only want them because they might be useful, or some other purpose they've got, or they need new socks, or they need new shirts … they're quite a burden to other people, because you start off by wanting them to have good homes, all the things that are left over from another person's life, and then you end up by saying "Oh, let's just get rid of them." The more I talk about it the more it is because they are things that belonged, they are people's lives that you're just – then they go back to being just their commodity value – and people are saying "No, I don't want them. They're not worth anything to me." And that is hurtful to the memory of the people who had owned them.

The priority when disposing of collected items, of preserving their symbolic meanings, and resisting transformation into commodities, was often signaled by reference to the need to find "a good home." Even when June had been forced by lack of space to sell some of her items at a weekly bric-a-brac market, she was still hoping for this:

> A lot of it is very beautiful and should be appreciated, and probably should be moved on to someone who would love it. Because even in a small way, on a Friday, if somebody comes along and goes "I've got one of these, I'd love another," I think "that's going to a good home." Whereas, I've got a thing about people who are looking for something that's cheap, and they just want to add a few bob on it and move it to the next person.

Paul voiced similar reservations about a fellow collector and friend, who was also a dealer:

> I know Ned would love to erm, inherit, if you'd call it – all these, because there'll be quite a few things in there that he'd love to have. Part of me wouldn't want him to have them, because I know he buys and sells in a more – that he's more businesslike about his record collection than I am.

A "good home" therefore is a way of referring to a "suitable" recipient, someone who will recognize and share the value that was constructed at the point the item was taken out of the "use" system and placed into the "sign" system, along with others, to create something unique. It is the opposite of what have been called "divestment rituals," designed to empty goods of meaning prior to exchange.[41] Amongst my interviewees, good homes had been found in a number of ways: by gifting as a rehearsal of bequeathing; by splitting the collection with a former spouse and fellow-collector; and by selling to another collector through clubs, magazines or specialist auctions.

But Ellen was not alone in being forced to risk transformation back into commodity status by consigning items redolent with symbolic meaning, conferred by their relationship with others (other people and other objects), to the uncertainties of "generalist" rather than "specialist" second-hand markets. As we saw from Gordon's classic collector's tale of the Persian sword, at the point of acquisition, collected items become repositories of a unique combination of ingredients: the creative imagination through which the collector conceives of the object as part of a collection of beautiful things; expert knowledge (of "things," and of markets); time devoted to the search; and the "serendipity" that brings these together in the place where the object is waiting for the "bargain" to be created. When disposal becomes an imperative, collectors may find that they have more limited access to some or all of the resources deployed in processes of acquisition.

The dilemma of modes of disposal, other than "finding a good home," was that either the profit embedded in the bargain had to be "circulated" along with the object, or the collector had to become a dealer. My earlier work showed how acquisition was patterned according to "pockets of time" which had to be accessed via intra-household negotiations of various kinds. Disposal, according to the kinds of practices acceptable to collectors, is likely to be a much more time-consuming business, and not one that can be fitted into available "pockets." The trouble with the alternative, of entering the system of commodities, is that it is a "business," and this was not what my interviewees saw themselves as engaged in. In other words, the disposal by sale of a collected item nicely reveals the cash nexus which has hitherto been glossed over:

> It's always been difficult to get rid of things at what you regard as being a real price … if you own your own business and you're flogging stuff, then all the profit is yours, whereas you sell things in auction, all the buyers' premiums – and there's now sellers' premium – so you know, it er, I've always felt that to be a little bit of a rip-off … you try and sell them through a dealer, and they say, "Well, I'll offer you fifty per cent of what the thing's actually worth." So again, I regard that as being a bit of a rip-off too. So I've never, I never try to deal in that way. If I did deal, then obviously I would be doing it in my own right as a dealer, and I've never really been that interested. [Gordon]

Gordon, Barry and Liz perhaps came closest to the traditional "connoisseur" model of collecting, in that they were very knowledgeable about their objects and corresponding specialist markets, but lacked time and inclination to enter the market as dealers. June, also expert enough to have been invited to give talks about her collections, had begun trading in a small way, but was very discriminating about who she would sell to. There is certainly further research to be done about how such transactions are negotiated. Dennis, however, was on the point of transition between collecting and trading, and I suspect that he exemplifies a new breed of modern popular collectors, who not only appreciate the qualities of the objects they collect, but have an eye to the entrepreneurial opportunities available. He had fewer reservations about dealing than other interviewees, but his knowledge was much more tentative. And when we look at the source of his knowledge, the crucial role of the media becomes apparent. He did spend time talking to traders at car boot sales, but he had acquired much of what he knew from reading the popular magazine *Collect It!* and would be guided in his "sweep" of the car boot sale by whatever appeared in this magazine. Pointing to various items within its pages, he proudly recounted how many of each he had. Many of his collections had been acquired in an attempt to predict or even create markets in collectables. There had always been an element of speculation involved in Dennis's acquisitions, not over what the "right" price might be, because he never paid much, but in forecasting the collectables of the future. The dilemma he and his partner faced, when lack of space dictated their disposal, was that there was very little information available, in the magazine or elsewhere, about where to sell his low-cost "collectables." There are no Miller's guides to trading in different second-hand markets:

[Doreen:] There's not anything written about Sizeler [*sic*], or Wade, or Sylvac. I've been to the library and got books. [Dennis:] I don't know whether we'll put the bloody lot in an auction. I don't know where to sell it ... ["You've never been tempted to get somebody who does know in to value it for you?"] No, they probably haven't got as much knowledge as what I've got. It's not knowing what it's worth, it's knowing where to get rid of it that's the problem ... I've never really looked into it. I don't know where to get rid of stuff, because I've never got rid of any.

Later he revealed that he had in fact sold a fair number of items to a dealer. It seemed that the fact that the dealer was also a friend, and Dennis could represent the sale in altruistic terms, rather than as a purely commercial trans-action, lessened the blow of not being able himself to realize the full monetary value he had (apparently correctly) predicted they might have as collectables:

I have sold once to a dealer, but he was a friend. I think he spent four hundred odd quid with me, and I totaled up and I let him have it cheap. It had cost me thirty-two pounds to buy it. He'd get at least twelve hundred for it. ["But that doesn't bother you?"] No. I did it to help him out.

Discussion and Conclusions

An examination of disposal as a neglected, almost taboo subject in the study of consumption in general, and of collecting in particular, uncovers the interaction between the social, cultural and economic aspects of the circulation of second-hand goods. Illustrated by the qualitative data presented here, the approach provides a framework for considering issues such as the variety of models of popular collecting; new developments in the sociology of consumption; the importance of the concept of "the bargain" in modern popular collecting; the unpredictability of pricing; types of trading; the role of the media in stimulating, even creating, specialized second-hand markets; and processes of "moving on."

My interviewees illustrated various models of popular collecting, including "collecting by default," where acquisitions are primarily via gifts; "traditional collecting" marked by the development of knowledge and expertise and progressive specialization; and "speculative collecting," which borders on dealing. They also exemplified a number of models of disposal, including unintentional disposal, via breakages; temporary disposal in which unwanted gifts are hidden and displayed at different times; rational disposal, to serve further specialization and a continuing career; and enforced disposal, resulting from shortage of space, divorce and death or its contemplation. Each of these presented its own peculiar difficulties, centering around the transformation of objects from symbolic to commodity status, and of individuals from collectors to more or less reluctant traders.

Uncovering their dilemmas and the practices used to address them goes some way toward rectifying the criticism of the sociology of consumption, at least in the UK, that its understandings of material culture have too often been derived from the starting point of the cash nexus, as opposed to examining the way objects are lived with in material culture, the way people's "quasi-social relationships with objects attach them to their culture and their social life, linking past and present, mediating direct human relationships and indirect cultural ones"[42] (although there is at least one early sociological exception to this[43]). Anthropological studies on the other hand, have tended to focus on the social and cultural aspects of things,[44] at the expense of understanding the place and meaning of the cash nexus within these relationships. A study of collecting seems to me to offer invaluable opportunities to examine the interplay of both sets of processes. Further research might focus on a case study of an individual's pattern of buying and selling over time, or attempt to trace the biography of an individual item. The latter is clearly important at the elite end of the spectrum, where provenance is so important, but has been less explored at the popular level.

Regardless of whether they could or could not afford to buy at the prices asked by smart retail outlets, most of my present-day popular collectors often sourced their acquisitions at car boot sales, markets, fairs and auctions. The "bargain" was very important to them. It made the hunt, in these "fluid" markets, more exciting, and also validated their developing skill in their chosen areas. But as Dennis demonstrated, this same fluidity makes entering the arena as a potential trader much more complex. There are no guide books on trading in different second-hand markets. Trade "insiders" have much more invested in keeping the consumer dream of the bargain alive than in encouraging new trader entrants, and the media play a crucial role in this. This is illustrated by the BBC TV program, *Bargain Hunt*. Although buyers at local auctions still consist in large part of dealers, who then "move on" their purchases through shops, fairs, export and to private collectors, *Bargain Hunt* is based on a reversal of this order: a competition to see which of two teams of amateurs can make most profit at auction, selling goods they selected and purchased earlier at an antique fair. After watching the teams make their purchases, viewers with access to the Internet can also win small antiques prizes by predicting on-line which items will make a profit and which a loss. In fact, 40 percent of contestants do make a profit.[45] This may be because, as one very bitter antiques fair trader explained to me, as we watched the program presenter set up a piece to camera, selected traders can be persuaded to drop their prices dramatically in exchange for the publicity.

More mixed messages about the unpredictability of pricing in these markets come from newspapers, where regular accounts appear of ordinary members of the public who have tried their hand at second-hand trading. Headlines such as "Is it goodbye to the bargain basement?," "From Boot to Loot" and "Don't move clutter – sell it"[46] actually lead in to stories of disappointment and disillusionment as people discover the realities of the labor involved, and the mythical nature, for most, of claims to easy money. For consumers, even formerly reliable sources of bargains can let you down: the first story cited above was by a journalist who was furious to discover that a large white damask tablecloth she was about to purchase in a charity shop cost more than a similar new version from a smart department store. Her investigations revealed the process of "professionalization" charity shop retailing has undergone.

There is undoubtedly convergence between alternative and mainstream kinds of trading, with both increased regulation of the former, for example, tax inspectors swooping on car boot sales to track down those who do not declare their earnings, and organizers of such events trying to keep them exclusively for "genuine booters."

There is also a degree of repetition, with largely unchanged stock appearing on some stalls at successive antique fairs.[47] Nevertheless, my observations at markets and fairs reveal that they bring together a hugely disparate group of traders, from veteran professionals for whom the fair is only one amongst a number of trading arenas, to retired people who have taken up amateur trading, and a fair sprinkling of occasional hobbyists, like June. The fact that not all of these amateurs have profit as their primary motivation[48] preserves unpredictability. This heterogeneity in terms of the diversity of goods on offer, the mixture of people and their motivations, the opportunities for bargains and for sociability, and the chance of finding something to treasure keeps the collector sufficiently enchanted to revisit second-hand trading sites again and again.[49]

I began with collectors, but focusing on the disposal aspects of the process reveals that, even via this most acquisitive group of consumers, goods constantly re-enter the circulation system. It also highlights the fact that collecting is one potential route into trading, if only at the level of "mobile" sites like markets and fairs. Modern mobile trading in second-hand goods

Figure 9.3. Notices on the gates of a regular car boot sale held at the Cattle Market in Derby

such as antiques and collectables is an under-investigated area, not only because of the supposed ease of entry and an opportunity structure for new entrepreneurs, and flexibility for more established traders, but also because of the extremely lucrative business for the major players behind the scenes – like the *Daily Mail* group of newspapers, which runs some of the biggest regular events in the UK and Europe.[50] In addition to the social factors we have seen here – the importance of domestic space, and changes in family formation – which act as drivers to circulation, the role of the media should not be underestimated. Second-hand goods may not be advertised on TV (recent ads by the Internet trading site "ebay" in the UK apparently feature new goods), but the links between auction houses, publishing, high-status retailers and program presenters suggest that the industry uses the mass media very effectively to stimulate these specialized second-hand markets, as well as to create new ones.

Dennis and other hopeful collector-traders may (or may not) be helped in knowing how best to "move on" items from their collections by the latest TV program to appear in the UK. Entitled *Flog It!* it is fronted, like the others, by an established retail trader in antiques. Despite the "barrow boy" connotations of its title, its aim is not to make traders of us all, but rather to stimulate the return to circulation of currently "hidden" collectables. Whatever the program's impact on disposal turns out to be, we might conclude that there will never be a shortage of supply in the circulation of this special category of second-hand goods. After all, all collectors and collections will, at some time or another, be "moving on."

Acknowledgment

I am indebted to my fellow sociologist and friend Teresa Keil for her invaluable encouragement and support in this and all my academic endeavors.

Notes

1. *Daily Telegraph* (May 16, 2002).
2. Reported in *Guardian* 2 (February 13, 2002).
3. S.M. Pearce, *Collecting in Contemporary Practice* (London, 1998).
4. P. Blom, *To Have and To Hold* (London, 2002).
5. W. Durost, *Children's Collecting Activity Related to Social Factors* (New York, 1932).
6. Russell Belk, *Collecting in a Consumer Society* (London, 1995).
7. Tim Dant, "Consumption Caught in the Cash Nexus," *Sociology*, 34, (2000), pp. 655–70.
8. Grant McCracken, *Culture and Consumption: New Approaches to the Symbolic Character of Consumer Goods and Activities* (Bloomington, IN, 1988).
9. N.K. Hayles, "Boundary Disputes: Homeostasis: Reflexivity, and the Foundations of Cybernetics," *Configurations*, 2, 3, (Baltimore, MD, 1994), pp. 441–67.
10. Susan M. Pearce, "The Urge to Collect," in Susan M. Pearce (ed.), *Interpreting Objects and Collections* (London, 1994), pp. 157–9.
11. N. Aristides, "Calm and Uncollected," *American Scholar*, 57, (1998), pp. 327–36.
12. S.M. Pearce, *Collecting in Contemporary Practice* (London, 1998); R. Belk, M. Wallendorf, J. Sheery and M. Holbrook, *Collecting in a Consumer Culture: Highways and Buyways* (Provo, UT, 1990), pp. 3–95; Russell W Belk, *Collecting in a Consumer Society*.
13. Daniel Miller (ed.), *Acknowledging Consumption: a Review of New Studies* (London, 1995), p. 39.
14. D. Miller, P. Jackson, N. Thrift, B. Holbrook and M. Rowlands, *Shopping, Place and Identity* (London and New York, 1998).
15. T. Edwards, *Contradictions of Consumption: Concepts, Practices and Politics in Consumer Society* (Buckingham, 2002).
16. G. Bagnall, "Consuming the past," in Stephen Edgell, Kevin Hetherington and Alan Warde (eds.), *Consumption Matters* (Oxford, 1996), pp. 227–47.
17. Angela McRobbie, "Second-hand Dresses and the Role of the Ragmarket," in A. McRobbie (ed.), *Zoot Suits and Second-hand Dresses* (Basingstoke, 1989), p. 36.
18. See D. Crispell, "Collecting Memories," *American Demographic*, 60, (November 1988), pp. 38–41, and G. Roberts, "A Thing of Beauty and a Source of Wonderment: Ornaments for the Home as Cultural Status Markers," in Gary Day (ed.), *Readings in Popular Culture: Trivial Pursuits?* (New York, 1990), pp. 39–47.
19. Colin Campbell, *The Romantic Ethic and the Spirit of Modern Consumerism* (Oxford, 1989).
20. Sharon Boden and Simon J. Williams, "Consumption and Emotion: the Romantic Ethic Revisited," *Sociology*, 36, (2002), pp. 493–512.
21. J. Elsner, and R. Cardinal, *The Cultures of Collecting* (Cambridge, MA, 1994).
22. A.D. Olmsted, "Collecting: Leisure, Investment or Obsession?" *Journal of Social Behaviour and Personality*, 6, (1991), pp. 287–306; R. Hatton and J.A. Walker, *Supercollector, a Critique of Charles Saatchi* (London, 2000).
23. Pearce, *Collecting in Contemporary Practice*.
24. N. Gregson and L. Crewe, "The Bargain, the Knowledge and the Spectacle: Making Sense of Consumption in the Space of the Car-boot Sale," *Environment and Planning D: Society and Space*, 15, (1997), pp. 87–112; W. Arrowsmith, *Antiques Fairs in England* (Bromsgrove, 1999).

25. Miller et al., *Shopping, Place and Identity.*
26. G. Lucas, "Disposability and Dispossession in the Twentieth Century," *Journal of Material Culture*, 7, 1, (2002), pp. 5–22.
27. M. Douglas and B. Isherwood, *The World of Goods: Towards an Anthropology of Consumption* (London, 1979).
28. Martin O'Brien, "Rubbish Values: Reflections on the Political Economy of Waste," *Science As Culture*, 8, (1999), pp. 269–95.
29. M. Thompson, *Rubbish Theory: the Creation and Destruction of Value* (Oxford, 1979).
30. Martin O'Brien, "Rubbish-Power: Towards a Sociology of the Rubbish Society," in Jeff Hearn and Sasha Roseneil (eds.), *Consuming Cultures, Power and Resistance* (Basingstoke, 1999).
31. Alan Beardsworth and Teresa Keil, *Sociology on the Menu* (London, 1997).
32. Susan Strasser, *Waste and Want. A Social History of Trash* (New York, 1999).
33. Susan Porter Benson, "Gender, Generation and Consumption in the United States: Working-Class Families in the Interwar Period," in Susan Strasser, Charles McGovern and Matthias Judt (eds.), *Getting and Spending: European and American Consumer Societies in the Twentieth Century* (Cambridge, 1998), pp. 223–40.
34. Jackie Goode, "Collecting Time: the Social Organisation of Collecting," in Graham Crow and Sue Heath (eds.), *Social Conceptions of Time: Structure and Process in Work and Everyday Life* (Basingstoke, 2002), pp. 230–45.
35. Daniel Miller, "Consumption and Its Consequences," in Hugh Mackay (ed.), *Consumption and Everyday Life* (London, 1997), pp. 13–64.
36. Daniel Miller, *The Dialectics of Shopping* (Chicago, IL, 2001).
37. Raphael Samuel, *Theatres of Memory*, Vol. 1: *Past and Present in Contemporary Culture* (London, 1994), p. 113.
38. E.g., M. Mauss, *The Gift: The Form and Reason for Exchange in Archaic Societies* (London, 1950).
39. Paul Martin, "'I've Got One Just Like That!' Collectors, Museums and Community," *Museological Review*, 1, (1995), pp. 77–86.
40. J. Finch and L. Hayes, "Gender, Inheritance and Women as Testators," in Lydia Morris and E. Stina Lyon (eds.), *Gender Relation in Public and Private: New Research Perspectives* (Basingstoke, 1996), p. 135.
41. McCracken, *Culture and Consumption.*
42. Dant, "Consumption Caught in the Cash Nexus," p. 4.
43. Jennifer Platt, "Economic Values and Cultural Meanings: the Market for Antiques." Paper presented to the British Sociological Association Annual Conference, (1978).
44. I. Kopytoff, "The Cultural Biography of Things: Commoditization as Process," in Arjun Appadurai (ed.), *The Social Life of Things: Commodities in Cultural Perspective* (Cambridge, 1988), pp. 64–94.
45. *Bargain Hunt* presenter on "Have I Got News For You," BBC2, June 1, 2002.
46. *Weekend Telegraph*, February 6, 1999; *Observer*, May 2, 1999; and *Daily Telegraph*, March 4, 2000, respectively.
47. Media creations of new categories of collectables, for example, collecting increasingly recent "eras," is one solution to the problem of scarcity. Miller's mini guides are currently up to "Collecting the '70s."
48. P. Van Der Grijp, "Passion and Profit: the World of Amateur Traders in Philately," *Journal of Material Culture*, 7: 1 (2002), pp. 23–47.
49. Gregson and Crewe, "The Bargain, the Knowledge and the Spectacle," pp. 87–112.
50. "dmg world media," a "global exhibition, publishing, and new media company," is a subsidiary of the *Daily Mail* group of newspapers. For the year to September 2004 it reported a total revenue of US $298.5 million and a profit of US $57.7 million. Art and Antiques is one of its four core sectors: in addition to an antiques and publishing arm of the business, "DMG Antiques Fairs" is the largest promoter of antiques shows in Europe, running over 100 events a year in the UK and France. They also own twenty-three antique trade and public fairs in the USA, and North America is their fastest-growing market for Art and Antiques, predicted to account for 50 percent of total revenue by 2003.

10

THE SECOND-HAND CAR MARKET AS A FORM OF RESISTANCE

Bernard Jullien

In seeking to explain consumption behaviors, much research in the area of social sciences is based on a presumption that consumers have preexisting preferences that they use to evaluate alternatives in choosing what to purchase. Mary Douglas has proposed an alternative in which consumption is based not on preferences, but on their opposite. She explains this as follows:

> Inquiries about consumption patterns have focused on wants. The questions have been about why people want what they buy. Whereas, most shoppers will agree, people do not know what they want, but they are very clear about what they do not want. ... To understand shopping practices we need to trace standardizes hates, which are much more constant and more revealing than desires.[1]

This is a key element to understanding the existence and functioning of second-hand markets when they exist. An analysis of the supply and demand of these markets enriches our understanding of consumption behaviors in general. By not participating in the market for new products, suppliers and purchasers in second-hand markets are expressing a negative evaluation of the primary marketplace. By participating in the second-hand market, however, they are also acting positively in creating an alternative marketplace. It is therefore proposed that social science should not restrict its analysis of second-hand markets by considering them simply as derived markets with lower prices. Rather, what is proposed is a reflection on the role of second-hand markets as socio-economic structures made up of groups of professional actors and specific consumption relationships with the goods in question.

An examination of second-hand markets from this perspective requires careful definition of and access to data on the demand for new and used goods. In the automobile market, for example, the level of income may be taken as the major explanatory variable for the decision to buy a new or used car. Nonetheless, a large proportion of households with the means to acquire a new car choose not to do so. Conversely, a certain segment of the new-car market is composed of households for whom such a purchase is a significant investment in relation to their relatively modest incomes. The analytical approach that is proposed in this chapter is to view the behavior of these two groups as worthy of further investigation rather than to dismiss it as a curiosity.

In other words, the second-hand good cannot simply be defined as a lower-priced version of the new product. The second-hand product offers both the possibility of a good "deal" and access to a more "suitable" marketplace for entire populations of professional actors and households. For various reasons, these suppliers and consumers are not integrated into the mainstream market that is structured around the sale of the new product. While there is undoubtedly a strong financial dimension to this "suitability", there is more to second-hand markets than this dimension alone.

The car is symbolic of much of the ambivalence that surrounds second-hand markets. On one level, the configuration of the second-hand car market depends on that of the new-car market and the efforts made by manufacturers to manage the interactions between both these markets. The ongoing difficulties they encounter, however, can be seen as evidence that there is another level of activity in which consumers and professionals are free to create alternatives outside of the market under the management of the car manufacturers. In trying to understand the interaction of these two different dimensions of the second-hand car market, it is important to recognize that there have been evolutions over time and that there are important differences between how the interaction has emerged in different geographical regions. This recognition in turn requires us to consider both how car manufacturers have addressed the issue of used cars from a historical perspective and to investigate how different actors in different markets around the world have proved adept at taking advantage of the various forms of social and economic spaces left open to them by manufacturers in the second-hand car market.

The first part of this chapter will show how the used-car market has always been a concern for car manufacturers and that it continues to demand their attention. Three specific cases are examined: the US during the period 1910–40, France during the period 1930–60 and Europe during the period 1995–2005. Comparing the solutions proposed in the earlier two periods with more recent initiatives leads one to conclude that the ongoing indecisiveness of car manufacturers in relation to used cars has permitted the emergence of an autonomous alternative secondary marketplace.

The second part of the chapter will look in more detail at this alternative automobile market. Again, three specific cases will be examined in detail: the US in 1996–7, emerging countries during the period 1995–2005 and France during the period 1995–2005. We will see that the used-car market in each case possesses its own distinct group of professional actors, who are serving different types of customers to those of car manufacturers. These differences relate not only to purchasing power but also to the customer's relationship with the automobile.

Car Manufacturers in Search of a Role in the Used-car Market: Three Case Studies

Despite the fact that the vast majority of business conducted in the car industry concerns second-hand cars, manufacturers have had great difficulty managing the business challenges posed by used cars. The three cases studies that follow illustrate that their inability to integrate activities linked to second-hand cars has been an ongoing problem for both US and European car manufacturers.

The US in 1910–40: an Emerging and Unresolved Problem

The period 1910 to 1940 is when automobile manufacturers in the US put in place the management processes required to manage their relationships with their distributors. It was during this time that the fundamental commercial issues to be resolved in the market were emerging and the solutions chosen then continue to dominate today's distribution landscape. The question of how to deal with the second-hand car market was one of these fundamental issues.

Following a number of unsuccessful attempts to manage final distribution directly, Ford developed its most efficient distribution system toward the end of the 1910s. A network of company-owned wholesalers supplied its independent dealers and agents nationwide. This was a more integrated system than in most other companies at the time and Ford was thus able to exercise a higher level of control over the activities of its distribution channel members than the competition. Henry Ford mistrusted sales'people in general and the company's attitude toward its distribution network was typically that of the dominant supplier imposing its will on weaker partners. The company, for example, obliged its intermediaries to accept an exclusive contract with the Ford Motor Company.

By contrast, the chief executive of General Motors at that time, Alfred Sloan, appears to have had a less antagonistic attitude toward the firm's distribution network. Although it is often used as a counter-example to the Ford model, GM had also chosen to distribute its automobiles through a network made up of many independent firms. In 1939, for example, GM had 17,000 dealers and agents employing 125,000 people. For both firms, the underlying reasons for not integrating distribution are the same. Firstly, doing so would have required a level of investment that was judged far too high. Secondly, the competence common to successful automobile manufacturers was their mastery of economies of scale in manufacturing, and the management of thousands of specific distribution operations did not benefit from this type of competence. The market itself was changing, however. A key change was linked to the growing diffusion of the product itself. In 1908, when

Ford's first Model T was introduced there was one car for every twenty households. By 1920, the proportion had increased to one car for every three households. The distribution network was increasingly called upon to accept trade-ins in order to sell a new car, and General Motors appears to have adapted more quickly to the impact that this was having. Alfred Sloan himself is quoted as saying:

> when the used car came into the picture in a big way in the 1920s as a trade-in on a new car, the merchandising of automobiles became more a trading than an ordinary selling proposition. Organizing and supervising the necessary thousands of complex trading institutions would have been difficult for the manufacturer; trading is a knack not easy to fit into the conventional type of a managerially controlled organization.[2]

Despite its growing complexity, both GM and Ford chose to operate in the automobile marketplace via a network of independent distribution businesses. Even though Sloan appeared to appreciate that the skills needed to trade were different to those needed to sell, GM did not manage to avoid the same conflicts that Ford faced in attempting to manage its relationship with its dealership network.

A detailed study of legal documents submitted to the Fair Trade Commission (FTC) between 1921 and 1941 highlights the main types of problems faced by GM in this regard as the FTC was regularly called upon to resolve conflicts between GM and its dealers.[3] A significant area of recurring conflict between GM and its dealership network concerned the question of trade-ins. As the automobile market in the 1920s became one in which many consumers were seeking a replacement vehicle, the task of selling a new car became increasingly linked to the trade-in conditions the dealer was able to offer. However, in the eyes of manufacturers, it was still the new car that was the focus of management attention as new technologies emerged and needed to be integrated into new models to remain competitive. The second-hand car was seen as a necessary evil, incurring losses that dealers tried to minimize. While this initially only worried dealers, trade-ins finally began to concern manufacturers. They realized that, on the one hand, the value of trade-ins would have an impact on the financial solidity of their dealers and, on the other, they could harm their ability to sell new cars effectively. In effect, if the losses incurred from the trade-in business became too significant in comparison to the margin the dealers were afforded on new car sales, dealers with low levels of profitability would be tempted to sell fewer new cars. Quotas and threats to cut off franchises appeared to help reduce this temptation to some extent. Nonetheless, manufacturers pushed for measures to destroy second-hand cars to limit the extent of the problem they posed and, in 1933, they managed to get government support for such measures.

As this did not suffice to resolve the problem, however, dealers were forced to try to win back from buyers of new cars the losses they incurred from having to buy the used car. Two main approaches were used, which inflicted long-lasting damage on buyers' faith in car dealers. The first consisted of the creation by dealers of what were known as "bureaus." They served to diffuse information about trade-in offers made to clients to avoid bidding up the price. The second was the vagueness surrounding the final price of different models, in particular if credit was been used to finance the purchase. This allowed dealers to rely on the ambiguity of the price of the new car to win back the money they may have lost on the trade-in.

As a result of these questionable practices, a long series of complaints and judgments led to the introduction of a series of regulations that required the details of the manufacturer's selling price and taxes and transport costs to be posted on a sticker on the car's windscreen and that regulated publicity concerning interest rates on purchase financing. However, despite these regulatory measures, there is such a variety of different elements involved in the sale of a new car that it has proved practically impossible to predict and regulate the manner by which dealers and/or manufacturers attempt to dissimulate final prices for new cars.

These distribution conflicts were faced not only by GM in the 1920s and 1930s, but also by the Ford Motor Company in the 1930s. The company was initially somewhat sheltered from the question of trade-ins as the primary business was to roll out the highly successful Model T to as many US households as possible. By the end of the 1920s, however, the trade-ins were beginning to arrive en masse in Ford dealerships. Competition from GM had also led to a strategic shift to multiple models and an annual model change by the 1930s, and Ford dealers were also thus facing issues of inventory management when demand for the increasingly diversified range of products did not exactly match what was anticipated.

Overall, what emerges from the analysis of events during this period in the history of automobile distribution in the US is the importance of the key decision taken by automobile manufacturers at this time to delegate responsibility for distribution of their product. This decision was accompanied by a certain disdain for the difficulties of dealers and a suspicion that they were not always choosing to behave in a way that maximized the interest of manufacturers. A major point of conflict in the problematic relationship that emerged between dealers and manufacturers was that of second-hand vehicles. What has tended to happen is that manufacturers have subsequently attempted to regain control of certain aspects of distribution by careful measurement and reward systems for certain aspects of the dealerships' commercial activities, but there are certain areas where the original hands-off approach remains dominant. The business of second-hand car sales is one of these, and car dealerships in the US are relatively free to conduct this business as they see once it does not impinge on their ability to sell new cars. The same distribution network is thus home to a mixed set of rules. At one extreme, these rules involve the firm application of a centralized and heavily coordinated marketing and sales culture. In the middle, there is a much looser set of obligations and far less support in relation to after-sales service. And, at the other extreme, dealerships are virtually entirely independent in relation to their activities involving second-hand cars.

France in 1930–60: the Recurring Question of Used Cars

The questions that were being asked in the US in the 1920s emerged in France in the 1950s.[4] Up until this point, there had been two key periods in the history of the automobile industry in France when the question of used cars preoccupied manufacturers. The first was in the 1930s, when there was much debate about the problem of "market saturation," and the second was in the period immediately following the Second World War, when the concern was that markets would be undersupplied due to manufacturing shortages.

Historical analysis has highlighted the dominance of the American manufacturers during the Ford and Sloan years in the United States.[5] To a large degree, European automobile manufacturers trailed behind their American counterparts, as they proved singularly incapable of democratizing what was still viewed as a luxury good. Other manufacturers had shown the way with the success of the Mathis, Rosengart and Simca models in the 1930s, but the biggest French manufacturers were only developing their first credible small-car projects in 1935. In the end, a joint decision was taken to abandon them as the manufacturers were worried that their loss-making agents would not have the means to finance a successful launch.[6] Boulanger, who was appointed director general of Citroën in 1936, relaunched the 2CV project and the new model was introduced in the foire automobile in Paris in 1939.

Under the aegis of Pierre Michelin, Citroën conducted the first market studies to be conducted in the French automobile market. These studies actually integrated the second-hand car market in order to consider how the company could broaden the appeal of cars to lower income markets. Between 1935 and 1940, only 10 percent of the 210,000 cars sold annually were new cars. As can be seen from the Table 10.1, the vast majority of consumers buying their first car bought one that cost less than 10,000 francs, meaning that they bought an affordable second-hand car.

Between 1935 and 1940, the range of new cars available from French car manufacturers was not adapted to the potential demand of consumers purchasing their first car. Only 2.6 million new cars were sold in a country with a population of 41 million and the vast majority of these were to existing car owners. Within Citroën, the lessons were clear. To broaden the appeal of car ownership and develop a more significant presence on the market, the relevant segment was made up of customers who were only able to afford a

Table 10.1. Cost of first car purchase (new and used) between 1935 and 1940

	Number	%
Less than 2,000 francs	50,400	24
From 2,000 to 5,000 francs	67,200	32
From 5,000 to 10,000 francs	52,500	25
From 10,000 to 15,000 francs	18,900	9
From 15,000 to 20,000 francs	18,900	9
More than 20,000 francs	2,100	1

Source: *Bulletin intérieur Citroën*, 1/07/1946 – quoted in Jean-Louis Loubet, *Citroën, Peugeot, Renault et les autres: soixante ans de stratégie* (Paris, 1995), p. 301.

second-hand car. The model that would appeal to this segment had to be priced at between 5,000 and 10,000 francs.

This is an interesting historical period as it shows how the access to car ownership has tended to occur through the purchase of a second-hand car. It also highlights that car manufacturers equate the broadening of car ownership with the need to sell more new cars. If this is not the case, the lack of new cars arriving on the marketplace limits the availability of second-hand cars, and the growth of the number of automobiles on the road is only possible by extending the ages of cars on the road.

The French car industry had numerous projects for the production of a mass market automobile during the period of postwar reconstruction, but it was obliged to wait until 1948 for permission from the authorities. In addition to the damage that the war had inflicted on roads as well as fuel and car distribution channels, the state was faced with a shortage of raw materials. The production of cars was not seen as a priority and, when a growth in car production was finally allowed in 1947, it was in order to develop exports that were to finance the Monnet Plan. Nonetheless, the need and desire for cars were both present in the marketplace. Since 1939, the number of automobiles on the road had been reduced by one million cars. Market studies conducted at the time concluded that there were three high-potential segments. These were the medium- and high-range car, as existed before the war, but, in addition, the popular car segment.

Curiously, the most successful models were the biggest ones whose, target market was clients who had operated in the black market during and after the war and who were the only potential clients for the small quantity of new cars that were sold during these early post war years. The first cars that had been sold were 90,000 military vehicles sold by the British and American army in 1946. Light trucks followed and, from the end of 1946, a small quantity of cars began to arrive on the marketplace. In 1946, only 67,000 of the 619, 000 cars registered were bought in that year. The shortage of raw materials had led the authorities to develop a system of purchasing licenses and not everyone could buy a car. A black market was quick to develop and a nine-year-old used car could end up for sale at a price 50 percent above that of a new version of the same model. It was during this phase of its development that the French car retailing business acquired a reputation of being a business for profiteers and racketeers. This also explains in part why French households traditionally mistrust car dealers and, where possible, avoid having to deal with them by selling and buying directly via small ads.

From a regulatory perspective, this specific period is also indicative of a long-running difficulty facing public policy makers in relation to the used car market situation. It is an alternative market that is very difficult to regulate and it is, in fact, subject to very little regulation. Policy makers, like manufacturers, have found it difficult to develop a solid and defensible position in relation to the used-car market and its customers.

The post war years of shortages in France were followed by ten years of euphoric growth in output and household purchasing power. As predicted by Michelin in the 1930s, the small affordable car proved hugely popular and was sold to customers buying their first car. The French market thus became a market with significant levels of product renewal. At this point, the distribution network was faced with the problem of trade-ins, and their relationships with both clients and manufacturers suffered. French manufacturers were aware of the American precedent[7] and the potential impact on their networks of these evolutions and of the need to develop new competences. They did not, however, appear to be ready to take significant action. From time to time, when the problem became insurmountable and began to have an impact on the commercial success of a new model, the manufacturers introduced financial incentives and support.

In this regard, two specific examples are of interest.[8] The first occurred in 1958, when the ID19 and DS were proving difficult to resell in the second-hand market. Citroën copied an earlier initiative of Simca's by adopting a second-hand 'quality label' to assist in their resale. The label offered the equivalent guarantee to that of a new car for ID and DS models in a good state of repair and the manufacturer financed the guarantee and a part of the repair bill. These measures were extended to other models in the years that followed and Renault also went on to create its own used-car guarantee, called "Garantie OR (Occasion Renault)."

The launch of its 204 in 1965 was Peugeot's move into a more generalist market position and, as it did not have cars in this market segment, its dealers found themselves forced to accept as trade-ins other marques that were difficult to sell on through their own outlets. Peugeot initially tried to resolve the problem with financial support but eventually it was forced to develop a network of used-car centers to part with the stock that had been acquired.

These two examples show that the strategic intentions of manufacturers in France, as elsewhere, were not far from Sloan's philosophy of delegation of distribution outlined earlier. They were not trying to integrate used-car sales and develop an adapted commercial strategy. Their major concern was to ensure that problems linked to used car sales did not have a negative impact on their primary business, which was to sell new cars through their dealership networks. Moving beyond this would involve competences and risks that, from their perspective, were best left to the distribution network. The network, during this period, was in fact developing its own practices in the vacuum left by manufacturers.

Thus, even in relation to the relatively minor part of the second-hand market that does pass through the official distribution network of manufacturers, the norm that emerged during this period was to operate outside of the mainstream manufacturer's world with its standards and specific marketing and segmentation practices developed to promote the sale of new cars. Dealers have thus a long history of interacting with a series of professionals and clients far removed from the market for new-car sales.

Europe in 1995–2005: Solutions to the Recurring Problem?

In the last decade of the twentieth century, car manufacturers initially appeared ready to reconsider their traditional lack of interest in second-hand cars. Up until this point, as we have already seen, the major preoccupation had remained the sale of new cars and trade-ins were accepted as a necessary evil. The distribution channels of manufacturers only represented a small fraction of the trade in second-hand cars and they did not see this business as profitable. In reality, they had not sought to develop any specific commercial approach to this segment of the car market and they had left the business to alternative players thus abandoning a significant proportion of motorized households and the after-sales service that went along with the sale of a second-hand car.

No radical change was undertaken during this decade but a number of factors had led to a growing level of interest in Europe for second-hand cars during the 1990s. In Anglo-Saxon markets, an alternative form of commercialization of relatively new second-hand cars was emerging. The improvement in reliability was facilitating the emergence of a viable guarantee and financing system for second-hand cars that made them more credible substitutes for new cars. Loyalty strategies were transferred from business markets to consumer markets by offering leasing and credit services and these increasingly involved calculating the likely depreciation of the vehicle and proposing a buy-back solution. The generous discounts offered on the initial sale demanded careful management of the profitability of the subsequent buy-back. Overall, during this period, the official manufacturers networks in Europe were losing market share in the after-sales service business. In 2002, the removal of the block exemption protecting manufacturers' monopoly position in the supply of spare parts served to speed up this process. Competition from independent chains was increasingly successful and manufacturers were searching for alternative sources of profitability for their distributorships. The problem was compounded for distributors as their margins from new-car sales were already at an all-time low as manufacturers sought to dissuade the entry of new competitors into the European market.

All of these factors contributed to the development of a series of proposals that would standardize the approach of the distribution network to the commercialization of second-hand cars. A key element in this strategy was the development by manufacturers of "quality labels" for second-hand cars. Although such initiatives were relatively unsuccessful in the US, their adoption was relatively widespread in Europe. To a large degree, automobile manufacturers are in a far more dominant position in relation to their distribution network in Europe compared to the situation in the US. Dealers in Europe thus appeared more willing to overcome their doubts about the competence of manufacturers in relation to used cars and many adopted the quality labels and the associated business program for second-hand cars.

To some degree, these initiatives show that automobile manufacturers were willing to accept the reality of the existence in the marketplace of an alternative automobile world that had up to this point been outside of their control and which they had chosen to ignore. One way of analyzing this change in their attitude and behavior toward this segment of the market is to recognize its link to the evolution of income inequality in Western societies since the 1980s. As these inequalities increase, so too does the proportion of households whose only access to motorization is the purchase of a second-hand car. As the relative importance of this segment of the market grows, automobile manufacturers find it increasingly difficult to ignore.[9]

A similar analysis appears to have played a major role in the debate concerning the regulation of the European market for car distribution. It appeared initially that the policy makers' primary concern was the price of new-car sales, but their attention was quickly drawn to the apparent inconsistencies in the arguments of the automobile manufacturers that there is a "natural link" in the car market between sales and after-sales service. As automobile manufacturers had for decades been blatantly neglecting second-hand car sales and disregarding any link that there may be with their after-sales service, which was likely to be even more important as the product aged, it proved very difficult for them to defend their insistence on the "natural link."

In the case of second-hand car sales, which represent the majority of transactions in Europe, buyers do not expect a link to exist between the sale of the product and repairs and service that take place after the sale has occurred. When a customer buys a second-hand vehicle, there is no expectation that the seller has revised or repaired the vehicle in question. The seller, in turn, does not require that the buyer return to the original, more expensive supplier of spare parts in order to guarantee a certain level of after-sales service. The organization of the second-hand market is thus significantly different to the organisation that dominates the world of new-car sales that the automobile manufacturers were trying to defend.

Overall, the second-hand car market offers a more realistic view of the automobile marketplace and its practices than the view afforded by that of new-car markets. There is much more to the automobile world than the problems faced by automobile manufacturers and their distribution networks as they try to sell more new cars. In the second-hand car markets, manufacturers are not the dominant force and the competition appears to have established itself in a more central role in responding to consumers. Recent developments in Europe have helped us see this automobile "underworld" more clearly, and the second-hand car market has established itself as a strategic, commercial and regulatory priority. This adds to the argument that the manufacturers' perspective is insufficient to develop a comprehensive understanding of second-hand automobile markets and pushes us to evaluate them from the alternative perspective.

Consumers and Professionals Developing Alternatives

As we have seen, car manufacturers are not unaware of the importance of the used-car market to their business and to that of their networks. However, they have proved consistently unable to develop a successful model to integrate the activities of the used car market into their overall business model. To a large degree, this inability to deal with the used-car market is a result of an early decision made in the industry to delegate responsibility for the management of the commercial interdependence of the two markets to the distribution network. This has left car manufacturers with very imperfect knowledge of the behavior of consumers in relation to used cars, and their attempts to take control of their dealers' activities in this market have been met with skepticism on the part of the dealers concerned. Three more case studies are examined in this second part of the chapter with the objective of presenting the perspective of the main actors in the second-hand car market. These cases are the US during the period 1996–97, emerging countries during the period 1995–2005 and France during the period 1995–2005.

The US in 1996–97: the Emergence of Superstores

At the end of the 1980s, the car distribution market in the US was subject to significant upheaval as a result of the entry of a number of new firms specializing in the sale of second-hand cars. It was not until 1996–97 that the strategies of the different actors clearly emerged, and their subsequent success has been mixed. However, the ambitions of the new entrants and their initial success are evidence of the gap in the automobile market that had been left by car manufacturers. By replacing the more informal methods used for trading used cars that were in existence up until that point, these firms saw an opportunity to build a profitable and sustainable business that the car manufacturers had chosen to ignore.

While the firms involved were quite different from one another, they were all responding to the same environment. The regulatory constraints that weigh heavily on operators in the new market are inexistent in the used-car market. In addition, despite the fact that the automobile market in its entirety is relatively stagnant, used-car sales represent a more significant volume than that of new-car sales. In the US, the ratio has stabilized at approximately 2.5, meaning that, for every new car sold, 2.5 second-hand cars are sold. As the vehicles themselves had become more reliable and as the manufacturers had extended the lifetime of their guarantees, it became more feasible to create a commercial range of good-quality used cars. A final contributory factor to the attractiveness of a structured used-car alternative was the relative price increase in the new-car market. In 1979, for example, the price of a new car represented 18.1 times the median monthly income of a US household. By 1996, this figure had risen to 27.5.[10]

A final key environmental factor to be considered by the new entrants was the level of competition they would face from existing firms. In this respect also, the opportunities appeared to outweigh the risks. The purchase of second-hand cars was either direct from seller to buyer via small ads or passed through one of two professional channels. One of these was a network of 23,000 dealers whose primary business was the sale of new cars and the other was a network of 63,000, independent dealers who suffered from a poor reputation in the eyes of car buyers. Their vehicles were generally viewed as unreliable and their sales methods were perceived as aggressive and were regularly the subject of criticism.[11]

New entrants into this fragmented market were also able to take advantage of the arrival on the used-car market of a relative abundance of good-quality used car in 1996 and 1997. These cars appeared as a result of the boom in the leasing market, which began in the US in 1996 and that quickly went on to represent 25 percent of new-car sales.[12] In 1996, 1.7 million vehicles were leased and 3.1 million in 1997, and the appearance of these vehicles on the used car market within the following two years allowed new entrants to develop a large range of good-quality cars.

It was in this context that the innovative concept of superstores emerged. These stores were made up of a number of branded stores that offered a large stock of second-hand cars that were between one and five years old. The details of what was available were accessible on touch-screen computers and the cars had been subject to a series of controls that allowed the store to offer a guarantee. The prices were clearly marked and were non negotiable, thus avoiding the need to haggle and the subsequent doubts about the price that was eventually agreed. Employees in the stores were remunerated not on the basis of sales but on the basis of customer satisfaction.

CarMax was the first brand of these superstores to become widely known in the US in 1996. The firm was a pioneer in the development of the superstore concept and its origins lay in its parent group's background as a retailing giant in the area of consumer electronics. The initial idea was to transfer knowledge from the group's competence in its original market by exploiting the similarities that existed between the two activities. Four elements were seen as key to the success of the new concept: large-scale advertising budgets, the recruitment and motivation of a sales force, the need to master the financial aspect of the business and the strategic nature of the servicing and repair services. The first store was opened in 1993 and in 1996 it was decided to develop CarMax into a national brand. CarMax expanded its network of "car supermarkets" in which consumers could choose among a range of between 500 and 1,200 vehicles. The objective was to sell 3,000 cars per year in each location[13] and to become market leader in the US.

The rapid expansion of the CarMax brand was accompanied by the arrival on the market of copycat firms. The most significant of these was Driver's Mart, a firm created by a number of "megadealers" with a very similar business model to that of CarMax. Most of the other new entrants were small-scale operations and were focused on specific market niches. HPR Automotive Superstore, for example, developed a smaller version of the superstore for towns with a population of approximately 100,000 people. Ugly Duckling and Smart Choice were two firms who chose to specialize in the financing and sale of used-cars to the low-income segment of the population that was typically seen as a credit risk by credit organizations. The vehicles on sale were priced at less than $10,000 but the interest rates on finance were close to 30 percent.

In the same period, an alternative model was developed by the firm Republic, which went on to become the leading player in automobile distribution in the US market. Its strategy of integration has permitted the firm to become a profitable and fast-growing business. The initial move into the business occurred through the acquisition of two large car-rental businesses in 1996. In 1997, the group began to buy up car dealerships in order to access the "buybacks" that car manufacturers had been guaranteeing to promote sales of new cars. These cars were then used to supply quality used cars to the group's superstores. In establishing itself in each of these different distribution activities, the firm was achieving its stated objective of satisfying all motoring needs of consumers: acquisition, rental and leasing of new or used cars.

In fact, Republic was seeking to maximize the revenue associated with every vehicle that the group acquired from a manufacturer. Following its acquisition, each vehicle could be rented and/or sold on three or four different occasions with Republic, maximizing its returns on both the financing and the repair of the vehicle throughout its lifetime. To do so, Republic had to establish its brand and its physical presence in the fifty different markets that make up the overall US market at the same time as it rationalized the supply chain and set up the holding company that would provide the centralized financing service. In addition to the economies of scale offered by such a structure, the broad offering of Republic was seen as a way of protecting the group from cyclical downturns in individual businesses. The group's president thus pointed out in 1997 that history has shown that a drop in new-car sales is accompanied by a growth in used-car sales. Thus, recession or no recession, Republic will continue to receive its monthly repayments.

Not all these new entrants have survived into the new millennium, but many have.[14] The dynamism of the US market during this period is evidence that there are commercial opportunities in the used-car market. Despite the refusal and/or inability of car manufacturers to exploit them, these existed nonetheless and other players proved adept at benefiting from them.

Emerging Countries in 1995–2005: Second-hand Car Networks Dominant

Emerging markets provide another example of the marginalization of the used-car world by car manufacturers. Since the 1980s, a number of new product development projects have been the central preoccupation of car manufacturers in the plans for emerging markets. The launch of the Renault Logan in autumn 2004 represents the concretization of one such project. However, the reality of the marketplace in such countries is very similar to the French market in the 1920s. The vast majority of households can only aspire to car ownership through the purchase of a second-hand car with an average price far more adapted to their purchasing power than that of a new car. Manufacturers are primarily concerned with establishing the necessary conditions to ensure new-car sales and the survival of their nascent sales networks. Similarly, policy makers have tended to focus their attention entirely on new-car sales when they set up incentives for car manufacturers to invest or when they develop regulations relating to car-related issues such as taxation and pollution.

A simple visit to India or to a country in central or northern Africa suffices for a motorist from the developed world to perceive the key explicative factors of the distance that separates car manufacturers from car users in these countries. It is patently obvious that the sale of a new car is relevant to only a tiny minority of citizens of the developing world, where motorization rates are three to four times less than in the developed world. The majority of households who do have a car have acquired it as an old or very old second-hand car. Once a car enters on the road in these countries it is kept on the road through multiple changes of ownership over a period of decades. Very little is known about the transactions in question, as they are often not registered. What is known is that in these countries the ratio of new cars to used cars is between 1 to 10 and 1 to 20, compared to between 1 to 2 and 1 to 8 in the developed world. Similarly the average age of the number of automobiles on the road is between 6 and 9 years in the developed world and it is over 15 years in central and northern Africa.

As the number of vehicles in circulation ages, it also increases in volume and thus offers users more opportunities to access a form of motorization that is far removed from what is available from the car manufacturers. One important form of purchase that occurs on this alternative marketplace is that of spare parts. Manufacturers and distributors know that there is little opportunity to sell spare parts in emerging markets, even though this is a key element of the profitability of their business in developed markets. They tend therefore not to stock them and an alternative system of supply is inevitable. These may or may not be totally legal as they may be selling counterfeit spare parts or parts that have been recuperated in a piecemeal fashion from a variety of sources. They fill in the gap in the marketplace left by manufacturers who are either charging too much or who do not have the spare part in stock. Certain states have actually refused to recognize the right to intellectual property protection in relation to spare parts in the hope of supporting the industrial development of their mechanical industry. Recent studies in Morocco have shown that sub-suppliers of automobile manufacturers who have been dropped as selection criteria become more stringent have chosen to move into the production of spare parts as the market offers interesting levels of profitability.[15]

The same reasoning reappears in relation to repair services. The norms, rates and recommendations that the representatives of the manufacturers are required to apply are far removed from the needs and purchasing power of most car users. An informal car repair sector has thus evolved in large towns. The organization of work, skills and technical equipment appears to have allowed these actors to develop a range of adapted services. Thus alternative models to those dominated by the ideas and practices of the manufacturers have emerged to occupy a predominant role in the automobile market of these emerging countries.

The national number of automobiles on the roads grows "naturally" as a result of the difference that exists between the number of new cars that enter it and the number of older cars that are destroyed. In developing countries, however, the market for new-car sales is restricted to only 1 to 5 percent of the population and the difference between sales and removals from the market is too small to explain the growth of the number of cars on the road. In fact in these countries, there is often a level of importation of used cars that is more important than the sale of new cars. This importation may be organized by the manufacturers themselves in search of secondary markets for products that need to be sold off for commercial or technical reasons. Most of the cars that are imported into developing countries, however, are older models and pass through unofficial channels. They may involve, for example, emigrants who live abroad for economic reasons, such as Turks in Germany, or local car professionals who buy cars in developed countries and take care of the paperwork to import them legally. Thus a large part of the clientele for the car auctions that were developed in France in the 1980s were professionals, such as these who bought up vehicles that were at the end of their lease period. Such vehicles are sold off at approximately 40 percent of their value as new cars. These are then repositioned at the top end of the local used-car market in developing countries, where most imported used cars are ones that failed their technical control procedure in their market of origin.

Since the devaluation in 1994 of the West African currency, it appears that this business has grown exponentially and has become, for example, the principal economic activity of Benin. This country reexports 90 percent of the vehicles it imports to neighboring countries. Initially, the business was created by students whose scholarships had lost virtually all their value, and their success inspired numerous professionals, who went on to build informal trading structures. A report in the French press concerning the automobile business in Cotonou in Benin described the amazing number of different trades that have emerged. These include children carrying batteries to recharge cars that have been driven from Europe. There are specialists who transport the cars from the boats in which they arrive and specialists who are waiting to spot the best deals. In addition, there are painters and welders and drivers to take the car on to its destination. There is a further substratum of economic activity that involves stripping items such as rear-view mirrors from cars when they arrive off the boat and then setting up shop to sell them to the new buyers of the "stripped" cars before they leave the port.[16]

The incentives to import are of course increasing as the purchasing power of the inhabitants of these countries falls. As was noted in relation to the devaluation of the currency in Gabon in 1995, fewer and fewer citizens of all social classes are in a position to gain access to the level of finance necessary to buy a new car. It is believed that a "moving coffin" is better than being on foot even if many buyers of these ancient cars find themselves having to pay out again very quickly for repair work.

An official in the customs service of Gabon is quoted as saying that the country is not in a position to fight against counterfeit spare parts as the country does not have a car industry and in the end the local consumer ends up paying less.[17] This attitude exemplifies the problems that face public policy makers in emerging countries such as Benin and Cameroon in relation to the dynamic market for the sales and servicing of second-hand cars. They are trying to balance the social argument for motorization of their citizens with the need to fight the illegal aspect of some of this activity, at times with the implicit support of their own customs and security services. In addition, there is an opportunity cost in terms of lost import duties[18] and the manufacturers and their representatives put them under pressure to act against these alternative channels.

The current balance appears to weigh in favour of the continued existence of the alternative distribution models for used cars that have emerged over the last ten years in these countries. The state services concerned are relatively powerless and the borders between states are permeable to the unregulated car trade. Added to this scenario are the dynamic force and inventiveness of the participants in the alternative model, which to some extent is comparable to the situation in France, which is to be discussed in the following section.

France in 1995–2005: Alternative Car Usage Systems

In France, the relative amount of new-car sales to second-hand car sales is not as disproportionate as it is in the developing world. However, the difference between the average unitary values for new cars and those of second-hand cars in the French market is striking. This occurs because the majority of second-hand cars sold in France are over five years old and, at this age, cars have lost approximately 70 percent of their value. This is a fairly clear indication that the populations buying a second-hand car and a new car are different, with the exception of those households buying an almost new or very recent used car. This means that they need to be approached in a distinctively different manner by professionals in the automobile market.

The first step in understanding the evolution of the volumes and the structure of the used-car market is to analyze the nature of the existing used-cars. The French number of cars on road is growing by 2 to 3 percent per annum and is aging. The average age of the car owned by a French household has increased from 5.8 years in 1980 to 7.5 years in 2000 and is going to be over 8 years in 2006. This corresponds to a total number of new cars registered of roughly 2 million. This is not matched by the number of 1.5 million cars withdrawn from circulation, as the age of such cars is tending to increase from an average of 12.5 years.

As these cars on roads are the basis for second-hand car sales in France, it is logical to expect the average age of used cars bought and sold to have increased also and to imagine a growing disparity between the average unitary value of a used car and a new car. However, recent vehicles are still over-represented, with cars of less than 5 years representing only 35 percent of the number of cars on the road but 40 percent of the transactions, and, as a result, the average age of second-hand cars sold in France remains below that of the overall French automobiles. To understand this phenomenon, it is important to distinguish between the registration of new car sales to individual buyers and the registration of new car sales to companies. In France, what are called "direct sales" to firms represented 38 percent of all new car sales in 2001 and 46 percent in 2006. These cars tend to be kept only for a short period but during this time they clock up a high mileage. The larger the proportion of the overall market that is represented by this type of sale, the more active the second-hand car market will be. These company cars in France make up 37 percent of the second-hand market for cars of less than five years and only 12 percent of the overall second-hand market. To understand the level of activity in the second-hand market, however, it is also necessary to integrate the length of time that individual buyers keep their cars. In France in 2000, households owned a total of 26.5 million cars and acquired 6.25 million. This equates to an average period of retention of 4.25 years.

The French market represents an average level of activity compared to the UK, for example, where the regulatory and commercial environments have generated a higher level of activity. At the other extreme, the Italian and Spanish markets are far less active.[19] The French market has thus become a relatively active business in which the manufacturers' dealerships coexist with specialist operators. They both continue, however, to ignore an important segment of the market – that of the old and the very old vehicles that are aging the French cars on the road. The three principal channels that serve the second-hand car market in France are the manufacturers' dealerships, the professional used-car channels and direct sales from consumer to consumer, generally via the small ads, representing respectively 35 percent, 15 percent and 50 percent of the overall market. Naturally, these different channels are not represented to the same degree for different types of cars and what competition there is that exists between them is limited by a strict division of labor among the various actors. In the second-hand car market, which is essentially a market whereby individual sellers sell to individual buyers, the manufacturers' dealerships have become more active in the sale of the more recent vehicles, leaving it up to the many specialists in the nonstructured sector of used-car sales to provide an alternative offering for households looking to buy older cars.

The demand for second-hand cars in France is far more important in terms of volume than the demand for new cars. There is thus a major gap between the reality of automobile consumption and the typical analysis of motoring spending that is presented by professionals in the industry and, in particular, by the manufacturers' dealerships. From the manufacturers' perspective – as distinct from that of their dealerships – the demand for used cars is potentially a problem insofar as it may encroach on the demand for new cars. This happens when the used car is viewed as a substitute for a new car to be used in the same way and requiring a similar amount of investment that would be required to purchase a new car. While this is a reasonable possibility and has been growing in significance as a commercial proposition for the past ten years, it is not generally valid when the purchase of a used car is being considered. For most motorized households, the purchase of a second-hand car is the alternative when a new car purchase is beyond their means. Studies have shown that there is a relatively limited overlap between household purchases of new and used cars. The results show where there is hesitation or switching behavior on the part of households who at times buy a new car and switch to a used car or vice versa. Thus, it is estimated that for every 100 households in the market for a replacement vehicle, 20 to 25 percent are already new-car buyers and remain as such, 50 to 55 percent are used-car buyers and remain as such and the remaining quarter switch from one category to another. Among this final group, a small majority switch from being used-car buyers to new-car buyers but over 10 percent of households changing their cars switch from a new car to a used car, in order to move up-market in one-third of the cases studied. In terms of the replacement of new cars by used cars in a country such as France, where households buy and sell approximately 5.5 million vehicles, the overlap is thus calculated at somewhat less than one million purchases.

While the growing substitutability of used cars for new cars that they have contributed to creating is attracting a lot of attention from car manufacturers, it is only part of the story. Overall, the very large majority of used cars are sold for amounts that clearly differentiate the demand for used cars from that of new cars. To make a useful comparison, we first remove the used-car transactions involving very recent used cars of less than three years of age. Depreciation for such cars is around 40 percent and they represent the 20 to 25 percent of transactions that are the "overlap" mentioned above. The average transaction value of the remaining three-quarters of transactions is less than 15 percent of the average value of a new-car purchase. Clearly, the figures are so disproportionate for the majority of used-car sales that they cannot be seen as substitutes for new cars. Neither can used-car sales be described as the same demand satisfied differently – it is truly an alternative form of demand, which represents some 4 million vehicles per year in the French market.

It thus emerges clearly that for a very important proportion of households, the ownership and running of an automobile is a purchasing obligation that is not matched by anything on offer from the professional network put in place by the manufacturers. These households have subsequently been obliged to invent a specific subsystem for consumption that is on the margins of the structured automobile market and in which traditional car marketing has little meaning. In reality, the marketing of new cars is concerned with products and services that these households may encounter in five to ten years when the new cars have moved on to become second-hand, third-hand or fourth-hand purchases. By this time, their initial characteristics will have become significantly altered through wear and tear, and service and repair work will have long since been done by garages outside of the official dealership network. In addition, these households' car-related spending is dominated by spending related to use, and their choice of car is based on a desire to limit the risks of further outlay by seeking out a good relationship with a car repair outlet or buying a solid, reputable product.

Thus the consumer behavior exhibited by these households, which are in the majority, does not correspond to that which is used by the manufacturers to build their car development strategies and to promote their products and services. Three main factors explain these differences:

- For these consumers, the purchase cost of the car is relatively marginal as part of their overall automobile outlay and it is the consumer's estimation both of the car's ongoing usage costs and of the risk of unanticipated service and repair costs that is of primary importance, rather than the product's technical or aesthetic characteristics.
- As they are usually unable to afford guaranteed used cars, these buyers seek out a more subjective level of reassurance by relying on interpersonal relationships. The primary motivation in choosing a used

car that emerges from professional research studies is consistently the advice of the garage owner or personal relationship with the seller, and the brand or model of car is secondary.

- The marketing tools used by manufacturers to promote their new cars are based on segments whose characteristics are, by very definition, unlike those of used-car buyers as their target markets tend to be made up of new-car buyers who already buy from their dealer networks or those of their competitors. As there is little overlap between this group and the larger group of used-car buyers in the population, the "concepts" they develop to launch their new cars and their services are not adapted to used-car buyers. In addition to socio-economic differences between the two groups, there is also an important distinction between the time frame of the original and the used-car purchase. Over the last fifteen years, car manufacturers have been updating their product ranges more regularly, based on their belief that consumer needs are changing more and more quickly. Given that most cars will in fact be in the hands of the majority of their users on average five years after their initial market launch, the efforts made by manufacturers to adapt to the needs of the original purchasers are likely to be of limited impact.

For these reasons, it is seen as crucial to recognize the distinction in motivations between new-car buyers and used-car buyers. The latter group consists of buyers who, in general, are not choosing between car brands or models based on their image. To gain further insight into the motoring behavior and spending patterns of different segments of the French population, an analysis was conducted of the annual household budget survey. It highlights that not only do different forms of consumption coexist but, to a large extent, they are interdependent.

The data in Table 10.2 compare the manner in which the richest households in France consume automobile products and services with the contrasting behavior of the poorest households. These two series of figures show clearly the co-existence of two usage systems. While it is difficult to survive in a social or economic sense in France without access to a car, Table 10.2 highlights how different socio-economic classes acquire this access in radically different ways.

In the first column, representing the purchasing behavior of the poorest households, it is clear that the majority of the spending relates to the running cost of the automobile, mainly accounted for by fuel and repair costs. The car consumption behavior of these poor households can be typified as the purchase of a second-hand car that is usually old and heavier in fuelconsumption than more recent models. It is more likely to be in poor repair and will not be likely to be covered by a guarantee as many of the purchase transactions are made between individuals. Clearly, these households are generally not customers of the dealership networks of manufacturers. It is estimated that approximately 20 percent of the expenditure of poorer household on their cars ends up in these official networks.

Table 10.2. Structure of motoring expenditure in the French market

	Poorest 20%	Richest 20%
New-car purchases	16.7%	38.9%
Used-car purchases	21.7%	22.3%
Petrol	39.5%	23.9%
Other usage costs	22.1%	14.9%

Source: Author's calculations based on *INSEE Household Budget Survey*, 1995.

The data in the other column indicates that the most significant proportion of the spending on automobile products and services by the top 20 percent of French households relates to the purchase of new cars. They tend to own more cars overall and are more likely to be multi-car-owning households and to purchase "recent used cars" if they are buying a second-hand car. Sales of new vehicles to this 20 percent of the population alone represented one-third of overall new-car sales in the French market in 1995.

Conclusion

The automobile market differs from other mass markets, such as those for food or consumer electronics, for example, in that the structured marketplace does not serve the entire range of household demand. This difference is growing as cars become more reliable permitting the used-car market to meet an ever-increasing proportion of the motoring needs of the marketplace. While car manufacturers and their distributors have succeeded in meeting the needs of certain car buyers, the above analysis of different historical periods and different geographical locations has shown that the vast majority of the participants in the second-hand car market continue to operate outside of the structured marketplace. With the notable exception of the American superstores of the late 1990s, the market opportunites left open by car manufacturers have not attracted organized alternative suppliers into the used-car market.

As a result, the different forms of access to motorization are only partly organized and controlled by the official channels. As is highlighted by the analysis of both developing and developed countries, the used-car market and associated markets such as those of car repair exhibit a form of "self-organization" that flourishes in the relatively spacious margins that persist outside the narrow confines of the structured market of the car manufacturers. The study of these subsystems is of interest to the social sciences not simply because they permit large sections of the population to avoid the exclusion that would result if their access to motorization were reduced to what is on offer from car manufacturers. The emergence, persistence and variety of alternatives to the official channels is also evidence of a voluntary refusal on the part of a large proportion of consumers and professionals to participate in the new-car market. In choosing to buy a second-hand car, large numbers of consumers are continuing to resist the persistent commercial efforts of car manufacturers to attract them as new-car buyers. Such potential consumers for new cars could be described as defying the segmentation studies, the new-product development process and the sophisticated marketing techniques of manufacturers in favor of an alternative less structured marketplace that nonetheless offers them a more appropriate series of choices.

Viewed in this way, the used car market illustrates clearly the observation of Mary Douglas that "people do not know what they want, but they are very clear about what they do not want."

Notes

1. Mary Douglas, *Thought Styles – Critical Essays on Good Taste* (London, 1996), p. 83.
2. Richard S. Tedlow, *New and Improved, The Story of Mass Marketing in America* (Boston, MA, 1999), p. 162.
3. Sally Clarke, "Closing the Deal: GM's Marketing Dilemma and its Franchised Dealers, 1921–1941," *Business History*, special issue *The Emergence of Modern Marketing*, 45: I, (January 2003), pp. 60–79.
4. See Jean-Louis Loubet, *Citroën, Peugeot, Renault et les autres: soixante ans de stratégie* (Paris, 1995).
5. See Patrick Fridenson's chapter in Jean-Pierre Bardou, Jean-Jacques Chanaron, Patrick Fridenson, James M. Laux, *The Automobile Revolution: The Impact of an Industry* (Chapel Hill, NC, 1982). First edition *La Révolution automobile* (Paris, 1977).
6. Patrick Fridenson, in Jean-Pierre Bardou et al., *La révolution automobile*, p. 171.
7. C. Gautrelet announced to his dealerships in 1962 that they would soon be like Americans and would no longer sell cars but would trade and exchange them, quoted in Loubet, *Citroën, Peugeot, Renault*, p. 321.
8. Ibid., pp. 369–70.
9. For a detailed analysis of this phenomenon, two sources are recommended. The first is Alain Lipietz, *La société en sablier – Le partage du travail contre la déchirure sociale* (Paris, 1995). The second is Julie Froud, Colin Haslam, Sukdhev Johal, Bernard Jullien, Karel Williams, "Les dépenses de motorisation comme facteur d'accentuation des inégalités et comme frein au développement des entreprises automobiles: une comparaison franco-anglaise, in Gabriel Dupuy and François Bost (eds.), *L'Automobile et son monde* (Paris, 2000), pp. 75–96.
10. *Wall Street Journal*, June 12, 1996.
11. In the US, it is said to be easier to end your relationship with your spouse than with your car salesman.
12. *Automotive News*, October 7, 1996.
13. This figure is calculated by an analyst from CS Boston and is reported in the *Wall Street Journal*, June 12, 1996, p. 3.
14. Bernard Jullien, "Internationalisation of Car Service Firms and Changes in Distribution," in Michel Freyssenet, Koichi Shimizu and Giuseppe Volpato (eds.), *Towards the Globalization of Automobile Firms? Internationalization Strategies and Trajectories* (London, 2003), pp. 95–116.
15. Brahim Bachirat, Loubna Boulouadnine and Nisrineal Lembarek. "L'industrie automobile au Maroc: potentiels et dynamiques des relations clients/fournisseurs," in Twelfth GERPISA International Colloquium, Paris, June 9–11, 2004.

16. Arnaud de La Grange, "Cotonou et les mille et une voitures," *Le Figaro*, June 25, 2003.
17. Luc Ngowet, "Libanais d'Afrique – Gabon: le lucratif créneau des véhicules d'occasion," *RFI*, July 24, 2003.
18. Léopold Chendjou, "Le Cameroun roule en occasion," *Le Messager*, n°. 1404, August 23, 2002. The author notes that official imports have fallen by 48 percent representing a loss of between 5 and 6 billion CFA francs in the past year.
19. Bernard Jullien, "L'après-vente – Derrière l'occasion, la pièce, l'entretien et la réparation, la réalité des consommations et des offres automobiles: la diversité et la difficulté des constructeurs à y faire face," in EBG, *L'Automobile* (Paris, 2003), pp. 498–534.

11

UTOPIA POSTPONED?

THE RISE AND FALL OF BARTER MARKETS IN ARGENTINA, 1995–2004

Ruth Pearson

Barter – the exchange of goods and services outside the formal economy – is an activity which, it is generally assumed, has long since been surpassed in the vast majority of the economies in the contemporary world. Not only in industrialized economies but in developing countries also, where money has become the standard instrument of facilitating economic exchange between people and enterprises, national – and international – currencies that operate as the generalized medium of exchange have become a standard feature of economic activity, from highly internationalized trading to local food or produce markets. Even poor rural households, which until the mid-twentieth century produced much of their food for own consumption, have found themselves pulled into a mainstream economic system, which over several centuries has increasingly required cash – for taxes (e.g., Southern Africa), for commodities and in recent decades as Structural Adjustment Policies have become orthodox economic medicine to cure sick economies, for user charges on health and education.

For many the notion of "marketization" has become synonymous with "monetization," so that there is a general assumption that, when people's livelihoods become wholly or even partially dependent on the sale of goods and services in the market, then any kind of parallel or exchange transactions will disappear. However, such an approach is in essence ahistorical. It takes a modernization view of development and industrialization that assumes a universal linear movement from direct kinds of exchanges or barters in pre-monetary economies to "modern" monetized economies in which all exchange is organized through a specific monetary currency. Moreover, in spite of evidence to the contrary, there is also an implicit assumption that transactions concern commodities directly produced or purchased; there is little appreciation of the role that transactions in second-hand goods plays in the livelihoods of the poor. This is particularly true in the burgeoning informal sectors of developing countries, which is where the majority of the world's population trade and seek their livelihoods.

Of course, the history of money – let alone livelihoods and markets – suggests otherwise. Firstly, it is clear that some exchange has continued to be organized in parallel or instead of particularly monetary systems. Analysis of women's livelihoods for example has long demonstrated that in most countries of the world exchange of goods and labor for cash has not been the only means whereby they have ensured their households' subsistence or survival.[1] In rural societies reciprocal exchange of labor, often organized through communal institutions such as work parties, was the norm until the 1950s.[2] Increased diversification of household livelihoods, however, had the effect universally of reducing direct exchange with kin members and pressurizing people to engage in a whole range of trading and exchange relationships with a wide rage of people, either for cash, for wages or directly for food or agricultural inputs.

However, in urban households, the transition to a fully monetized economy has been much more rapid and much more thorough. This is true in the (post) industrial economies of North America and Western and Northern Europe and it has become so in the newly industrialized economies of East and South East-Asia and South America.

This was nowhere more true than in Argentina. By 1950 the majority of the population lived in cities or other kinds of urban settlements; because of its specific history only a small proportion was dependent on the land and most of these earned a wage in the extensive pampas (prairies), which produced wheat and beef for export to the region and beyond. Argentina, known variously as the granary of the world because of its role as agricultural exporter of staples to Northern countries, and as the "Paris of Latin America" referring to its absence of indigenous population (because of aggressive-land grabbing military exploits of the sixteenth and seventeenth centuries, followed by mass European immigration throughout the nineteenth and twentieth centuries) and also in recognition of the elegance, modernity and wealth of the city of Buenos Aires and other urban centers.

But, in spite of these claims, Argentina could not convincingly be described as a misplaced Northern society, located in the global South. Poverty has always coexisted with public and private opulence, and the *villas miserias* – Argentina's version of unplanned, unserviced squatter settlements – could be found on the outskirts of the capital and other cities, as well as increasingly within the metropolitan areas. The inhabitants of these shanty towns generally comprised those who had been marginalized by Argentina's relative prosperity. Ever since the first Peronist governments of the 1950s, working people, including blue-collar workers and agricultural workers, had striven to be at the center of Argentina's economic policy. In spite of successive – and often bloody – military coups, the economic structures reflected the two major political interests in the country – the landed oligarchy, which long benefited from their land ownership and the rewards of the agricultural export sectors, and the trade union organizations, representing their mass membership from the *sin camisas* (shirtless) working class. A protected economy until the last decade of the twentieth century, Argentina developed a significant domestic industrial capacity, together with an inefficient economy and rampant inflation.

The system began to demonstrate fatal symptoms of dysfunction in the last two decades of the twentieth century. Resolute adoption of neoliberal policies, which were highly dependent on foreign capital, produced meltdown, rather than the sustainable development that was necessary to maintain living standards and deliver growth and prosperity. In the 1990s, at the behest of the International Monetary Fund, Argentina opened up its financial and capital markets and privatized state companies. The protective trade barriers established in the 1960s and 1970s in the heyday of the structuralist policies advocated by the United Nations Economic Commission on Latin America (ECLA) were dismantled. And, to respond to endemic high levels of inflation, which reached over 2000 percent at the beginning of the 1990s, the government pegged its currency, the peso, to the dollar in 1991, on the basis of free convertibility. But, although this fixed parity system allowed President Menem's government to control inflation and economic growth was healthy in the first years of the 1990s , the system prevented the government from printing money; so to raise public revenue – on the basis of a notoriously low corporate tax base – the government sold off state enterprises and borrowed heavily abroad, leading to the takeover of large and key sectors of the economy by foreign companies. High interest rates attracted short-term capital, as the government's foreign debt ratcheted up from US$120 million in 1991 to US$240 billion in 2001.

Whilst these policies delivered respectable growth rates in the early 1990s – an average of 7.7 percent a year between 1991 and 1994[3] – the social and economic security of the waged workforce was under extreme pressure. As domestically owned companies collapsed, former state enterprises were rationalized and the new foreign owners of Argentinean businesses indulged in asset stripping and profit repatriation, supported by the 1:1 dollar parity unemployment rates rose to over 30 percent according to official figures, and many previously secure working-class and lower-middle-class employees lost their jobs. The universal social security system on which Peronism had traditionally based its appeal and support might have been expected to support these workers with pensions and social security benefits. However, this too was to fall apart, besieged by corruption, underfunding and the general effect of the economic collapse affecting all parts of the country.

By the second half of the 1990s the Argentinean economic bubble was beginning to burst. The Asian financial crisis of 1997–8 affected financial markets globally; when the Brazilian *real* plummeted in 1999, the *peso* was unable to devalue, since it was still tied to the US dollar – leaving Argentine exports vastly more expensive than those from neighboring Brazil The subsequent decline in world prices for agricultural products and the global economic slowdown at the end of the millennium again reduced Argentina's ability to earn much needed foreign exchange in export markets, making it impossible to finance the escalating dollar-dominated debts.

The Rise of Barter Markets – 1995–2000

The birth of Argentina's barter markets and the formation of the national network the *Red Global de Trueque* can be understood in the context of economic decline in the country outlined above. The swelling numbers of the "new poor" were stranded in an economy that, unlike the case in many developing countries, had little "informal sector" activity that could act as a safety net for those excluded from the regulated formal labor market. The barter markets can be understood partly as a way of inventing a market that would serve the function of the informal economies in other less regulated economies and specifically would facilitate trade without formal currencies; and most pertinently one in which all kinds of commodities, including second-hand clothing and household and other goods, as well as home-grown and produced goods and personal services, could be traded outside the main formal economy.

The plight of the new poor struck a chord with a number of activists who were seeking to develop community-based strategies that could be counter-poised to the dominant practices, which they saw as imposed by the exigencies of global capitalism. Argentina has always had its share of social visionaries who have proposed solutions to social and economic problems. But the generation that had grown up in the wake of the "dirty war" of the 1970s when the military junta inflicted all manner of human rights abuses on the population, and then witnessed the waste and suffering of the Malvinas adventures (which eventually brought about the downfall of the repressive military regime) were intent on finding constructive and "inclusive" solutions rather than following the confrontationalist policies of the left opposition of previous decades. One such group was the PAR (*Programa de Autosuficiencia Regional*), which was a nongovernmental organization (NGO) responsible for what became the largest experiments in community currencies in the twentieth century.

What was interesting about this scheme is that it took its inspiration from the writings of Silvio Gessell, a German businessman who had lived for many years in Argentina and other parts of South America. Gessell explained in his once famous book *The Natural Economic Order* his views on the nature of money, how it functions in the economy and how it should be reformed. He originated a plan for issuing a type of currency that would not be hoarded. Gessell believed that the value of money should depreciate with time, like the value of goods it is supposed to represent.[4]

Gessell's ideas were implemented in a series of schemes introduced in Germany in the face of spiraling inflation after the end of the First World War and similar (short-lived) schemes were in Austria. A more lasting application was the WIR business circle, which was founded in Zurich in 1934 and has survived and prospered up to the present time. In 2000 WIR had almost 7,000 participants and operates on the basis of providing a solidarity-based currency, which offers an alternative source of credit to support small and medium-sized businesses.[5]

In the post-Second World War period there have been various developments of community currencies in the Western world. The best known are the LETS – Local Economic Trading Systems – the brainchild of a Canadian, Michael Linton.[6] These have become well established in Canada and the UK and particularly in New Zealand and Australia but remain for the most part small-scale. In the United States the Ithaca Hours currency, developed by Paul Glover in New York State in 1991 as a response to the first Gulf War, is an adaptation of the LETS model. The Ithaca scheme also uses a community-issued currency, rather than direct barter between individuals on the basis of a recorded credit and debit account, which is how most LETS schemes operate. By 2002 the Ithaca scheme claimed a circulation of US$85,000, with over 500 participating businesses and thousands of members.[7]

Although inspired by various historical writings on social credit and interest-free money, the organization and shape of the Argentine barter system evolved independently. The system operates on the basis of producing a (quasi) currency with which to enact exchanges between members of the network; but from the start the vision was of a barter market – a system of exchange between people rather than the faceless market of contemporary capitalism and the name *treuque* (barter) has remained central to its identity. The objective was to facilitate the exchange of goods and services between individuals who were excluded from the mainstream consumer markets in urban Argentina at the end of the twentieth century, which meant people who could not look to sell their professional or industrial skills in exchange for wages and salaries, people who were thoroughly urbanized and could not access other forms of self-provisioning outside monetized exchange systems. This scheme gave these excluded groups the opportunity to convert their unwanted possessions into purchasing power for essential goods and services; that is, it provided a system whereby second-hand goods could command a "price" outside the main monetary systems and be converted into the ability to acquire other items required for family survival. And all this not in a pre-industrial, pre-modern society but in the sophisticated – if divided – urban areas of 1990s Argentina.

History of the *Red Global de Trueque* (Global Barter Network)

The organization of barter exchange between residents of urban Buenos Aires can be traced back to the activities of an environmental NGO, the Regional Self-Sufficiency Programme (PAR) cited above. This organization had been originally established in 1989 in Bernal in the Province of Buenos Aires and was dedicated to the development of a series of "intermediate technology" projects, such as organic food production, alternative sources of energy (such as solar and biomass), and recycling of domestic waste. Its objective was to develop a series of enterprises that could contribute to improving the quality of life of the community in terms of the social, economic and ecological environment and would deliver sustainable development based on the utilization of unutilized local resources.[8]

However, with time, the orientation of the organization changed. Rather than concentrating on the development of technologies that could be utilized in such projects, the organization became more interested in promoting the economic independence of the local region and in providing a framework for revalorizing environmental, economic, cultural and technical resources. Because of the double effect of economic globalization and the neoliberal deflationary policies of the Argentinean governments of the 1990s, the group became more and more interested in initiatives that would provide a self-help network for people struggling to make sense – and a living – in a rapidly declining economy. This widened into an ambition to create a protected economic space for people who were not able to keep themselves afloat as their economic environment became more and more difficult in the stringent economic circumstances of an economy at the mercy of – and at odds with – the economic orthodoxy of the time.

The idea for an alternative "market" where people could exchange their own produced or surplus (previously owned) goods – or even services that had no buyer in the formal market – first arose amongst a group of friends and neighbors of the PAR organizers, based in Bernal. Apocryphally, a surfeit of quince pears grown on a neighbor's roof initiated the concept of exchanging surplus produce for other home-produced or home-grown items. For several months a group of people met in a friend's garage and directly exchanged – or bartered – items such as bread, foodstuffs, fruit and vegetables, cakes and handicrafts, all of which had been produced by the barterer.

The initial form which the *Club de Trueque* took sounds quaint, if not comical. According to their own account:

> [A]fter much discussion a group of some 60 people carried out the following activities: One by one we entered a part of the room where we would leave different products such as cakes, pasties, pizzas, articles of clothing and handicrafts, to which were attached their "prices" in *creditos*. We would then go out and come in again in the role of consumers noting the value of our purchases on our individual ticket. During the weekend we would hide away in our house for hours in order to transfer the information on to the spreadsheet – which proved to be an interminable task.[9]

This clumsy system reflected the ways in which the early LETS schemes operated in North America and the UK, where each local scheme kept an account of transactions and members' overall credits or debts. However, in Argentina the interest and the need, for a parallel market grew quickly and, once there were other clubs in operation in addition to the original one in Bernal, it became clear that this convoluted and labor-intensive system of keeping accounts was not practical – because it was too time-consuming – or desirable – because it would make new clubs dependent on the administration of the original Bernal *nodo* (the term for an individual local club or cell which became part of the Global Barter Network). One of the founders, Rueben Ravera, came up with the idea of producing a token or voucher to facilitate exchange – or trading – between the participants. The voucher, in effect a community-issued "money," allowed the system to develop from direct barter to multi-reciprocal barter, which permitted a three-stage exchange – your produce for a voucher, your voucher for someone else's product. This was the birth of the social currency, denominated in units called *creditos*.

Following these initial steps, and thanks to extensive publicity from the television and the print media, as well as the international press, the idea of a simple voucher or token that could operate like money caught the imagination of many people. Even though the objective of the scheme was to facilitate the exchange of surplus or unused goods and services, as well as the recycling of local resources for mutual benefits, the utilization of a quasi-monetary unit was the catalyst in the growth of the scheme.

Barter Clubs Expand 1996–2000

During the five years up until the political and economic crisis in 2001, the Barter Clubs enjoyed considerable expansion and success. Within a year of the first club, a network of some twenty clubs were operating in the Buenos Aires area and by 1998 it was reported that there were more than 150 clubs active in different parts of the country, involving between 80,000 and 100,000 people involved in "barter" transactions of food, clothes and household items. The goods traded came from a range of sources. Originally the exchange was in surplus items already available in the home – effectively second-hand clothing, domestic equipment, as well as (predominantly food and handicraft) items prepared specifically for the barter markets. People also offered fruit and vegetables grown in their gardens for sale. But, as time went on, other sources of goods were being traded. By 2000 surplus or remaindered wholesale and retail stock that could find no buyers in the peso markets were being off-loaded through the barter clubs. And as the economic situation deteriorioated factories, which were facing severe shortages of working capital due to the acute liquidity shortages that accompanied the economic and political crisis of 2001, took advantage of the existence of the barter network and its alternative exchange currency to both pay some of its wages bills in *creditos* as well as accept credits for the sales of surplus stocks. As the barter network expanded, more sophisticated products were drawn into its orbit; for instance, at a market in Bernal in 2000, I saw computer hardware, printers and consumables for sale as well as DIY tools and ecologically designed water filters.

During these years exchange and trading in services was also encouraged. Each local *nodo* published a weekly or monthly list of services offered – for example plumbers, decorators, computer repairs, catering, gardening, cleaning and childcare. In some *nodos* professionals including doctors, dentists and lawyers advertised their services and on the trading day would set up a stall either to take orders for future services or to provide instant attention – such as eye testing, checking blood pressure, or dental hygiene and diagnosis.

By the beginning of 2000, one of the founders, Carlos de Sanza claimed that there were up to 400,000 members of barter clubs (counting both direct members and family relatives of participating members) and the annual amount of *creditos* in circulation was of the order of 4–6 million. Given that nominally there was equivalence between a *credito* and a peso and there was still at that date parity between the peso and the dollar, this could be said to be equivalent to a circulation of US$4–6 million, a scale of trading with alternative currencies that was unprecedented in any of the experiments in community currencies that had been developed anywhere in the world in the twentieth century.

Relationships with the government, particularly at the local and provincial levels, had been positive from the beginning, unlike other experiences in Europe between the wars. The Bernal group, which became the center of operations for the whole Global Barter Network, operated from an empty ex-textile mill in Quilmes, which was made available by the local city authorities. In 1997 the *Programa Social de Trabajo* (Social Programme of Employment Promotion), jointly financed by the Secretariats of Industry, Trade, Tourism and Employment, supported a mega-market – the first National Day of Multi-reciprocal Barter. This was held in a large exhibition hall in the province of Buenos Aires and served to facilitate meetings and exchange between members of different *nodos*, as well as to introduce the idea and mechanisms of the barter network to potential new participants and to get media coverage and publicize the support of the local government. This event was replicated on an annual basis until 2001. The local agencies also supported the publication of a regular periodical. The 10 or so issues of *Trueque*, which carried information about local *nodos*, training, and events in Argentina, as well as news and communications from other countries in Latin America, North America and Europe, bore the logos of both the *Red Global de Trueque* and the *Programa Social de Trabajo*. The same agency also supported a program of training and support for the network in the city of Buenos Aires.

Before long the Federal Government was also providing technical and financial support for the network. The Department for Small and Medium Enterprises lent its support to the national barter fair in March 2001, having established a program of national support for the network, primarily aimed at supporting enterprises operating in this alternative economy.

In the face of increasing unemployment and failure of enterprises across the scale, the *Red Global de Trueque* was welcomed to the extent that it appeared to offer a cushion for the unemployed and a potential source of creation of new jobs as well as the provision of a safety net for those left without any income in the escalating crisis, all of which was welcomed in that it could help maintain the government's political support and legitimacy. Although no tax revenue is collectable from *trueque* transactions, a regulation issued by the tax department in March 2000 regularized the situation of *creditos*, allegedly making them legal tender outside the confines of the actual markets held by the local *nodos* or the occasional regional and national *ferias*, resulting in a number of regular businesses including law firms, bus and taxi companies, auto repair shops and psychologists, beginning to accept *creditos* as payments. *Creditos* also became acceptable by a handful of towns in payment of local taxes and it was reported that a judge ruled that a man could make his monthly child support payments in barter currency as well.[10]

The Bubble Bursts – 2001–2003

But, as the months of 2001 rolled on, the number of barter clubs, the number of people participating in the barter markets and the amount of parallel currency in circulation grew exponentially. Excited print and electronic journalists were constantly recording the phenomenon of *el Trueque Argentino*. As the political system veered out of control, the economy was under severe pressure. Factories and businesses were closing down at an escalating rate, leaving even more of the "new poor" not only without employment but also without a monetary safety net of a pension or unemployment benefit. More and more households left without an income turned to the barter network to ensure the short-term survival of their households. Interestingly, many of the newest recruits were less than enthusiastic about their participation, seeing their fall from participation in the mainstream economy as a source of shame and fear.

Participation was further boosted after bank deposits were frozen in December 2001 as successive short-lived governments tried to preserve the dollar to peso parity introduced by Menem in 1991. Whilst this measure was intended as an anti-inflationary policy to ensure that government could not pursue money-printing policies (since in theory the emission of the peso had to be backed by dollar reserves), the policy proved to be untenable. Foreign debt, both public and private, escalated – debt obligations were forecast at US$20 billion against a foreign reserve in the Central Bank of only US$ billion, after the sudden flight of about US$20 billion dollars just days before the government froze all withdrawals.[11] So, by the end of 2001, the Argentinean government was forced to take stringent measures in an attempt to comply with IMF requirements and maintain the dollar parity. These policies included swingeing social spending cuts, reductions in monetary levels of wages and salaries and the *corralito* (a partial freeze on bank accounts to shore up the value of the peso).[12]

As the economic crisis in Argentina worsened throughout the first half of 2002, the shortage of cash in the economy provided a fertile ground for the expansion of the barter system. The *Buenos Aires Herald* reported (February 28, 2002) that there were then some 2.5 to 5 5 million Argentineans frequenting some 4,500 barter clubs across the nation, trading everything from food and clothes, to cars, property and holiday trips, with about 40 to 50 million *creditos* of barter vouchers in circulation. Interestingly, many contemporary sources, especially journalists,[13] assumed that the barter clubs and their social currency had been a spontaneous response to the crisis – like the *piqueteros*, who were constructing road blocks to demand money from vehicular traffic, or the local assemblies or those occupying factories – all three of which are a post-crisis phenomenon.[14]

But it is certainly true that the nature of the crisis and the political and economic aftermath, which lasted through the whole of 2002, did have a fundamental effect on the nature and effectiveness of the barter club network. Given that the Argentine population had experienced a range of non-standard currencies earlier in their history – with official currency replacements, from pesos, to new pesos, to *autrals* back to pesos – and had lived with the official parity of the peso and the dollar since 1995, which meant that prices and more significantly bank accounts could be held in a foreign currency, they were used to a certain flexibility in terms of what they considered as money for immediate exchange. In the Northern provinces of Salta, Tucaman and La Rioja, the provincial governments issued bonds to pay their public employees in the 1980s;[15] (in spite of the central government's efforts to prohibit them because they were deemed to be inflationary by adding to the amount of money in circulation, they continued to be utilized in a number of northern provinces well into the 1990s).[16] As the effects of the restrictions on access to bank deposits severely reduced the amount of cash in circulation in 2002, many different sorts of quasi-money were being created by mainstream economic institutions. Provincial bonds were rediscovered by provincial governments – including Buenos Aires province, which began paying its 150,000 state employees in new *patacones* bonds, accepted by commercial outlets such as McDonald's and shopping malls – forcing President Duhalde to promise the visiting US Treasury Secretary Paul O'Neil in August 2002 that he would eliminate the fifteen provincial currencies currently in use as a local substitute for the peso.[17] Whilst such bonds were in opposition to orthodox neoliberal policies, it was reported that even the World Bank had resorted to paying out "funny money" in order to finance its "Heads of Household" poverty alleviation scheme in the country.[18]

It is also true that the initial government support, together with the influx of many downwardly mobile skilled manual or white-collar workers into the ranks of the dispossessed "new poor" extended *Trueque*'s constituency beyond the bottom-up participants in what had been an ecologically oriented system to effect the circulation of second-hand and inactive goods and services. By mid-2002 participation in the barter markets had become a mechanism whereby the cash-starved (but not necessarily assetless) Argentineans attempted to maintain a standard of living commensurate with their idea of their class position, by off-loading their consumer goods on to an increasingly problematic alternative market. One journalist commented, "While the poor barter for basic food and clothing, former members of the middle class are increasingly using the *trueques* in their struggle to maintain the lives they were accustomed to – trading for cars, apartments, beauty treatments and even hotel stays on the beach."[19] The same report recorded the offer for sale in a Buenos Aires barter market of a Louis XV bed, while purchasers were seeking a car battery for an Argentine-manufactured Ford and a fax machine. Professional people such as dentists and lawyers actively sought *credito* customers since their normal market was frozen with the *corallito*. The expansion was so rapid that by mid-2002 some journalists were claiming that up to 20 percent of the population were involved in trading in barter clubs.[20]

However, as many people, both external observers and those connected with the barter networks predicted, the rapid expansion of the barter markets spelt disaster. One of the founders, Ruben Ravera, reported that by March 2002 the Quilmes barter club had 400 salaried members – paid partly in credits and 500,000 members of the club. Divisions in the organization had already emerged and by April 2001 a rival network – the *Red de Trueque Solidario* (RTS – Solidarity Barter Network) had broken away from the main network – the RGT – over differences about the organization and philosophy of the network. The RTS accused the RGT of turning the club into a for-profit business, of charging fees in standard hard currency and of deviating from their goal of local self-sufficiency and popular democracy.[21]

During 2002 the RGT recognized that they had lost control of the movement in the context of the rapid growth. By mid-2002 the organization reported that there were 5,800 *nodos* with more than a million direct members, up from 400,000 in 2,000 *nodos* in October 2001. However, by the end of December the numbers had declined dramatically – to an estimated one-third of the late 2001 level. The organization had suffered a whole series of attacks; merchandise was stolen from the markets, outside groups – some suspect sections of the Peronist party – infiltrated the networks and utilized large volumes of currency to support their political cliental system in the absence of their traditional forms of funding, which was responsible for a large part of the inflation and weakening of the *credito* currency. The media was flooded with reports of betrayal and corruption by the leadership. Although these were without foundation, it was more difficult to shrug off accusations of mismanagement as the emission of new currencies into the market escalated causing inflation and lack of confidence. The worst problem was the large-scale counterfeiting of the *credito* vouchers; according to de Sanza at one point 95 percent of the vouchers in circulation were fake. The injection of worthless vouchers pushed prices up by a factor of more than 40 percent; the barter "price" of cooking oil rose from 7 to 300 *creditos* and flour skyrocketed from 3 to 140.[22] Other proscribed practices also began, such as charging interest on *credito* on debts and selling vouchers.[23]

The End of Barter in Argentina?

A chastened and philosophical leadership is currently trying to reestablish the barter system in Argentina, according to its original vision of facilitating recycling of goods and other factors of production that have been marginalized from the mainstream markets. In trying to learn from the debacle of the recent years, it is introducing strict controls on currency emission and utilization and providing more extensive training and participation from the membership. It has established a not-for-profit foundation and its activities are more transparent and open to scrutiny.

But the experience in Argentina in the last few years echoes that in mid-Europe in the 1930s and 1940s as well as in the UK and North America in recent decades, suggesting that alternative moneys can only coexist with dominant currencies and centralized financial systems on the basis of small-scale and locally controlled systems, where the adherence of those using the currency is continually reinforced by the rules and experience of participation – such as the LETS systems or the Ithaca Hours system in the USA. But there are also other potential implications. Whilst the demise of the RGT in 2002–3 can rightly be attributed to the rapid escalation in the scale of the system, the mismanagement – or naiveté – of the organizers and the opportunism and criminality of political activists and government officials, there were also other factors. It was also apparent that as the economic crisis bit deeper those genuinely facing poverty – rather than downward social mobility – found it increasingly hard to find articles – or services – to barter. Whilst initially participation could be secured on the basis of running down stocks of nonessential items, the production of new items and even the selling of services became increasingly constrained. To bake cakes required the purchase of flour and eggs, etc. – difficult with no formal currency; to run a hairdressing business required supplies of electricity, water and basic tools and supplies, only obtainable in the mainstream peso market. But, as prices within the barter market rose, the poor had fewer and fewer stocks of second-hand goods to trade and few options to produce other goods or services to earn stocks of the social currency required for trading in the alternative barter market. Once people's stocks of tradable goods had been exhausted, the market conditions militated against the possibility of ongoing participation in such a market.

So can we conclude that methods to facilitate the circulation of goods and services outside the dominant monetized markets of urban populations are doomed to failure and that barter is indeed a historical anachronism that has no place in the twenty-first century? Clearly a lot of the problems stemmed from the political and economic context of Argentina at the end of the last century. But there were also some interesting and important lessons – not least that it is possible to facilitate the circulation of second-hand goods, particularly among those who have suffered a relatively rapid drop in their income and living standards. As a recent communication from the RGT leadership indicates, "the reactivation of the barter market network is slow and we still have a problem to recuperate our credibility, but evolution is positive!" Perhaps the utopian vision of a humanized market based on barter has only been postponed.

Notes

In addition to the sources listed, research information for this chapter draws on transcripts of interviews carried out by the author in March 2001, undertaken in connection with an Open University Video, entitled Funny Money,? which was produced for an Open University Course U213: International Development: Challenges for a World in Transition. A fuller account of these interviews is carried in Ruth Pearson "Argentina's Barter Network: New Currency for New Times?" *Bulletin of Latin American Research*, 22:2 (2003) pp. 214–30. Additional information was obtained by further interviews with the founders of the Global Barter Network in November 2002 (see note 23 below), and from regular email exchanges.

1. The importance of nonmonetary exchange in the survival strategies of low-income women is emphasized in Caren Grown and Jennifer Sebstad, "Towards a Wider Perspective on Women's Employment," *World Development*, 17 (1989), pp. 937–53.
2. According to oral interviews with older Afro-Colombians in the southwest of Colombia, the reciprocal labor system, known as *minga*, prevailed until the individualization of farming household livelihoods in the 1950s. More detail can be found in Valerie Roberts, "Building Social Capital through Micro-credit: the Impact of a Rural Credit Programme on Borrower Livelihoods," unpublished PhD thesis, School of Development Studies, University of East Anglia, July 2002.
3. Figures are taken from: BBC Business: Q&A Argentina's Economic Crisis April 2, 2002; downloaded on July 16, 2002 from http://news/bbc.co.uk/hi/english/business/newsid.
4. An account of Gessell's ideas can be found in Thomas H. Greco, *Money: Understanding and Creating Alternatives to Legal Tender* (White River Junction, VT, 2001) p. 62.
5. Ibid., pp. 67–8.
6. Information on the growth of various community-based currencies such as LETS and Ithaca Hours etc. can be found in Richard Douthwaite, *Short Circuit: Strengthening Local Economies for Security in an Unstable World* (Dublin, 1996), and Greco, *Money*. See also David Boyle's comprehensive *Funny Money: In Search of Alternative Cash* (London, 1999), and G. Seyfang, "Community Currencies: Small Change for a Green Economy – An Evaluation of Local Exchange Trading Systems (LETS) as a Tool for Sustaining Local Development," *Environment and Planning A* 33, 6 (2001), pp. 975–96.
7. See Caroline White, Update on Ithaca Hours, (2002) available from www.feasta.org/documents/shortcuircuit/sc3/IthcacaHours.
8. A full account of the development of the *Red Global de Trueque* can be found in a pamphlet published by PAR: Carlos De Sanza, Horacio Covas and Heloisa Primavera, *La experiencia de la Red Global de Trueque en Argentina* (Buenos Aires, 1998). This forms the basis of many subsequent histories of the network.
9. Ibid., p. 4.
10. This is reported in David Adams, "No Pesos? No Problem," *St. Petersburg Times*, March 18, 2002; available from www.sptimes.com
11. Figures taken from Sue Branford, "The Land of Plenty Runs Dry," *New Statesman*, October 1, 2002, pp. 32–3.
12. See Clara Auge, "Argentina: Life after Bankruptcy: Barter, Demos, Theatre and a Dictionary of Crisis," *Le Monde diplomatique*, September 2002; available from http://mondediplo.com/2002/09/13.
13. See Duncan Green, "Report of Visit to Argentina," policy Unit, CAFOD 2003; available from www.cafod.org.uk/archive/policy/argentina.
14. The following paper discusses all three phenomena: Pete North "'Have Confidence and Cast Your Nets into Deep Waters' – Community Responses to Neo-liberalism in Argentina," paper presented at the session "Alternative Geographical Imaginations: Networks, Resistance and New Spaces of Engagements," Association of American Geographers, New Orleans, March 2003.
15. See Greco, *Money*.
16. Ibid p. 82.
17. See Auge, "Argentina," note 4, p. 5.
18. See Green, "Report of Visit to Argentina."
19. See Adams, "No Pesos? No Problem," p. 2.
20. This was claimed in a BBC2 documentary called *Cry for Argentina*, transmitted BBC4 September 24, 2002, and is repeated in many other journalists' reports.
21. Jeff Powell, "Petty Captilism, Perfecting Capitalism or Post-capitalism? Lessons from the Argentinian Barter Network," ISS Working Paper Series No. 357 (2002) contains an extensive discussion of the differences between the RGT and the RST.
22. See A. Gaudin, "Argentina – Bursting the Barter Bubble," February 17, 2003. Available from www.lapress.org.
23. Much of the information about the demise of the *Red Global de trueque* is drawn from discussions in Buenos Aires between the author and the RGT founder members, Carlos de Sanza, Ruben Ravera and Horacio Covas, during November 2002.

12

Charity, Commerce, Consumption

The International Second-hand Clothing Trade at the Turn of the Millennium – Focus on Zambia

Karen Tranberg Hansen

The international second-hand clothing trade grew rapidly toward the end of the twentieth century, fueled by the opening up of markets in many Third World countries and Eastern Europe. Today, Africa is the single largest market for this export from the West. This chapter provides a brief overview of shifts in the international second-hand clothing trade from the post-World War Two years and on through the present, identifying some of the actors involved: major charitable organizations who receive donated clothing, textile recyclers/graders, who collect and sort surplus clothing for domestic and export markets, commercial middlemen, brokers and shippers. Turning the focus on Zambia, where second-hand clothing has been a popular commodity since the late 1980s, the chapter sketches the wholesale, retail and distribution arrangements that link segments of this trade across the country and beyond. It then explains how the West's castoff clothing is transformed into new garments on its journey from the textile recycler's warehouse to the retail space and onward through dress practices in how, when and where the body is put together with clothing. Drawing on research I conducted in Zambia between 1992 and 1999,[1] the chapter showcases how traders and consumers work actively to give new lives to the West's used garments, in the process remaking their meaning.

The Second-hand Clothing Trade

The second-hand clothing trade in domestic markets in Europe has a long history, as the chapters in this volume vividly demonstrate. Well into the nineteenth century, used clothing constituted the effective market for much of the population except the very rich. Second-hand clothing was sourced and traded across vast distances.[2] By the first half of the eighteenth century, the Netherlands and London were centers for the wholesale trade in used clothes, with exports to Belgium, France and South America. The export trade reached the colonies as well, including North America, Australia and Africa. By the late nineteenth century in Paris, reasonably priced ready-wear competed so effectively with second-hand clothes that the used-clothing trade became limited to exports, especially to colonial Africa.[3]

The second-hand clothing trade may have a long history but not one of unbroken continuity between past and present. Concerning exports to Africa, I suggest at least a three-phase process marked by changes during the mid- to late nineteenth century, followed by shifts in the 1940s and in the 1980s. The profitable potential of the second-hand clothes market in colonial Africa was seized after the two world wars, when surplus army clothing was exported by used-clothing dealers in America and Britain and on the Continent. The availability of army clothing and men's work clothing from the early production of ready-wear are among the reasons why the histories of second-hand clothing consumption in Africa are distinctly gendered. In effect, the generally slower development of women's ready-wear affected this process.[4] Men's greatcoats and jackets came first and only in the interwar period did women's wear begin to enter used-clothing consignments for export. But the substantive growth of the African second-hand clothing market is a phenomenon postdating the Second World War, a product of both supply and demand: a vast surplus of still wearable used clothing in the West and growing desires and needs for clothes in Africa, where socio-economic transformations catapulted more and more Africans into new markets as consumers. The purchase of second-hand clothing became part of clothing consumption practices that included tailor-made and mass-produced garments. These practices were influenced by purchasing power ("class") and cultural norms for what was considered to be appropriate wear for women and men.

The Charitable Connection

Developments in the export trade in second-hand clothing since the Second World War have depended to a great extent on the clothing collection of major charitable organizations who supply both domestic and foreign second-hand clothing markets. The charities have a long and changing, involvement with second-hand clothing. In both Europe and the United States at the end of the nineteenth century, philanthropic groups collected and donated clothes to the poor.[5] Post-World War Two shifts in income distribution and growing purchasing power enabled more consumers than ever before to buy not only new, but more, clothes, including fashions and styles oriented toward specific niches, for example, teenage clothing, corporate and career dressing and sports and leisure wear. Such dress practices produced an enormous yield of used, but still wearable clothes, some of which ended up as donations to charity.

Many charitable organizations began emphasizing store sales in the late 1950s, among them the Salvation Army, for which the sale of used clothing was the single largest source of income in the United States.[6] The charitable organizations dominated the second-hand clothing retail scene in the 1960s and 1970s. They were joined during the 1980s by a variety of specialist second-hand clothing stores operating on a for-profit basis with names that rarely feature words like "used," "second-hand" or "thrift." Although most of the specialty stores cater to women, some stock garments for both sexes, there are stores for children's apparel and men's stores have appeared as well. Most of these stores target specific consumers, for example young professionals who may want high-quality clothing at modest prices or young people keen on retro and vintage fashion, punk and rave styles. Some stores operate on a consignment basis, others source in bulk from second-hand clothing vendors, or both. Some of these businesses donate garments that do not sell well "to charity," and some also dispose of their surplus at bulk prices to commercial second-hand clothing dealers.

The charitable organizations are the single largest source of the garments that fuel today's international trade in second-hand clothing. They include, in the United States, the Salvation Army, Goodwill, St. Vincent de Paul and Amvets and, in Europe, Humana, Oxfam, Terre and Abbey Pierre, just to mention a few. Because consumers in the West today donate much more clothing than the charitable organizations can possibly sell in their thrift shops, the charitable organizations resell their massive overstock at bulk prices to commercial second-hand clothing dealers. While the spectacular increase in second-hand clothing exports to Africa since the mid-1980s has taken place alongside the growth of the international humanitarian aid industry, this export is less about charity than it is about profits. Used clothing as outright donations in crisis and relief situations plays a very minor role in an export process that is overwhelmingly commercial. What is more, clothing donated for crisis relief often ends up sold commercially in local markets.

The Commercial Connection

Because every piece of clothing has many potential future lives, textile recycling is a lucrative business. The textile recycling industry comprises salvagers and graders, fiber recyclers and used-clothing dealers, brokers and exporters. "Used clothing" includes not only garments but also shoes, handbags, hats, belts, draperies and linens. In recent years, soft toys, for example teddy bears, have found their way into this export. The textile recyclers sort and grade clothing and apparel into many categories, some for the domestic vintage or upscale market and others for export; some for industrial use as rags and others for fiber. Blue jeans, especially Levi Strauss 501, the original button-fly jeans created in 1853 for miners and cowboys in the American West, are popular in Japan. Wool garments used to be exported to Italy to the wool regeneration industry in Prato, near Florence.

Among the more than 300 commercial firms in the textile recycling industry in the United States in the mid-1990s, approximately fifty large textile salvagers did the bulk purchasing by trailer load or in bales from both charities and for-profit organizations and shops. At factory setups, the collected garments and apparel are then sorted. The employees unbind the bundles and do a first sorting into resalable clothes and rags. Torn and stained items are put away, only to appear at a later stage of the process as industrial rags (wipers) or to be ground into fiber for car insulation, rugs or blankets. Vintage clothing is set aside. Since the mid-1990s, buyers, for example from Urban Outfitters, regularly visit the recyclers, traveling across the United States in their search for vintage apparel, some of which is recycled into "new" clothing and some sold as vintage. Japanese buyers also travel between these firms, purchasing garments with particular appeal to the youth market.

A second sorting distinguishes numerous categories by garment and fabric type. The categories reckon with changing seasonal demands, different markets and occasionally with customer specification. After the final sorting, the better grades are exported to Central American countries such as Costa Rica, Honduras and Guatemala and to Chile in South America. The lowest grade goes to African and Asian countries. Most recyclers compress sorted garments into 50 kilogram bales while some press unsorted bulk clothing into bales weighing 500 or even 1,000 kilograms. The bales are wrapped in waterproof plastic, tied with metal or plastic straps, placed in containers and shipped. Most of the large textile recyclers in the United States who are involved in buying and reselling for export are located near port cities along either coast and the Great Lakes. In Europe, for historical and geographical reasons, the chief commercial sorting capacity is available in the Netherlands and Belgium with easy access to the world's major ports. Among the world's largest importers and exporters of second-hand clothing, commercial firms in these countries sort and grade tons of second-hand clothing exported in bulk from Germany and Scandinavia, where the local capacity to handle this stage of the process is limited. In efforts to save labor costs, some of these firms have moved their sorting operations to former East Bloc countries, among them Hungary.

The second-hand clothing trade is an unusual industry because of the uneasy relationship between "charity" and commercial interests and the ways that each of these are organized. In the West today, the second-hand clothing trade in both domestic and foreign markets is dominated by non-profit charitable organizations and private textile recycling/grading firms, often family-owned. The extensive interactions of the charitable organizations with the textile recyclers/graders add a commercial angle to their dealings about which there is little substantive knowledge. At the same time, growing environmental concerns in the West in recent years have enhanced both the profitability and respectability of this trade and given its practitioners a new cachet as textile salvagers and waste recyclers.

World Exports and Imports

The second-hand clothing trade constitutes an immense, profitable, but barely examined worldwide commodity circuit that exports millions of dollars' worth of used clothing abroad. It grew more than seven fold over the last two decades, from a value of US$207 million in 1980 to US$1,483 million in 1999.[7] The United States is the world's largest exporter in terms of both volume and value, followed in 1999 by Germany, Belgium–Luxembourg, the United Kingdom and the Netherlands. Between 1990 and 1995 alone, United States worldwide exports of this commodity doubled, from a value of US$174 million to US$340 million,[8] declining in 1999 to US$288.[9]

The countries of sub-Saharan Africa are the world's largest second-hand clothing destination, receiving in 1999 thirty percent of total world exports, worth US$426 million, up from US$117 million in 1990.[10] There are several Asian countries among the large net importers of second-hand clothing, including Malaysia, Singapore, Pakistan and India. The large importers include such Middle Eastern countries as Syria and Jordan and several countries in Latin America. Sizable exports go not only to developing countries but also to Japan, the Netherlands and Belgium–Luxembourg, which all engage in both import and reexport of this commodity.

African used-clothing markets undergo changes not only because of civil strife and war but also because of legislation guiding the entry or prohibition of second-hand clothing imports. Monetary policies affecting exchange rates influence the ability of local wholesalers to import. Some countries have at one point or another banned imports, among them Côte d'Ivoire, Nigeria, Kenya and Malawi. Some countries have restrictive policies, for example South Africa, which only allows import of second-hand clothing for charitable purposes rather than for resale. Some small countries, like Benin, Togo and Rwanda before its civil wars, are large importers and active in transshipment and reexport. And, although second-hand clothing imports are banned in some countries, there is a brisk trans-border trade in this commodity.

Zambia's second-hand clothing trade dates back to the colonial period, when imported used clothing reached Northern Rhodesia, as Zambia was called then, from across the border with the Belgian Congo, now the Democratic Republic of Congo. Direct importation of this commodity was prohibited in Zambia during the first decades after independence in 1964. When restrictive import and foreign exchange regulations were relaxed in the mid- to late 1980s, the second-hand clothing trade grew rapidly. The name *salaula* came into use at that time. It means, in the Bemba language, approximately "selecting from a pile by rummaging" or, for short, "to pick." The name describes vividly the process that takes place once a bale of imported second-hand clothing has been opened in the market and consumers select garments to satisfy both their clothing needs and their clothing desires.

Import and Wholesale

Second-hand clothing consignments destined for Zambia arrive by container ships in the ports of Dar es Salaam in Tanzania, Durban in South Africa and Beira in Mozambique, from where they are trucked to wholesalers' warehouses in Lusaka, the capital. Lusaka is the hub of the *salaula* wholesale trade, though some firms have upcountry branches. At the warehouse, marketeers,

Figure 12.1. Sign on gate to wholesaler shop of second-hand clothing in Lusaka, Zambia. Photo: Karen Tranberg Hansen, 1997.

vendors and private individuals purchase bales of *salaula*. They in turn distribute and sell their goods in urban and rural markets, hawk them in the countryside and transfer them in rural exchanges in return for produce, goats, chicken and fish. *Salaula* is also sold from private homes in urban middle- and high-income residential areas and some traders bring second-hand clothing to city offices and institutions like banks to sell on credit.

The value consumers in Zambia attribute to *salaula* is created through a process of recommodification that involves several phases.[11] In the United States and Europe the sorting and compressing of second-hand clothing into bales in the recycler's warehouse strip these garments of their prior social life. The decommissioned value of the West's unwanted but still wearable clothing is then reactivated on local terms in transactions between overseas suppliers and local importers. Through subsequent transformations the meanings shift in ways that help redefine used clothing into "new" garments. These transformations begin in communications between exporters and importers and in on-site visits, continue at the wholesale outlet and in public markets and they are made visible in how consumers put themselves together with *salaula*. In addition to these processes through which the register of meaning of clothing shifts, there are also physical and material changes, involving alteration, mending and recycling.

The sorting and grading of second-hand clothing prior to export is guided not only by the West's categories of garment distinctions but also by specifications from the importer's end. The big wholesalers try to reckon with the changing cultural and seasonal demand that place a local mark on what at first sight appears to be a clothing universe determined by the West. These local terms are the seasonally varying terms for what sells, when and where

Figure 12.2. Fifty kilogram bales of imported second-hand clothing from the United Kingdom at wholesaler's warehouse, Lusaka, Zambia. Photo: Karen Tranberg Hansen, 2002.

and the culturally shifting terms for what is proper dress. Style terms enter as well, both regarding fabric and what is considered "the latest."

Once bales of second-hand clothing have been stacked in the warehouse and customers specify the type of bale they want to buy, the transformation process continues. Customers assess their nonreturnable bales with exacting care before contemplating a purchase. They scrutinize the plastic wrap and inspect the straps to determine that the bale has not been tampered with. The purpose of the customer's scrutiny in the warehouse is to ascertain that the bale has arrived "fresh" from its Western source, untouched by dealer interference and thus offering a range of "new" items.

Second-hand Clothing Markets

Zambia is one of the world's least developed countries. This was not always the case, but the economy has been on a downward slide since the mid-1970s.[12] Between 1980 and 1994, Zambia received several structural adjustment loans from the World Bank and its sister agency, the International Monetary Fund. Yet Zambians today are poorer, on a per capita basis, than they were at independence from British colonial rule in 1964. Given this decline, the significance of second-hand clothing is not surprising. But economics and poverty do not adequately account for the popularity of *salaula*. People in Zambia want to cut a good figure and buying their clothes "from *salaula*" is a means toward that end.

The shop window of Zambia's second-hand clothing trade, the big public markets, creates an atmosphere much like the West's shopping malls, where

Figure 12.3. "Changa changa" (baby clothes) seller at Chawana market, Lusaka, Zambia. Photo: Karen Tranberg Hansen, 2002.

consumers can pursue almost unlimited desires with an abandon not possible in the formal stores, where they are often dealt with offhandedly or are pressured to purchase. In these markets, the transformation of the West's cast off clothing into new garments, initiated in interactions at the point of wholesale, continues. The process of redefinition hinges on the meaning of the term *salaula* – selecting from a pile in the manner of rummaging. Practices that express this are evident, for example on "opening day," when a bale is cut open, its contents individualized into distinct objects of exchange, counted and assessed for quality and price. At this moment, when the clothes are ready to enter into another cycle of consumption, it is important that they have not been meddled with. Both traders and customers prefer to open bales in public, so that customers can select on the spot. A bale that is opened within full view in the market is considered to contain "new" garments. If it were opened privately at home, the trader might put aside choice items, causing customers to suspect that they are presented with a second cut and not "new" clothing.

On first sight, these *salaula* markets meet the nonlocal observer's eye as a chaotic mass of second-hand clothing hung up on flimsy wood contraptions, displayed on tables or dumped in piles on the ground. That view is deceptive. A variety of informal rules organize vending space and structure sales practices. Both vendors and customers know these practices. A prospective customer looking for a specific garment will go to a particular part of the market. The vendors of men's suits, for example, one of the most expensive items in the second-hand clothing markets, tend to be located in a part of the outdoor market that is near to major thoroughfares such as a main road passable by automobiles. So are vendors of other high-demand garments, such as women's skirts and blouses and the best-selling item of all, at least in

Zambia, baby clothes. There are spatial clusters of vendors selling shoes and, during the winter in the southern hemisphere, cold-weather clothing. These demarcations are not static as vendors sometimes change inventory.

The display on most second-hand clothing stands is carefully designed. High-quality items are hung on clothes hangers on the makeshift walls. A clothes line or a wood stand may display a row of cotton dresses. Everything that meets the eye has been carefully selected with a view both to presentation and sales strategy. Sales are accompanied by lively discussions and price negotiations. The piles on the ground include damaged items and garments that have been around for a while without being sold. Such items are sold "on order," that is, several pieces at a discount and they are often purchased by rural customers who plan to resell them in the villages.

Near the high end of the second-hand clothing stalls of the second-hand clothing markets and near the major roads of this market section cluster the "boutiques," where the desire for "newness" is particularly evident. Boutiques in these markets sell specially pre-selected items, coordinated to form matched outfits that are stylish. They tend to be operated by young vendors who "pick," in the language of the market. Once other traders open bales, the pickers descend on them, selecting choice garments, which they buy on the spot. Then they make up, for instance, women's two-piece ensembles, men's suits and leisure wear. Most of the boutique operators I met were young men who were very skilled at choosing their stock, with a fine eye for what might sell, a great sense of style and a flair for making stunning combinations. In recent years, the clothes displayed in the boutique section of Lusaka's *salaula* markets have been hung up "fresh" from the bale, that is, with wrinkles and folds. In the opinion of traders and customers alike, pre-washed and ironed clothing leaves the suspicion that the clothes might be "third-hand," meaning previously worn by Zambians.

Salaula Consumption

Consumers in Zambia go to second-hand clothing markets for many reasons. White-collar workers of both sexes in Lusaka's city center often spend their lunch hour going through the second-hand clothing stalls, sometimes making purchases at whim. Others go to find just that right item to match a particular garment. Some women who tailor in their homes search the *salaula* markets for interesting buttons, belts and trim to accent garments. And some go to purchase garments with the intention to resell. Today in these markets, more women's clothing is available than men's. Women are also more frequent shoppers than men, who at times are reluctant to be seen in the clothing markets and let their wives do the shopping. The vast majority of customers shop from *salaula* for clothing for themselves and their families. They come into the city center from residential areas like those in which I examined clothing consumption and where roughly two-thirds of all households supplied most of their members' clothing from *salaula*. Only the very tiny high-income group in Zambia, the *apamwamba* (a Nyanja term meaning "those on the top"), has an effective choice in the clothing market. For them, shopping "from *salaula*" is definitely a pastime.

Today, dealings with second-hand clothes extend across most segments of Zambian society except the *apamwamba*. My 1995 survey of clothing consumption practices fleshes this out in more detail.[13] Roughly two-thirds of the survey households in high-income areas of Lusaka, for example, met most of their clothing needs from *salaula*; in addition to buying *salaula*, more than half of these households also made regular use of a tailor; and the *apamwamba* sources clothing everywhere, including from second-hand clothing markets. These observations can be further specified in terms of age, gender and socio-economic background.

The least well-off of my survey households met most of their clothing needs from *salaula*, save for children's school uniforms and shoes; yet parents and guardians often buy parts of school uniforms, such as stockings, shirts, cardigans and shoes, from *salaula*. Nurses, whose dress allowance does not come close to the costs of a uniform, sort through *salaula*, searching for lab coats. Many young men buy their first suit from *salaula*. Adult women in better-off households obtained their clothes both from formal shops and tailors, men bought from shops, whereas most of the clothes for children and young adults were purchased at *salaula* markets. The *apamwamba* bought clothing everywhere; they also frequented, but did not depend on, the *salaula* market when searching for a specific garment to complement their wardrobe or when buying clothes for country relatives or their household staff. In fact, they sourced most of their own garments from the "outside." A mid-level public-sector executive in her late thirties, for example, explained to me in 1995 that she bought most of her clothes from "suitcase traders." Suits from South Africa were popular office wear that year, as was "American clothing," brought back by persons who visited the United States. In recent years, Dubai, Bangkok and Hong Kong have been popular destinations for suitcase traders.

My clothing consumption survey depicts a well-dressed adult as a person wearing garments that are well taken care of, with well-matched accessories that extend the good look of the clothes, carefully groomed hair, makeup enhancing the natural features and poised manners and comportment. Clothing attention is highly focused on creating a smooth line, including such details as fabric quality and texture, folds/draping and trimmings. The exception is women's *chitenge* (colorful printed cloth) dresses which are becoming more elaborate and increasingly constructed. The general concerns about clothing are with the length of the skirt, the exposure of the body, the pattern of the blouse/shirt, the cut of the jacket and the style of trousers. Women's clothing should not be tight and short and men's should be neither too loose nor scruffy. This clothing ideal produces elegance and dignity in a "look" that is neat and polished, not too casual, flamboyant or extravagant. And such ensembles can be readily assembled from *salaula*. In fact. a person in his or her *salaula* best is barely distinguishable from a person in store-bought clothing.

While *apamwamba* wardrobes are more expensive, containing clothing and apparel that has been obtained from a wider variety of sources then those of medium-income people, the norms of what constitutes a well-dressed person, depending on age, sex and the situation, are pretty much shared across the income/class spectrum. Designer labels are not household names save among the *apamwamba*. Among ordinary consumers I have found hardly any concern with brand-name clothing. Most stores and boutiques selling ready-made clothing obtained their garments from low-cost producers, largely non local, without brand names. Only in T-shirts, baseball caps and running shoes had faked brand-name products made their appearance.

This is to say that, by and large, income and class distinctions are not very marked in clothing consumption because of the ready availability of *salaula*. A few years ago, when he described how women "pounce on the latest import mania," a male news feature writer remarked on this. "When it comes to fashion," he noted, "the women in our cities are classless." As he explained, "the issue of class does not come in because women from both down-and-out and affluent families are in the race."[14] Indeed, clothing competence in putting oneself together with style, quality and fit is so keenly developed that it is mainly through shoes and accessories that the second-hand status of garments and apparel reveals itself to the discerning observer. This contrasts with rural people who have less exposure to *salaula* and often were identifiable by their ill-matched clothes. Their "lack of style" is a result of the limited rural availability of garments, combined with a tendency of urban traders to offload unpopular *salaula* designs, colors and fabrics on country people. This began to change in the late 1990s as the *salaula* circuit reached consumers throughout the country. Even rural dwellers have begun to complain about the poor quality and styles of clothes the *salaula* traders from town are selling to them.

Clothing Competence

The enormous crossover appeal of second-hand clothing can be explained not merely in terms of its affordability to poor people but above all by reference to the importance people in Zambia attribute to dressing and dressing well. Dressing and dressing up, is both an end and a means. This preoccupation with the dressed body involves an aesthetic sensibility that brings discerning skills from a variety of sources to bear on creating an overall look that mediates experiences of pride and well-being.

Clothing consumption is hard work. When shopping for *salaula*, consumers have a number of things in mind, depending on whether they are covering basic clothing needs or satisfying specific desires. The scrutiny of *salaula* takes time. Color coordination is keenly attended to and there are issues of size and fit to consider. Regardless of income group, most consumers considered "value for money" a major selection criterion, discerning "good value" in terms of quality and fashion/style. Low-income consumers in both Lusaka and the provinces paid careful attention to garment durability/strength, whereas young urban adults looked for "the latest." This is their own term and it comprises influences from South Africa, Europe and North America as well as from specific youth cultures. In effect, *salaula* fashions bring consumers into a bigger world: the world of awareness, of now. Consumers draw on these influences in ways that are informed by local norms about bodies and dress.

The attraction of *salaula* to clothing-conscious Zambian consumers goes far beyond the price factor. Consumers want clothing that is not common. "Clothes from *salaula* are not what other people wear," one woman said to me when explaining why clothes from *salaula* are viewed as "exclusive." The clothing sensibility such statements convey hinges on social constructions of gendered and sexed bodies, comportment, personal grooming and presentation. It manifests itself in a visual aesthetic that is created in context. In short, this meaning/value/sensibility does not inhere in the garments themselves but is attributed to them in social interaction.

Clothing competence includes knowledge not only of which garments to wear but also of how to wear them in specific contexts. Clothing practices and performance comprise one juncture where sociocultural norms take on authorship over the West's used clothing.[15] *Salaula* is pulled apart, resewn, altered and put on in ways that physically and culturally fit Zambian bodies. What is being transformed is not necessarily the garment but its meaning. This is to say that the body is the site on which cultural ideals are constructed through dress.[16] For example, many young adult men who were close to graduating from secondary school were reluctant to wear jeans for fear of being mistaken for street vendors. They have higher job aspirations for themselves. This contrasts with the search of young male barbers and vendors for oversize jeans from *salaula* to create the "big look" they associated with the opportunity and daring of a world away from home. And some young adult women, uneasy of approaching sexual maturity, told me how they "hated" wearing dresses because they make them look old and, worse still, dresses make them look like mothers.[17] In short, social and sexual identity is lodged in the way the body is worn through clothing.[18]

Conclusions

What begins as charity with donations of used clothing in the West becomes a whole industry that draws in countries like Zambia not as passive receivers of the West's surplus clothing but as actively involved in making it their own. The relationship revolves around a process of recommodification, in which the meaning of second-hand clothing is appropriated on local terms. My emphasis in this chapter has been on how the local value of imported second-hand clothes is created through a variety of processes that strip this imported commodity of its prior life and redefines it, readying it to enter new lives and relationships. This is the magic of clothing at work, dissolving prior distinctions in the reworking of the new lives of clothes.

Zambia's *salaula* markets meet the non local observer's eye as a chaotic mass of second-hand clothing. This deceptive view hides many layers of market segmentation, both in terms of where used clothes are available for sale and of how they are displayed and sold. A variety of informal rules organize vending space and structure sales practices. Because both vendors and customers know these practices, they are clothing-savvy.

The clothing competence consumers demonstrate when shopping "from *salaula*" brings discerning skills to bear on creating a total look with a pleasing visual aesthetic that is culturally acceptable. Shopping from second-hand clothing markets is not a process of random clothing selection but a strategic exercise that draws on specialist, practical and localized knowledge. Retailers and customers who create and share this knowledge operate within a frame of a culturally accepted dress profile. Against this backdrop, second-hand clothing markets make available an abundance and variety of clothes that allow consumers to add their individual mark on the culturally accepted clothing profile. Far from being a passive imitation in which consumers in Zambia dress more like the West, it is a form of cultural improvisation in which the meaning and value of second-hand clothing are constructed anew on local terms.

Notes

The research on which this chapter is based began in Zambia with preliminary work during the summers of 1992 and 1993, extensive field and archival research in Zambia during the calendar year 1995, research on and interviews with textile recyclers in Europe and the United States during the summer of 1996 and spring and summer 1997 and returns to Zambia during the summers of 1997 and 1999. The research was supported by faculty grants from Northwestern University and awards from the Social Science Research Council (USA) and the Wenner Gren Foundation for Anthropological Research. Most of this chapter's discussion is developed in more depth in my book (Karen Tranberg Hansen, *Salaula: The World of Second-hand Clothing and Zambia* (Chicago, 2000)). Later observations were made during the course of ongoing research on another topic in Zambia every summer since 2000.

1. Hansen, *Salaula*.
2. Beverly Lemire, *Dress, Culture and Commerce: The English Clothing Trade before the Factory, 1660–1800* (London, 1997).
3. Philippe Perrot, *Fashioning the Bourgeoisie: A History of Clothing in the Nineteenth Century*, trans. Richard Bienvenu (Princeton, 1994 [1981]), p71.
4. Ellen Leopold, "The Manufacture of the Fashion System," in Juliet Ash and Elizabeth Wilson (eds.), *Chick Thrills: A Fashion Reader* (Berkeley, 1993), pp. 100–17.
5. Madeleine Ginsburg, "Rags to Riches: the Second-hand Clothes Trade 1700–1978," *Costume*, 14 (1980), pp. 121–35, 128.
6. Edward H. McKinley, *Somebody's Brother: A History of the Salvation Army's Men's Social Service Department 1891–1985* (Lewiston, NY, 1986).
7. UN (United Nations), *1995 International Trade Statistics Yearbook*. Vol. II: *Trade by Commodity* (New York, 1996), p. 60 and *1999 International Trade Statistics Yearbook*. Vol. II: *Trade by Commodity* (New York, 2000), p. 117. These statistics must be interpreted with many qualifications. There is a widespread tendency to under-report both the value and the volume of shipments for export in order to reduce shipping costs and import tariffs. The main statistical source, the United Nations international trade statistics, are not complete. Not all countries report to the United Nations. Even if they do report, they might under-

value the extent of trade. And, when they exist, many import statistics are misleading because of extensive smuggling.

8. UN, *1995 International Trade Statistics Yearbook*, Vol. II, p. 60.

9. UN, *1999 International Trade Statistics Yearbook*, Vol. II, p. 117.

10. UN, *1995 International Trade Statistics Yearbook*, Vol. II, p. 60 and *1999 International Trade Statistics Yearbook*, Vol. II, p. 116.

11. Igor Kopytoff, "The Cultural Biography of Things: Commoditization as Process," in Arjun Appadurai (ed.), *The Social Life of Things: Commodities in Cultural Perspective* (Cambridge, 1986), pp. 64–91, 73.

12. Marcia Burdette, *Zambia: Between Two Worlds* (Boulder, CO, 1988).

13. The clothing consumption survey comprised a total of 107 interviews in private households in Lusaka, deliberately over-sampling high-income households (thirty-two in low-income households, twenty in medium-income households and fifty-five in high-income households). I also carried out nine interviews on clothing consumption in the Luapula Province.

14. *Times of Zambia*, "Fashions are Irresistible" (feature article by Michael Andindilile). September 6, 1990.

15. Marilyn Strathern, "Foreword: the Mirror of Technology, " in Roger Silverstone and Eric Hirsch (eds.), *Consuming Technologies: Media and Information in Domestic Spaces* (New York, 1992), pp. vii–xiii, xiii.

16. Terence S. Turner, "The Social Skin," in Catherine B. Burroughs and Jeffrey Ehrenreich, (eds.), *Reading the Social Body* (Iowa City, 1993), pp. 15–39 (reprint from Jeremy Cherfas and Roger Lewin (eds.), *Not Work Alone: A Cross-Cultural View of Activities Superfluous to Survival* (London, 1980).

17. Karen Tranberg Hansen, "Gender and Difference: Youth, Bodies and Clothing in Zambia," in Victoria Goddard (ed.), *Gender, Agency and Change: An Anthropological Perspective* (London, 2000), p. 200.

18. Jennifer Craik, *The Face of Fashion: Cultural Studies in Fashion* (London, 1994), p. 56.

CONCLUSION

Laurence Fontaine

Far from being supposedly marginal, these essays allow us to see the true economic, social and symbolic importance of the circulation of second-hand goods. This book has focused mainly on garments, which were the major goods of these circulations. Personal belongings, luxury objects, arms and lastly cars have also appeared in the chapters, but we lack analyses of other second-hand items that were in circulation. If the market for books has already been partly studied, we know very little of the market in art and of the re-use of materials in the building industries. In fact, categories of second-hand objects should be analyzed according to their relationship with the kind of market in which they were circulating, the actors who dealt with them, and their changing value as consumer goods.

We have seen that in early modern Europe, textiles were a highly valued commodity. They were used for making clothing as well as paper, used in the army and in hospitals. To fill these different needs and to supply these industries, from the time of the Renaissance on, these markets were operating at every level of trade: local, regional and international. Garments, for instance, were never discarded, but were always sold, rented, pawned or given as presents. They fueled an important trade that involved a number of middlemen: shop keepers, clothes-brokers, peddlers, auctioneers, pawn-brokers and women resellers. Each of these stood at the intersection of several markets and various clienteles. While some were members of recognized and regulated occupational groups, like corporations, or less regulated ones, like the networks of migrants, others were occasional but omnipresent agents of this trade, like women or servants, and still others exercised unlawful or criminal activities, all participating to a greater or lesser extent in both the official and the illicit economy. Therefore, these markets, animated by a wide variety of actors, also take a wide variety of forms. However, no single pattern emerges. Instead, there were different combinations at different times, both legal and illegal, depending on the location, the needs of the poor and the desires of the rich.

Women were central to these markets, as clothing is one of the basic components of the household economy, and the essays have given many examples of their involvement in the various facets of the trade. Women can be found in guilds, but their proportion varied greatly throughout Europe. In some regions, such as the northern European countries or Scotland, they held the monopoly on appraisal of deceased goods, and sometimes even of their sale at auction.[1] They were also everywhere at the heart of a small-scale credit system, as pawnbrokers or as go-betweens for others.

The involvement in the trade by diasporas is at the root of the links with the international markets, since their networks enabled them to bridge the gap between the different spaces and clienteles. They were in the best position to bring about commercial activity across local, regional and international networks, since they had merchants in all these spaces, and the spaces were interconnected. In early modern cities like Paris, Rome or Venice,[2] for example, people of Jewish origin supplied the shops with luxury garments, furnishings and jewelry to rent out to travelers, diplomats and courtesans, at the same time as they collected cast off clothes for re sale to the local populations, and gathered stock of worn-out clothing to supply the various rag industries. We have seen networks of migrants of diverse origin in every chapter dealing with the organization of the trade. But up to now, too little work has been done on these networks of merchants, though there is nowadays a growing interest in migrant business connections.

In addition to the lack of utilisable statistics before the contemporary period, there is still too little information about the way legal and informal economies intermeshed to be able calculate the volumes in circulation or to estimate the number of people who made their living from second-hand trades. As far as clothing is concerned, a number of market constants appear in the essays on Europe throughout the pre-industrial period. Local markets were primarily an urban phenomenon: the bulk of the second-hand clothes markets were concentrated in the towns and cities, and that is where the poor could afford to shop. Outside the large cities, while clothing always changed hands easily, the pathways followed are harder to detect. The street was long the major site for the reselling trade, occupied by peddlers, individuals in need of money and thieves seeking to get rid of their loot. In addition, there is every indication that specialization was not routine, and that all small shopkeepers, in particular tailors and innkeepers, but also bakers and ironmongers, served as middlemen.[3] With the eighteenth century, the second-hand clothing trade moved into shops and appeared in smaller and smaller towns. In the nineteenth century, the urban geography of the second-hand trade was profoundly redrawn by the creation of specialized markets relegated to the outskirts of towns. In the countryside, on the other hand, repairing, restyling and charitable circuits stemming from the legacies of the rich and from parish work continued to dominate.

The major break occurred in the twentieth century, when, following the Second World War, mass production of ready-to-wear garments put an end to the scarcity of clothes. The overall improvement in people's income added to the clothing boom, to reduce the numbers of needy and increase the numbers of those who could give in turn. The flow was suddenly reversed, and commercial routes gave way to charitable networks, which became the departure point for second-hand goods entering the different markets. The diasporas capable of linking local and international circuits still benefited from these changes. At the end of the nineteenth century, some charitable organizations whose nation wide operation was too vast for them to manage the flow of merchandise they received, turned to the professional second-hand clothes dealers. It was in this way that the diasporas dominating the second-hand market in pre-industrial Europe gained control of the new transoceanic routes, along which the bales of old clothes circulated.[4]

Throughout Europe, up to the dawn of the twentieth century, customary monetary practices, which led people to hoard their money rather than putting it into circulation, as much as the scarcity of currency, fostered the development of an economy based on the circulation of goods. This circulation was fueled, due to the general weakness of the industries, by every possession, including every kind of garment. Moreover, many examples attest to the practice of giving items of clothing as a token of appreciation to servants, children's nurses, women who cared for the sick, and those who kept vigil with the deceased; and court records show that, where such gifts were not given, they were readily replaced with money.[5] Furthermore, servants regularly resold the clothes given them by their masters. Thus many of the items that were not worn ended up with the second-hand clothes dealers, which goes to show that such items actually were regarded more as a part of the salary than as a gift, demonstrating clearly their role as an alternative currency. Another important function that comes out of the book lies in the role of these goods as a major tool of credit for the population. These practices, be they informal or institutionalized, are a very little explored area.[6]

Finally, the value of all objects and textiles made them the habitual target of thieves. A whole criminal economy grew up around textiles, for instance, with its "fences," its resellers and its tailors. This economy was just touched upon in the essays, and in the light of this economy of the second-hand, studies should be carried out to understand their social and economic role. Many indications show that it was a widespread practice, and point to the role played by women, partly because the punishment they received was less harsh, and partly because most of the objects stolen were items of clothing, and these goods fell into their sphere.[7] Little is yet known about the practice of receiving stolen goods. It seems that receiving or harboring stolen goods was widespread among the population, and it was a low-visibility crime. In every period, people readily acquired stolen goods, even if they disapproved of and feared burglary. Likewise, there was a discrepancy between the complaints lodged and the sentences meted out for theft, which were harsh, and the willingness of law makers and the police to fight the receiving of stolen goods, toward which they were much more lax. Furthermore, the principal receivers were usually legitimate merchants, who went unbothered by the law. Criminal records also show that the police tolerated and used the women resellers, thus sharing this acceptance of the receiving of stolen goods. Some worked in groups in conjunction with police informers, others managed to have it both ways, acting as informers and as resellers of stolen clothes.[8] Eighteenth-century Edinburgh already had its Dickensian world in which thieves, dealers in second-hand goods and pawnbrokers played hide-and-seek with the law. Analysis of police files shows that their network extended as far as London, where they knew shops that would buy stolen goods.[9]

In all these forms of the circulation of second-hand goods, the illegal economy was closely intertwined with the legitimate sector, and behind these unlawful circulations one could see the survival strategies of the poor, as well as the business strategies of the merchant. The fact that the circulation of objects was added to all the other kinds of exchange, from the most official to the highly forbidden, is a distinctive feature of the circulation of second-hand goods. The book has shown how city-dwellers put stolen objects back into circulation, as well as their use of the official pawnshop to store their valuables. This appropriation of the pawnshop, well documented for nineteenth-century England,[10] seems, with the examples given here of Renaissance Rome and of Enlightenment Paris, to go back to the very creation of the pawnshops. The appropriation of economic institutions by the working classes, alongside the interlocking of the informal economy with the regulated economy, should be pursued.

The importance of recycling and of re-use in the system of the *ancien régime*, as in certain sectors of the contemporary world, invites us to think that the major feature of this economy is in fact circulation, as opposed to the developed world of today, which is dominated by production. The inability of the car industry to integrate the issue of the buying and selling of second-hand vehicles allows us, moreover, to reflect upon what one could call the change from an "economy of circulation," to one of production. Up to the twentieth century in Western countries, circulation predominated over production and the old and the new worked well together. Since the end of the nineteenth century, and overall during the twentieth century, production has become a fundamental characteristic of western markets. One might wonder if this new role of production isn't responsible for this separation of the new and the used, and if this separation, which has profound repercussions, as we have seen, on the hierarchies of value that objects carry, isn't, in turn, at the root of the inability of the car industry, until very recently, to integrate the buying and selling of second-hand cars into their sales strategies.

A major result of the book is to have illuminated the blurred boundaries between money and merchandise, as well as between new and second-hand, and between gift, charity and commerce. This absence of clear-cut boundaries was for a long time unproblematic for society, and the history of their separation is an underlying narrative of the book.

The porous boundaries between money and merchandise illuminate the fluidity of the world of the merchant, showing how ill-defined the occupation of merchant was. Anyone could call himself a merchant, set up on a street corner, and sell his wares without arousing suspicion. What such economic practices tell us is that people were more accustomed then to bartering, to reselling, to handling objects with an eye to their potential resale value, than they are today: they possessed a culture that the salaried inhabitants of the twenty-first-century developed countries have lost.

Charity has proved to be another very good example to trace the merging of these categories. The reselling of charity goods by the poor began to pose a problem in the nineteenth century, and charitable organizations began marking the clothes they gave with indelible ink, so as to show their provenance and to curb their resale.[11] At the same time, there was a growing tendency to question whether charity was an effective response to poverty, and in England, for example, a tendency to ask for a payment for the clothes emerged. The theory of utilitarian philanthropy maintained that charity was degrading, and that gifts were never received in the spirit in which they were offered. This idea gave rise to the sponsored sales known as "jumble sales," which became familiar in England at the turn of the twentieth century.[12] These were followed by the charity shop, which changed the way the poor were perceived, as, instead of being on the receiving end, they were now customers. And so there came about the second-hand clothing shops open to allcomers, whose prices were set somewhere between jumble sale and trade, and whose profits went to fund charitable activities, in addition to providing very inexpensive clothing for the genuinely poor. In reality, market elements intervened even in the collection of clothing, and charity sales were usually held in the form of auctions. As charitable organizations have outgrown their capacity to cope with the influx of gifts and the demands of managing them with volunteers alone, they have been drawn to using market principles. Progressively, collecting, sorting and selling are handled by professionals, who return a proportion of their profit to the society. In 1976, the Great Charity Clothing Scandal showed that the professionals working for the Children's Research Fund, a Liverpool-based charity, earned £75,000 during 1974–5, with £15,000 going to the Society and £60,000 to the collectors. Karen Tranberg Hansen has shown how, treading the line between the fear of scandal and the need for the market, these charitable organizations have grown in the last few decades. While most of the clothing is given to the charities by individuals, 75 percent of what is received is sold to specialist professionals.[13]

Finally, the book has given us access to the ways in which populations have appropriated second-hand objects over the centuries, showing the roles played by second-hand and old goods in defining and reorganizing identities, and these transformations speak of the changing values of objects and of the importance of understanding their changing cultural meanings.

We have seen that in societies accustomed to the scarcity and antiquity of objects, second-hand was the norm for exchange; and re-use, a customary practice. The spread of Enlightenment ideas, with their emphasis on trade, currency and progress, as well as the birth of fashion, with its constant demand for the new, not to mention the Philosophes' urging to rehabilitate luxury living as a driving force of exchange and provider of work, gradually raised the status of the new and valorised the replacement of objects and wardrobes, to the detriment of their conservation and re-use. Later, progress in the field of medicine brought a new awareness of the dangers presented by previously worn clothes, the difficulty of cleaning them, the massive diffusion of clothing-borne vermin, and thus threw suspicion on cast-off clothes and, in particular, items of unknown origin. Even today, for health reasons, Spain and its former colonies have slapped prohibitive restrictions on the import of second-hand clothes, though importers and exporters regularly circumvent them.[14]

Parallel to the popularity of the new valorization of antiques has spread down through society from the aristocracy. This second appropriation led to the birth of the antique. Although from the eighteenth century possession of new objects gradually came to confer more status than ownership of old items,[15] eighteenth-century aristocratic gentlemen used an ideological antipathy to luxury as a means of expressing their political leadership, antipathy that was appropriated later by middle-class reformers to gain access to the formal institutions of power. At the same time, the European nobility took a number of institutional measures to protect its patrimony from creditors and maintain family continuity, even in the absence of direct heirs. A culture of the aristocratic house thus arose, and its material environment came to be regarded as sacred.[16] When, in the nineteenth century, political power became solidly installed in the middle class, souvenirs of aristocratic splendor became much sought-after items, the power of money being legitimized by the tradition evoked by this life style.

From this fascination with the old sprang a new interest in the specialized markets that preoccupation with modernity had relegated to city outskirts. These markets became new, vaguely disturbing hunting grounds for the new collectors – lone hunters who needed cunning to unearth the object and acquire it at the best price. The collector's aim was to know, even before the seller, that the coveted article had already changed categories: that it had moved from second-hand to antique; and the art of the deal lay in acquiring it at the second-hand rate. The nineteenth-century flea markets thus became a *rendezvous* for those out for a stroll, amateurs and tourists; newspapers and novels fondly described the Sunday-morning jaunts, evoked the accumulation of second-hand objects, each with its own biography, "a tale perhaps of sorrow and sadness and want." They imagined the life of the hundreds of trousers, jackets and other coats and mantles that had once been the property of dandies, criminals or sailors, where all levels of society – war, prison and hospital – intermingle.[17] But not all came to buy: they also came to enjoy the show, and the pleasures of the imagination it developed. Long an aristocratic pastime, collecting became a more democratic activity in the twentieth century, and the new collectors in turn invented new venues of exchange, and new relations with objects. But analyzing this "circulation economy" from the point of view of the objects has shown that their career doesn't stop with their exit from the market, and their entry into the world of collecting, of inheritance, or the domain of the sacred.

One last twist in the evolution of the second-hand brings castoff clothes full circle, to once again become a raw material, as in pre-industrial Europe, when women cut down old clothes for re-use. This transformation can be seen in the ways in which second-hand clothing is appropriated by the poor and the rich. We have seen how in African cities sellers and buyers have created an original style from *salaula*. Alternatively, the standardization of production in the industrialized world has enhanced the value of one-off items as well as second-hand ones. Young people in the 1960s were willing to pay more for faded jeans to show their rejection of the consumer society. Today, other young people want to feel unique, and strive for the most outlandish dress in order to stand out. In modern-day Japan, for example, these youngsters seek to satisfy their rejection of traditional conformity by appropriating second-hand clothes as a raw material; they then layer, assemble and restyle them to create a singular self. So great is the demand that one second-hand clothes supermarket, Hanjiri, has opened a store in the high-fashion quarter of Harajuku, offering the new raw material needed to make this experimental look. Perfumed candles and techno music envelop the clientele wandering among the racks of patched work clothes, tattered suede jackets or calico dresses.[18] The values with which second-hand objects are invested are at the heart of their acquisition by the populations of both yesterday and today. This story, drawn in the main from the essays and bibliography available in the book, is still far from being fully written.

Finally, the decision to build the project on comparison has proved to be a fruitful way of going about it. Indeed, working in the very long term – from the Middle Ages to the contemporary world – has two big advantages: it has enabled us to show changes in the categories of discourse and, by comparing highly contrasting realities, it has obliged us to constantly rethink the categories we use and the questions we need to ask, for the same realities mean different things in different contexts.

The problems posed by charity clothing in the development of poor countries, and those raised by the return to the barter system in Argentina in the last few decades, both of which are discussed in this volume, are good examples of how the same reality takes on different meanings when the context changes, and how comparison helps refine the analysis. For instance, some blame the export of used clothes to the Third World for destroying local garment industries and ultimately retarding development; others believe, on the contrary, that the economic effects induced – such as jobs in warehousing and sorting, in cleaning, repairing and restyling and distributing, ranging from the wholesalers to the small market vendors, not to mention the savings in household expenditure on clothing – help developing countries boost their productivity, in spite of the negative impact of this trade on the clothing industry. The problem posed by these contemporary forms of circulation could be included in a reflection on the history of industrialization in early modern Europe, where used-clothing markets largely dominated the clothing sector before the nineteenth century, implying at the same time a weakness in the textile industries. Comparison with pre-modern Europe ought to enable us to recast the question in a more complex manner.

The return of the barter system, in the form of the exchange of goods and services in contemporary Argentina, is another comparison that holds a rich lesson, in that it brings out the political dimension of economic choices. In Europe, the separation of economics from politics was one of the necessary conditions for establishing democracy, as it made it possible to sever the bonds of loyalty attaching to both gifts and debts. This separation relied in part on the market and on paper money to bring about the depersonalization of transactions and promote individual freedom. In the last decade, in a developed country like Argentina, opponents of the government have resorted to barter and other substitutes for official currency – economic forms regarded as archaic – in an attempt to put the country on a new political footing and to avoid the corruption that was currently driving it to ruin.[19] These two examples, the first of which poses a question that was unthinkable in the eighteenth century, and the second, which shows the complexity of the connections between politics and economics, raise a number of issues that go beyond the analysis of the circulation of second-hand objects alone, to show the role of this circulation in unexpected areas.

In showing the diversity and complexity of the second-hand markets: diversity of the actors, because everyone – men and women, aristocrats as well as poor people – used them; complexity of the circulations, since goods circulated between the towns and the countryside, between regions and countries, between the generations, and between the social classes; complexity of the markets and the non market circulation, because second-hand objects circulated within and outside traditional markets, this book has opened new fields of research. In this resale economy, all roles are fluid, and such categories as official, informal and illegal blend readily into each other. This topic helps us to think in terms of fluidity and exchanges between diverse economies, and to grasp the role of changing values in their evolution.

Translated by Nora Scott and Jackie Goode

Notes

1. Elizabeth Sanderson, , "Nearly New: the Second-hand Clothing Trade in Eighteenth-Century Edinburgh," *Costume*, 31 (1997), p. 40. Wood Merry Wiesner, "Paltry Peddlers or Essential Merchants? Women in the Distributive Trades in Early Modern Nuremberg," *The Sixteenth Century Journal*, XII: 2 (1981), pp. 3–13.
2. Patricia Allerston, "The Market in Second-hand Clothes and Furnishings in Venice, c. 1500–1650," PhD thesis, European University Institute, Florence, 1996.
3. Sanderson, "Nearly New," p. 47; John Style, "Clothing the North: the Supply of Non-elite Clothing in the Eighteenth Century North of England," *Textile History*, (1994).
4. Madeleine Ginsburg, "Rags to Riches: the Second-hand Clothes Trade 1700–1978," *Costume*, 14 (1980), pp. 121–35, p. 125.
5. Sanderson, "Nearly New," p. 39.
6. For England, see the works of Beverly Lemire and in particular "Petty Pawns and Informal Lending: Gender and the Transformation of Small-scale Credit in England, circa 1600–1800," in Kristine Bruland and Patick O'Brien (eds.), *From Family Firms to Corporate Capitalism: Essay in Business and Industrial History in Honour of Peter Mathias* (Oxford, 1998), pp. 112–38.

7. Olwen Hufton, *The Poor of Eighteenth-century France 1750–1789* (Oxford, 1974). Garthine Walker, "Women, Theft and the World of Stolen Goods," in Jennifer Kermode and Garthine Walker, *Women, Crime and the Courts in Early Modern England* (London, 1995), pp. 81–106 and Patrice Peveri, "Techniques et pratiques du vol dans la pègre du Paris de la Régence d'après les archives du procès de Louis-Dominique Cartouche et de ses complices," Thesis for the École des Hautes Études en Sciences Sociales, 1994.

8. Daniel Roche, *La Culture des apparences. Une histoire du vêtement XVIIe–XVIIIe siècle* (Paris, 1989), pp. 318–19.

9. Sanderson, "Nearly New," pp. 42–3.

10. Melanie Tebutt, *Making Ends Meet. Pawnbroking and Working-class Credit* (London, 1984).

11. Ginsburg, "Rags to Riches," p. 126.

12. Ibid., p. 130.

13. Steven Haggblade, "The Flip Side of Fashion: Used Clothing Exports to the Third World," *Journal of Development Studies*, 26:3 (1990), pp. 505–21, p. 510.

14. Ibid., p. 24 and appendix 6 on restrictions and taxes imposed on used-clothes imports according to countries, pp. A53–A59.

15. Grant McCracken, *Culture and Consumption* (Bloomington, IN, 1988), p. IX: "suddenly, high-standing individuals could find more status in things that were new than in things that were old; with novelty in the ascendant, patina fell into eclipse."

16. Christophe Duhamelle analyzed this phenomenon for Germany in *La Noblesse d'Église: famille et pouvoir la chevalerie immédiate rhénane, XVIIe–XVIIIe siècles* (Paris, 1994).

17. Daniel Kirwan, an American journalist describing Petticoat Lane, after giving a vivid description, concludes: "take two hundred men, women and children, mostly of the Jewish race, and here and there a burly Irishman sitting placidly smoking a pipe amid the infernal din; and shake all these ingredients up well, and you have a faint idea of what I saw in Rag Fair," quoted by Christopher Breward, *The Hidden Consumer. Masculinities, Fashion and City Life, 1986–1914* (Manchester, 1999), p. 123. Twenty years later, in 1890, James Greenwood, describing the same scene, switched his emphasis to the market as show, as a space given over to leisure and social interaction. Ibid., p. 124.

18. Philippe Pons and Brice Pedroletti, "La Génération Shibuya," *Le Monde*, April 10, 2001, p. 14.

19. Several articles in the *International Journal of Community Currency Research*, vol. 4 (http//www.geog.le.ac.uk/ijccr/).

BIBLIOGRAPHY

Adams, David. "No Pesos? No Problem," *St. Petersburg Times*, March 18 2002; available from "No Pesos? No Problem," *St. Petersburg Times*, March 18, 2002; available from www.sptimes.com

Adler, Ken. "Making Things the Same: Representation, Tolerance and the End of the Ancien Regime in France," *Social Studies of Science,* 28 (August 1998), pp. 499–545.

Ago, Renata. "Di cosa di può fare commercio: Mercato e norme sociali nella Roma Barocca," *Quaderni Storici*, 91:1 (1996), pp. 113–33.

_____. *Economia barocca: Mercato e istituzioni nella Roma del Seicento* (Rome, 1998).

_____. "Il linguaggio del corpo," in Carlo Marco Belfanti and Fabio Giusberti (eds.), *La Moda* (Turin, 2003), pp. 117–48.

_____. *Il gusto delle cose. Una storia degli oggetti nella Roma del Seicento*, (Rome, 2006).

Aigrefeuille, Charles. *Histoire de la ville de Montpellier depuis son origine jusqu'à notre temps*, 4 vols. (1882; reprint, Marseille, 1976).

Allen, Ruth Alice and, Sam B. Barton. *Wage Earners Meet the Depression* (Austin, TX, 1935).

Allerston, Patricia. "The Market in Second-hand Clothes and Furnishings in Venice, c. 1500–1650," PhD thesis European University Institute, Florence, 1996.

_____. "Reconstructing the Second-hand Clothes Trade in Sixteenth- and Seventeenth-Century Venice," *Costume* 33 (1999), pp. 46–56.

_____. "Clothing and Early Modern Venetian Society," *Continuity and Change,* 15:3 (2000), pp. 367–90.

Aretino, Pietro. *Ragionamento*, (first edition 1534) (Milan, 1984).

Aristides, Nicholas. "Calm and Uncollected," *American Scholar*, 57 (1998), pp. 327–36.

Arnold, Thomas F. *Renaissance at War* (London, 2001).

Aron, Jean-Paul. "Débris," in *Le Mangeur du XIXᵉ Siècle* (Paris, 1973).

Arrowsmith, William. *Antiques Fairs in England* (Bromsgrove, 1999).

Auge, Clara. "Argentina: Life after Bankruptcy: Barter, Demos, Theatre and a Dictionary of Crisis," *Le Monde diplomatique*, September 2002; available from http://mondediplo.com/2002/09/13.

Bachirat, Brahim, et al. "L'industrie automobile au Maroc: potentiels et dynamiques des relations clients/fournisseurs," Twelfth GERPISA International Colloquium, Paris 9–11 Juin (2004).

Bagnall, Gaynor. "Consuming the Past," in Stephen Edgell, Kevin Hetherington and Alan Warde (eds.), *Consumption Matters* (Oxford, 1996).

Bailey, Sarah Barter. "The Royal Armouries 'Firework Book'," chapter 5 in Brenda Buchanan (ed.), *Gunpowder: The History of an International Technology* (Bath, 1996), pp. 57–86.

Baillien, Henry. *Inventaris van de Fondsen van de stad Tongeren, de ambachten en genootschappen en weldadige instellingen* (Brussels, 1964).

Bakke, E. Wight. *The Unemployed Worker: A Study of the Task of Making a Living without a Job* (New Haven, CT, 1940).

Barbier, Frederic. , "Bouquinistes, Libraires Spécialisés," Roger Chartier and Henri-Jean Martin (eds.), *Histoire de l'édition française*, vol. 3, *Le Temps des éditeurs, du romantisme à la belle époque* (Paris, 1990).

Bardou, Jean-Pierre et al. *The Automobile Revolution: The Impact of an Industry*, (Chapel Hill, 1982). First edition: *La Révolution automobile* (Paris, 1977).

Bassompierre, François de. *Journal de ma vie: Mémoires du maréchal de Bassompierre*, 4 vols. (Paris, 1870–7).

Baumel, Jean. *Montpellier au cours des XVIe et XVIIe siècles. Les guerres de religion (1510–1685)* (Montpellier, 1976).

BBC Business: Q & A Argentina's Economic Crisis April 2, 2002; downloaded on July 16, 2002 from http://news.bbc.co.uk/hi/english/business/newsid.

Beardsworth, Alan and Teresa Keil. *Sociology on the Menu* (London, 1997).

Béaur, Gérard. *Histoire agraire de la France au XVIIIe siècle* (Paris, 2000).

Becq, Annie. "Artistes et marché," in Jean-Claude Bonnet (ed.), *La Carmagnole des Muses. L'homme de lettres et l'artiste dans la Révolution* (Paris, 1988), pp. 81–95.

Beer, Carel de (ed.). *The Art of Gunfounding: The Casting of Bronze Cannon in the Eighteenth Century* (Rotherford, 1991).

Beks, G. "Dutch Arms for France 1635–1640," in Jan Piet Puype and Marco van der Hoeven (eds.), *The Arsenal of the World: The Dutch Arms Trade in the Seventeenth Century* (Amsterdam, 1996), pp. 36–41.

Belk, Russell. *Collecting in a Consumer Society* (London, 1995).

Belk, Russell, M. Wallendorf, J. Sheery and M. Holbrook. *Collecting in a Consumer Culture, Highways and Buyways*, (Provo, 1990).

Benedict, Philip. "The Huguenot Population of France, 1600–85," in *The Faith and Fortunes of France's Huguenots, 1600–85* (Aldershot, 2001), pp. 34–120.

Bennett, Judith M. *Ale, Beer, and Brewsters in England: Women's Work in a Changing World, 1300–1600* (New York, 1996).

Benson, Susan Porter. "Living on the Margin: Working-class Marriages and Family Survival Strategies in the United States, 1919–1941," in Victoria de Grazia (ed.) with Ellen Furlough, *The Sex of Things: Gender and Consumption in Historical Perspective* (Berkeley, CA, 1996), pp. 212–43.

_____. "Gender, Generation, and Consumption in the United States: Working-class Families in the Interwar Period," in Susan Strasser, Charles McGovern and Matthias Judt (eds.), *Getting and Spending: European and American Consumer Societies in the Twentieth Century* (Cambridge, UK, 1998), pp. 223–40.

_____. *Household Accounts: Working-class Family Economies in the Interwar USA* (Ithaca, NY, 2007).

Béranger, P.-J., *Chansons de P.-J. Béranger*, 1814–1835 (Paris, 1861).

Berg, Maxine. "New Commodities, Luxuries and their Consumers in Eighteenth-Century England" in Maxine Berg and Hellen Clifford (eds.), *Consumers and Luxury. Consumer Culture in Europe, 1650–1850* (Manchester and New York, 1999), pp. 63–85.

_____. "From Imitation to Invention: Creating Commodities in Eighteenth-Century Britain," *Economic History Review*, LV (2002), pp. 1–30.

Bernardi, Philippe. "Récupération et transformations: les produits dérivés de la brique et de la tuile dans le bâtiment au Moyen Age," in *La brique antique et médiévale. Production et commercialisation d'un matériau* (Rome, 2000).

Bernier, Theodore. *Histoire de la ville de Beaumont* (Mons, 1880).

Berra, L. "Cinque letter inedite," *Archivio Storico Lombardo*, 20 (1890), pp. 366–8.

Bigo, Raymond. "Aux origines du Mont de Piété parisien," *Annales d'histoire économique et sociale* (1932), pp. 113–26.

Black, Jeremy. *A Military Revolution? Military Change and European Society, 1550–1800* (Atlantic Highlands, 1991).

Bloch, Marc. "Pour une histoire comparée des sociétés européennes," *Revue de synthèse historique*, Dec. 1928; reprinted in *Mélanges historiques* (Paris, 1963), vol. 1, pp. 16–40.

Blom, Philip. *To Have and To Hold* (London, 2002).

Blondé, Bruno. "Domestic Demand and Urbanisation in Brabant: Demographic and Functional Evidence for Small Towns of Brabant," in Peter Clark (ed.), *Small Towns in Early Modern Europe* (Cambridge, 1995), pp. 229–49.

Blondé, Bruno, Hilde Greefs and Ilja Van Damme. "Consumers and Commercial Circuits: Mapping the Retail Sector in Early Modern Antwerp," unpublished paper for the Fourth European Social Science History Conference, Session: Material Culture and Commercialsation: Shopping, Second-hand Market, Theft, February 28, 2002.

Boden, Sharon and Simon J. Williams, "Consumption and Emotion: the Romantic Ethic Revisited," *Sociology*, 36, (2002), pp. 493–512.

Boulton, Jeremy. *Neighbourhood and Society: A London Suburb in the Seventeenth Century* (Cambridge, 1987).

Bourdieu, Pierre. *La Distinction* (Paris, 1979).

Boyle, David. *Funny Money: In Search of Alternative Cash* (London, 1999).

Branford, Sue. "The Land of Plenty Runs Dry," *New Statesman*, October 1, 2002, pp. 32–3.

Braudel, Fernand. *Civilisation matérielle, économie et capitalisme, XVᵉ–XVIIIᵉ siècle*, 3 vols. (Paris, 1979).

Brennan, Thomas. "Town and Country in France, 1550–1750," in S.R. Epstein (ed.), *Town and Country in Europe* (Cambridge, 2001), pp. 250–71.

Breward, Christopher. *The Hidden Consumer. Masculinities, Fashion and City Life, 1986–1914* (Manchester, 1999).

Brewer, John. *The Sinews of Power: War, Money and the English State, 1688–1783* (Cambridge, 1988).

_____. *The Pleasures of the Imagination: English Culture in the Eighteenth Century* (London, 1997).

Brewer, John and Roy Porter. *Consumption and the World of Goods* (London, 1993).

Bruneel, Claude, Luc Delporte, and Bernadette Petitjean (ed.), *Le dénombrement général de la population des Pays-Bas Autrichiens en 1784* (Brussels, 1996).

Burdette, Marcia. *Zambia: Between Two Worlds* (Boulder, CO, 1988).

Burt, Roger. "The Transformation of the Non-Ferrous Metals Industries in the Seventeenth and Eighteenth Centuries," *Economic History Review*, New Series, 48 (February 1995), pp. 32–3.

Callot, Jacques. "Destruction of a Convent." No. 6 of *The Large Miseries of War*, 1633.

Calvi Giulia and Isabelle Chabot (eds.), *Le ricchezze delle donne: diritti patrimoniali e poteri familiari in Italia: 13.–19. secc.* (Turin 1998).

Camerano, Alessandra. "Donne oneste o meretrici?" *Quaderni Storici*, 99:3 (1998), pp. 637–75.

Campbell, Colin. *The Romantic Ethic and the Spirit of Modern Consumerism* (Oxford, 1989).

Caron, Jean-Claude. *Générations romantiques. Les étudiants de Paris et le Quartier Latin (1814–1851)* (Paris, 1991).

Carroll, Stuart. *Noble Power during the French Wars of Religion: The Guise Affinity and the Catholic Cause in Normandy* (Cambridge, 1998).

Cavan, Ruth Shonle and Katherine Howland Ranck. *The Family and the Depression: A Study of One Hundred Chicago Families* (Chicago, 1938).

Certeau, Michel de. *L'Invention du quotidien* (Paris, 1980).

Chabod, Federico, "Stipendi nominali e busta paga effettiva dei funzionari dell'amministrazione milanese alla fine del Cinquecento," in *Miscellanea in onore di Roberto Cessi* (Rome, 1958), vol. 2, pp. 188–363.

Chagniot, Jean. *Guerre et société à l'époque moderne* (Paris, 2001).

Chambre de commerce de Paris, *Statistique de l'Industrie à Paris résultant de l'enquête faite par la chambre de commerce pour les années 1847–48* (Paris, 1851).

Chendjou, Léopold. "Le Cameroun roule en occasion," *Le Messager*, n°. 1404, august 23, 2002.

Choné, Paulette. "Les Misères de la guerre ou 'la vie du soldat': la force et le droit," in Paulette Choné, Daniel Ternois, Jean-Marc Depluvrez, and Brigitte Heckel (eds.), *Jacques Callot, 1592–1635* (Paris, 1992), pp. 396–410.

Cibin, Patricia. "Meretrici e Cortegiane a Venezia nel '500," *Donnawomanfemme: Quaderni Internazionale di Studi sulla Donna*, 25–26 (1985), pp. 79–102.

Clark, Gracia. *Onions Are My Husband: Survival and Accumulation by West African Market Women* (Chicago, 1994).

Clarke, Sally. "Closing the deal: GM's marketing dilemma and its franchised dealers, 1921–1941," *Business History*, special issue *The emergence of modern marketing*, volume 45, I (2003), pp. 60–79.

Clark-Lewis, Elizabeth. *Living In, Living Out: African American Domestics and the Great Migration* (Washington, DC, 1994).

Cobb, Richard. *La Mort est dans Paris* (Paris, 1985), pp. 170–1.

Code de la toilette, Manuel complet d'élégance et d'hygiène, contenant les lois, règles, applications et exemples, de l'art de soigner sa personne, et de s'habiller avec goût et méthode (Paris, 1828).

Cohen, Lizabeth. *Making a New Deal: Industrial Workers in Chicago, 1919–1939* (Cambridge, 1990).

Conner, Philip. *Huguenot Heartland: Montauban and Southern French Calvinism during the Wars of Religion* (Aldershot, 2002).

Cooley Angell, Robert. *The Family Encounters the Depression* (New York, 1936).

Coquery, Natacha. *L'Hôtel aristocratique: le marché du luxe à Paris au XVIIIᵉ siècle* (Paris, 1998).

———. "The Language of Success: Marketing and Distributing Semi-luxury Goods in Eighteenth-century Paris," *Journal of Design History*, 17:1 (2004), pp. 71–89, Special Issue: *Disseminating Design: The French Connection*.

Corvisier, André and Jean Jacquart, (eds.). *Les Malheurs de la guerre. I: De la guerre à l'ancienne à la guerre réglée* (Paris, 1996).

Coryat, Thomas. *Crudities* (orig. 1611), Reprint (Glasgow, 1905).

Craik, Jennifer. *The Face of Fashion: Cultural Studies in Fashion* (London, 1994).

Crispell, Diane, "Collecting Memories," *American Demographic*, 60 (November 1988), pp. 38–41.

Croft, Pauline. "Trading with the Enemy, 1585–1604," *Historical Journal,* 32 (June 1989), pp. 281–302.

Crouzet, Denis. *Les guerriers de Dieu. La violence au temps des troubles de religion, vers 1525 – vers 1610 (*Paris, 1990).

Cunningham, Andrew and Ole Peter Grell, *The Four Horsemen of the Apocalypse: Religion, War, Famine and Death in Reformation Europe* (Cambridge, 2000).

Dambruyne, Johan. "Stedelijke identiteit en politieke cultuur te Gent," in Hugo Soly and Johan Van de Wiele (eds.), *Carolus. Keizer Karel V 1500–1558* (Ghent, 1999), pp. 110–21.

_____. *Mensen en centen. Het 16de-eeuwse Gent in demografisch en economisch perspectief* (Ghent, 2001).

Danneel, Marianne. "Handelaarsters in oude kleren in de 16de eeuw te Brugge," *Brugs Ommeland,* 25 (1985), pp. 203–18.

Dant, Tim. *Material Culture in the Social World* (Buckingham and Philadelphia, 1999).

_____. "Consumption Caught in the Cash Nexus." *Sociology,* 34, (2000), pp. 655–70.

Davis, Robert C. *Shipbuilders of the Venetian Arsenal: Workers and Workplace in the Preindustrial City* (Baltimore, 1991).

De Brouwer, J. *Geschiedenis van Lede. Het dorpsleven, het parochieleven, het volksleven* (Lede, 1963).

de Kezel, Luc. "Grondbezit in Vlaanderen 1750–1850. Bijdrage tot de discussie over de sociaal-economische ontwikkeling op het Vlaamse platteland," *Tijdschrift voor Sociale Geschiedenis,* 14 (1998), pp. 61–102.

De Peuter, Roger. *Brussel in de 18de eeuw. Sociaal-economische structuren en ontwikkelingen in een regionale hoofdstad* (Brussels, 1999).

De Potter, F. *Gent van de oudsten tijden tot heden, geschiedkundige beschrijving der stad,* VI (Roeselare, 1969) (Ghent, 1882).

De Saegher, E. *Notice sur les archives communales d''Ypres et documents pour servir à l''histoire de Flandre du XIIIe au XVIe siècle* (Ypres, 1898).

De Sanza, Carlos, Horacio Covas and Heloisa Primavera. *La experiencia de la Red Global de Trueque en Argentina* (Buenos Aires, 1998).

de Schaepdrijver, Sophie. "Some Remarks on the Urban History in Belgium," *Journal of Urban History,* 23 (1997), pp. 647–57.

Deceulaer, Harald. "Guildsmen, Entrepreneurs and Market-segments. The Case of the Garment Trades in Antwerp and Ghent (Sixteenth to Eighteenth Centuries)," *International Review of Social History,* 43 (1998), pp. 1–29.

_____. "Entrepreneurs in the Guilds: Ready-to-wear Clothing and Subcontracting in late Sixteenth- and early Seventeenth-century Antwerp," *Textile History,* 31:2 (2000), pp. 133–49.

_____. "Urban artisans and their countryside customers: different interactions between town and hinterland in Antwerp, Brussels and Ghent (18th century)," in Bruno Blondé, Michèle Galand and Eric Vanhaute (eds.), *Labour and Labour Markets between Town and Countryside (Middle-ages–Nineteenth Century)* (Turnhout, 2001), pp. 218–35.

_____. *Pluriforme patronen en een verschillende snit. Sociaal-economische, institutionele en culturele transformaties in de kledingsector in Antwerpen, Brussel en Gent, ca 1585–ca 1800* (Amsterdam, 2001).

_____. "Consumptie en distributie van kleding tussen stad en platteland. Drie regionale patronen in de Zuidelijke Nederlanden (zestiende-achtiende eeuw)," *Tijdschrift voor Sociale Geschiedenis,* 28 (2002), pp. 439–68.

Deceulaer, Harald and Marc Jacobs. "Qualities and Conventions. Guilds in Eighteenth-century Brabant and Flanders: an Extended Economic Perspective," in C.E. Nunez (ed.), *Guilds, Economy and Society* (Sevilla, 1998), pp. 91–107.

Deceulaer, Harald and Bibi Panhuysen. "Schneider oder Näherinnen? Ein geschlechtbezogener Vergleich der Bekleidungshandwerke in den Nördlichen und Südlichen Niederlanden während der Frühen Neuzeit," in Wilfried Reininghaus (ed.), *Zunftlandschaften in Deutschland und den Niederlanden im Vergleich* (Münster, 2000), pp. 85–106.

Déguignet, Jean-Marie. *Mémoires d'un Paysan Bas-Breton* (Le Relecq-Kerhuon, 2000).

Dejongh, Guy and and Erik Thoen, "Arable Productivity in Flanders and the Former Territory of Belgium in a Long-term Perspective (from the Middle Ages to the end of the Ancien Régime)," in: Bas van Bavel and Erik Thoen (eds.), *Land Productivity and Agro-systems, Middle Ages–20thCentury. Elements for Comparison* (Turnhout, 1999), pp. 30–64.

Delort, André. *Mémoires inédits d'André Delort sur la ville de Montpellier au XVIIe siècle (1621–1693)* (Marseille, 1980).

De Nolf, J. "Socio-professionele structuren binnen de Brugse samenleving rond het midden van de achttiende eeuw," in Jos de Belder, Walter Prevenier and Chris Vandenbroeke (eds.), *Sociale mobiliteit en sociale structuren in Vlaanderen en Brabant* (Ghent, 1983), pp. 79–102.

Dermigny, L. "De la Révocation à la Révolution," in Philippe Wolff (ed.), *Histoire du Languedoc*, 2nd ed. (Toulouse, 2000).

Detio detto Colloredo, Valentino. *Caso Lacrimoso e Lamentevole. Di Cecilia Bruni Muranese Cortegiana in Venetia à San Paterniano* (Macerata, Ronciglione, 1621) (BAV Capponi Stampati, v 683, int. 32).

DeVault, Marjorie. *Feeding the Family: The Social Organisation of Caring as Gendered Work* (Chicago, 1991).

DeVries, Kelley. "Gunpowder and Early Gunpowder Weapons." In Brenda Buchanan (ed.), *Gunpowder: The History of an International Technology* (Bath, 1996), pp. 121–35.

Dhondt, Luc. "Plattelandslijnwaad en stadskatoen tegen en even na 1800. De organisatie van een oude en van een nieuwe industrie. Een memorie uit 1808 en haar relevantie," *Handelingen van de Geschied-en Oudheidkundige Kring van Oudenaarde*, XXXII (1995), pp. 89–149.

Diefendorf, Barbara B. *Beneath the Cross: Catholics and Huguenots in Sixteenth-century Paris* (Oxford, 1991).

Discry, F. *Notice historique et nouvel inventaire des archives de la ville de Huy* (Huy, s.d.).

Douglas, Mary. *Thought Styles – Critical Essays on Good Taste* (London, 1996).

Douglas, Mary and Isherwood, Baron. *The World of Goods: Towards an Anthropology of Consumption* (London, 1979).

Douthwaite, Richard, *Short Circuit: Strengthening Local Economies for Security in an Unstable World* (Dublin, 1996).

Dubois, R. *La Ville de Huy au XVIIIe siècle* (Huy, 1895).

Du Cros, Simon. *Histoire de la vie de Henry dernier duc de Montmorency. Contenant tout ce qu'il a fait de plus remarquable depuis sa naissance jusques à sa mort* (Paris, 1643).

Duhamelle, Christophe. *La Noblesse d'Église: famille et pouvoirdans la chevalerie immédiate rhénane, XVIIe–XVIIIe siècles* (Paris, 1994).

Durost, Walter. *Children's Collecting Activity Related to Social Factors* (New York, 1932).

Earle, Peter. *The Making of the English Middle Class: Business, Society and Family Life in London, 1660–1730* (London, 1989).

Ebeling, Dietrich and Wolfgang Mager (eds.). *Proto-Industrie in der Region. Europäische Gewerbelandschaften vom 16. bis zum 19. Jahrhundert* (Bielefeld, 1997).

Edwards, Peter. *Dealing in Death: The Arms Trade and the British Civil Wars, 1638–52* (Stroud, 2000).

Edwards, Tim. *Contradictions of Consumption: Concepts, Practices and Politics in Consumer Society* (Buckingham, 2002).

Elderton, Marion (ed.). *Case Studies of Unemployment Compiled by the Unemployment Committee of the National Federation of Settlements* (Philadelphia, 1931).

Elias, Norbert. *La Société de cour* (Paris, 1985).

Elsner, John, and Roger Cardinal. *The Cultures of Collecting* (Cambridge, 1994).

Eltis, David. *The Military Revolution in Sixteenth-Century Europe* (New York, 1995).

Epstein, S.R. "Introduction," in idem, *Town and Country in Europe, 1300–1800* (Cambridge, 2001), pp. 1–29.

Fabre, Ghilsaine and Thierry Lochard. "L'impact urbain de la contre-réforme à Montpellier (1600–1706)," in Anne Blanchard, Henri Michel, and Elie Pélaquier (eds.), *La Vie religieuse dans la France méridionale à l'époque moderne* (Montpellier, 1992), pp. 55–78.

Fairchild, Cissy. "The Production and Marketing of Populuxe Goods in Eighteenth-century Paris," in John Brewer and Roy Porter (eds.), *Consumption and the World of Goods* (London, 1993), pp. 228–48.

Farr, James R. *Artisans in Europe, 1300–1914* (Cambridge, 2000).

Feigenbaum, Gail. "Gamblers, Cheats, and Fortune-Tellers," in Philip Conisbee (ed.), *Georges de La Tour and His World* (New Haven, 1996), pp. 149–81.

Ferguson, R.B. and N.L. Whitehead (eds.), *War in the Tribal Zone: Expanding States and Indigenous Warfare.* (Santa Fe, 1992).

Ferrante, Lucia. "Il valore del corpo: ovvero la gestione economica della sessualità femminile," in Angela Groppi (ed.), *Il Lavoro delle Donne*, (Rome and Bari, 1996), pp. 206–28.

Finch, Janet. and Lynn Hayes. "Gender, Inheritance and Women as Testators," in Lydia Morris and E. Stina Lyon (eds.), *Gender Relation in Public and Private: New Research Perspectives* (Basingstoke, Hampshire, 1996), pp. 1138–40.

Findlen, Paula, *Possessing Nature. Museums, Collecting, and Scientific Culture in Early Modern Italy* (Berkeley, 1994).

Fine, Ben and Ellen, Leopold. *The World of Consumption* (London, 1993).

Fontaine, Laurence. "Pierre Rullier colporteur horloger-bijoutier savoyard au XVIIIe siècle," in Martin Körner and François Walter (eds.), *Quand la montagne aussi a une histoire. Mélanges offerts à Jean-François Bergier*, (Berne, 1996), pp. 167–75.

_____. *History of Pedlars in Europe*, trans. Vicki Whittaker, (Cambridge and Durham, 1996).

Fontaine, Laurence and Jürgen Schlumbohm (eds.). *Household Strategies for Survival, 1600–2000 : Fission, Faction and Cooperation* (Cambridge, 2000).

Fontaine, Laurence and Jürgen, Schlumbohm. "Introduction," in idem (eds.), *Household Strategies for Survival 1600–2000: Fission, Faction and Cooperation* (Amsterdam: IISG, 2000), pp. 1–18.

Forty, George. *They Also Served: A Pictorial Anthology of Camp Followers through the Ages* (London, 1979).

Franchini Veronese, Francesco. *La Veronese. Caso compassionevole* (Macerata, 1619). Biblioteca Apostolica Vaticana. Capponi, Stampati v 683, int. 85.

Froud, Julie, Colin Haslam, Sukdhev Johal, Bernard Jullien, Karel Williams. "Les dépenses de motorisation comme facteur d'accentuation des inégalités et comme frein au développement des entreprises automobiles: une comparaison franco-anglaise," in Gabriel Dupuy et François Bost (eds.), *L'Automobile et son monde* (Paris, 2000), pp. 75–96.

Gaier, Claude. *L'Industrie et le commerce des armes dans les anciennes principautés belges du XIIIme à la fin du XVme siècle* (Paris, 1973).

Garrison, Janine and Paul Duchein, *Louis XIII et les 400 coups* (Toulouse, 2002).

Gaudin, A. "Argentina – Bursting the Barter Bubble," February 17, 2003. Available from www.lapress.org.

Ginsburg, Madeleine. "Rags to Riches: The Second-Hand Clothes Trade 1700–1978," *Costume*, 14 (1980), pp. 121–35.

Girard, Guillaume. *Histoire de la vie du duc d'Espernon* (Paris, 1730).

Goetstouwers, J.B. *Les métiers de Namur sous l'Ancien Régime. Contribution à l'histoire sociale* (Leuven-Paris, 1908).

Goode, Jackie. "Collecting Time: the Social Organisation of Collecting" in Graham Crow and Sue Heath (eds.) *Social Conceptions of Time: Structure and Process in Work and Everyday Life* (Basingstoke, 2002), pp. 230–45.

Greco, Thomas H. *Money: Understanding and Creating Alternatives to Legal Tender* (White River Junction, VT, 2001).

Green, Duncan. "Report of Visit to Argentina," Policy Unit, CAFOD; 2003; available from www.cafod.org.uk/archive/policy/argentina.

Gregson, Nicky and Louise Crewe. "The Bargain, the Knowledge and the Spectacle: Making Sense of Consumption in the Space of the Car-boot Sale," *Environment and Planning D: Society and Space*, 15, (1997), pp. 87–112

Grown, Caren and Jennifer Sebstad. "Towards a Wider Perspective on Women's Employment," *World Development*, 17 (1989), pp. 937–53.

Guicharnaud, Hélène. *Montauban au XVIIe 1560/1685. Urbanisme et architecture* (Toulouse, 1991).

Guillaumin, Gilbert-Urbain. *Dictionnaire universel théorique et pratique du commerce et de la navigation* (Paris, 1859–61), "Vêtements confectionnés," pp. 1759 ff.

Guilmartin, John Francis Jr. *Gunpowder and Galleys: Changing Technology and Mediterranean Warfare at Sea in the Sixteenth Century* (Cambridge, 1974).

Gutman, Myron P. *War and Rural Life in the Early Modern Low Countries* (Princeton, 1980).

Gutton, Jean-Pierre. *La Société et les pauvres. L'exemple de la généralité de Lyon (1534–1789)* (Paris, 1971).

Hacker, Barton C. "Women and Military Institutions in Early Modern Europe: a Reconnaissance," *Signs: Journal of Women in Culture and Society*, 6 (1981), pp. 643–71.

Haggblade, Steven. "The Flip Side of Fashion: Used Clothing Exports to the Third World," *Journal of Development Studies*, 26:3 (1990), pp. 505–21.

Hale, J.R. *War and Society in Renaissance Europe, 1450–1620* (Baltimore, 1985).

Hall, Bert S. "The Corning of Gunpowder and the Development of Firearms in the Renaissance," chapter 6 in Brenda Buchanan (ed.), *Gunpowder: The History of an International Technology* (Bath, 1996), pp. 87–120.

_____. *Weapons and Warfare in Renaissance Europe: Gunpowder, Technology, and Tactics* (Baltimore, 1997).

Hansen, Karen Tranberg. "Gender and Difference: Youth, Bodies and Clothing in Zambia," in Victoria Goddard (ed.), *Gender, Agency and Change: An Anthropological Perspective* (London, 2000), p. 200.

_____. *Salaula: The World of Second-hand Clothing and Zambia* (Chicago, 2000).

_____. "The World in Dress: Anthropological Perspectives on Clothing, Fashion, and Culture," *Annual Review of Anthropology*, 33 (2004), pp. 369–92.

_____. "Helping or Hindering? Controversies around the International Second-hand Clothing Trade," *Anthropology Today*, 20 (2004), pp. 3–9.

Hansotte, Georges. *La Clouterie liégoise et la question ouvrière au XVIIIᵉ siècle* (Brussels, 1972).

Hart, Marjolein 't. "Town and Country in the Dutch Republic, 1550–1800," in S.R. Epstein (ed.). *Town and Country in Europe, 1300–1800* (Cambridge, 2001), pp. 80–105.

Hatton, Rita and John A. Walker. *Supercollector, a Critique of Charles Saatchi* (London, 2000).

Hayles, N. Katherine. "Boundary Disputes: Homeostasis: Reflexivity, and the Foundations of Cybernetics," *Configurations: A Journal For Literature, Science, and Technology* 3 (1994), pp. 441–67.

Hélin, Etienne. "Prix des céréales à Luxembourg," in J. Ruwet, F. Ladrier, E. Hélin and Leo Van Buyten. *Marché des céréales à Ruremonde, Luxembourg, Namur et Diest au XVIIᵉ et XVIIIᵉ siècles* (Leuven, 1966), pp. 185–280.

Heller Committee for Research in Social Economics of the University of California and Constantine Panunzio. *How Mexicans Earn and Live: A Study of the Incomes and Expenditures of One Hundred Mexican Families in San Diego, California,* (Berkeley, CA, 1933).

Héroard, Jean. *Journal de Jean Héroard,* ed. Madeleine Foisil, 2 vols. (Paris, 1989).

Hoffmann, Philip T., Gilles Postel-Vinay and Jean-Laurent Rosenthal, *Des marchés sans prix. Une économie politique du crédit à Paris, 1660–1870* (Paris, 2001).

Honig, Elisabeth Alice. *Painting and the Market in Early Modern Antwerp* (New Haven and London, 1998).

Hudson, Pat. *The Industrial Revolution* (London, 1992).

Hufton, Olwen. *The Poor of Eighteenth-century France 1750–1789* (Oxford, 1974).

Hunt, Margaret. "Women, Credit and the Seafaring Community in London 1700–1740," paper presented at Session C 59 of the 12th International Congress on Economic History, Seville, 1988, Les Femmes et les Pratiques du Crédit (XVIIe–XIXe siècles), coordinated by M. Berg, L. Fontaine and C. Muldew.

Il Vanto e il Lamento della Cortigiana Ferrarese (Venice, 1538).

Installé, Herman. *Patriciërs en ambachtslui in het stadsbestuur te Mechelen onder Maria-Theresia. De sociale status van burgemeesters en schepenen (1740–1780)* (Mechelen, 1982).

International Journal of Community Currency Research, vol. 4, several articles. (http//www.geog.le.ac.uk/ijccr/).

Jacobs, Marc. "De ambachten in Brabant en Mechelen (12ᵈᵉ eeuw–1795)," in *De gewestelijke en lokale overheidsinstellingen in Brabant en Mechelen tot 1795*, II (Brussels, 2000), pp. 91–107.

Jacobs, Marc and Marianne Vanbellinghen. "Ambachten in de Zuidelijke Nederlanden (voor 1795). Een bijdrage tot de samenstelling van een bibliografische lijst van studies verschenen in de 19ᵈᵉ en 20ˢᵗᵉ eeuw," extra edition of *Oost-Vlaamse Zanten*, LXXIV (1999), pp. 187–320.

Jones, Colin. "The Military Revolution and the Professionalisation of the French Army Under the Ancien Régime," in Clifford J. Rogers (ed.), *The Military Revolution Debate: Readings on the Military Transformation of Early Modern Europe* (Boulder, 1995), pp. 152–5.

Jouanna, Arlette. *Le devoir de révolte. La noblesse française et la gestation de l'État moderne, 1559–1661* (Paris, 1989).

Jullien, Bernard. "Internationalisation of Car Service Firms and Changes in Distribution," in Michel Freyssenet, Koichi Shimizu and Giuseppe Volpato (eds.),

Towards the Globalization of Automobile Firms? Internationalization Strategies and Trajectories (London, 2003), pp. 95–116.

_____. "L'après-vente – Derrière l'occasion, la pièce, l'entretien et la réparation, la réalité des consommations et des offres automobiles: la diversité et la difficulté des constructeurs à y faire face," in EBG, *L'Automobile* (Paris, 2003), pp. 498–534.

King, Steven and Geoffrey, Timmins. *Making Sense of the Industrial Revolution. English Economy and Society 1700–1850* (Manchester, 2001).

Klapisch-Zuber, Christiane. "Le complexe de Griselda. Dot et dons de mariage au quattrocento," *Mélanges de l'Ecole française de Rome. Moyen Age – Temps Modernes*, vol. 94 (1982), pp. 7–43.

Kleinschmidt, Harald. "Using the Gun: Manual Drill and the Proliferation of Portable Firearms." *Journal of Military History* 63 (July 1999), pp. 601–29.

Knell, Simon, J. (ed.) *Museums and the Future of Collecting* (Aldershot, 1999).

Kopytoff, Igor. "The Cultural Biography of Things: Commoditization as Process" in Arjun Appadurai. (ed.), *The Social Life of Things: Commodities in Cultural Perspective* (Cambridge, 1986), pp. 64–91.

Krause, Keith. *Arms and the State: Patterns of Military Production and Trade* (Cambridge, 1992).

Krenn, Peter and Walter J. Karcheski, Jr. *Imperial Austria: Treasures of Art, Arms and Armour from the State of Styria* (Perth, 1998).

Kuechler, Susanne and Daniel Miller (eds.), *Clothing as Material Culture* (Oxford, 2005).

Kunzle, David. *The Early Comic Strip: Narrative Strips and Pictures in the European Broadsheet from c.1450 to 1825* (Berkeley, 1973).

La Grange, Arnaud de. "Cotonou et les mille et une voitures," *Le Figaro*, June 25, 2003.

Ladrier, F. "Prix des céréales à Namur, XVIIe–XVIIIe siècles," in Ruwet, J., F. Ladrier, E. Hélin and L. Van Buyten, *Marché des céréales à Ruremonde, Luxembourg, Namur et Diest au XVIIe et XVIIIe siècles* (Leuven, 1966), pp. 281–342.

Lane, Frederic Chapin. *Venetian Ships and Shipbuilders of the Renaissance* (Baltimore, 1934).

Langer, Herbert. *The Thirty Years' War*, translated by C.S.V. Salt (New York, 1990).

La prise et transport des bleds; et autres provisions des habitans de la Rochelle. Par Monsieur le duc d'Espernon ensemble l'empeschement des eaux douces en ladite ville, & l'incommodité qu'elles apportent aux Habitans. Les préparatifs des Vendages. Les deffaictes qui se sont faictes és lieux circonvoisins. Et generalement tout ce qui s'est passé à ce subject jusques à present (Paris, 1621). [BNF, 8° Lb³⁶ 1740.]

L'Arrive de l'armee du roy, devant la ville de Montauban, avec trente mille hommes. Et les furieux escarmouches faictes entre monsieur le duc de Mayenne & les assiegez (Paris, 1621). [BNF, 8° Lb³⁶ 1741.]

La Vita et Miseranda Fine della Puttana (Venice, c. 1650). Civica Raccolta Stampe Bertarelli, Milan. Popolari Profane, Volumetto Albo C66 and Popolari Profane, 11F 2, 3, 4, 5.

Leenders, Geert. "De beroepsstructuur op het platteland tussen Antwerpen en Brussel (1702–1846)," in Jan Craeybeckx and Frank Daelemans (eds.), *Bijdragen tot de Geschiedenis van Vlaanderen en Brabant. Sociaal en economisch* (Brussels, 1983), pp. 167–228.

Lemire, Beverly. "Peddling Fashion: Salesmen, Pawnbrokers, Tailors, Thieves and the Second-hand Clothes Trade in England, c. 1700–1800," *Textile History*, 22:1 (1991), pp. 67–82.

_____. *Dress, Culture and Commerce: The English Clothing Trade before the Factory, 1660–1800* (London, 1997).

_____. "Petty Pawns and Informal Lending: Gender and the Transformation of Small-scale Credit in England, circa 1600–1800," in Kristine Bruland and Patick O'Brien (eds.), *From Family Firms to Corporate Capitalism: Essay in Business and Industrial History in Honour of Peter Mathias* (Oxford, 1998), pp. 112–38.

_____. "Consumerism in Pre-industrial and Early Industrial England: the Trade in Secondhand Clothes," *Journal of British Studies,* 27:1 (1998), pp. 1–24.

Lemire, Beverly, Ruth Pearson and Gail Campbell (eds.). *Women and Credit: Researching the Past, Refiguring the Future* (Oxford: Berg, 2002)

Leopold, Ellen. "The Manufacture of the Fashion System," in Juliet Ash and Elizabeth Wilson (eds.), Chick Thrills: A Fashion Reader (Berkeley, 1993), pp. 100–17.

Le Roy Ladurie, Emmanuel. "Difficulté d'être et douceur de vivre : le XVIᵉ siècle," in Philippe Wolff (ed.), *Histoire du Languedoc,* 2ⁿᵈ ed. (Toulouse, 2000), pp. 247–8.

Lescazes, Jean-Jacques. *Le Memorial historique, contenant la narration des troubles, et ce qui est arrivé diversement de plus remarquable dans le païs de Foix et diocèse de Pamiés, depuis l'an de grâce 1490 jusques à 1640* (1644; reprint, Pamiers, 1989).

Les Commentaires du soldat du Vivarais (1908; reprint, Valence, 1991).

L'Estat du siege contre Montauban par l'armée Royale de sa Majesté contre ceux de la Rebellion. Avec les remarques des fortifications de la Place, & scituation d'icelle. Et generalement ce qui s'est passé par Mr. le Duc de Mayenne, jusqu'à present. Le tout extraict des Memoires escriptes au Camp Royal, le 12. Aoust 1621 (Paris, 1621). [BNF, 8° Lb³⁶ 1730.]

Leydi, Silvio. "Milan and the Arms Industry in the Sixteenth Century," in Stuart W. Pyhrr and José-A. Godoy (eds.), *Heroic Armor of the Italian Renaissance: Filippo Negroli and His Contemporaries* (New York, 1998), pp. 25–33.

_____. "Les armuriers milanais dans la seconde moitié du XVIᵉ siècle. Familles, ateliers et clients à la lumière des documents d'archives," in José-A. Godoy and Silvio Leydi (eds.), *Parures triomphales. Le maniérisme dans l'art de l'armure italienne* (Milan, 2003), pp. 25–55.

Limberger, Michael. "Merchant Capitalism and the countryside in the West of the Duchy of Brabant (fifteenth–sixteenth centuries), in: Peter Hoppenbrouwers and Jan Luiten Van Zanden (eds.), *Peasants into Farmers? The Transformation of Rural Economy and Society in the Low Countries (Middle ages–Nineteenth century) in Light of the Brenner Debate* (Turnhout, 2001), pp. 158–78.

Lipietz, Alain. *La société en sablier – Le partage du travail contre la déchirure sociale* (Paris : La Découverte/Poche, 1995).

Loubet, Jean-Louis. *Citroën, Peugeot, Renault et les autres: soixante ans de stratégie* (Paris, 1995).

Lourens, Piet and Jan Lucassen. ""Zunftlandschaften" in den Niederlanden und im benachbarten Deutschland," in Wilfried Reininghaus (ed.), *Zunftlandschaften in Deutschland und den Niederlanden im Vergleich* (Münster, 2000), pp. 11–41.

Lucas, Gavin. "Disposability and Dispossession in the Twentieth Century," *Journal of Material Culture,* 7 (March 2002), pp. 5–22.

Lynn, John A. "Food, Funds, and Fortresses: Resource Mobilization and Positional Warfare in the Campaigns of Louis XIV." in John A. Lynn (ed.), *Feeding Mars: Logistics in Western Warfare from the Middle Ages to the Present* (Boulder, 1993), pp. 137–59.

_____. "How War Fed War: the Tax of Violence and Contributions during the *grand siècle,*" *Journal of Modern History,* 65 (June 1993), pp. 286–310.

_____. *Giant of the Grand Siècle: The French Army, 1610–1715* (Cambridge, 1997).

Madonna Maria Luisa and Mario Bevilacqua. "The Roman Families in Urban development," in Peter van Kessel and Elisja Schulte (eds.), *Rome and Amsterdam. Two Growing Cities in Seventeenth-Century Europe* (Amsterdam, 1997), pp. 104–23.

Marais, Jean-Luc. *Histoire du don en France de 1800 à 1939. Dons et legs charitables, pieux et philanthropiques* (Rennes, 1999).

Marec, Yvon. *Le "clou" rouennais des origines à nos jours (1778–1982) du Mont de piété au Crédit municipal. Contribution à l'histoire de la pauvreté en province* (Rouen, 1983).

Martin, Jean-Clément. "Le commerçant, la faillite et l'historien," *Annales ESC*, 6 (1980), pp. 1251–68.

Martin, Paul. "I've Got One Just Like That!" Collectors, Museums and Community," *Museological Review*, 1, (1995), pp. 77–86.

Mathias, Peter. *English Trade Tokens: The Industrial Revolution Illustrated* (London, 1962).

Mauss, Marcel. *The Gift: The Form and Reason for Exchange in Archaic Societies* (London, 1950).

McCracken, Grant. *Culture and Consumption* (Bloomington, 1988).

_____. *Culture and Consumption: New Approaches to the Symbolic Character of Consumer Goods and Activities* (Bloomington, Indiana, 1998).

McKendrick, Neil, John Brewer and J.H. Plumb, *The Birth of a Consumer Society: the Commercialization of Eighteenth-century England* (London, 1982).

McKinley, Edward H. *Somebody's Brother: A History of the Salvation Army's Men's Social Service Department 1891–1985* (Lewiston, NY, 1986).

McRobbie, Angela. "Second-hand Dresses and the Role of the Ragmarket," in Angela McRobbie, (ed.), *Zoot Suits and Second-hand Dresses* (Basingstoke, 1989).

McRobbie, Angela (ed.). *Zoot-Suits and Secondhand Dresses: An Anthology of Fashion and Music* (Boston, 1989).

Mercier, Louis Sébastien. *Tableau de Paris*, ed. Jean-Claude Bonnet, 2 vols., (Paris, 1994) (original edition published between 1781 and 1789).

Meulemans, Arthur. "Leuvense ambachten III. De Oudkleerkopers," *Eigen Schoon en de Brabander*, 40 (1957), pp. 60–8, 134–42, 185–94, 301–14, 365–75.

Miller Daniel (ed.), *Acknowledging Consumption: A Review of New Studies.* (London and New York, 1995).

Miller, Daniel. "Consumption and Its Consequences," in Hugh Mackay (ed.), *Consumption and Everyday Life* (London and Milton Keynes, 1997).

_____, *A Theory of Shopping* (Cambridge, 1998).

_____. *The Dialectics of Shopping*, (Chicago, IL, 2001).

Miller, Daniel, P. Jackson, N. Thrift, B. Holbrook and M. Rowlands. *Shopping, Place and Identity* (London and New York, 1998).

Morsa, Denis. "L'urbanisation de la Belgique (1500–1800), taille, hiérarchie et dynamique des villes," *Revue du Nord*, LXXIX (1997), 303–30.

Mortimer, Geoff. *Eyewitness Accounts of the Thirty Years War 1618–48* (New York, 2002).

Muldrew, Craig. "'Hard food for Midas': cash and its social value in early modern England," *Past and Present* 170 (2001), pp. 78–120.

Muzzarelli, Maria Giuseppina. *Guardaroba medievale: vesti e società dal 13. al 16. secolo* (Bologna, 1999).

Nadaud, Martin. *Léonard, Maçon de la Creuse* (Paris, 1998).

Necker, J. *De l'administration des finances de la France*, (Paris, 1784).

Nenadic, Stana. "Middle-rank Consumers and Domestic culture in Edinburgh and Glasgow, 1720–1840," *Past and Present*, 145 (1994), pp. 122–56.

Neuschel, Kristen B. "Noble Households in the Sixteenth Century: Material Settings and Human Communities," *French Historical Studies*, 15 (Autumn 1988), pp. 611–12.

Ngowet, Luc. "Libanais d'Afrique – Gabon: le lucratif créneau des véhicules d'occasion," *RFI*, July 24, 2003.

North, Pete. "Have Confidence and Cast Your Nets into Deep Waters' – Community Responses to Neo-liberalism in Argentina," paper presented at the session "Alternative Geographical Imaginations: Networks, Resistance and New Spaces of Engagements," Association of American Geographers, New Orleans, March 2003.

Nougaret, Jean. "La contre-réforme à Montpellier: la traduction architecturale," in Anne Blanchard, Henri Michel, and Elie Pélaquier (eds.), *La vie religieuse dans la France méridionale à l'époque moderne* (Montpellier, 1992), pp. 79–134.

Nouveau Tableau de Paris au XIXe siècle (Paris, 1834–1835).

O'Brien, Martin. "Rubbish Values: Reflections on the Political Economy of Waste," *Science As Culture*, 8, (1999), pp. 269–95.

_____. "Rubbish-Power: Towards a Sociology of the Rubbish Society," Jeff Hearn and Sasha Roseneil (eds.), *Consuming Cultures, Power and Resistance*, (Basingstoke, 1999).

Olmsted, Allan D. "Collecting: Leisure, Investment or Obsession?" *Journal of Social Behaviour and Personality*, 6, (1991), pp. 287–306.

Palmen, Erik. "Dordt en zijn ommelanden," in W. Frijhof, H. Nusteling and M. Spies (eds.), *Geschiedenis van Dordrecht van 1572 tot 1813* (Hilversum, 1998), pp. 173–93.

Palmer, Alexandra and Hazel Clark (eds.), *Old Clothes, New Looks: Secondhand Fashion* (Oxford, 2003).

Panhuysen, Bibi. *Maatwerk. Kleermakers, naaisters, oudkleerkopers en de gilden (1500–1800)* (Amsterdam, 2000).

Paret, Peter. *Imagined Battles: Reflections of War in European Art* (Chapel Hill, 1997).

Parker, Geoffrey. *The Army of Flanders and the Spanish Road, 1567–1659: The Logistics of Spanish Victory and Defeat in the Low Countries' Wars* (Cambridge, 1972).

_____. "Early Modern Europe," in Michael Howard, George J. Andreopoulos, and Mark R. Shulman (eds.),*The Laws of War: Constraints on Warfare in the Western World* (New Haven, 1994) pp. 40–58.

_____. *The Military Revolution: Military Innovation and the Rise of the West, 1500–1800*, 2nd ed. (Cambridge, 1996).

Parrott, David. *Richelieu's Army: War, Government, and Society in France, 1624–1642* (Cambridge, 2001).

Pearce, Susan M. "The Urge to Collect" in Susan M. Pearce (ed.), *Interpreting Objects and Collections* (London, 1994), pp. 157–9.

_____. *Collecting in Contemporary Practice* (London, 1998).

Pearson, Ruth "Argentina's Barter Network: New Currency for New Times?" *Bulletin of Latin American Research*, 22:2 (2003) pp. 214–30.

Perrot, Philippe. *Les Dessus et les dessous de la bourgeoisie, une histoire du vêtement au XIXe siècle* (Paris, 1981).

_____, *Fashioning the Bourgeoisie: A History of Clothing in the Nineteenth Century*, trans. Richard Bienvenu (Princeton, 1994 [1981]).

Personal Narratives Group (ed.). *Interpreting Women's Lives: Feminist Theory and Personal Narratives* (Bloomington, IN, 1989).

Peveri, Patrice. "Techniques et pratiques du vol dans la pègre du Paris de la Régence d'après les archives du procès de Louis-Dominique Cartouche et de ses complices." Thesis for the École des Hautes Études en Sciences Sociales, 1994.

Philips, Carla Rahn. *Six Galleons for the King of Spain: Imperial Defense in the Early Seventeenth Century* (Baltimore, 1986).

Platt, Jennifer. "Economic Values and Cultural Meanings: the Market For Antiques." Paper presented to the *British Sociological Association Annual Conference* 1978.

Poisson, Georges. "Des châteaux à visiter au début du XVIIe siècle," *XVIIe siècle,* 118–19 (1978), pp. 3–23.

Pomian Krzysztof. "Collezione," in *Enciclopedia Einaudi*, vol. I (Turin, 1978), pp. 330–64.

_____. *Collectionneurs, amateurs et curieux. Paris, Venise XVIe–XVIIIe siècle* (Paris, 1996).

Poncelet, Edouard. *Les Bons Métiers de la cité de Liège* (Liège, 1900).

Pons, Philippe and Brice Pedroletti. "La Génération Shibuya," *Le Monde*, April 10, 2001.

Pontano, Giovanni. *I libri delle virtù sociali*, Francesco Tateo (ed.), (Roma, 1999).

Poulot, Dominique. "Une nouvelle histoire de la culture matérielle?" *Revue d'Histoire Moderne et Contemporaine,* April–June (1997), pp. 344–57.

Powell, Geoffrey. "Petty Capitalism, Perfecting Capitalism or Post-capitalism? Lessons from the Argentinian Barter Network." ISS Working Paper Series No 357 (2002).

Prak, Maarten. "The Politics of Intolerance: Citizenship and Religion in the Dutch Republic (Seventeenth to Eighteenth Centuries)," in R. Po-Chia Hsia and H. van Nierop (eds.), *Calvinism and Religious Toleration in the Dutch Golden Age* (Cambridge, 2002), pp. 167–74.

Prims, Floris. *Geschiedenis van Antwerpen*, XI, 2 (Brussels, 1927).

Puype, Jan Piet and Marco van der Hoeven (eds.). *The Arsenal of the World: The Dutch Arms Trade in the Seventeenth Century* (Amsterdam, 1996).

Raison-Jourde, Françoise. *La Colonie auvergnate de Paris au XIXe siècle* (Paris, 1973).

Rapport de l'Exposition Universelle de 1867 à Paris, 35e classe, *Habillement* (Paris, 1868).

Recit veritable de ce qui s'est passé aux trois nouvelles sorties de ceux de Montauban. Furieusement repoussés, chassés, & battus par messieurs les duc de Mayenne & comte de Bassompierre (Paris, 1621). BNF, 8° Lb³⁶ 1742.

Recueil des Ordonnances des Pays Bas Autrichiens, III (Brussels, 1873).

Redlich, Fritz. *The German Military Enterpriser and his Work Force: A Study in European Economic and Social History.* 2 vols. [*Vierteljahrschrift für Sozial- und Wirtschaftgeschichte.* Beihefte 48.] (Wiesbaden, 1964–1965).

Renson, G. "Sociaal-economisch leven te Halle in de 17de eeuw," *Eigen Schoon en de Brabander*, 66 (1983), pp. 345–60.

Rey, Alain, ed. *Dictionnaire historique de la langue française* (Paris: Dictionnaires Le Robert, 1992), vol. 2, p. 1163.

Rivoli, Pietra. *The Travels of a T-Shirt in the Global Economy: An Economist Examines the Markets, Power, and Politics of World Trade* (Hoboken, NJ, 2005).

Roberts, Gweneth. "A Thing of Beauty and a Source of Wonderment: Ornaments for the Home as Cultural Status Markers," in Gary Day (ed.), *Readings in Popular Culture: Trivial Pursuits?* (New York, 1990), pp. 39–47.

Roberts, Michael. *The Military Revolution.* (Belfast, 1956).

Roberts, Valerie. "Building Social Capital through Micro-credit: the Impact of a Rural Credit Programme on Borrower Livelihoods." Unpublished PhD thesis, School of Development Studies, University of East Anglia, July 2002.

Roche, Daniel. *Le Peuple de Paris* (Paris, 1981).

_____. La Culture des apparences. Une histoire du vêtement XVIe–XVIIIe siècle (Paris, 1989).

Rogers, Clifford J. (ed.). *The Military Revolution Debate: Readings on the Military Transformation of Early Modern Europe* (Boulder, 1995).

Romano, Ruggiero and Ugo Tucci (eds.). *Economia naturale, economia monetaria*, in *Storia d'Italia, Annali*, n° 6 (Turin, 1983).

Ruwet, J. "Mesure de la production agricole sous l'Ancien régime. Le blé en pays mosan," *Annales ESC*, 19 (1964), pp. 625–42.

Saint-Blancard, Jacques de. *Journal du siège du Mas-d'Azil en 1625 écrit par J. de Saint-Blancard, défenseur de la place, contré le maréchal de Thémines*, ed. C. Barrière-Flavy (Foix, 1894). [Extrait du *Bulletin de la Société Ariégeoise des Sciences, Lettres et Arts*, 4 (1894).]

Samuel, Raphael. *Theatres of Memory*, Vol 1: *Past and Present in Contemporary Culture* (London, 1994).

Sandberg, Brian. "Bonds of Nobility and the Culture of Revolt: Provincial Nobles and Civil Conflict in Early Modern France, 1610–1635." PhD dissertation, University of Illinois at Urbana-Champaign, 2001.

Sanderson, Elizabeth. "Nearly New: the Second-hand Clothing Trade in Eighteenth-century Edinburgh," *Costume*, 31 (1997), pp. 38–48.

Sargentson, Carolyn. *Merchants and Luxury Markets. The Marchants Merciers of Eighteenth-century Paris* (London, 1996).

_____. "The Manufacture and Marketing of Luxury goods: the Marchands Merciers of Late Seventeenth- and Eighteenth-Century Paris," in: Robert Fox and Anthony Turner (eds.), *Luxury Trades and Consumerism in Ancien Régime Paris. Studies in the History of a Skilled Workforce* (Aldershot, 1998), pp. 99–137.

Savary des Bruslons, Jacques. *Dictionnaire universel de commerce, d'histoire naturelle et des Arts et Métiers*, 5 vols. (Copenhagen, 1759).

Schnapper, Antoine. , "Probate Inventories, Public Sales and the Parisian art market in the Seventeenth Century," in M. North and D. Omrod (eds.), *Art Markets in Europe, 1500–1900* (Aldershot, 1998), pp. 131–41.

Schneider, Jane, "Of Vigilance and Virgins: Honor, Shame, and Access to Resources in Mediterranean Society," *Ethnology*, n° 9 (1971), pp. 1–24.

Schneider, Jane (ed.), *Beyond the Myth of Culture* (London, 1980).

Schouteet, A. "Het ambacht van de oudkleerkopers te Brugge," *Handelingen van het genootschap voor geschiedenis gesticht onder de benaming Société d"Emulation te Brugge*, CVII (1970), pp. 45–57.

Schuurman, Anton. "Aards Geluk.Consumptie en de moderne samenleving," in: Anton Schuurman, Jan de Vries and Ad Van der Woude (eds.), *Aards Geluk. De Nederlanders en hun spullen van 1500 tot 1850* (Amsterdam, 1997), pp. 15–24.

Sekora, John. *Luxury: The Concept in Western Thought* (Baltimore, 1977).

Seyfang, Gill. "Community Currencies: Small change for a Green Economy – An Evaluation of Local Exchange Trading Systems (LETS) as a Tool for Sustaining Local Development" *Environment and Planning A* 33:6 (2001), pp. 975–96.

Shammas, Carole. "Changes in English and Anglo-American Consumption from 1550 to 1800," in John Brewer and Roy Porter (eds.), *Consumption and the World of Goods* (London, 1993), pp. 177–205.

Société Internationale des études pratiques d'économie politique, *Ouvriers des deux mondes*, (Paris, 1856–62), "Enquête n° 34. Auvergnat Brocanteur en Boutique à Paris."

Solinas, Francesco (ed.). *Le Straodinarie raccolte di Cassiano dal Pozzo: 1588–1657* (Rome, 2000).

Sparti, Donatella Livia, *Le collezioni Dal Pozzo. Storia di una famiglia e del suo museo nella Roma seicentesca* (Florence, 1998).

Spufford, Peter. *Money and its Use in Medieval Europe* (Cambridge, 1988).

Stabel, Peter. "Urban Markets, Rural Industries and the Organisation of Labour in late Medieval Flanders: the Constraints of Guild Regulations and the Requirements of Export Oriented Production," in Bruno Blondé, Michele Galand and Eric Vanhaute (eds.), *Labour and Labour Markets between Town and Countryside (Middle-Ages – Nineteenth Century)* (Turnhout, 2001), pp. 140–57.

_____. "De-urbanisation and Urban Decline in Flanders from 1500 to 1800: the desintegration of an urban system?," in D. McCabe (ed.), *Eurocit. European Urbanisation, Social Structure and Problems between the Eighteenth and Twentieth Century* (Leicester, 1995), pp. 87–108.

Stern, Steve J. *The Secret History of Gender: Women, Men, and Power in Late Colonial Mexico* (Chapel Hill, NC, 1995).

Storey, Tessa. 'Questo Negozio è Aromatichissimo,': a Sociocultural Study of Prostitution in Early Modern Rome," PhD, European University Institute, Florence, 1999. Forthcoming as a book with Cambridge University Press.

_____. "Fragments from the 'life histories' of jewellery belonging to prostitutes in early-modern Rome," in Roberta J.M. Olson, Patricia L. Reilly and Rupert Shepherd (eds.), *The Biography of the object in Late Medieval and Renaissance Italy* (Oxford, 2006), pp. 67–77.

Strasser, Susan. *Waste and Want. A Social History of Trash* (New York, 1999).

Strathern, Marilyn. "Foreword: the Mirror of Technology," in Roger Silverstone and Eric Hirsch (eds.), *Consuming Technologies: Media and Information in Domestic Spaces* (New York, 1992), pp. vii–xiii, xiii.

Styles, John. "Manufacturing, Consumption and Design in Eighteenth-Century England," in John Brewer and Roy Porter (eds.), *Consumption and the World of Goods* (London, 1993) pp. 527–54.

_____. "Clothing the North: the Supply of Non-elite Clothing in the Eighteenth Century North of England," *Textile History*, 25 (1994), pp. 139–66.

Tableau général du commerce de la France avec ses colonies et les puissances étrangères, Direction générale des douanes et des contributions indirectes. 1837 à 1846 (Paris, 1848).

Tarde, Alexis de. *Les Lois de l'imitation* (Paris, 2001).

Tebutt, Mélanie. *Making Ends Meet. Pawnbroking and Working-class Credit.* (London, 1984).

Tedlow, Richard S. *New and Improved, The Story of Mass Marketing in America* (Boston, Massachussetts, 1999).

Thompson, Michael. *Rubbish Theory: the Creation and Destruction of Value*, (Oxford, 1979).

Thornton, Peter. *The Italian Renaissance Interior: 1400–1600* (London, 1991).

Timmermans, Bert. "Een elite als actor op de kunstscène. Patronen van mecenaat in het zeventiende-eeuwse Antwerpen," *Bijdragen tot de Geschiedenis*, 83 (2000), pp. 3–35.

Tinayre, Marcelle. *Madeleine au miroir. Journal d'une femme* (Paris, 1912).

Touzery-Salager, Anne. *Les Châteaux du Bas-Languedoc: Architecture et décor de la Renaissance à la Révolution* (Montpellier, 1996).

Travaglini, Carlo M. "Rigattieri e Società Romana nel Settecento," *Quaderni Storici*, 22:2 (1992), pp. 415–48.

Truquin, Norbert. *Les Aventures d'un prolétaire à travers les Révolutions* (Paris, 1977)

Turner, Terence S. "The Social Skin," in Catherine B. Burroughs and Jeffrey Ehrenreich, (eds.) *Reading the Social Body* (Iowa City, 1993), pp. 15–39 (reprint from Jeremy Cherfas and Roger Lewin (eds.), *Not Work Alone: A Cross-Cultural View of Activities Superfluous to Survival* (London, 1980).

UN (United Nations). *1995 International Trade Statistics Yearbook*. Vol. II: *Trade by Commodity*. (New York, 1996).

———. *1999 International Trade Statistics Yearbook*. Vol. II: *Trade by Commodity* (New York, 2000)

Vallès, Jules. *Le Bachelier* (Paris, 1970 (1881))

Van Buyten, Leo. "De Diesterse Mercuriaal, XVIIe–begin XIXe eeuw" in J. Ruwet, F. Ladrier, E. Hélin and L. Van Buyten, *Marché des céréales à Ruremonde, Luxembourg, Namur et Diest au XVIIe et XVIIIe siècles* (Leuven, 1966), pp. 343–481.

Van Damme, Ilja. "Het vertrek van Mercurius of de semi-periferisering van Antwerpen in de tweede helft van de zeventiende eeuw," unpublished thesis for the degree of licentiaat, Katholieke Universiteit Leuven, 2001.

Vandenberghe, Yvan. *Jacobijnen en traditionalisten. De reacties van de Bruggelingen in de Revolutietijd* (Brussels, 1972).

Vandenbroeke, Chris. "Sociale en konjunkturele facetten van de linnennijverheid in Vlaanderen (late 14de–midden 19de eeuw)," *Handelingen der maatschappij voor geschiedenis en oudheidkunde te Gent*, XXXIII (1979), 117–74.

Van Der Grijp, Paul. "Passion and Profit: the World of Amateur Traders in Philately," *Journal of Material Culture*, 7 (2002), pp. 23–47.

Van der Wee, Herman and Peter D"Haeseleer, "Ville et campagne dans l'industrie linière à Alost et ses environs (fin du Moyen âge–temps modernes)," in Jean Marie Duvosquel and Erik Thoen (eds.), *Peasants and townsmen in Medieval Europe. Studia in honorem Adriaan Verhulst* (Ghent, 1995), pp. 753–67.

Van Honacker, Karin. *Lokaal verzet en oproer in de 17de en 18de eeuw. Collectieve acties tegen het centraal gezag in Brussel, Antwerpen en Leuven* (Kortrijk-Heule, 1994).

Van Isterdael, Herman. *Stad en baronnie Ronse (Ancien Régime)*, Rijksarchief Ronse, Inventarissen, 20 (Brussels, 1998).

Van Roey, Jan. "De sociale structuren en de godsdienstige gezindheid van de Antwerpse bevolking op de vooravond van de reconciliatie met Farnese (17 augustus 1585)," unpublished PhD thesis, University of Ghent, 1963.

Van Werveke. L.M., *Stad Nieuwpoort. Inventaris van het archief van het Oud Régime* (Brussel, 1937).

Vastesaeger, Siska. "Vrouwen in ambachten in Brussel in de achttiende eeuw," unpublished thesis for the degree of licentiaat, Vrije Universiteit Brussel, 1997–8.

Verbeemen, J. "Antwerpen in 1755. Een demografische en sociaal-economische studie," *Bijdragen tot de Geschiedenis*, 40 (1957), 27–63.

Vogel, H. P. "The Republic as Exporter of Arms 1600–1650," in Jan Piet Puype and Marco van der Hoeven (eds.), *The Arsenal of the World: The Dutch Arms Trade in the Seventeenth Century* (Amsterdam, 1996).

Voyage de M. le duc de Rohan en Vivarais, in *Les Commentaires du soldat du Vivarais* (1908; reprint, Valence, 1991), pp. 254–5.

Vries, Jan de. "The Industrial Revolution and the Industrious Revolution," *Journal of Economic History*, 54 (1994), pp. 249–70.

———. "Great Expectations. Early Modern History and the Social Sciences," *Review*, 22 (1999), pp. 121–49.

Vries, Jan de and Ad van der Woude. *Nederland, 1500–1815. De eerste ronde van de moderne economische groei* (Amsterdam, 1995).

Walker, Garthine. "Women, Theft and the World of Stolen Goods," in Jennifer Kermode and Garthine Walker, *Women, Crime and the Courts in Early Modern England* (London, 1995), pp. 81–106.

Van Damme, Ilja. "Changing Consumer Preferences and Evolution in Retailing. Buying and Selling Consumer Durables in Antwerp (c. 1648–c. 1748)," in Bruno Blondé, Peter Stabel, Jon Stobart and Ilja Van Damme (eds.), *Buyers and Sellers. Retail Circuits and Practices in Medieval and Early Modern Europe* (Turnhout, 2006), pp. 199–223.

Ward Helen. "Worth its Weight in Gold: Women and Value in North West India," PhD thesis, University of Cambridge, 1997.

West, Jenny. *Gunpowder, Government and War in the Mid-eighteenth Century* (Woodbridge, 1991).

White, Caroline. Update on Ithaca Hours (2002), available from www.feasta.org/documents/shortcuircuit/sc3/IthcacaHours.

Wiesner Wood, Merry. "Paltry Peddlers or Essential Merchants? Women in the Distributive Trades in Early Modern Nuremberg," *The Sixteenth Century Journal,* XII: 2, (1981), pp. 3–13.

William Trotter, Jr., Joe. *Black Milwaukee: The Making of an Industrial Proletariat, 1915–1945* (Urbana, IL, 1985).

Wolfe, Michael. "Walled Towns during the French Wars of Religion," in James D. Tracy (ed.), *City Walls: The Urban Enceinte in Global Perspective* (Cambridge, 2000), pp. 317–48.

Wood, James B. *The King's Army: Warfare, Soldiers, and Society during the Wars of Religion in France, 1562–1576* (Cambridge, 1996).

Woodward, Donald. "'Swords into Ploughshares': Recycling in Pre-Industrial England." *Economic History Review*, 2nd series, 38 (1985), pp. 175–91.

NOTES ON CONTRIBUTORS

Renata Ago is Professor of Early Modern History at the University of Rome "La Sapienza". She is the author of *Economia barocca. Mercato e istituzioni nella Roma del Seicento* (1998) and *Il gusto delle cose. Una storia degli oggetti nella Roma del Seicento* (2006).

Susan Porter Benson died on June 20, 2005. She was professor at the University of Connecticut. She is the author of *Counter Cultures: Saleswomen, Managers, and Customers in American Department Store* (1986) and of *Household Accounts: Working-Class Family Economies in the Interwar USA* (forthcoming).

Manuel Charpy is a teaching assistant to the École d'Architecture of Paris-La Villette. He is currently completing a *doctorat* on: *L'ordre des choses. Dispositifs techniques, cultures matérielles et modes des espaces privés, Paris, 1830–1914* at the Université de Tours. He is the author with Souley Hassane of *Lettres d'émigrés. Africains d'ici et d'ailleurs, 1960–1995* (2005).

Harald Deceulaer works in the Belgian State Archives. He is the author of a book on the clothing trades in the Southern Low Countries in the early modern period, *Pluriforme patronen en een verschillende snit. Sociaal-economische, institutionele en culturele transformaties in de kledingsector in Antwerpen, Brussel en Gent, 1585–1800* (2001).

Laurence Fontaine is Directrice de Recherches at the CNRS-EHESS Paris. She is the author of *History of pedlars in Europe* (1996), *Pouvoir, identités et migrations dans les hautes vallées des Alpes occidentales (XVIIe–XVIIIe siècles)* (2003) and has edited with Jürgen Schlumbohm *Household Strategies for Survival, 1600-2000: Fission, Faction and Cooperation* (2000).

Jackie Goode is a Research Fellow at the University of Nottingham, UK. She is the author of *Collecting Time: the social organisation of collecting, in Social Conceptions of Time: Structure and Process in Work and Everyday Life* (2002), and *Whose Collection is it Anyway?: an Autoethnographic Account of 'Dividing the Spoils' Upon Divorce, in Cultural Sociology* (forthcoming 2007).

Karen Tranberg Hansen is Professor of Anthropology at Northwestern University. She is the author of *Distant Companions: Servants and Employers in Zambia 1900–1985* (1989), *Keeping House in Lusaka* (1997), *Salaula: The World of Secondhand Clothing and Zambia* (2000). She is editor of *African Encounters with Domesticity* (1989) and co-editor with Mariken Vaa of *Reconsidering Informality: New Research from Africa* (2004).

Bernard Jullien is Assistant Professeur at the University of Bordeaux. He is the author of articles on distribution networks in the automobile industry.

Ruth Pearson is Professor of Development Studies at the University of Leeds. She is the co-editor of *Feminist Visions: Gender, Development and Policy* (1998), *Women and Credit: researching the Past; Re-Figuring the Future* (2002), *Corporate Responsibility and Labour Rights: Codes of Conduct in the Global Economy* (2002) and *Globalization, Export-Oriented Employment and Social Policy: Gendered Connections* (2004).

Valérie Piétri is Assistant Professeur at the university of Nice. She is the author with Germain Butaud of *Les enjeux de la généalogie (XIIe–XVIIIe siècle): Pouvoir et identité* (2006).

Brian Sandberg is an Assistant Professor of History at Northern Illinois University. He is currently revising a monograph entitled, *Heroic Souls: French Nobles and Religious Conflict after the Edict of Nantes, 1598–1635*.

Tessa Storey is at present research associate in the history of medicine at Leicester University. She is the author of *Carnal Commerce in Counter Reformation Rome* (forthcoming, 2008).

INDEX

Lightning Source UK Ltd.
Milton Keynes UK
UKHW020643020220
358006UK00007B/371

9 781845 452452